The Secret History of Western Civilization

The Secret History of Western Civilization

or

The Next Holocaust

February, 1993

Revised, June 2003

by

Anatoly (Tony) Kandiew

Order this book online at www.trafford.com
or email orders@trafford.com

Most Trafford titles are also available at major online book retailers.

Printed in the United States of America.

ISBN: 978-1-4120-8644-8 (sc)
ISBN: 978-1-4122-0445-3 (e)

Trafford rev. 01/02/2015

Trafford PUBLISHING www.trafford.com
North America & international
toll-free: 1 888 232 4444 (USA & Canada)
fax: 812 355 4082

Contents

Acknowledgments

I am very grateful for the assistance I got in publishing this book. In particular, to Marinella, my former wife, who encouraged me to write. To Emilia, my mother, who encouraged me to publish. To Emma, my sister, who allowed me to use her art for my covers. And, last but not least, to Angelo Rombola, my long-time friend, who helped me edit this book and who made many useful suggestions.

Tony Kandiew
20th September 2003

1

First Day

Today I decided to get a good night's sleep. The day was long and exhausting. I labored all day cleaning my office, filing my papers from my prior projects and preparing for my next major activity. The new project is called 'Market Timing.' In a nutshell, it asks the question: "Is there a best way to select a stock or bond or any other financial instrument?."

Actually, the problem has two aspects. The first is: is there a 'better' way to select financial securities, and if so how? The second aspect is: once a 'best' selection method has been found, is there a best way to manage a portfolio of issues?

Needless to say, the solution to any aspect of this problem would be extremely profitable to investors. I have found a few clients who are interested in solving this problem on a rational basis, i.e., using a model or a series of models to determine the best choice. Then, if the problem can be solved or improved on a rational basis from existing methods, these models could be used time and again to improve selection and portfolio performance.

My clients have pooled some resources and backed this limited project, not necessarily believing that the problem can be solved precisely. But, it was felt the opportunity of even a reasonable approximation or an improvement in their existing methods would pay for this venture very quickly. Thus, this limited project was set up to investigate the nature of the problem. Since the problem is potentially solvable, there is much interest in solving it.

On the other hand, the problem has many vocal opponents who take every opportunity to undermine the rational attack to find a potential solution. Instead, they recommend trade 'patterns' as the only means of selecting issues and managing portfolios.

Unfortunately, trade patterns are 'visible' after the fact or after the market action. Therefore, the key to the problem is to find these patterns before the market action occurs. Thus, the financial industry is divided between the 'believers' in a rational solution and the 'disbelievers' who promote other techniques.

Armed with these doubts and opportunities, I cleaned my office and prepared myself for the new project. I felt that a fresh look at the problem in the morning would be more productive.

So, my wife Marinella and I decided to feast tonight. I stopped work early -- the afternoon was shot anyhow. By the time I had cleaned my office and filed my papers I was not in the state of mind to tackle a new and complex problem.

My wife is of Italian ancestry and an excellent cook. To her, each meal must begin with a plate of pasta. It is followed with a main dish of meat or fish with a salad and then capped with a desert. Naturally, each meal must be accompanied with wine.

We rationalize our choices. Some rationalizations are based on news or background information, other rationalizations are based on taste or preference. Still others are based on customs.

My favorite pasta is pasta in white sauce. Here, heavy cream is used as a basis for the sauce. A few diced clams are mixed in for taste and seasonings are added to complete the dish. My wife prepares this appetizer only on rare occasions. To her, milk products with pasta borders on sacrilege. To me, pasta and milk product are compatible combinations.

My favorite meat is lamb. Beef has received a lot of bad press and I tend to shy away from it. Almost daily we hear how hormones are added to the feed of cattle and tend to produce side-effects in humans. Pork and chicken need to be overcooked to be safe to eat. Cases of trichinosis and salmonella are plentiful in the news. On the other hand, lamb can be served rare, medium or well done. We both prefer our meat in the medium range.

Since lambs require a pasture, they feed naturally. Each time I eat lamb I picture lush rolling hills from New Hampshire or some other idyllic place. Therefore, the hormone problem can be minimized with lamb.Since lamb is not a carrier of trichinosis or salmonella it is relatively safe, even when served rare. The specific lamb dish is not that important to me. Of course, a nice rack of lamb is a feast when Marinella puts her mind to it. But, a leg of lamb or even lamb 'steaks' are a delight. Lamb requires garlic to enhance the taste. Our culture frowns on garlic -- at least to some degree. This of course is mainly because we are based on an Anglo-Saxon role model. Teutonic culture minimizes the use of garlic. And lamb without garlic is like a fish out of water.

When we choose fish for our main dish we both prefer fresh whole fish. That is, a fish with its head and tail. Over the years my wife perfected a recipe which is a delight. The whole fish is steamed and a sauce is prepared on the side. The sauce consists of: oil, soy sauce, minced garlic and scallions. The sauce is heated almost to the boiling point and then poured over the steamed fish.

Our preference of fish preparation restricts us to certain types of fish -- salmon, grouper, sheep-head and a few others. This is because the fish must be of a certain size. Usually no more than two pounds. However, any fish up to two pounds prepared this way becomes a culinary marvel.

Generally speaking we prefer red wine. Usually a Bordeaux, Beaujolais, Chianti, Bordolino or Barollo is just fine. Our favorites are: a good Chateau-Neuf du Pape for me and a Barollo for her. Of course, a good classic wine can become expensive. Then, depending on our resources and the occasion, we resort to table wines. Even domestic table wines (California-based wines) are now quite good. We prefer, however, French or Italian table wines.

Wines, in particular red wines, have many mystiques attached to them. At some time this was probably used to differentiate the 'wine snobs' from the casual wine drinkers. According to many wine experts, only three producers of wines are consumable in the first place: French, Italian and now California wines. This is because the basic ingredients, the grapes, require not only a lot of attention and expertise to cultivate, but a specific climate is also required. This climate is most favorable in France, Italy and California. Without the base quality of the product, the grapes, all other factors become secondary. Naturally then, the most valued wines are associated with various regions of these countries and with a particular grape.

Wines which are pure in the sense that only one type of grape is used -- are called premium wines. When a blend of grapes are used, they are called table wines. Premium wines are always prominently advertised on the label on the wine bottle.

Since climatic conditions change from year to year, the quality of the grapes changes also. Therefore, the quality of the grapes is judged according to the year; hence the most favorable years we call simply: vintage years.

However, we find it also to be true that many vintage years are overrated. Frequently we can find a reasonable vintage to be far superior to a commercially accepted quality vintage wine. This only proves that wines -- as many other products are sold-- not bought. Some wine connoisseurs say that this is directly proportional to the type of hangover and its duration. Since we have seldom more than two or three glasses of wine at dinner, we use other factors to arrive at our rating.

Much ado is made about the 'breathing' of wine. A bottle is opened and potential consumers stare in great anticipation at the open bottle. Since there is no hard and fast rule how long a wine should breathe, we allow from two to five minutes.

On occasion we have been to parties when red wine was served. Then, a bottle would be opened and the wine would be allowed to 'breathe.' All guest would then be expected to comply with this ritual. Since nobody in the know likes to disappoint the host, the opened bottle just stands there until some unsuspecting soul takes the courage and pours a glass of wine. Once the spell is broken, all other guests usually follow suit. Of course, the basis of this ritual is the aroma.

The aroma serves to identify the grape or conversely any by-products in the wine. Some wineries add sugar to help the fermentation process. This produces a heavy fermentation aroma. Needless to say, it is sacrilege to add sugar in order to produce a good wine. Some wineries add sugar to camouflage the grape itself. By definition, then the quality of the grape was inferior to start with. The aroma will frequently tell the story.

We tend to sniff the wine, usually in private, to make sure that the aroma is pleasant and familiar. If it is, we call it a good aroma. If it is not, we either tell the merchant or delete the brand or year from our purchase list.

We also examine other characteristics. Once the wine is poured we lift the glass towards a light to examine the color. Again, the color must be familiar and consistent with the wine we are about to drink.

Most wines are clear and uniform in color. However, some of the best wines have sediments. Disturbing the sediments disturbs the clarity of the wine. Then, particles and sometimes even pieces of the sediment can be observed floating when the wine was not properly handled. A good look at the clarity assures us when the wine is ready to be consumed. Before we drink a red wine, we like to test its body. Again, this is a ritual performed only on red wines. We pour half a glass of wine and rotate it gently so that the wine spreads to the top of the glass. As the wine recedes it should leave 'columns,' which can be readily observed. These columns are a sign of the body of the wine.

When the red grapes are diluted excessively, columns will not appear. When the red grapes are not diluted the columns will be very pronounced. Since a certain amount of dilution is desirable this dilution can be readily tested this way.

Once our red wine passes these tests, we are ready to drink it in small to medium sips. Of course red wine needs food and helps the digestive process. Some say it breaks down the fats and helps our body to digest the food better.

We concentrate more on how well the wine matches or complements the taste of our main meal.

Since meats are not as delicate as fish, red wine goes best with meat. Red wine will overpower the taste of fish and therefore it has become fashionable to choose red wine for meats and white wine for fish. Of course, sometimes it is prudent to overpower the taste of fish and use red wine. However, we try to avoid this with company because it is a no-win situation.

If you choose a red wine with fish, this tells your host that the fish is bad -- if you know what you are doing. And, if you choose red wine out of ignorance -- then your ignorance is a clear sign to the host and guests.

Of course white wines are more delicate. Many of the tests do not apply to them. Aroma, clarity and taste are the dominant factors. Again, the aroma should be pleasant and consistent. Particles are not expected in white wine. Therefore, there should be none. The color should be white to a slight yellow-orange. The taste should not be vinegary or too sweet. Sweet tastes are normally signs of added sugar, sacrilege to oenophiles. When the taste is too vinegary, the wine is probably spoiled and not fit for consumption.

We choose our wine according to the main meal. We try to make our meals relatively homogeneous. We do this because we do not like to switch from white to red wines in the course of a meal. Opened bottles of wine spoil very quickly. Hence, we keep a bottle closed until the wine is to be consumed.

The temperature is the dominant factor for a wine to spoil. Red wines are supposed to be kept at room temperature or about seventy degrees Fahrenheit. When the temperature rises above 78 degrees, red wine spoils easily. Therefore, wines are kept in a cellar. In the absence of a cellar wine coolers should be used.

While it may be fashionable in some circles to provide a variety of appetizers with the main meal, we prefer one simple pasta appetizer. Of course, Marinella has literally a thousand and one way to make pasta different. In that sense, our appetizer is always different from day to day. We also prefer to match the meal to one wine. Usually this is both an economic and taste consideration. A good wine is usually the most expensive part of the meal. Then, it is only prudent to match the meal to the wine and not the other way around.

A salad, in a traditional sense in this country, is a tossed salad. Lettuce, tomatoes, cucumbers and onions are the main ingredients.

Marinella prefers a tomato salad. That is, slices of vine-ripe tomatoes, covered with slices of mozzarella, basil and a little olive oil. Here the key ingredient, of course, is basil.

For desert we use fruits, mostly peaches and/or cheese. Again, fruits and cheese go well with most red wines and are an appropriate close for a good meal.

So, today is lamb-steak night with pasta in white sauce.

While Marinella prepares the meal, I set the table and we chit-chat about the day's events as we get ready for dinner. The entire meal takes less than one hour to prepare and then we feast.

In many ways, the characteristics of a wine and a meal, parallel the characteristics of the market timing problem. The difference being that wine and food has been prepared for thousands of years and the characteristics have become self-evident. Rational financial analysis is a new field, in fact for all practical purposes it started only in 1973. Therefore, the characteristics are not that obvious and still questioned by many investors.

Today, the meal preparation was not much different from many other days, except that, during this meal we touched on Greek mythology. We often discuss how well and complete the Greek pantheon was structured. How humanity's basic wants and needs were reflected by it. Yet how the purely selfish attributes were hidden and not flaunted.

After we finished our meal, we cleaned up and retired. I fell asleep right away. Maybe an extra glass of wine was the reason, maybe the intensity and pre-occupation of my work was the culprit, but in any event I was sound asleep instantly.

2

Hermes

A figure is approaching from the distance. As the figure comes closer I begin to make out its shape. The figure is dressed in veils. The veils are in the form of a dress and the veils float as the figure approaches me. I think it is the figure of a woman.

As the figure comes closer I begin to make out her features. She comes closer still and now she is right next to me. She is beautiful.

Her hair is pitch-black, yet radiant, loosely falling on her neck line. Her face is white and oval without a blemish. Her eyebrows are black and pronounced. Her eyes are brown, deep brown. Her eyelashes are black and almost touch her eyebrows. Her nose is straight, classic I thought, and a perfect match to her face. Her mouth is small and smiling. She has little dimples on her chin and cheeks.

I take a closer look. This time I scan her face, her body and her feet. Her feet are bare. Curious, no shoes, I notice.

My first impression is: what is she doing all dressed up, yet without shoes? Did it matter that she has no shoes?

It does not matter to me. Another scan, and I am amazed at her beauty. Her figure is perfect. Her dress of veils only pronounces the contours of her body. It is perfect.

I am stunned. I keep looking at her -- probably with my mouth wide open. I can not believe her presence.

"Hello," I say.

"Hello, hello, hello..." she replies.

"Have you come to me..." I say nervously.

"Come to me, come to me, come to me,..." she replies.

I moved toward her. But, instantly she moved away. She was still smiling and looking at me, yet moving away at the same time. It seemed to me that she was motioning me to follow her. Yet each time I moved closer, she moved away. Thus we began floating away. I kept moving closer to her and she continued moving away at the same instant. As I moved faster towards her, she moved faster away from me. No matter how hard I tried to get closer to her, that very instant she moved away at the same speed. The effect was movement through endless space, just she and I.

I tried to talk to her again, but I could not form a sound. I was numb. Maybe, I thought, I should stop chasing her. Maybe my motion prevented me from speaking. If I would stop, maybe I could talk to her again -- so I thought -- but an uncontrolled force drove me onward. I was not in control of this force.

And so we travelled through space until we came to a small valley surrounded by low hills carpeted with deep green grass. Bright sunshine covered the entire valley. How curious I thought. Not a dark spot in the entire valley. Not even a shadow.

Even stranger was the fact that there was not a single tree in the valley, only a small brook winding its way through the hills. Near the brook was another figure faintly visible, toward whom we seemed to be headed.

As we came closer the figure became clearly visible to me, an old man sitting on a stone, apparently waiting for us.

Sure enough, my companion floated to his side and the next instant I landed next to her. Finally, I thought, we are back on firm ground. The journey was over.

Before I could say anything, the old man motioned, and my female companion resumed her flight and quickly disappeared out of my sight. I seemed to be frozen. I could not move.

The old man looked at me and said: "How was your journey?" What journey I thought? I thought it was more of a chase which ended in a kidnapping.

Yet I replied: "Fine."

I took another look at the old man and tried to figure out who he was. He wore a strange old hat with a large rim. On the hat was a band. And, on the band were all sorts of small figurines, labels and tiny trinkets. He wore a worn out sleeveless vest, blue jeans, white socks and sandals. I had no idea who he was. I only knew I had never seen him before. Nor did his appearance impress me in any way. I mustered some courage and asked, "What am I doing here?"

The old man looked at me and replied: "We are interested in your work. We want to re-assess its impact on us."

What work could he be possibly be interested in? Who was us? I looked him straight in the eyes and asked: "May I ask who you are?"

He looked at me with piercing eyes and said: "I have many names. The name you are most familiar with is Hermes. I used Echo to bring you here to discuss your work with me."

"I will be more than happy to discuss my work, but how could it be of any interest to you?" I inquired.

"Well, my friend, when Prometheus created humanity, he created the third generation of mortals. The other generations had perished because they had very limited intellects. Zeus thought this creation was a bad idea, but he tolerated it because they were mortals and we Olympians were immortal. When Prometheus stole the fire and became the champion for his creation, Zeus punished him. But he left humanity alone, for it was clear that mortals had to worship and serve us. Initially, they did. But in time, these mortals have taken away our powers. Little by little, piece by piece they defied our commands. Now only a few mortals worship us altogether. We paid little attention over the eons to you mortals. Now, we have decided to take an active interest and work with you from here on in to avoid our mutual extinction. In order to do that, we need to re-assess the impact of your work."

"How can the work of mortals affect you so much?" I asked.

"Let me give you an example. I used to be in charge of commerce, communications, travel and I also had many other responsibilities. Now, you mortals have invented the printing press, discovered electricity, built radios, installed television and use computers everywhere. Over the ages my powers have been restricted a great deal. I am not needed any more. I am no longer worshipped -- I have become an old man. Of course I am immortal and I can transform myself into a young man. But my state of existence is that of an old man. Therefore, my manifestation to you is that of an old man."

"If that is the case -- why was Echo so beautiful?" I asked.

"As you may know, Echo was a home-body and a chatter-box. She was not beautiful at all when she served Hera. Hera punished her chattering by allowing her only to repeat the questions or parts of any questions asked. But Echo's powers have increased as mankind's inventions and innovations grew. Look around you -- how many of your species worship her! How many members of your species only repeat what was said before. As more members of your species worship her -- her physical powers are increasing also.

"We have great disorder in our ranks. Once the gods were powerful, now many are reduced to mere shadows of their previous glory. Our current hierarchy is nearly bankrupt; we need to re-organize and re-structure the Olympians. We did not expect to be in this dilemma. But now we are forced to be more proactive where humanity is concerned."

"Why are you dressed the way you are?" I asked.

"In the communications area I have lost control. You have wizards now who are nearly as good technically as I am. Of course, there is a real opportunity now for me to leap-frog ahead of your species. However, in the commerce area I am still far ahead of any member of your species. The backbone of commerce is financial analysis, and this field is dominated by the United States. I wanted to appear familiar to you," he answered.

"Why was Echo dressed the way she was?" I asked.

"I felt Echo should reveal herself to you with her full powers. Each veil is a form of truth which your species promotes. The first few veils are the dominant scientific beliefs. They change when Echo is in motion. Yet while they change -- they remain the same. The next veil is another scientific truth -- it is less volatile to change. Therefore, it is restricted by the first veil and so on. The contours of her body -- or the real truth -- are almost visible only if your species takes the time and effort to sort out the intervening truths. Since at this time your species is not inclined to do so, your perception of truth is only visible to your species as broad outlines rather than the stark or rigid reality," he replied.

"Why was her body so beautiful?" I asked.

"You and your species are taught that truth is beautiful. Therefore, her body is the most desirable body to your mind. Of course, I can show you the basic error in your thinking. I explained this error once to Moliere and he wrote a play along these lines." He paused.

"Please explain," I asked Hermes.

"Do you consider your mother to be beautiful?" he asked.

"My mother is old, she aged with time. She had many misfortunes in her life, yet she overcame all of them. For her age and her lot in life..., yes I would consider her beautiful," I replied.

"I did not ask for your rationalizations or your personal feelings. I simply asked if she is beautiful. Well..., is she?" he pressed on.

"Well, in absolute terms, her physical appearance lost some of her previous beauty. But her inner beauty grew with time..."

"Again..., stop rationalizing..., just tell me if she is beautiful?" he interrupted.

"Well, on that basis, she is not beautiful," I admitted.

"Then, if she is not beautiful, she must be ugly. This of course is a consequence of your own prevailing logic using the reflection principle. Apollo worked with Aristotle closely to define the rules of logic, but in the end Aristotle succumbed to his own interpretations which have a few flaws. Logic is the primary tool we gave humanity to arrive at a truth. Therefore, when you speak the truth -- you should be calling your mother ugly. Yet you call her beautiful? Have you no respect for the truth?" he said.

"But I am a Christian, I am taught to honor my mother and my father. Is that wrong?" I asked.

"Not at all. You are throwing buzzwords at me. It has nothing to do with Christianity or any other religion. All religions are explanations of the same cosmic order and its generative process. However, the cosmic order can only be kept when the social order is in harmony with the cosmic order. We reveal this mystery to the human race in terms they can understand at a particular time. But the capacity of the human mind is limited and we have a hard time revealing this interaction to the human race in its entirety. All too often our message is lost or muddled, and results in paradoxes and inconsistencies.

"From time to time we choose a human to update this interaction. You call them seers, innovators, prophets and founders of religions. But most of the time our message is distorted or perverted. If it is distorted in the beginning, then that religion is short-lived. Sometimes it is distorted downstream when the cosmic message is used to compete for temporal powers. There the cosmic message appears to be incompatible with temporal reality. Periodically, about every 600 years or so on your time scale, we try to revamp the entire perspective. But unfortunately, each revision produced new religions, and we are unable to reconcile their specific polarities at this time. Of course, the cosmic order can be expressed with numbers and their harmony. We taught Pythagoras this mystery, we even taught the scribes how to encode the sacred writings so that untruths can be recognized. We even encoded these relationships in sacred structures in order to preserve them for posterity -- but humanity has lost the code and has defiled our works," he said.

Hermes got up from the stone. He stretched his legs and looked into the sky. Then he turned to me and continued.

"The human race is entering a new era. Humanity called the last major cosmic revision the 'Reformation.' Since then, 600 years have nearly passed. Humanity had the opportunity to tinker with many new forms of governments, with new social experiments and new cosmic interpretations. Humanity is now ready for a new cosmic revision. There is more urgency to this revision because physics, the self-proclaimed technical interpreter of the cosmos is gaining more attention. But, mankind's models are linear and have only a minute resemblance to the non-linear interactions of the cosmic forces. They are moving humanity on a collision course with nature. We know that technicians can not be trusted in matters of metaphysics to convey universal truths. They bamboozle humanity with a few esoteric formulations, draw a few simplistic conclusions and steer humanity in the wrong direction. Only much later, after the theories have been found to be deficient or inconsistent, are they discarded. Meanwhile, great harm can be inflicted on nature, on the cosmic order and on the human race. Technicians tend to sensationalize particular phenomena which are insignificant in the cosmic process when viewed in their totality," he said.

Hermes paused and I had the distinct feeling that he was waiting for a question.I was intrigued with his characterization of the United States with respect to financial analysis. How could I put my question to him properly?

"You said something about the United States which interests me a lot. You said that it is the financial leader. Yet we have a very strong recession now. Our primary antagonist, the Soviet Union, collapsed. Germany has been re-unified. Now Germany and France are poised again to build a United Europe -- that is a new Holy Roman Empire.This new Empire could stretch from the Atlantic to the Pacific. What Napoleon and Hitler failed to achieve by war, may be achieved by economic advantages. Should this happen the United States will be in a real predicament. Then, Great Britain will overtly deny her ties to America and join that new Empire.And, we could face economic encirclement andisolation..." I paused to catch a breath. Then, I continued.

"Japan has a huge trade surplus with the United States despite her financial woes. Meanwhile, China is flexing her economic muscles. Hong Kong has been returned, Taiwan is threatened and new economic powers have risen on the Pacific Rim: Korea, Singapore and Malaysia. And, let us not forget Australia. Just recently the United States came under attack with the destruction of the World Trade Center. We have identified the culprits and we got ready to take action against them. But then, our former friends in Europe refused to back our actions. Why do you say that the United States is the leader in the financial markets?" I asked.

"Your question has many parts. Let me make a few points and then we can discuss them briefly," he replied.

"The future wars will be fought on the economic battlefields; traditional military action will be the exception, not the norm. Therefore, it is imperative that the financial forces must be understood. Then, there are the following considerations:

"First, the United States is centrally located in the world markets. Second, the United States is the market maker for practically all financial instruments. Third, the instrument of the future are options and derivatives. The only meaningful work on options and derivatives is done in the United States. Finally, the United States is the leader in computers and communications technology. These factors alone make the United States the leader in the financial industry," he replied.

"Our world is a sphere. How could any geographical area be the center?" I asked.

"You know that any problem has potentially many good solutions. The best solution, of course, is an analytic solution or a formula. While a formula is the best solution, it is also the worst solution. This is because a formula implies specific boundary conditions which are implied and not stated explicitly. All too often a formula is thought to be universally true. Change the boundary condition and the formula is worthless. Hilbert demonstrated this with his spatial geometry." He paused.

"Of course the trick in using Hilbert's method is to find the spatial functions which characterize the solution space in the first place. A bad choice of functions will create singularities. The most effective way to remove the singularities is to choose a better set of functions. That is, a better formulation of the problem. Other methods will work, but they are inferior.

"To see how the United States is the center of the financial markets -- use time-zones to establish the pre- and after-markets in a global market scenario. That is, plot the exchanges in terms of their time displacement from each other and see which geographical market cluster has the best opportunity to create a pre- and after-market. If you do that, you will see that the United States is the geographical center of the world markets," he stated.

"To see that the United States is the market maker in the world markets add up the daily volumes for each exchange, multiply each trade by its contract value, normalize the result to any currency and you have a measure of the world impact. Again, if you do that, you will find that the United States, with its exchanges, is by far the largest player in the market. Therefore, the United States is the market maker in the world markets.

"Of course the variety of instruments is also a factor. Just enumerate the number of different instruments traded in the United States. Compare this with any other nation or even groups of nations in similar time zones and again you will see that the United States has the greatest diversity," he paused.

"Finally, you yourself demonstrated that all instruments interact. Therefore, the class of problems being attacked in the United States is clearly much more comprehensive than in any other time zone or nation.

"This is why both Apollo and Athene have taken up permanent residence in the United States and refuse to join us on Mt. Olympus. Even Poseidon, who built himself a castle near London not so long ago, is moving his headquarters to California," he lamented.

Hermes mused for a while and then continued: "In fact, most Olympians have residences in the United States now. Apollo moves constantly between Chicago, New York, Berkeley, Houston and some place near Daytona. Athene spends most of her time in the Washington D.C. area. Sometimes she goes to Annapolis, New York and Denver. On occasion both are very hard to find. There is a lot of secrecy in the United States, you know. Demeter is mostly in Kansas and Minnesota. Aphrodite lives primarily in Los Angeles but visits often Miami. Artemis spends a lot of time near Philadelphia. Occasionally she goes to Boston and Orlando. Only Hera remains on Mt. Olympus with her companions. The place is now quite deserted and run down. Hephaestus refuses to leave Mt.

Vesuvius to fix up Mt. Olympus. We could have a grand party if he did -- just as we used to have in the past. Ares moves around a lot. He is as busy as ever. First, he went to Rome, then to Paris, then to Berlin and then to St. Petersburg. Now he roams near Babylon and is thinking of moving his residence to Samarkand. Hades, of course, is still in Rome -- his residence has been very stable for the last 1500 years. Dante gave him a lot of publicity and he is highly revered in Rome. Hestia had a permanent residence in Peking, but just recently she moved to Delhi, India and spends a lot of time in Bangladesh. Bacchus still has a wonderful place near Bordeaux and another near Florence. But even he is thinking of building a summer place in the San Bernadino valley. Zeus roams in the far east, mostly in Thailand. I think he is looking for a flat in Hong Kong or in Tokyo. He has a knack of anticipating the future hot spots."

There was clearly more to his explanation. He looked at me and saw that I was waiting anxiously for his continuation.

"Where were we?" he continued.

"Options," I said.

"Yes, of course. You know that options are the oldest and most volatile instruments.Bacchus told Thales of Miletus to study the relationship of the cosmic cycles and how they affected the crops on earth.Once Thales was pointed in that direction he could observe how the grape crops and the need for grape presses were related. The cosmic forces gave Thales a nine month lead time to compute the cosmic impact on the grape crop. One year that relationship became clear to Thales as it applied to his region. He mustered enough courage and bought the right to use all the presses in his region for a nominal price. When harvest time came, the grape presses were in his control. Now he could charge a premium for their usage. He did, and made a tidy sum in the transaction.

"Of course, I am only outlining the process. If you want more detailed answers you will have to talk to Apollo and Bacchus. Even Athene can shed some insight on this subject," he reflected a little while, then he continued.

"The problem with options, of course, are not only the technical difficulties in computing the correct premiums involved but also the enforcement of a contractual obligation. Obviously, when either the technical aspects or the contractual obligations are inconsistent or not enforceable the instrument is worthless.

"This happened more than once. Probably the most notorious case was the tulip bulb disaster in Amsterdam. And ever since the tulip bulb disaster, options, as financial instruments, have received a lot of bad press. Therefore, options, as financial instruments, must still overcome the perceived riskiness of the past," he said.

"The Chicago Board Option Exchange (CBOE) found a reasonable approach to deal with the contractual aspects of the problem. Black and Scholes developed a reasonable technical solution to the problem, but their solution applies only to limited type options and well defined financial markets.

"American and European options are different. Many aspects of their formulation are still crude. Fungibility is a key ingredient in the option market. Thus the basis to the problem, can almost be solved now. Of course, a better solution to the option problem is a prerequisite to the market timing problem you are working on.

"As you pointed out in one of your papers, the option market drives the stock market. And the stock market maintains a parity with the corporate bond market. Yet the corporate bond market is driven by the US Government bond market. Of course, the municipal bond market is also driven by the US Government bond market, and in the midst of these market activities is the convertible bond market. A major component for pricing convertibles is the fair value of the implied option component. I am so glad that someone is trying to unify these markets," he smiled.

"I did not forget the futures market. In fact as you will progress even further in your work, you will see the real importance of the futures markets. In particular the financial futures market. And then,the importance of the currency markets," he said.

"As you know the ratio of interest rate rates for two countries imply their expected inflationary rates. That ratio also implies the interest rate parity with respect to the spot and forward rate. It also implies the expected change in spot rates. This class of relationships, while crude in many ways, are also known as the Fisher effect," he paused again.

"I should not speak to you in these terms because I might steal the thunder from Apollo and Athene. All I wanted to do is to show you again how the United States is so pivotal in the world markets, both geographically and as its prime market maker," he paused again.

"In the computer field there is no doubt that the United States was both the inventor and prime architect. I am glad that you pointed out the importance of Franklin and Lucasievicz. But I have a problem with Seymour Cray. He does not listen to me each time we converse. He only follows the inspirations of Apollo and Athene. I am getting a little bit upset with him -- he keeps ignoring my marketing advice," he paused again.

"Of course, Babbage and Turing have little to do with the computer industry. For that matter, if we were to delineate the invention of computers to include devices driven by external power, I prefer Archimedes as the originator of the field. But then, of course, we would have to sort out many mechanical devices. Then, the abacus would win as the forerunner to computers.

"I accept your delineation with Franklin and the prerequisite of electricity, but you left out many other contributors," he said.

I turned to him and replied: "I know, I did not mean to be disrespectful -- my book was getting to be too large. I even said that in my book. In addition, the editing was taking up a lot of my time. My intent was only to point out the fallacies of Penrose and Hawking."

"Penrose and Hawking are only instruments of a higher plan. You must inform your citizenry of their geopolitical ambitions. In particular, how they encircle the United States with Japan, Canada and Mexico and deny her access to the world markets.

"England and the United States are heads-on competitors. Yet each time England paints itself into a corner with her geopolitical ambitions, she runs to the United States for help. So far the United States has been a willing gladiator for England, but this will change soon. You will see it in your life-time. Mark my words," he assured me.

"Well, what's done is done. Let us see if we can set an agenda so that the Olympians have a chance to talk to you," he seemed to be finished.

He looked at the sky, motioned with his hand and I woke up.

I was disoriented at first. I touched my surroundings and felt soft objects. A pillow, a blanket -- they were all next to me. My right arm had a tickling sensation -- as if I was resting my head on it for too long. As a matter of fact I was.I stretched my right arm and the tingle began to subside.

It was still dark outside. I glanced at my clock and saw it was nearly four o'clock in the morning. Time to get up I thought. Time to get back to the market timing problem.

I got out of bed, picked up my clothing and gently left the bedroom so that I would not disturb my Marinella. I closed the bedroom door, put on my robe, went to the kitchen and prepared the coffee. While the coffee was brewing I went to the bathroom and got ready for the new day.

3

Hera

I fell asleep right away. At first I felt a darkness which enveloped me. Next, I felt I was floating away on my own. All of a sudden I was back in the valley, near the brook from the night before. I did not notice him at first, but there he was, Hermes beckoned me closer.

"So, how was everything today?" he asked.

"Frustrating," I replied.

"I got my new professional Quick Basic compiler from Microsoft and after a full day's work of installing it and converting my modules, I found out that it is not suitable for my machine configuration. Then, I had to back-out all changes and continue developing with the prior version. A real mess," I said.

"Why don't you upgrade your computer?" he asked.

"Right now I am short on cash. The real estate market is very bad. I can't sell any of my properties," I responded.

"Besides, I think I am waiting subconsciously for the next generation of PC's before I am ready to buy a new system. I am waiting for machine speeds to double, hard disk capacity to quadruple and the price to drop by at least 20%," I continued.

"Well, I'm sure you will find a way to reach your objectives." Then, he continued.

"Did I cover your concerns last night?"

"Not really -- you did not discuss the geopolitical implications for the United States for her immediate future."

He looked at me sternly. I had the distinct feeling he was a bit annoyed at my question.

"I did not want us to get entangled in the rhetoric,innuendo and downright fallacies which are accepted as real currency in your world." He said.

"History is written by the victors, not the vanquished. History is written to please the individual in power and thus gain his favors. History is also intertwined with religion making history difficult to rationalize. However, if you insist, let me give you a brief outline and then you may pick the particular topic which is dear to you.

"Let me begin with the major historians and their perspectives. I will enumerate them in chronological order so you can see the evolution.

"The first historian in Western Civilization was Homer. He wrote three important histories: The Iliad, The Odyssey and Menelaos.

"The Iliad deals with the destruction of the great city of Troy, which was built by Poseidon. With the ruin of Troy many great civilizations perished: Achaean, Aegean, Cretan, Etruscan, Hittite and so on. There, Homer tried to meld the Achaean Civilization, which was derived from Egypt and Phoenicia, with the new Doric invaders. Today you call this the Greek Civilization...

"The Odyssey deals with the exploration of the Atlantic Ocean. When it was rewritten in Latin, however, the action was shifted to the Mediterranean Sea.

"Rome refused to accept that there were other civilizations beyond the Straits of Gibraltar. This, despite the fact that every seaman knows that even from a dingy, there are only a few locations where land is not visible in the Mediterranean Sea. This changed Homer's history to a fantasy and it received little serious attention for a long time. Yet, when examined closely, there are passages which clearly show that the action took place in the Atlantic.

"Menelaos deals with the exploration of the Indian Ocean. That history is lost to you in the present, but it is referred to in the Odyssey -- when Telemachus went to see Menelaos, who had just returned from his expedition, which also lasted nearly 10 years. Strabo mentions this in his 'Geography.'

"These early histories were written in poetic form. Of course, not everyone was suitable to be a poet; therefore, Herodotus introduced a new style, prose. Which is a narrative style. We did not like his new style at all, but it caught the fancy of your race, and from then on practically all histories were written in prose. We did not like prose because it left out the interaction of the gods -- us -- and focuses only on the deeds of man.

"Thucydides introduced a new style, currently called 'Eyewitness Accounts.' His history set the norm and style from then on. Accordingly, many modern historians call Herodotus 'a story teller,' while Thucydides is called a historian. With only one major exception: The Old Testament, the first book of the Bible.

"Its style is a hybrid between Homer and Herodotus. It is the history of the Hebrews and their relationship with their God, but that history has two faults. First, there is no author, i.e. it is the work of a committee. And, most importantly, we Olympians lost our identity. Only Zeus was promoted while the other Olympians were demoted to angels. The Old Testament introduced a new technique -- codification, called 'Theomatics' today. The reason it was codified was simple. Prose is much easier to alter and falsify than poetry. It does contain, however, much of the common wisdom of its time and many of the cosmic truths we were teaching all along.

"Livy wrote the definitive history of Rome. In order to make it more respectable, Livy added about 200 years of fictitious history -- all the Etruscan Kings. This was proven only recently using a new technology -- carbon dating -- coupled with the archeological work in Rome; and had it not been for Polybius, Livy would have written that during the Second Punic War each battle was a victory for Rome, even though Hannibal, with only a small contingent of men, roamed the Italian peninsula for 17 years undefeated, despite Rome's inexhaustible supply of new recruits each year. But Livy's history pleased the Roman Emperors, guaranteeing him a place in Western Civilization.

"Cassiodorus Senator wrote the definitive history of the Goths. At that time they ruled Italy from Ravenna, not Rome. However, they were Arian Christians and when their King Theodoric died, Emperor Justinian used Belisarius and Narses to evict them, forcing them to leave for Gaul and Spain, joining their kinfolk there. Cassiodorus identified the many nations who made up the Goths: Alans, Amazons, Angles, Gepids, Jütes (Jutes), Macedonians, Normans, Sassons, Scythians, Slavs, Suevi, Wends and so on.

"In fact, the Slavs and Goths had merged into one people before the Trojan war. This is recorded in their mythology which was also consistent with what Strabo had written about earlier. But, this identification did not suit the Roman Empire. So, his book was discounted and eventually eradicated. All you have left is the recollections of Jordanes. His book is called 'Getica.' But be careful when you read it. It has been altered to suit the Germans," Hermes smiled pensively.

I was fascinated with the tidbits Hermes was throwing at me. I saw him rolling his eyes and I could sense that he was trying to start a new topic. Then, he continued.

"Tomorrow and the following days,I will talk about Christianity,the plight of the Goths and how this affects your country. Today,I will finish the historical thread of Western Civilization and give you time to think about it. Otherwise we will not get to the agenda I had in mind.

"Christian tradition has it that the priest of a congregation is called 'Papa' or 'Father.' This is a very good custom for it binds the congregation to their spiritual leader.

"In 800, the Roman Empire was near extinction. Spain had been conquered by the Moors and the Arabs were at the gates of Constantinople.This is when the Papa of Rome decided to form his own brand of Christianity and break away from the main Church. You call it the Roman Faith -- or Catholicism. The problem was, Roman militarism was replaced with Christian monasticism around 330. The new Western militarism did not evolve until the Crusades when it was directed and organized by the Pope...

"But, in order to do so, he needed a protector. That protector became Charlemagne. Thus, a Concordat was made. The Concordat, an agreement in perpetuity between Charlemagne and his descendants and the Papa of Rome and his successors, can not be invalidated by any man or earthly authority. The Papa of Rome would be called Pope and his protector would be the Emperor of the 'Holy Roman Empire.' Thus, on Christmas Eve in 800, this concordat was ratified. Charlemagne was proclaimed Emperor of the Holy Roman Empire and the Papa became Pope.

"Today, it is called 'The German Concordat.' This is so, because the Carolingian line came to an end and the last successor was called Louis the German. This is how the House of Hohenstaufen came to power. Eventually, this 'baton' passed to the House of Habsburg, and there it stayed until the Holy Roman Empire was dismantled by Napoleon. This concordat gave the Germans the right to rule all other nations, to conquer all heathens and to exterminate all non-Catholics -- all in the name of Catholicism. However, Gaul -- you call it France today -- was diametrically opposed to this, but only because they were excluded.

Thus, from then on, France headed one coalition while the Emperor of the Holy Roman Empire led the other. They were at odds with each other over the centuries until Hitler's time. Hitler then conquered France, and France under Petain, became an ally of Germany in their attempt to conquer the Soviet Union. Of course, Hitler's effort at conquest failed, Germany was defeated and divided in such a way that she would never again be a threat to humanity.

"Marshal Petain and General Charles DeGaulle made a pact, however, just before France was defeated by Germany. DeGaulle went to London to rally the 'Free French.' This way, no matter who won, France would be saved. Thus, when the end was near, France rallied behind DeGaulle and France emerged victorious in the war.

"Today, France and Germany are partners again. They run the new European Union jointly. And, look at their success! All European nations want to be part of this Union, even the break-away republics of the former Soviet Union. The only hold-out, so to speak, is Russia. Russia is trying to cut the 'best-deal' between the European Union and the United States. Thus, you are right. If Russia joins the European Union, that Union will stretch from the Atlantic to the Pacific.

"There is still one major problem. Russia is not a European nation. They are the descendants of the former Tartars who ruled their land, and their Christian Faith, their form of Orthodoxy, is a heresy. I will cover this another time in more detail.

"Meanwhile, France was settled by the Goths displaced by the Huns. The Goths saved Western Civilization at Chalons-sur-Marne where Attila was defeated. Then, they ran Gaul for a few centuries. You know them as Merovingians, attracting the Norman Goths who likewise settled in France, allowing that country to have more Gothic descendants than they have Gaels. Fortunately, most of the Goths intermarried and accepted the Roman Faith. Those that did not were mercilessly exterminated -- such as the Albigense and others. The dynasty started with Mirveche or Meervech (meaning Peace-assembly) and they rose to power with Clovis. But, Clovis was his Latin name. His original name was Cholodoveche or Chlodovech (meaning Cold-assembly.) That is, Clovis was a compromise candidate of the Goths and Franks.

"In 1066, the Normans of France conquered England, ruling in England until Queen Ann died when the Norman line died out. Leibnitz had prepared for that eventuality and argued successfully in the Emperors court that the next legitimate successor was the Elector, the Duke of Hannover, his employer. Thus, when Queen Ann died, the German took over the rule in England as George I bringing with him his entire Hanoverian entourage, and they rule Great Britain to this day. Of course, they tried to disguise their lineage. They did that by changing their names during the First World War. The House of Hanover became the House of Windsor, and the Battenbergs became Mountbattens, and so on. With the Germans in power in England, history had to be adjusted to suit the new German masters. Gibbon per force made a few 'minor corrections' to the prior history. There were two aspects which needed to be 'corrected.' First, the original Gothic invaders had to made German -- to establish the lineage of the new rulers and to solidify their claim. Second, the Goths had to 'disappear' from the political scene in Europe. This he accomplished in his history entitled 'The Rise and Fall of The Roman Empire.'

"The original Sassons, described by the Venerable Bede, Gibbon called Saxons. Thus, the Anglo-Saxon myth was created. By then, the Gothic Angles had been conquered and were Germanized, and -- as far as the remaining Goths was concerned -- they simply disappeared from the political scene in Europe (according to Gibbon) and the Slavs appeared. Gibbon's history thereby eliminated all the nasty consequences of lineage and ethnicity.

"Keep in mind that the Germans were never seafarers. Not at the time of Tacitus, who vividly describes their panicky fear of the open sea, and not today. They never had a navy to speak of; not even in the modern era. The best they could do to combat Great Britain was to build submarines. Technically speaking, a submarine is a different weapon system. Occasionally the Germans built a modern cruiser or battleship during the wars, but as soon as it was launched and reached the open sea it was attacked and destroyed by the British. For example:Graf Spee,Scharnhorst, Gneisenau and so on. They were all used as 'single fortresses.'

"Finally, I should mention here in passing, that there are two other Concordats. That is, there are three of them that involve nations. As I mentioned before, the first is the German Concordat.The second is called the French Concordat and the third is called the Italian Concordat. I have explained the first. The second Concordat was made during the reign of Francis I in the 16th century of your time frame (1515). In that Concordat Francis I negotiated an agreement whereby the French pay a fixed sum of money to the Pope in perpetuity, and in exchange their King can install his own Bishops, also in perpetuity. This paved the way for the rise of nationalism in France. The third Concordat was made between Mussolini and the Pope. The Papal States were a thorn in the side of a unified Italy. When the Italian State was formed in 1865 the Papal States were simply taken away from the Papacy. Thereupon, the Pope locked himself up in the tower and refused to associate with his flock. Mussolini formulated the notion of the Vatican, an autonomous State for the Pope within the State of Italy solving the religious dilemma. Now his descendants are active in modern Italian politics...

"I hope you can readily see that the new European Union will not have the problem which the Holy Roman Empire had. France is allied with Germany. Italy is in favor of the Union and allied with Germany. The Pope is of much less importance now than he was before. England is almost ready to join the Union -- only the remnants of her former Commonwealth are keeping her out today; but as soon as Australia and Canada leave the Commonwealth, England will have no choice but to join the European Union. This realization alone pushes her into the arms of the European Union today...

"The only country which will hold out on purpose will be Switzerland. They hope to be the tax-haven for that Union," Hermes concluded.

I could see he was practically out of breath with his monologue, but after a long pause, he started again.

"Today, I have an agenda in mind. We will visit Hera and then we will see what we should do next."

He stretched out a rod and motioned me to hold on to one end. As soon as I had a good grip on it, we were off.

We moved swiftly. I could see nothing. I could not see anything below us, or above us, or even in front of us. I had to squint my eyes to compensate for the air pressure. My eyes were watering. Otherwise the ride was quite comfortable. I felt I was weightless as if we were floating through space. I don't remember how long we floated, but a sudden jerk brought me back to my awareness. We were standing in a palatial hall of white marble. Two oval staircases curved up to a platform on the second floor. The staircases were also of marble. The platform opened to two corridors, one on each side. A gleaming railing protected the open spaces all around.

Beyond the railing on top, golden doors were staring down the hall. In the center was a double door. All others were single doors. The first floor had twelve golden doors on each side of the center. In the center, below the staircase, was also a set of double doors. Between the doors were six marble benches, three on each side. The floor was white marble.

I noticed that the hall had no windows, yet is was as bright as daylight in the hall. What an incredible structure I thought. So simple and yet so powerful. So overwhelming.I turned to Hermes and saw a faint smile on his face. He was apparently pleased by my admiration.

"Hephaestus is a real craftsman, is he not?" Hermes asked.

Before I could reply, he continued. "The second floor has the banquet room in the center, some servants quarters and the guest rooms down the hall. On the first floor we have our cosmic room in the center, an extensive library to the left, and many general purpose rooms all around. You probably noticed that the hall has no windows yet is quite well lit. Actually,Apollo helped Hephaestus a little bit.Apollo created a miniature fusion reactor to create light and solved some load and stress problems for the building. Sometimes Hephaestus is stubborn, he prefers to work with marble and gold...

"The fusion reactor was placed by Apollo on the ceiling in the hall. If you look closely, you will see a small yellow ball in the ceiling," and he pointed his finger at the center of the ceiling in the hall. "We have a number of rooms like this. The marble comes mostly from Sicily. The doors are solid gold. This project took Hephaestus a whole year to complete..."

"We enjoyed this place for a long time," he continued. "But then, Hera converted one of the rooms into a computer room and many of the Olympians refuse to come here. Of course, eventually all Olympians will have to cope with computers...

"Let's go into the computer room. Hera is there with her companions. They are expecting us." He turned toward one of the rooms on the first floor and motioned me to come along.

We came to one of the doors and Hermes stopped.

"Come here..., open the door...," he told me.

I stepped forward and noticed that the gold frame of the door was inlaid with gold plates. The plates were sculptured. They depicted men and women, war scenes... I had no time to look closer. I was stunned. The art-work was incredible. Minute and precise, every detail was clearly visible up close. If I could only spend a few moments to look and absorb...

Instead, I reached for the door handle, pushed it down and pulled the door towards me. Again, I was surprised. It required no effort at all; the slightest pull opened the door.

"Now, that's craftsmanship..., is it not?" I heard Hermes say. "Do you appreciate the ease of usage?" I heard him.

As I opened the door I could see a number of persons in the room. About a dozen or so. Mostly females, I thought, as I took a quick peek into the room. Their dress was curious. Most of the females wore dresses similar to the one I saw Echo wear. They wore dresses of veils. The veils were almost transparent. The contours of their bodies were practically visible from my angle. I was not sure what to make of this. Should I stay behind and let Hermes lead the way? I was intimidated. How would I be able to speak with them?

"The truth is revealing, is it not?" I heard him say.

Hermes went quickly through the door and motioned me to follow him. He went directly towards a female seated behind a marble desk with a white box on one side of her desk. She was focusing on a white box. Thank heavens, I thought, this female wore a tunic draped around her body. I can cope with that, I thought. To be even more inconspicuous, I concentrated my vision on the desk.

"Hera, I brought you the fellow who created XL. You wanted to talk to him," I heard Hermes say.

Hera looked up from her desk, motioned to Hermes to come closer and said: "I'll be right with you. We have a slight emulation problem on the modified super-computer. I'll need a minute or two on my terminal."

"Ganymede, bring two chairs for our visitors," I heard her say.

A young man from the crowd moved towards us and pushed two white chairs in front of Hera's desk.I had not noticed the chairs before.They looked like white plastic and were not at all noticeable at first. Hermes and I sat down. The chairs were very comfortable. They were not plastic. Hermes noticed my curiosity.

"Ivory," I heard him say.

I took a look at the room, just the part directly in front of me. I noticed white cabinets with flashing lights -- computers I thought. But there were no cables. The computers had white covers and blended in with the white marble of the room. How did they possibly do it?

To install the connecting cables, to provide the power to drive all this machinery in the room must have been a formidable task. Again, Hermes seemed to read my mind. I heard him say: "Hephaestus and Apollo installed this equipment. Did they not do a good job?" he asked.

"Outstanding," I said softly.

Hera was finished with her work. She turned to me and asked: "How do you like the color coordination in my house? Mostly white, beige and gold," she said.

"It is beautiful!" I exclaimed. Hera seemed pleased.

"Do you think that a super-computer can actually solve the non-linear problems of Class I?" she asked.

"I think so. I am using..."

"Well, I am not so sure. Some time ago we talked to Heesch and his solution method for the four color problem. He felt certain that he would be able to solve the problem with a CDC 6600. We installed a super-computer in this room, and even speeded it up a little bit, four fold. But, when we reached twenty-nine irreducible border colorations it was obvious that the super-computer did not have the speed to solve the problem within the next 200 years. We have deferred the quest for a solution for a while.I am not certain if you will not run into a similar problem with your machine and your solution method for nonlinear problems of Class I" she said.

"But then we have to accept randomness as a potential solution alternative," I replied.

"We know that. Remember, nothing is random in the cosmic sense. That is why we brought you here. However, while nothing is random, this does not mean that there are simple analytic solutions either," she replied.

"We have nursed the human race for nearly 5500 years in their approach to solve problems. The first rational approach was finally taught by Pythagoras. Then, it took another 2000 years for the human race to include zero in their solution space. Descartes had a very hard time conveying this message. True, once the idea was accepted and refined with Euler, Hilbert was able to solve linear systems quite handily. The transition from linear systems to non-linear systems is not that difficult, but I am not so sure that your approach will receive a great deal of attention in the beginning. New ideas appear to be difficult to grasp by the human race. Besides, when Dedekind defined the real numbers with his cut, he actually created havoc. We encoded the relationship of the real numbers to the transcendental, irrational and whole numbers in our megalithic constructions for posterity. Napoleon, however, changed our weights and measures with his metric system and our measures: feet, cubits and stadia were lost in the megalithic monuments. I am so glad you formulated this relationship in your paper 'Extended Number Bases.' " She paused.

I was not sure if an answer was expected of me. So, I kept my silence. I was thinking of a good question to ask, but before

I could start Hera continued.

"We tackle mostly social problems here. We created two rational models: One analyzes the problem from the genus, based on a family unit. The other is a holistic approach and begins with the migration problem of the human race. In your terminology the first is a bottom-up approach and the other is a top-down approach. Eventually, both models should produce the same results. We are very close in reconciling the two models. A few differential equations which couple the two models still create singularities. In addition, the modern era ushered in a new migration problem. We call it the 'reverse migration' problem for lack of a better word." She opined.

"Of course in the family unit model, religion, economics, education and the form of government are the dominant variables. Abuse of these variables leads to crime, divorce and social decay." She paused again.

"In the migration model the conquest horizon is by far the most dominant variable. Traditionally,entire nations migrated and destroyed civilizations which opposed them or offered the greatest economic rewards. The invader was usually a barbarian or not a Greek and had to overpower the opponent with sheer numbers. In modern times this form of migration is no longer viable.Strong nations have developed powerful weapons systems and can annihilate any potential invader of this type. Some nations even assume the role of a policeman to prevent this kind of upheaval. Thus, the new form of conquest will shift to the economic battle scene. You call this the balance of power and regions of influence. We are not so sure that this concept will work in the long run. The migration problem had an advantage. When the invader succeeded, its citizenry remained relatively homogeneous and old ideas were swept away. The disadvantage was that intellectual progress suffered a setback. For example: Rome and the Goths," she paused.

"There are a number of exceptions of course.There are always exceptions. Alexander and Napoleon committed Hubris and we intervened against them.

"To Alexander we sent Clotho and she cut him down in the prime of his life. To Napoleon we sent Nemesis and his military exploits ended with dismal defeats. Military leaders tend to commit Hubris most of the time. Then, their fate is sealed. Usually we use Nemesis to show them their folly. Therefore, military leaders cannot be trusted in matters of politics,"she paused and looked at me sternly.

"What about Hitler and Stalin?" I asked.

"Hitler, of course, was an entirely different problem. Initially, he convinced us of his limited intentions. We even felt that he was justified to some degree to correct the wrong from the prior war. But as his plan unravelled and it became clear that he not only committed Hubris but also Genocide we had no alternative. We felt we had to support Stalin against Hitler in order to preserve the human race. Poseidon swayed most of us. Only Ares stayed with Hitler. In retrospect, we should have punished both even more severely..."

"What about religious leaders?" I interrupted.

"Our models show that religious leaders, as a class, are even worse. Theocracy of any form is tyranny of the highest order. To begin with it enslaves the women. It relegates them to second class citizens. All major religions exploit them, even today..."

She continued: "Modern migrations are of a different nature. They are essentially for economic reasons.Underprivileged nations need to off-load some of their citizenry,or economically deprived individuals seek their fortune in a rich or potentially rich country. The nature of these migrations is totally different. The base of a nation becomes dishomogeneous and can lead later-on to disharmony," she paused.

"How do we solve this problem?" I asked.

"A good question. The solution we have is also a non-linear problem, but it is of Class II. We don't know if our solution will find much active support...

"You see, in a traditional hierarchy the delegated power increases with the hierarchy. That is, power and hierarchy are directly related. In a non-linear system of Class II, power and hierarchy are inversely related. What binds this order is parity, and parity establishes equilibrium." She looked at me again.

"We discussed these notions with Aristotle, St. Augustine, Machiavelli, Smith, Marx and Wilson. However, each time the intent was perverted. It was used for personal or national glorification and the quest for supremacy...

"Aristotle wrote about it in 'The Athenian Constitution.' However, he restricted the solution needlessly to apply only to Greece and to small city states. That is, he explained the problem in a local sense and suggested drastic measures to deal with anomalies: banishment, slavery and so on. He accepted a number of axioms we did not advocate. First, the axiom of a ruler and the ruled. We have a hierarchy, do you see any slaves in my house?Do you see chains or whips or other instruments of torture? Of course not. In fact it is barbaric to use brute force. There are much better ways to discipline the unruly. Next, he accepted the axiom that the male is superior to the female. Consequently men were educated while women were not...

"Look at me, I am in charge in this house and many males are inferior to me in our hierarchy.If he had used us as a role model then these two fallacies could have been avoided.

"What about Saint Augustine?" I asked.

"St. Augustine saw an opportunity to promote a cult into a religion. He preached freedom, yet kept many slaves in his household. He preached fidelity, yet practiced debauchery. He preached poverty, yet lived in luxury. Most of all, he promoted the notion of taking the possessions and property of non-believers. In other words, he was a real hypocrite. He was the primal cause of man's inhumanity to man. Had we not been so preoccupied with the wars at that time, we would have addressed this situation right away.

"For example, in 'On Christian Doctrine II, 40,' St. Augustine says: 'Whatever was rightly said by heathens, we must appropriate for our uses.' This included not only their writings but also their property. He justified the carnage caused by the early Christians, when they became the dominant religion of the Roman Empire and gave license to cause further destruction in the future. Is this what Jesus taught? I see no trace of it in His teachings.

"As you can see, the Church of Jesus became institutionalized, and once it became a bureaucracy that institution served itself and not the teachings of Jesus..."

"How about Saint Thomas Aquinas?" I asked.

"St. Thomas Aquinas transcribed the works of Aristotle adding only a few Christian comments. In other words, he was the original plagiarist. But the Roman Faith did not perceive it that way, so he became very popular.

"He lived in the 13th century (1225-75), right after the Fourth Crusade (1204), when Constantinople had been plundered and destroyed by fellow Christians. The Crusaders brought back the works of Aristotle and many other Greek authors to Venice, Genoa, Florence and Rome. There, these works were sold at bargain prices by the Crusaders. These books ushered in the Renaissance.

"I don't like two aspects of his work, called 'Summa Theologica.' First, is the fact that he plagiarized Aristotle.

Second, because he degraded women in his work, but that was a consequence of his plagiarism. In the Greek culture, women played an inferior, submissive role. To begin with, they were not educated -- that was reserved only for men. Consequently, they were unable to run the household.They were used to bear children, that's all.

"The Greek agenda for men was something like this: at age 8 they were sent to school; at age 12, they entered the academy; at age 16, they served the military until age 45. Then, they were free to marry and raise a family. Consequently, old men married young girls -- age 14 or so. The life expectancy of men was about 80, while the life expectancy of women was barely 40..."

"How about Machiavelli?" I asked.

"Machiavelli, was basically a nationalist. He saw powerful nations being forged in his time. He used our discussion to formulate the required actions for a strong and successful Prince. Again, he placed more emphasis on history than on the nature of the problem. The inverse relationship of power and hierarchy was not emphasized in his book..."

"And, Adam Smith?"

"Adam Smith overemphasized the economic base in his 'Wealth of Nations.' His fallacy was similar to Aristotle's. Smith used England as a statistical sample and his conclusions are distorted in the global sense. Again, the problem was addressed, but only in a local sense..."

"And, Karl Marx?"

"Marx concentrated on parity in 'Das Kapital.' And his conclusions led him to the realization that an inversion of the hierarchy was necessary in order to establish the inverse relationship. Therefore, his conclusion was that this inversion could only be accomplished with a revolution. He should have realized from the beginning, of course, that Communism is not practical and not workable. Plato tried it in Sicily. He tried it against our advice. It was a dismal failure after only a short time. Economic bankruptcy forced him to leave the island hastily. And, economic bankruptcy brought down the Communist Empire..."

"And, Woodrow Wilson?" I asked.

"Woodrow Wilson, was the first to formulate the solution in a global sense.He promoted and established the League of Nations, which was an off-shoot of the 'Holy Alliance,' which Czar Alexander I, promoted in Paris and Vienna. However, that body had no economic, political or military powers at all.

"Their success or failure depended only on the good will of the participating members. When Japan invaded Manchuria with England's covert consent and Mussolini invaded Ethiopia also with England's covert consent, it became clear to the participating nations that the League of Nations was only a paper tiger, a forum for England to practice geopolitics. What was lacking were the notions of parity and enforcement which would have made that body stronger. Charismatic dictators seized onto this weakness and exploited it," she finished.

"How about the United Nations?" I asked.

"If it were not for the United States, it would do just as badly as the League of Nations. After the last great war, the United States became the strongest and wealthiest nation. It carried the burden of the UN for the most part. One nation alone, however, can not police, subsidize and be the role model forever. Other nations must participate more effectively. All nations have their time and place in the cosmic order. The mechanisms are not in place to do that effectively in the UN.

"As a result, each nation joins a block of nations to lobby their common interests. Most of the time the interests are selfish and perverted. Much of the effectiveness of the UN is purely imaginary. If a better hierarchy were established and parity could be demonstrated, many of the inefficiencies would be resolved. The emphasis must be more on social, ecological, and economic variables and how they maintain parity with political and military variables, rather than on ideological follies," she said.

After a long pause, she started again.

"I am the protector of the family. I am dismayed at America. The basic family unit is falling apart. The traditional values have been subverted -- America's family values as defined by her founders. A divorce rate of 50% or more leads to promiscuity, which in turn leads to anarchy. Same sex marriages are an abomination. They are against the nature of humanity. The models we have show this beyond any doubt. If this trend continues,America will not survive very long as a super-power.

"Historically speaking, this is why the Greek Civilization imploded -- it fell apart from within after 300 years, while the Roman Empire lasted over 1600 years. The Holy Roman Empire, despite all the other faults, survived 1000 years because they valued and preserved the family unit. The Communist regime imploded, to a large extent because of their disregard for family values. It is an abomination when the most desirable job for a young girl is perceived to be a 'hard currency prostitute.' This was the most recent finding in a poll conducted in present day

Russia."

She looked at Hermes and asked: "What else is on your agenda?"

"I think our next stop should be Bangladesh," Hermes replied.

Before I could thank Hera for her time, Hermes pushed the rod into my hand. Instinctively I held on to it and we vanished from the palace. Again, I had the sense of moving through space. We landed in our familiar place, in the valley, in no time at all.

Hermes sat down on the rock and started.

"This will be our base. I will give you a debriefing the next time we meet. This way you have an opportunity to collect your thoughts and questions, while I will schedule our next visit from here. Is that ok with you?"

"That is perfect." I replied.

"In that case, let me take you to an aspect that is closely linked to Hera."

With that, he shoved his rod into my hands and we were off.

4

Hestia

We came to an abrupt halt in a mud puddle in a rice field. On the rice field were many people, all bent over. They were either pulling weeds or planting seedlings. At first I was not sure which, because in one hand they held a bunch of small green plants and the other hand was submerged in water. It soon became clear that they were planting.

In front of us stood a tall lady wearing a beige sarong. Only her face, her arms and the lower part of her legs, from her knees down, were visible. Her face was beautiful and she had a deep tan. A few strains of blonde hair curled up on her forehead.

"I have only a few moments for you," she said to Hermes.

"I expect a difficult childbirth and my help will be required," she continued.

She turned to me and said: "I have brought you here to show you how misapplied technology makes the lot of women worse now than eons ago. Your race talks about equality and equal rights for women, yet only the most menial tasks are delegated to women. No matter what the standard of living of a country, no matter what the spectrum of job opportunities is -- only the lowest jobs are made available to them. Nations, religions and institutions who mistreat their women do not deserve to be part of the human race."

I did not know what to say. She seemed to be angry with me. I did not create this problem, I thought to myself. How could I possibly remedy this situation? She seemed to read my mind and resumed.

"Our intent was to create man and woman as social and economic partners for life. Over the years man appointed himself to be the provider or the dominant economic force in this partnership and relegated women to a menial social role. We tolerated this arrangement provided that parity was maintained within the family unit. As economic conditions began to change and take on a more significant impact, man created more jobs for himself. Each new job was more powerful than the one before, leaving fewer job opportunities for women. This axiom became the rule and nobody questions it even today," she said.

"The first job man created for himself was that of a warrior. Women are not well suited physically to be warriors, you know that. Therefore, the parity was upset from that moment on. Once man discovered the reflection principle he created a new job, that of a priest. Did man offer this job to his partner? Oh, no... Only on rare occasions did man offer this job to women, but even then only as a perversion of the job. Man has tried systematically to keep women in bondage and for his pleasure. This perversion must stop. My workload has increased to the limits of my power because of the folly of man. If this trend is not reversed, I will petition for an intervention and change of the socioeconomic responsibilities for the human race," she paused.

"How could I possibly help?" I heard myself say meekly.

"Problem solving should not be done in a vacuum or as a gratification for the intellect. When problems are solved for gratification, perversion is inevitable. The solution of a problem must be holistic or universal. A universal solution requires a set of abstractions or axioms. Therefore, universal solutions can only exist when the basic problem does not involve motion or change. Consequently, problems involving motion or change are only universally valid if they are solved in the holistic sense. However, the capacity of the human race is very restricted. Therefore, even the most simple problems involving motion or change are beyond the capacity of your species. You may find approximations which will work in a very restricted environment. You call them boundary conditions. But these solutions are not universally true," she stated.

"Would you please explain this further," I asked.

"The predominant problem of your species we call your 'free lunch' syndrome. When your race discovered war as a preoccupation, slavery was the perversion. When slavery was abolished, it was done so not for humanitarian reasons. Not at all. It was done because an even greater form of servitude was feasible.

The age of industrialization also required many mindless workers. Thus, the notion of slavery gave way to a new form of exploitation. Since your race reverses the roles of each intended subjugation you call it employment. In the name of peace you make war. In the name of liberty you subjugate. Even your major industries find the inversion of your terminology useful to disguise their intent. What you call Life Insurance, is really Death Insurance and so on. Now you created computers. Is this not potentially another form of perversion?" she asked.

Before I could formulate a question, she continued. "Look at your educational process. The most universal truths have the weakest names. You call them 'Theorems.' The weakest universal truths you call 'Laws.' For example: 'The Pythagorean Theorem' remained valid for the last 2600 years. Meanwhile, 'The Laws of Motion' are practically not usable, even today. You still can not solve 'The Three Body Problem' with them,..."

"Excuse me," I interrupted, "... how about Sir Isaac Newton's formulation of the 'Fundamental Law of Attraction?'" I asked.

"To begin with, Newton called his chapters: 'Axioms, or Laws of...' Later transcriptions omitted the word 'axioms' and so the word 'laws' came into use. Newton's first three laws of Physics are really two. His second and third law describe the same phenomenon. They only differ by a differential going from law 2 to law 3 or by an integral going from law 3 to law 2. Galileo described law 1 and law 2 in great detail in his 'Two Sciences.'

"Archimedes invented what you call today 'Integral Calculus,' while Leibnitz developed 'Differential Calculus.' Newton stole Leibnitz's work and called it his own, but he changed the word 'differential,' which Leibnitz used, to 'fluxion.' Present day Calculus uses the word differential not fluxion. This is because, when Newton was asked to define a fluxion, he could not, while Leibnitz could define his differential precisely...

"This leaves the 'Fundamental Law of Attraction.' Archimedes formulated the 'Law of Levers.' And the 'Fundamental Law of Attraction' is nothing but a rewrite of the law of levers. Here it is: Archimedes formulated that in a see-saw, which is the trivial case for levers, the following law is valid -- two bodies m1 and m2 are in balance from the fulcrum when they are r1 and r2 distances apart. That is, to have balance, this law must hold.

$$\frac{m1}{r1} = \frac{m2}{r2}$$

"Now make that a homogeneous equation. That is, rewrite it, so that all known terms are on one side and call if F. Then you have:

$$F = \frac{m1}{r1} - \frac{m2}{r2}$$

"Now rewrite the right-hand side as a fraction. Then you have:

$$F = \frac{m1*r2 - m2*r1}{r1*r2}$$

"Now factor out m1*m2 on the right hand side. Then you have:

$$F = \frac{m1*m2*(r2/m2 - r1/m1)}{r1*r2}$$

"Now give that bracketed expression, that 'fudge-factor,' a name. Call it g and rewrite the equation. Then you have:

$$F = g * \frac{m1*m2}{r1*r2}$$

"Let's fix the denominator by factoring out another r1. Then you have:

$$F = g * \frac{m1*m2}{r1*r1*(r2/r1)}$$

"Now bury the bracketed expression into g and call it G. Then you have:

$$F = G * \frac{m1*m2}{r1*r1}$$

"Now there is only one r involved so you can drop the subscript. (Or factor out r squared.) And what do you have?

$$F = G * \frac{m1*m2}{r*r}$$

"Now give G, that fudge-factor, a grandiose name, such as, 'Gravitational Constant,' and you have lulled yourself into believing that you can solve celestial problems, with a law which you call the 'Fundamental Law of Attraction!' What nonsense...

"But," I interrupted, "...with that law, no matter how bad it is, we solved and explained many phenomena, such as the ebb and tide, and many gravitational problems..."

"That is not the issue.." Hestia interrupted me, "...the ebb and tide was explained by Archimedes a long time ago. I object on two counts. First, it is a law Archimedes formulated, not Newton. Second, the fact that you believe that you have solved the law of attraction of celestial bodies -- this alone prevents humanity from finding the correct formulation which governs the attraction of celestial bodies. The reason this law 'works' occasionally-- and only for two bodies -- is, when you have a see-saw situation among the celestial bodies at a split-instant. That is, it only works in the steady-state or only in the trivial case.

"This kind of deception is practiced in all your sciences, not only in Physics. For example: In economics your species formulated the law of 'Supply and Demand.' This is not a law. It is only a conjecture. It even works from time to time. But as you can see, it is not universally true. The Utilities and Oil Companies violate that law all the time. What gives you the audacity to call it a law?" she asked.

"We are in search of the truth. When we determine a cause and effect relationship we tend to call it a law. Is that wrong?" I asked.

"Your species is incapable of finding or determining the absolute laws. These laws can only be revealed to your species by us. However, our revelation is only meaningful to your race when it can be understood by your race. That is, your race has the capacity to understand the revelation. Therefore, we reveal the same truth in terms your species can understand at that time.

"The search for truth is an endless cyclic process. It begins with chaos, or the unstructured truth. In order to classify chaos, you choose a few axioms or boundary conditions and classify the chaos according to your axioms. This process you call the analytic or rational method. Eventually chaos is restricted in this way and you have an ordered or structured truth. However, the very axioms or boundary conditions restrict the absolute truth. Since the derived truth is too restrictive you begin to relax the boundary conditions or axioms to make the restricted truth more complete. Just look at Euclid and Lobachevsky.

"This process you call 'fuzzy-logic.' When sufficient boundary conditions have been relaxed or axioms deleted, you come back to chaos but on a different phase of the cycle. That is, you arrived at chaos again, but now viewed from a different perspective. What do you do then? You begin the process all over again. New axioms are chosen and applied, and a new truth is derived. But again the structured truth is not absolute. Therefore, you apply fuzzy-logic and end up with chaos once more but again at a different phase of the cycle.

"Therefore, time is the differentia of each truth, it is endless. Since your race is mortal, your race is incapable of determining the real truth which is myriads of myriads cycles away from the initial phase. All you see is the projection of each phase, and your race calls that the truth," she paused.

"Is there no hope for the human race?" I asked.

"Not at all," she said. "We are the cosmic order and the human race is part of this order. We gave your race a spark of our immortality in your soul. Therefore, the truth is in your soul and not your rational mind. To maintain the harmony of this order your soul and mind must be at harmony and understand your capacity. Religions and mythologies are only manifestations of the cyclic process described before. Religions are the current cycles you understand or which have been revealed to you and you choose to believe. Mythologies are the religions from the past, or the cycles you have passed. They all reveal the same truth. But that truth is contingent on your capacity to understand it. Therefore, the true acquisition of truth must unify and reconcile each prior cycle with the present. When you place too much emphasis on your rational mind, you are likely to commit Hubris and defy the cosmic order. Then, you commit perversions on nature and on yourself making us more likely to intervene and punish your misdeeds..."

I woke up. I had overslept. Daylight was breaking into our bedroom. I looked around and there were white sheets, a white blanket, two beige pillows and a gilded headboard. Curious I thought. I got up, took my things and left the bedroom to prepare the coffee.

5

Hephaestus

I fell asleep and found myself at the spot from the nights before. Hermes was there, waiting for me.

"What did you think of Hera and Hestia?" he asked me.

"Let me say that I appreciate your time and effort in this quest. Please thank Hera and Hestia for the time they spent with me. I am absolutely thrilled with this experience. My problem is, I don't know when to speak and when to be silent. I certainly don't want to offend anybody. I enjoyed the conversations immensely. Is there a purpose in the order we see your peers?" I asked.

"Of course there is a purpose of the order in which you are seeing the Olympians. Hera is the ruler of the home, her prime role is to maintain harmony. She is the generative aspect of the cosmos. All problem definitions begin with her. Lately, she devotes a lot of time studying the impact of a solution on the Olympians and on the human race. She feels our destiny and your existence are so much intertwined that they can be no longer separated. Hera took on many of the executive functions of our species.

"Hestia is the ruler of childbirth or the evolution of a solution. Her mission is very difficult these days. She is too close to the actual daily problems. She is saddled with day to day operational responsibilities. She does not have the time to reflect on the impact of a solution. Because of that she is always on the defensive," he explained.

Then he continued pensively, " The fact that Hera did not mention the complex numbers, did not seem to bother you at all?"

he asked.

I thought a moment about Hera's conversation, then I remembered why I did not ask any question in her presence. So I answered Hermes.

"In fact, I am glad you brought this up. I was so overwhelmed with her personality and her surroundings that I forgot to ask her a few pertinent questions. I just assumed she was talking about Euler's classification of numbers, was she not?"

"Of course she was," Hermes replied. "You see, Euler's classification defined all numbers precisely. Euler's equation binds the five most important numbers in the cosmic order; e, π, i, 1 and 0 with the equation:

$$e^{\pi * i} - 1 = 0$$

"This equation is of primary importance. You can readily see that the complex number i is only used as a phase shift for all other numbers into another dimension. The nature of all numbers in your 'real world' is well defined with Euler's classification. Thus numbers can be phased from one dimension into another. That is, the shift, and hence the multiplicity of roots can be seen from the formula:

$$e^{\Theta * i} = \cos(\Theta) + i * \sin(\Theta)$$

"Since the sine and cosine have a periodicity of 2 π, each solution has an infinity of solutions -- all of which are 2 π apart. Of course, in your world you use only the first spacial solution which you call the 'principal branch.' Thus, all sciences which use mathematics must incorporate π, e, i, 1 and 0 when they attempt a formulation for the real world. In other words, not only the primitives but also all their multiplicities. That is, the number 1, stands for all integers. The number 0 for all roots in an equation, i for the phase shift. While π and e are in a class all of their own. Of course, some day you will discover how to include the other transcendental numbers," and Hermes paused.

"How was your day?" he inquired.

"Well, today I started to down-load the available trade and fundamental data my clients have. What a mess. Many data elements are missing. The historical data is very short and the instruments are fragmented. It will be some time before the data will be complete and in the required form," I said.

"Well,..." he started again "I am sure you'll find a way to resolve this," then after a pause:

"I promised to brief you on the other aspects which affect the United States and the European Union. One of them is religion. But, before I start, do you have any questions about the historians I covered last night?"

"As a matter of fact I have. You did not mention Josephus, Nestor, Sturluson, Voltaire, Niebuhr and Mommsen. Are they not important?"

"Not at all. They are very important but they are more of the special case variety...

"Josephus has become important only recently, in your time. Before that he was ignored because his history deals with the 'Jewish Wars.' Many consider him an apologist for the Jewish Nation. He was a Roman citizen, but he was also a Jew.

"However, he had access to an older version of the Old Testament which is now lost and is substantially different from the version used in the Septuagint translation. His version is more accurate. This was discovered only last century.

"Nestor was a very well educated Greek monk, who was sent from Constantinople to Kiev to 'set the records straight,' in the 11th century. He was a contemporary of Yaroslav (Jaroslav) the Wise and Harold of Norway. At that time, the Swedes, Norwegians and Danes had their roots still in the Ukraine, Belarus and Novhorod (Novgorod). That is, he came to sow the same kind of disinformation among the Ostrogoths as Rome was sowing among the Merovingians or Visigoths. Remember, the policy of Constantinople and Rome was to cut the umbilical cord between the Ostrogoths and Visigoths. And in addition, to cut their umbilical cord with the Nordic countries. That is, the Slavs had to be given a new identity, just like the Merovingians.

"In Kiev, there was a large monastery called The Monastery of the Caves. So, he was sent there where he wrote the history of the martyrs Boris and Hlib (Gleb).Some say that he also initiated the Kievan Chronicle.

"When Nestor died, another monk from Greece was sent to Kiev to continue his work. His name was Sylvester. He became abbot of the Monastery of the Caves, wrote a 'Slavonic History' and continued the Kievan Chronicle. The upshot was, these two monks were able to cut the umbilical cord between the Ostrogoths and Visigoths, and between the Ostrogoths and the Scandinavian countries. In this new incarnation they became Slavs.

"Snorri Sturluson was an Icelandic Poet in the 13th century. We loved him a great deal. We recognized in him another Homer. Another historian who could write history in a poetic style. This endeared him to us.

"His goal was to write a history of the Norsemen, but by then there was so much disinformation about the Goths and Norsemen that it was impossible to find references of any kind. So, we urged him to take the ballads and songs which were still circulating, and piece them together into a history of the Goths. This he did. His book is called the 'Heimskringla.' This book has become the definitive history of the Norsemen-Goths for the time period of 600 to 1200. Before that, the ballads and songs were very sparse. The work was laborious and he did not finish it. In any event, that became the only and most accurate history for that period.

"As a by-product he found -- to his own amazement -- that a bard from Iceland could travel in Spain, France, England, Denmark, Norway, Sweden, Novhorod, Belarus and the Ukraine, speak only the Icelandic tongue and be understood there. That is, disinformation about the Goths was not yet complete, despite the policies of Rome and Constantinople.

"Voltaire is more famous for his plays. He lived in the 18th century. He wrote the history of Louis XIII and Louis XIV. What propelled him to fame was his historical novel about Charles XII. After that he wrote the 'definitive history of Russia;' but to the specifications provided by the Russian regime. He coined the word Russia. They call their country Rossija to this day.It is derived from the Dutch word Ross or horse which was coined by Peter I who called his realm 'The Land of Horses.'

"Voltaire made a lot of money with his Russian history (which is not really a history at all but a whitewash of the Czarist Regime in Russia.) Of course, all Russians love him because his history put Russia on the map of Europe.Consequently, every Russian historian of note has a dedication to Voltaire.

"Mommsen was a German. He debunked Livy, and as you know, Germany is a newly created state. It was created after the Franco-Prussian war in 1871. In Versailles, in the Hall of Mirrors, the German State was created by proclamation. However, Mommsen's objective was to create the environment in which the Germans could steal the history of other nations in order to build their own. He chose to pick on the Goths, and simply declared them to be a Germanic people, which they are not. Tacitus, Pliny the Elder and Strabo attest to that. The movement of the Goths he called: 'Völkerwanderung.' This created a huge pot, a virtual grab-bag for disinformation.

"This theft opened the floodgates for Wagner who took the Gothic mythologies and created the 'Ring,' a series of four operas. In that entire operatic sequence there is only one German goddess: Erde.

"All other characters are from the Gothic pantheon. Hitler picked up on Mommsen's trail. He called his Germanization of the Gothic history: 'Kulturkampf.'

"Niebuhr was a Dane. He proved that all histories written before the 19th century were essentially false. Most were written to serve the ruler (Gibbon), the state (Voltaire and Gibbon), the Pope (Gregory of Tours) or a Bishop (Jordanes). He believed a new, fresh and more accurate history of Western Civilization was overdue..."

"Wait a minute," I piped in, "wasn't Mommsen a student of Niebuhr?"

"Yes he was. Niebuhr wanted the histories corrected while Mommsen altered the history to suit Germany's cause and identity. Their goals were diametrically opposed, but since they were contemporaries of sorts, I mention Niebuhr last. Unfortunately the histories written before Niebuhr and Mommsen's interpretation of history still dominate European text books. Especially, Western European text books. And, because the Germans rule in Europe, Mommsen provided them with the blueprint they needed.

"Now, let's discuss one of the items left from last night: Religion, in the new European Union. In Continental Europe, the United States is considered to be a Jewish State. England is different, because they are heretics in the eyes of the Vatican anyway, and the bounty for their conquest and conversion is still in effect. In France the various branches of the Baptists, Methodists, Quakers and others are being closed down because they are considered to be Jewish sects. Germany will not be far behind. The other religions are still tolerated, but their days are numbered. Europe will once again attempt to have one uniform religion in its realm..."

"Wait a minute," I interrupted, "...who writes about the bounty set on England by the Pope?"

"Practically every Spanish historian who writes about the 'Spanish Armada.' Of course, if you read only English accounts, then that information will not be there. England does not like to flaunt the fact that they are heretics.

"As I mentioned before, just like the Roman Empire tried to have only one branch of Christianity -- the Orthodox Faith -- the Holy Roman Empire tried to have only one form of Christianity--

the Roman Faith or Catholicism.

"This, of course, is due to the pressure applied by the Pope or Vatican. In fact, ever since Christianity became the religion of choice in the Roman Empire, it only tolerated one denomination. The same intolerance was practiced by Rome and her Popes. All others were, by and large, exterminated. The only acceptable Christian religions in Europe today are: Catholics, Orthodox and Lutheran Protestants.

"Catholicism came from Rome, after 600 AD -- after Emperor Justinian promoted the Bishop of Rome to Patriarch. It is now the Christianity of Western Europe. Orthodoxy, however, preceded the Roman Faith. It was the religion of choice of the Roman Emperors, who ruled from Constantinople. They converted Eastern Europe. Now they are called schismatic, ever since the Holy Roman Empire got the upper hand, militarily. The Lutheran Protestants won their right of existence from the Catholics in the 30 Years War. They are situated mostly in Central and Northern Europe. Germany is the dividing line. Southern Germany, Bavaria and Austria are Catholic while Northern Germany is Protestant.

"The English, however, are heretics, ever since King Henry VIII evicted the Catholics and installed his own brand of Christianity. It is called the Anglican Church.

"That is, the rule in Europe became: the ruler determines the religion. They guard their turf, so to speak, and do not allow further fragmentation. It is likely, therefore, that religious persecution is around the corner and may be more intense than ever..."

"Why do you say that?" I inquired.

"I will cover that in greater detail later-on. For now, just keep the following in mind. You have in America a great expression: 'follow the money trail.' Every religion needs money to exist, flourish and grow. This comes in the form of tithes, donations and bequests. Over the years many other forms of raising money were invented: selling indulgences, selling fragments of relics, selling holy water and so on. (Note that televangelists are popular in America.) If you allow the spread of sects, that revenue is gone. The coffers will be depleted. Then the religious hierarchy may be forced to work for its subsistence. This thought alone sends shudders down their spine.

"Let's examine how it evolved, because this will be important in tomorrow's discussion. After Titus destroyed Jerusalem in 70 AD, the Jews were dispersed throughout the Empire, and as Jews opened a Synagogue, a Christian church sprung up right next to it. That is, the early Christians followed on the coattails of the Jews. The reason this was so is because conversion was easiest when the convert was a Jew. This is why the Romans called the early Christians a Jewish sect.

"Two factors helped the Christians in their rapid growth. One was the fact that it was an urban religion. Christians led an exemplary life which attracted many Gentiles. In particular, when there was an epidemic of any kind -- which was so frequent that only large scale epidemics were recorded -- most residents fled the city, but the Christians stayed behind. They tended to the sick and earned their respect.

"The second factor was a dire shortage of women in the Roman Empire. The Gentiles mistreated their women. Abortions were common-place and in those days, an abortion was usually fatal for the woman. In addition, most gentiles wanted sons. Thus, when a girl was born, she was often abandoned or set out in the wild. Like it or not, as a result many Gentiles had to marry Christian women. This usually resulted in the conversion of the husband and then the entire family.

"Meanwhile, as Christianity grew by leaps and bounds this way, there was no single spiritual leader, allowing many forms of Christianity to evolve. When Emperor Constantine issued the 'Edict of Tolerance' in Milan, in 313 AD, there were at least 20 major branches of Christianity. Constantine was not a Christian, he was a sun-worshipper, but as Emperor of the Roman Empire he was also Pontifex Maximus: the head of every religion in the empire, including Christianity.

"As head of the Christian Church, Constantine appointed a Bishop for every 'metropolitan area' in the empire, which was both a military and cleric title. The Bishop was the leader of the local militia and administrator of the Faith. In the administrative sense, Christianity was a God-send to the Emperor because, Constantine now had someone loyal to him in every metropolitan area.

"Constantine then appointed a Patriarch, a leader of the Church, but his choice fell on Arius, the Bishop of Syria. Arius in turn demanded that all Christians in the empire convert to his brand of Christianity and most did. Only one Bishop objected and called Arius' brand of Christianity heresy. The objector was Bishop Athanasius from Alexandria in Egypt. His form of Christianity was called Orthodoxy. A bitter debate ensued between Arius and Athanasius. In the end each excommunicated the other.However, Arius had the emperor on his side and Constantine sent a small task force to Alexandria to fetch Athanasius forcing Athanasius to flee to Ethiopia. For 70 years, Athanasius kept evading his captors. It was not until Valens became Emperor that the Arian brand of Christianity was declared a heresy and Orthodoxy the only true Christian Faith. With Orthodoxy the only true faith, conversion was now required of all the Arian Christians. Many converted, but many more did not. The holdouts were declared heretics and were subsequently slaughtered, their property seized and their servants enslaved. During this rampage many large sects were still tolerated. Eventually, however, each sect was done away with. The policy of the Empire was to target one sect for extermination every decade or so. The first to be targeted were the Arian Christians, of course. This process took about 300 years. In the end, there was only one sect left -- the Monophysites. By then, Islam was on the rise. Thus, when the Emperor Heraclites tried to convert the Monophysites, they converted to Islam. With their conversion to Islam many of the richest provinces of the Roman Empire became Muslim, with the end result that Constantinople now faced the Muslims who stood ready to dismantle the Roman Empire in 673.

"In 800, of course, as Constantinople was at the brink of destruction by the Muslims. Roman militarism was replaced with Christian monasticism since about 330. Both East and West had only small mercenary forces, while Islam had a mighty army. Therefore, the Patriarch of Rome decided to break away from Orthodoxy and form his own brand of Christianity: The Roman Church and install a new militarism directed by the Pope. With that break, all the western provinces were lost to the Roman Empire. Christianity now had two Empires -- the old Roman Empire run from Constantinople and the new Roman empire -- the Holy Roman Empire, run from Rome. But both empires were weak and feeble. It is almost a miracle that both survived for as long as they did, and this only because they began actively converting the rest of Europe. Constantinople converted Eastern Europe and Rome converted Western Europe. Just look at the military history for that period. From 330 to 800, there were no military exploits by Roman legionaires only by Roman mercenaries, led by foreign generals. While for the same time span, 470 years, for the prior Roman history there were countless Roman expeditions. For example: Stilicho was an Alan Goth and commanded mercenaries; Aetius was a Roman but commanded the Scythians; Belizarius and Narses were Romans but commanded mercenaries and so on...

"The death blow for the Roman Empire in Constantinople came not from the Muslims but from Rome. In 1204, the Fourth Crusade took Constantinople. They sacked and dismantled it. Everything of any value was taken away. Eventually, Constantinople was re-conquered, but from then on her days were numbered. In 1453, Constantinople was finally conquered by the Muslims with the help of the Austrians. (The Austrians built the cannon which breached the walls of Constantinople. It was called: 'Die Dicke Berta.') Thus ended the Roman Empire. It had ruled the known world for over 1600 years: from about 200 BC to 1453 AD. Some Western historians call the Roman Empire, for the period from 800 to

1453, the Byzantine Empire. The fall of Constantinople ushered in the Renaissance in Italy as the last priceless possessions, mostly books, were sold in Florence, Genoa, Venice and Rome at bargain prices.

"It appeared as if the woes of the Holy Roman Empire were over. At last there was only one 'Roman Empire' with only one dominant Christian Faith: Catholicism. All other sects had been exterminated in the West even though large areas were still 'infested with heretics.' Against them Rome launched internal Crusades and the Inquisition. Spain was reconquered, the Moors and Jews were evicted from Western Europe. Then, Western Europe began evicting all Jews systematically: from France, from England and from the rest of the Holy Roman Empire. This is when we intervened.

"I summoned the Polish Barons one by one, Hubris went to see the Pope, Athene paid a visit to Martin Luther and Ares went to see Ivan the Terrible in his god-forsaken dungeon in the Kremlin." Hermes paused pensively. It seemed he was trying to piece the independent actions together. After a long pause, he continued. I urged the Polish Barons to accept Jagiello's offer. To marry off Princess Hedzwiga (Yadviga or Jadwiga) to Jagiello and to invite the Jews into their realm. Their main objection was that Hedzwiga was already married to Maximilian, the Austrian Duke. I told them that was no problem at all. Just pay the Pope and her marriage will be annulled. This they did. Hedzwiga's marriage was annulled and they married her off to Jagiello. Then, they invited the Jews to manage their money. What a match this was!

"Without firing a single shot, without drawing a single sword, Poland tripled in size. Poland became the largest and richest Kingdom in Europe: larger than Muscovy and richer than France and England combined. We felt Poland would rally the Goths and establish a great empire. Remember, the Ukrainian Hetman from the Don, Ermak, had not yet gifted his conquest of Siberia to Ivan the Terrible. But the Polish Barons became greedy, selfish and badly counselled by their Jesuit advisors. In the end, they brought on their own downfall. If it were not for Countess Maria Walewska, Poland would not exist today. Thus you can see, Poland's greatness and very existence is due not to her Kings or Barons but to two women: Princess Hedzwiga and Countess Walewska.

"Hubris had a great plan to cut down the powers of the Pope. All that money coming in from England, France, Spain, the Low Countries, Poland, Italian City States, German Dukedoms and from the Scandinavian lands swelled the coffers of the Pope. In England it was called 'Saint Peter's Pence.' Hubris made a suggestion to raise much more money to re-build Rome to the glory of the gods. Hubris knew that the Pope would turn his idea into a selfish purpose, and the Pope did. He sent out legates to all parts of his realm to sell indulgences. Meanwhile, Athene had prepared Luther. Martin Luther was a devout Catholic, but Athene gave him the spark of reason. So, when the indulgences were sold in his jurisdiction, Luther was outraged. Most of his congregation had pre-paid for their sins and did not bother to attend his church anymore. One day Luther wrote down his 95 objections, he called them -- 'Theses' -- and posted them on the front door of his church in Wittenberg. Of course this single act eventually led to the Reformation. We did not foresee the carnage it would cause. More than half the population of Western Europe perished in 'Holy Wars' before this matter was settled in 1648. The only good which came of it was that the Protestants, in particular the Lutherans, won their right to exist among the Catholics.

"Henry VIII from England, was the first to respond to Luther's Theses. He wrote a rebuttal and sent it to the Pope. A grateful Pope dubbed Henry 'The Saviour of Christendom.'

"Meanwhile, Poseidon intervened. He summoned the Emperor Maximilian and urged him to establish maritime laws and give all nations a piece of the action in the 'New World,' which Columbus had discovered in the West and the Portuguese had explored in the East. Maximilian asked the Pope for a hasty conference in Tordesillas in 1494 and they partitioned the world into 'Two Spheres of Influence and Exploitation.' The West was awarded to Spain and the East to Portugal. Of course once the news of this treaty became public knowledge, all seafaring nations began to scheme and to defy this treaty, primarily, England, France and the Low Countries. This partition enraged King Henry VIII of England and he took drastic steps. We sent Hera to appease him, but the King would not listen to her. Henry decided to punish the Holy Roman Empire and the Pope. In order to disguise his intent he asked the Pope for a divorce without the proper compensation. The Pope refused to grant it unless he paid the established fee. This was all Henry needed. He closed all the Catholic institutions and installed his own brand of Christianity. He called it the Anglican Church. With that bold stroke, he robbed the Pope of the revenue from England. The Pope retaliated by issuing an interdict. This had no effect because the Church was now controlled by Henry. Reluctantly the Pope posted a bounty for the conquest of England: two million Ducats in gold.

"That bounty is still in effect today. At that time, Philip II of Spain, tried to collect it. Hastily he put together a fleet of about 130 ships. He called it by a grand name: The Armada. But the Spanish Armada was not suitable to navigate the Atlantic Ocean. The bulk of the fleet were transport ships designed for the Mediterranean. The Armada was to meet in the Low Countries with the Duke of Parma and ferry his army across the Channel. When the Armada arrived the Duke was not ready, and the Armada could not wait indefinitely. By the time the Armada decided to return to Spain, the English blocked the Channel with a fleet of their own. There was a minor skirmish, but neither side lost any ships due to cannon fire. The Armada then made the fateful decision to circumnavigate England on their return voyage. As they passed Scotland, many of their ships began to fall apart in a storm. Many of the shipwrecked made it to Ireland where most of the seamen were clubbed to death. Less than 80 ships made it back to Spain, an ignominious end to the first attempt to collect the bounty.

"The second attempt was made by Napoleon. It failed also. However, Napoleon needed cash, so he sold the Territory of Louisiana to the United States, which doubled the size of your country. Ares advised Napoleon and I counselled President Jefferson.

"The last attempt was by Hitler. It failed also. This time Ares advised Hitler and Poseidon counselled Churchill. When Hitler was assured that he had a deal with the Duke of Windsor, he invaded the Soviet Union. Ultimately, the deal fell through, but, by then, Hitler could not turn back. Thus, the bounty is still there to be earned."

Then, Hermes changed the topic.

"Today we will explore another aspect. Hold on," he said as he stretched his rod towards me. I clutched it and we were off.

The next thing I knew we were in a huge warehouse or laboratory about forty feet above the main floor. Below, I could see six rows. Each row was approximately ten yards wide and one hundred yards long. The warehouse seemed to be the size of a football field and about sixty feet tall. A second floor, about forty feet above the ground, protruded around the warehouse along the walls into the otherwise open first floor. We were on the second floor. The second floor seemed to be offices with a hallway. Three staircases with railings were attached along the edges.

On the first row, to my right, were crates and boxes. They were all neatly stacked on top of each other in clusters. The clusters formed a row along the wall of the warehouse. Huge humanoid creatures carried boxes from the outside into the warehouse through oversized open doors and formed neatly stacked heaps at the end of the first row. Next there were two aisles with shelves stacked with parts and materials of all kinds, plus two rows of tables at which regular humans were busy working. On the other side of the warehouse were glass enclosed cubicles. They were filled with tiny humanoids and all sorts of equipment.

"Welcome to the Vesuvian Enterprises," I heard someone say from behind me.

I turned around. I noticed a smile on Hermes's face. Then, I saw a mighty man in his 40's or so, smiling at us. He was dressed in a three-piece business suit. It was gray and was made of silk. The fit was tapered, definitely Italian made, I thought. A gold tie with blue stripes glowed from his gray silk shirt.

"Let me take you around," he said.

He started to walk down the aisle. I noticed he had a slight limp on his left side. This had to be Hephaestus, I thought. He started to explain:

"This is the sixth floor of my workshop. I employ titans, giants, humans and dwarfs. Prometheus is in charge of the titans. Fasolt is in charge of the giants. Daedalus is in charge of the humans. And, Alberich is in charge of the dwarfs."

"On this floor we assemble computers. We test the components, we integrate them, and then we stress-test their performance characteristics. Occasionally, we speed them up a little bit, by a factor of sixty or three hundred sixty, depending on their primary use. The enclosed section is our quality control area. The finished products are delivered to Hera, Apollo, Athene, Artemis, Demeter, Hades and Zeus; all according to their need. Hestia, Poseidon, Bacchus and Ares have not yet computerized their affairs. Hestia, because she is too involved. Poseidon, because he seems to have found another alternative; Bacchus, because he is preoccupied with the karma of the cosmos; and, Ares because he refuses to accept computers as a new tool. Hades is in the midst of a conversion. His primary needs are mass storage requirements," he paused.

"I use a matrix management structure which I originated in Chicago, to improve quality and ease of usage. Each species is evaluated by me according to the quality of their work. It must be perfect in every respect. Since time and cost is not a factor, quality and ease of usage are my main constraints. I deliver the best and easiest products to use. Most are 'turn-key' systems. In fact, only Apollo and Athene require raw computing power and develop their own applications," he paused again.

"All our work is custom made. All our products are hand made or assembled. We do not use assembly lines, conveyors or robots. I have an unlimited supply of workers at my disposal. I call them 'Lulus' or 'Adams.' They serve me well. I teach them every skill they need to know. Conveyor belts degrade the pride and craftsmanship of my workers. My products are perfect to the most infinitesimal detail.That type of perfection is not possible with mindless machines," he stopped as if soliciting a challenging question.

Who could possibly challenge his method? I saw the detail and workmanship in Hera's palace. I was impressed beyond any comment. But, I had the distinct feeling that he was expecting a question from me.

"How are the other floors used?" I asked.

"The first floor still has my anvil and occasionally I still like to work with it. We use that floor mainly to finish the stone and marble for my customers. The second floor I use for body armor and occasionally we have some demand for it. Today nobody wears it any more. Now it is used mainly for decorations.

"The third floor is where we make fine gold jewelry or all gold products. It is still one of our busiest floors. The fourth floor is were we forge guns and weapon systems of the first kind. These are weapon systems which use gunpowder in one form or another. The fifth floor is used for weapon systems which use nuclear power. I am planning to de-escalate this activity. Once we nearly blew up Mt. Vesuvius. It is far too dangerous and the nuclear waste presents a real problem. I have found a corner in the universe were I safely tucked away the waste. But at the rate the human race is proliferating nuclear power and exploring the universe, they could accidentally disturb it, and who knows what could happen. Now I am planning for a seventh floor. Most of the groundwork has been completed. We have to plan well ahead of the human race, otherwise we could be in for some nasty surprises."

After a pause he continued. "Apollo asked me a number of times to relocate to the United States. I have looked for a suitable place. I should. My wife Aphrodite spends a lot of time near Los Angeles. But, I have not found a suitable mountain. I am considering Mt. St. Helen. But, each time I go there, I have a sort of longing for this place. I should find a way to move the movie industry back to Rome or Naples instead. However, each time I am ready, a new project prevents me from completing this task. At times I miss Aphrodite a lot and the travelling from here to Los Angeles is exhausting. I have been here a long time and I prefer to work in one place. She prefers more glamorous locations. The only site I would consider would be Hawaii. But she objects to Hawaii because her skin could burn and she may get wrinkles. In addition, I would have to change my wardrobe and I don't like that either. I like the local style the most. Lastly, different aspects want me in different places. Apollo wants me near Washington DC, or Houston, or Daytona. But, there are no suitable mountains in that area for my activity. I refuse to go completely underground," he said.

We reached the end of the walkway on one side of the floor. We were about to turn, when he turned to me and said.

"I heard you developed XL and now you are trying to solve the market timing problem. Let me give you a few words of advice and encouragement. Examine every detail before you embark on this venture. Make sure the method is precise and consistent with the holistic approach. Make the model dynamic and trade-sensitive. Include as many strategic tools as possible, so you don't have to retro-fit later on. Then, if you devote boundless energy, you will succeed -- if your model is easy to use. In other words, precision and craftsmanship are the key words in your endeavour, and ease of usage is what sells the product" I heard him say.

"Do you employ Gremlins?" I asked.

"Certainly. Finella and her Widgets work for Alberich. And, I might add, they do a fine job..."

For some reason, Hermes poked his rod into my hand. Instinctively I held on to it. As soon as I did, we were off and moving through space.

6

Poseidon

We were back in our familiar valley. Hermes got seated and started.

"Let me finish the topic I talked about earlier."

"Ok." I said as I nodded my head.

"This time let me step back in time as we look towards the East. In Moscow, Ares was advising Ivan the Terrible to make war against the Tartars. At first, Ivan was not receptive. He wanted to marry Queen Elizabeth of England, but his overtures were firmly rebuffed. Then, he agreed with Ares.

"By that time, 'The Golden Horde' had divided into four Khanates: Crimea, Kazan, Astrakhan and Sibir. The Khanate of Crimea was conquered by the Ottoman Turks in 1475. This made their presence only stronger since they could now rally the full power of the Ottoman Empire. Therefore, Ivan decided to attack the Khanate of Kazan. He conquered it, but it was such a horrible bloodbath that the Khanate of Astrakhan surrendered to Ivan without a battle. They knew they were next in line.

"The Khanate Sibir was then conquered by the Don Cossack Hetman Ermak and gifted to Ivan as Siberia. On the surface it appeared that Ivan had just expanded his realm by leaps and bounds, but the Crimean Tartars assembled an army of about 200 thousand strong and invaded Muscovy. They defeated Ivan's forces and hemmed him in, in the Kremlin. They then rounded up all non-Tartars in his realm, over 1 million of them, and drove them like cattle to the slave markets in the Crimea...

"Since that day, and until today, the bulk of the population of the Duchy of Muscovy is Tartar. This is why Ivan's successors used the Ukraine, Byelorussia and other minorities they conquered to re-settle the heartland of Russia to establish an equilibrium between the European and Mongol population. Neither Peter I, nor Alexander I, nor Nicholas II succeeded, even though they nearly depopulated the Goths.

"Stalin resorted to even more drastic measures. Not only did he depopulate the Ukraine and Byelorussia, he annexed portions of the Ukraine and Byelorussia into the Russian Republic. For example: In 1926, the Ukrainian Don and Kuban areas were annexed forcibly into the Russian Republic. Gorbachev and Solzhenitsyn are from the Don area, but I'll cover all that in more detail when we discuss the Goths." Hermes took a long pause.

I knew there was more on his mind, so I simply kept quiet. Finally, Hermes started again.

"While some of the old problems of the Holy Roman Empire have been resolved, there are too many new problems lurking in the background for a European Union to include Russia. To begin with, Siberia has many different religions, and as I have shown you, the European Union was always striving to be of one faith, of one denomination. After much bloodshed only three Christian denominations are begrudgingly accepted: Catholics, Protestants and Orthodox. In Siberia you have heathens, Muslims, Hindu and Buddhists.

"Europe is not well disposed to these beliefs. In addition, there are the ethnic considerations. By and large, present day Europe is Gothic-German-Celtic-Gaelic. They are similar races. Once they go beyond Byelorussia and the Ukraine, however, they will encounter Tartars, Chinese, Hindu and many other ethnic groups. Stalin held them together with an iron fist, with stark terror. I don't think the European Union can handle this problem. However, your country is ideally suited to accommodate these minorities. Unfortunately, however, your Presidents are advised badly. Many of their advisors are of Polish background and they are intensely anti-Russian. While the United States is the best ally for Russia, Russia may be painted into a corner and forced to join the European Union.

"What has Russia to offer? Incredible resources of raw materials: Oil, gas, timber, gold, diamonds and much more. As these raw materials will get scarcer in this century, both the United States and the European Union will seek to entice Russia into a partnership. And, don't forget, as the polar ice will recede this century, Russia will have many new ports. What has Russia to gain? A decent standard of living. The Communist regime deprived them for so long of the most basic necessities that they are ready to strike a deal with Hades to improve their lot. Do you agree with my assessment?"

I was stunned. All I could utter was, "Yes, I agree with you wholeheartedly..."

"In that case," Hermes interrupted me, "let's be on our way." As he shoved his rod into my hands.

With that, we floated once again through endless space. Eventually we came to a stop. When I opened my eyes we were in a large and spacious office.

The floor was a soft green marble with a bluish hue to it. The walls were also of marble and had large windows. Beyond the glass of the windows fish were floating, like in a huge aquarium. Dark green drapes offset the marble on the wall. Closer to one wall was a large desk. Huge windows flanked it on each side. I could not determine the material the desk was made of, but it seemed to be green with an irregular white pattern on it.The legs of the desk were carved dolphins pointing upwards and holding the flat desk top. The dolphins were carved from ebony. Behind the desk sat a huge elderly man in a dark green suit. What was striking about him was his hair and his beard. His hair engulfed his face. It looked like a lion's mane. His hair was mostly white with what seemed to be greenish stands interwoven throughout. He was ticking away with a small golden tripod on his desk. This had to be Poseidon, I thought.

"Finally," he roared.

"I was expecting you," he continued.

His eyes were piercing me. I had a very un-easy feeling.

"You think it is so easy to solve the market timing problem?" he roared again. Then he continued:

"I favor the intuitive approach for non-linear problems," he roared again. "Apollo has been nursing the human race to understand the simplest linear problems and look where you are. Almost no place. Even the simplest problems in counting give you endless paradoxes," he thundered as if he was enjoying himself.

"I taught the Babylonians and Egyptians to build massive and beautiful structures. Then Apollo had to come along and convince Pythagoras that the formulations had no rational basis. No rational explanation, he claimed! They allowed inconsistencies, he insisted. Rope-stretchers, you call them!" he seemed to laugh in his deep voice.

"Apollo had his turn for a while: Pythagoras, Eudoxus, Euclid and Archimedes all listened to Apollo. You call this the 'Golden Era of Greece.' All I had to do was to raise the consciousness of Zeno and your race entangled itself in endless paradoxes. Then, it was my turn again. Initially, I was on the side of Carthage against Rome. But, when Dido let Aeneas slip though her fingers, I sided with Rome against the rest of the barbarians and intellectuals. Look what empire I created. It could have lasted another 1000 years had Demeter not moved the Goths against Rome. But I convinced the Goths to follow the footsteps of Rome. They did. And I reigned for another 1000 years," he roared again.

"Then Apollo buttonholed Galileo who was in his mid-life crisis and the rational method was in favor again. Descartes, Leibniz and Euler were Apollo's disciples. So, I simply moved to England and taught Newton how to plagiarize the rational wave. Do you see what happened? Everybody eulogizes Newton, few if any know of Apollo's students. And, so it goes. Apollo tries to perfect the rational methods, and I counter with paradoxes or dualities of the problem. The intuitive approach can not be dismissed because it is humanity's only window to the immortals. This is the only avenue by which we can reveal the mysteries of the infinite in a consistent way and within the capacity of the human soul." He seemed pleased and paused to wait for a question.

I was not about to ask anything. I just stood there, I was highly intimidated. I did not dare to contradict his wisdom.

He tapped his tripod on the table and continued: "You think Leibniz solved many problems with 'Differential Calculus' and the use of differentials? He only circumvented the nature of the problem. I am going to counter this folly with 'fractals.' We'll see how long it will take your race to unravel these mysteries," he bellowed again.

After a while he continued. "Apollo almost won with Euler. Euler explained the nature of numbers so clearly and so precisely that even I was amazed at the precise definition. For a while I had to search high and low to find someone to show that Euler's formulation was not complete. I found Dedekind and he showed the nature of real numbers. Not that the concept was new in any way, Archimedes showed the macro behavior in his 'The Sand-Reckoner.' I only showed Dedekind how the reflection principle applies to the micro-behavior of numbers. The rationalization of analysis nearly collapsed. But then Apollo found Lebesgue and corrected the deficiencies. Now you have formulated the relationship of reals to transcendentals, irrationals and integers. Do you really think academia will accept your formulation?" he paused briefly and then continued in his stentorian voice.

"I must admit that right now Apollo has the upper hand. Analysis seems to be the mainstay of the educational hierarchy. So, for now I have institutionalized all schools, and look at what we have: The primary school system is polarized with the University system. Each wants to be credited with educational excellence. Naturally, the primary system must lose in this contest. They only teach students from the ages of 6 to 18. Whereas as soon as the University system became institutionalized, everybody from age 18 on until their senility sets in becomes a potential candidate for them. Thus, their mission becomes perpetual teaching and perpetual training. Of what? Of nothing practical of course, but only of a myriad of conjectures and suppositions! Now, I am looking for a sensitive statistician who can demonstrate the folly of the analytic approach in a different way. Chaos, in terms of probabilities versus the analytic solution. In terms of its likelihood of existence in the real world. The paradox of course is that -- if a solution is very precise -- it has no chance of existing. This is because the axioms must be rigid and inflexible. Then the axioms in themselves preclude the existence of that problem in any real sense. In a changing universe the axioms can-not be rigid, they must be variable. Therefore, a precise solution, while imaginable, is far removed from reality. On the other hand, chaos while always changing, has a determinable statistical likelihood of happening." He paused as if inviting yet another question.

"Which then is the better approach? A solution which is precise but has no associated real problem, or a solution which characterizes a real problem, is statistical in nature but has no precise formulation?" said he as he ticked away with his tripod on the table.

His question could not be answered. Because the first part of the statement said that precise solutions were only feasible for imaginary problems. Real problems had no precise solutions. The only admissible solutions to real problems were in terms of their likelihood of occurring. That is, the real world was a world of uncertainty, not of order and certainty.

"Keep this in mind as you work on the market timing problem towards a rational solution. I still prefer patterns to formulas. To me, a 'saucer,' a 'cup-and-handle,' a 'flag,' a 'trend' and the 'momentum' is all I need to know to be effective in the securities market," he continued to roar.

I did not wish to contradict him in any way. But I thought about the tools in error analysis. What relationship is there in error analysis with respect to a solution? I thought. I almost heard this question ticking away in my mind.

He smiled in a jovial way and roared on: "You think error analysis has the answer?" He seemed amused as he continued:

"You have a multitude of forms of error analysis. To Gauss, Apollo revealed the notion of a residual error for linear systems. To Hilbert, Apollo revealed the notions of eigenvalues and the stability characterization for linear systems. To Bernoulli, Apollo revealed statistical inferences. To Markov, Apollo revealed linked chain events. To Tesla, Apollo revealed how to harness electricity using alternating current. To Fermi, Apollo revealed the Fermi Surfaces and Quantum Mechanics. I could go on and on. Yet your race has made no attempt to reconcile and to determine their nature and interaction. All you produced was the atom bomb. The revelations of Apollo culminated only in destruction and misuse. You have polluted my realm. Can't you see that when you try to destroy me, you are destroying yourself?" he roared at me.

I was frightened. Please don't think, I thought to myself. Each thought was like a real question to him. He read my mind like an open book. There was no way I was going to antagonize him in any way. My eyes began to shift, first onto the desk top. Then I thought of a safer place still, the legs of the desk. Then I heard him roar again:

"I am not blaming you personally. I hope you understand this. I only want to raise your consciousness so as not to be too single-minded in your work. Keep a broader perspective," he rumbled with a much gentler voice.

I felt Hermes's rod in my hand. I clutched my end and we were gone.

7

Demeter

The next thing I know, we were standing in a silo gazing at a good-looking woman. She appeared to be in her forties, dressed in blue jeans and a brown and blue plaid blouse. Her hair was short, her face was round and there was a sadness in her eyes. She mustered a faint smile and said softly to me:

"Did Poseidon overwhelm you?" she asked softly. She did not wait for an answer but continued: "He usually does," as she answered her own question.

"I am Demeter. I have brought you here because I want you to see both the abundance and the despair your race has created," she said.

"I know both aspects. I create abundance in your crops, but I also know despair. My daughter, Persephone, was abducted by Hades and I searched for her for untold centuries. I was so desperate, I plagued this world with drought the likes of which was not seen before or since. Eventually, Hermes told me where she was. I got her back. But despite my efforts, I found out that Hades had married her without my consent. I struck a bargain with him. For nine months of the year, while Persephone is with me, I create abundance. For three months of the year, while she is with him, I make the earth sterile and dormant. You call this the seasons," she paused. Again, she resumed:

"I have repeated this process for eons. But now I have come to a dilemma. You see this farm,..." and she pointed her hand in one direction. She continued: "This farm has an abundant crop. You can see the grain in this silo,..." and she pointed her hand to the grain we were standing on. "Yet this grain will never reach the needy. It will be sold and stored on barges on the Mississippi river until it rots. This violates my intent,..." she paused. Then she turned and pointed her hand in the opposite direction and said:

"Over there is another farm. It also has an abundant crop. That farmer did not sell his crop in the futures market. Then prices collapsed. That farmer cannot recover his cost and faces ruin. This situation also violates my intent,..." she paused. Then she turned slightly again and pointed yet in another direction and said:

"Over there is yet another farm. It had an unusually bad crop. That farmer sold his crop in the futures market and was facing ruin for a while. But because the market collapsed, he was able to cover his contract, and made a handsome profit to boot. This also violates my intent,..." she paused. Then she faced me and continued:

"Financial instruments affect lives. They are not an intellectual game of hide and seek. The toils of labor are no longer rewarded. My efforts are in vain!

"I create abundance to feed the hungry when the soil and the forests are in harmony. Flora creates abundance for the basic needs in the forests. Yet your race ravishes the landscape, destroys this harmony, and is on a collision course with destruction and desolation...

"Once Mesopotamia was full of forests and rich soil. It was the 'Garden of Eden.' The gardens were full of fruits and flowers. But reckless devastation of the forests destroyed the soil. Now, only an arid desert dominates that landscape...

"Once Egypt had the means to feed your race. Needless devastation ruined that potential. Now, Egypt cannot even feed herself. I can go on and on. Lebanon, North Africa, Greece, Italy and Spain had abundant forests and rich soil. The trees were recklessly cut down, the soil turned barren and the human race was flirting with disaster.

"This process has not stopped. The United States, Mexico and Brazil are continuing the same folly...

"What do I have to do to teach your race harmony? For how long must I endure the destruction of my realm? If this continues for much longer I will turn the earth about its axis and make Mesopotamia the North Pole to give it some rest from your abuse." She seemed upset.

I was shocked. The mere thought of Mesopotamia as the North Pole sent chills through my body. The polar caps would melt. A flood would devastate humanity. What could I say to moderate her fury? I had to probe her reasoning.

"Are you suggesting that farmers must be financial wizards to survive in our economic markets?" I asked.

"Not wizards, but they must have some basic training in market fundamentals and they must have the tools to use the market effectively. In fact, in your day and age all educated people must have that knowledge and understanding. Otherwise you will be forever behind the 'eight-ball.' Indirectly, I am accusing your educational system.

"Every College has a kernel of courses which are required for graduation. That kernel of courses must include at least one year of market fundamentals with hands-on trading techniques. Otherwise you will not survive in this new world you have created for yourself and will be financially enslaved by others who have that experience. Let me explain...

"Until the Industrial Revolution, grain and wood were the primary staples for survival. Grain, to feed the population and wood, to build the ships to engage in trade.

"Athens is a classical example in antiquity. At one point they controlled the major grain centers of the known world: North Africa, Egypt and the Ukraine. During the Peloponnesian war, which lasted from 434 to 404 BC, Athens fought Sparta for the hegemony of Greece. Athens tried to expand their influence to Syracuse, in Sicily, which was controlled by Corinth. Corinth, however, was allied with Sparta. In 417 BC, they sent an expedition under Alcibiades to take Syracuse, to cut off the grain supply to Sparta. When they arrived, Alcibiades was replaced for reasons of jealousy in Athens and the expedition failed. The entire Athenian fleet was destroyed. With that defeat they not only lost their fleet, but also their control of North Africa. Within a few years they lost control of Egypt. For the next 12 years, however, the Ukraine shipped over 5 million bushels of grain annually to Athens and they never felt the pinch. It was not until 405 BC that the Spartans blockaded the trade route from the Ukraine, and within less than one year Athens was starved into surrender. Strabo explained that in great detail.

"The Age of Industrialization started with wood, then coal and then oil to drive the steam engines, turbines and motors. The last major war converged on oil as the principal and essential source of energy for any industrial power to exist. This is why Japan tried to take the oil-fields in Dutch Indonesia. Oil became a strategic resource. But oil is controlled by a handful of greedy oil barons who found it more convenient to keep the status quo and not develop new sources of energy. They find it more convenient to collaborate with the enemy than to develop new sources of clean energy. Now you have oil-cartels who can choke off your precious oil supply whenever they want: Saudi Arabia, Indonesia, Russia, Venezuela and so on. This despite the fact there is abundant energy for the taking. For example, the sun provides you all the energy you'll ever need, yet it is hardly used. Consider this: more energy falls on the transmission lines than the energy they transmit. Isn't this a travesty of misuse?

"Instead you develop alternate sources of energy which are extremely wasteful and harmful to you and your environment: Hydro-electric and nuclear. Both are capital intensive and both pollute the environment.

"Hydro-electric energy changes the flow of rivers which disrupt sea-life, contribute to major flooding, destroy architecture and ancient burial grounds. Why? Because dams have to be built, water levels have to be raised and the most fertile land has to be sacrificed for the sake of a few kilowatt-hours. Entire species of sea animals have been annihilated because they can not reach their spawning grounds or traditional habitats.

"Nuclear power flirts with an ecological disaster the likes of which you have not yet seen..."

"You mean like Chernobyl?" I piped in.

"Chernobyl is only the tip of the iceberg and look what it caused. The Ukraine has turned into an ecological wasteland. Her agricultural products are shunned world over. Her traditional trade has been ruined. But that is not the worst of it. The nuclear waste you are generating will choke you in the years to come. You will pollute your soil for centuries to come..."

"What is the answer?" I inquired.

"The answer is that you must find clean sources of energy: Sun, wind, corn, soy and others. From sources of energy which are in abundance or you can readily grow and harvest..."

"Wouldn't that make energy very expensive?" I opined.

"It is very expensive now. Within the next few decades, if oil prices increase at the rate they have in the past, they will triple in value. What will happen to your entire industrial complex if oil prices reach $100 a barrel?" She asked.

"Prices will soar." I replied.

"Yes, but disproportionately." She retorted. Then she explained.

"While the prices of a 'strategic commodity' go up linearly, all other prices go up exponentially. In the early 1960's, the median price of a barrel of oil was $10, today it is about $30-- a 300% increase or 3 times. At the same time, a home in Levittown Long Island was priced at $13,000; a small car such as a VW was about $1,100, a gallon of gas was 16 cents, and a quart of milk was 16 cents -- including delivery, and a postage stamp was 3 cents to mail a letter. Today that same house in Levittown is $250,000; the VW is $16,000; a gallon of gas is $2.00; a quart of milk is $1.89 -- excluding delivery, and a postage stamp is 37 cents. The median increases of these products increased roughly 3 raised to the power of e!

"The transcendental number e can be bracketed by the two integers 2 and 3. When raised to the power of e, they are roughly: 6.5 and 19.5. Now let's compare the increases in terms of their factors: the house in Levittown is 19.2 times; the VW is 14.5 times; the gallon of gas is 12.5 times; the quart of milk is 11.6 times and the postage stamp is 12.3 times! As you can see, the factors tend to cluster around 3 raised to the e power."

"That's very interesting," I exclaimed. "I never thought about it in these terms," I added.

"That's because your race does not think in terms of the transcendental numbers, but as you can see, they are very important. They come up naturally..."

"Where else do they pop up naturally?" I inquired.

"In Market-Timing, of course. Apollo taught me a method I use very extensively. It is not fool-proof, but it serves me well -- it is nearly 95% accurate using only a few well defined variables. Do you want to hear about it?..."

"By all means, tell me all about it," I interrupted.

"To begin with, all cycles use the number π and all accruals use the number e. I use only the following variables for equities: Closing Price, Trade Volume, three Weighted Moving Averages (Short, Medium and Long), the Amplitude and the Put/Call Ratio. Apollo uses far more variables, but his system is far to complicated for me.

"The actual daily closing prices are difficult to use. They are too erratic. Instead, I use their weighted moving averages for a proxy. This smoothes out the price movement and the most current trades become more significant. The most current trade gets the weight of n in an n-day moving average for the last trade. The prior trade gets the weight of n-1 and so on. The last trade in the average gets the weight of one. This way they are weighted in proportion to their significance.

"Statistically, it makes no difference if you use the closing price or the high price or the low price for the day, provided you use them consistently. You can not mix and match them to suit your purpose.

"Using the closing price I form my weighted moving averages. Their ratio must be a multiple of π. When my short weighted moving average is 7 trade days, then its corresponding medium weighted moving average is 22 trade days and my long moving average is 138 days. Their ratios are π and 2 π respectively. More often than not, I prefer to use 10, 32 and 200 trade days. Their ratio is also π and 2 π. That is, I make allowances for the integers to closely match up with the ratios of π.

"I superimpose my weighted moving averages with the daily trade data on a chart. I prefer to use the closing price. Then, the short weighted moving average hugs the trade data while the medium weighted average lags behind the trade action.

"Most of the time I only look at the short and medium weighted moving average. Then, I construct their amplitude. That is, the difference between the two weighted moving averages.
When the amplitude is increasing or positive as measured from the short to the medium weighted average, the stock is rising in value. Then there is no problem and you just ride with the market. Conversely, when the amplitude is negative, then the stock is declining. Again, as long as the amplitude gets larger, more negative, the price is falling and you can ride the market.

"Eventually, the amplitude begins to shrink. This is your first sign that the price movement is slowing down or even reversing. Now you have to look at the other variables.

"My favorite is the put/call ratio. When it is significantly over 1 -- say 2 -- then the market sentiment of the small investor is to sell. We know that the small investor is invariably wrong, therefore it is a bullish signal. Conversely, when that ratio is significantly under 1 -- say .5 -- then, the market sentiment of the small investor is bullish. Therefore, the market will decline. This covers about 70% of the cases you will encounter on a daily basis..."

"What if those ratios are not clear cut. What are finer thresholds," I asked.

"Between 1.25 to 1 and 1 to .75 they are only marginally valid, about 60% of the time. Between 1.99 to 1.25 and .75 to .51 they range from 75% to 95%, depending on their value. At 2 and above and .5 and below they are more than 95% accurate..."

"What happens when that ratio is between 1.25 and .75," I asked.

"This is the area when you can be 'whip-sawed.' It takes fortitude to keep your cool. The first thing I do is, I look at the volume. If the volume is normal then the trend will most likely continue. If the volume on that day exceeds the weekly volume, then there is cause for concern, and if the volume exceeds 3 weeks it is a sure sign of a reversal. Then I look at other indicators.

"Keep in mind, at the top or the bottom the volume is always exceptionally high. Yet each share sold is bought by someone else. The market is efficient..."

"Then, who is buying at the top and bottom?" I asked.

"If we knew that, we would have no problem at all. Unfortunately we only have inferences. Keep in mind the 'market-makers' are pitted against the investor. When they are buying, they are convinced the stock is undervalued and when they sell, they believe the stock is overvalued.

"Therefore, while at the top the investor is euphoric and the market maker cashes in. At the bottom, the investor panics and sells, then the market makers buy.

"It's that simple. Just go to any brokerage house and observe how they run their operation. A horde of small brokers sell the stock and when they collectively make some headway and move the price up -- a large broker, in the same company unloads for his client. The big fish eats the small fish most of the time..."

"Sounds to me like the labors of Sisyphus," I piped in.

"Precisely." Demeter replied.

"In any event, when I am in doubt, I look at my long weighted moving average. It tells me if I have encountered a market top or bottom.

"As I said in the beginning, I use only a small set of variables and they have served me well...

"Ask Apollo, what additional variables can be used. He will tell you for sure..."

I woke up in a cold sweat. Curious, I thought. Maybe I caught a slight fever. I took my things and left the bedroom to get ready for the new day.

8

Artemis

I was standing in front of Hermes at our appointed spot in the valley. He had changed his clothes. He wore a gray flannel suit, a white shirt, leather shoes and a striped red tie added some color. He wore no hat. His hair was curly, sort of blonde-grey and well trimmed.

Instead of the rod he held an umbrella in his right hand. In fact, he was drawing figures with the umbrella tip in a patch of dirt in front of him.

"You look great. Just like a corporate executive," I blurred out.

"Well, today we will be tangling the 'rat-race' and I don't want to be conspicuous," he said with a gentle smile on his face.

"What did you think of yesterday?" he continued.

"I must say, Hephaestus is well organized. No wonder he produces such quality products. Poseidon was, quite frankly, intimidating -- I was scared when he talked to me. I felt very insignificant in his presence. Demeter presented a point of view that lingered on my mind, which I could never articulate properly,..." I answered.

"Well, let's review the experiences...

"Hephaestus was demonstrating the layers of a problem. Each layer in turn needs precise and accurate staging or ordering. Each ordering has its own hierarchy and dependency. The current layer is dependent on the past: Experience, knowledge, requirements etc. The current layer must provide the interface to the future. That is, the solution of a problem of today must have sufficient open-endedness to accommodate solution alternatives for the future. While not every solution alternative can be anticipated, their eventual extension must be provided for...

"Poseidon was stressing the trend view and the contrarian view which is part of every problem. That is, the elusiveness of a solution due to the multitude of exceptions. The anomalies he talked about are real issues. They can-not be ignored. When anomalies are not accounted for in the solution alternative the solution itself is suspect. Finally, while you have been taught that an analytic solution is the best, it is also the most utopian approach. While statistical solutions are generally the least accepted solution alternatives, they are more universal in nature. Of course, in between an entire spectrum of solution alternatives is possible...

"Demeter tried to stress the purpose of a solution. A solution of a problem for purely self-gratifying purposes leads inevitably to misuse and then to disaster...

"So much for yesterday, and how was your day?" he asked.

"Quite good. It started out not good at all. But, by the end of the day I had the first meaningful results -- at least I think they are meaningful," I said.

"Alright, explain what you have found," he urged me on.

"I started with the options. I formed the complete option block for each time frame and for each issuer..."

"Did you include all exchanges?" he interrupted me.

"Of course. Some issues continue to trade on another exchange when they are active, even after their primary exchange has closed. But that was not my initial problem. When I keyed on the volume activity, I got nonsense. The major issues: GM, Ford, IBM and the like, appeared on every active list I formed for every trade day. While the active issues trading on secondary exchanges did not make my active list," I said.

He only smiled at me and said: "So, what did you do?"

"I realized that their trade volume needed to be normalized with respect to their shares outstanding. As soon as I did that, I was able to match up the active issues consistently with their activity, that is for most part -- not all mind you," I continued.

"That is only a matter of refining the threshold," he said. Then he prompted me again: "What else did you find?"

"Well, I was trying to find clear signals for the bull-spread, the bear-spread and the calendar-spread, and correlate them with respect to the motion of the stock into the future," I replied.

"What did you find?" he asked.

"Well, I found an excellent bull-spread correlation. I back-tested it to the inception of the data I have. It is about 87% percent accurate! I also found a much weaker calender-spread correlation, but when I back-tested -- it proved to be less than 70% accurate. This disappointed me a lot. However, I could not find a bear-spread correlation at all. This makes me wonder if my method is correct." I said.

"Don't jump to conclusions, at least not yet, ..." he said softly. He continued: "Bear-spread correlations will be only visible in a prolonged bear market. Thus, the question is: how far back do you have valid data?" he asked.

"1982," I replied.

"Well, that explains the lack of a true bear-spread correlation. The stock market was in an up-trend from 1981 until now. Hence, you will not find any bear-spread correlations at all," he said.

"How about, 1987?" I asked.

"I am surprised at you -- 1987 was caused by a shift of assets to produce a higher yield. A yield in excess of 10.5% for the bellwether bond is not sustainable in the stock market. Therefore, money switched from the stock market to the bond market and that was all. The down-trend lasted only one week. Then, the market recovered and marched upwards ever since. There was no chance to develop bear-spreads in such short a time. Wait until you have a prolonged bear-market for that...

"How about, 2001 through 2003?" I asked.

"Now there you should have seen a few bear-spreads. What did you see?" Hermes asked.

"It was so overwhelming. I could not believe it. It started in January 2000 and until June 2000. As far as I was concerned, this was not a bear-spread, it was a market collapse. It was not at all what I had expected, but only on the Nasdaq. After that and until now there were no regular bear-spreads at all," I answered.

"This should teach you a lesson. You provided for the contingencies, yet when they happened, you refused to believe them. That is the major problem with models. In order to use them effectively you must stick to them, you can not 'out-model' them to suit your purpose. Did you get caught in the market downturn?" Hermes asked.

"Indirectly. I have a private pension fund. When it started to decline I could do nothing about it. I had to sit by and watch it decline to pre 1992 levels. I lost more than 40% of my pension income, even though my portfolio was one-third bonds and two-thirds equities. This was the most frustrating experience I ever had. I was helpless. I knew what to do but could not do it." I complained.

"Don't feel bad, many other investors did much worse. The sad part is that many pension funds nearly collapsed. This forced many elderly to re-enter the job market, and that's very hard for the retired. It is very difficult for the elderly to recoup their losses, especially when they did not speculate and depend on the income. The last downturn should raise a red flag to the notion to put a portion of the Social Security contributions into the equity market.

"Keep in mind, the market makes major corrections almost on the spot. A regular investor has no chance when he tries to make changes when the market is in a tailspin. The market is pre-programmed to sell at predetermined levels. This can set off a chain-reaction. Then the telephone lines are tied up, the broker may not be available and everything that can go wrong will go wrong.

"The key is to be one step ahead of the market. You must concentrate on the period from November of 1999 and until September 2000. The Nasdaq collapse was strictly due to the '.com' bubble. It collapsed because the market will tolerate only so much red ink.

"Look at it from a positive side. Everybody who was in the bond-market or money-market did not feel the impact at all. Only the equity market was affected...

"However, I am surprised that you found such a low correlation for the calendar-spread. You should be able to get much better results. There have to be many greedy bastards who act on solid insider information," he seemed finished with his inquiry.

I still had a number of questions I had to ask him. So, I asked him hastily before we were off to our next place: "Wait, I need a few questions answered before we leave," as I blurted out.

"Why then did the rest of the market, especially on NYSE, have a downturn?" I queried.

"There were two major factors. First, it was a sympathetic reaction. When there is a major downturn on one exchange, it will have a similar effect on the other exchanges, even though it may be muted. Second, many accounting irregularities were exposed, such as Enron, Global Crossing, Worldcom and others. It will take years to unravel the gory details..."

"One more," I interrupted. "I don't believe in unstructured patterns as flaunted by Poseidon. I really think that there is a rational formulation for them. What do you think?" I asked Hermes.

"Well, what did you have in mind?" he asked.

"Let us begin with the most fundamental formulation of a stock price or value. Then we have: The stock value equals the present value of all future earnings, does it not?" I asked.

"Of course," he replied. "But, in the present -- the future earnings are not known, hence the value remains a mystery does it not?" he replied.

"That's true, but at least a trend can be projected, can it not?" I insisted.

"Of course, that's why successful portfolio managers look at the growth patterns of a company. The most important fundamental variables are earnings and sales -- nothing else. All other items can be manipulated, in particular, dividends..."

"You are absolutely right," I exclaimed. "I found a number of companies who declared large dividends in one year and the stock 'zoomed' to new highs. The next year the dividend was cut or even abolished and the stock tumbled to a new low."

"Bravo, you have just discovered one subtle way how stocks can be manipulated!" and he grinned at me.

"But this 'case' can be formulated precisely and this trap can be avoided by an astute investor," I said calmly.

"Ok, how can you detect and avoid this case?" he asked.

"Simple, demand that dividends be supported by the earnings growth and the earnings growth be supported by a growth in sales," I said.

I could see how he was quickly computing this relationship in his head. He lifted his head, his eyes were rolling and for a moment I thought steam might come out of his ears. Then, after a moment, he turned to me and said: "Yes, that would work, but these relationships are not linear. You must adjust for taxes and growth in expenses. But basically, this relationship is correct..."

"Now," I continued, "if this relationship is essentially correct, we can deal with 'classes' rather than with individual companies. As a matter of fact, I have classified my database into three broad categories, each with three subsets. The first I call growth companies, the second I call stagnant companies and the third category I call 'dinosaurs' or companies headed toward extinction. The growth companies and the dinosaurs are easy to spot. For the growth companies I used a twenty-five percent criteria for earnings and sales growth for the last three years. For the dinosaurs I used declining sales and/or declining earnings for the last three years, all others I called stagnant."

Hermes closed his eyes, lifted his head towards the sky and I had a distinct feeling that he was in a 'compute and sift' mode. Then he turned to me and asked: "So, what did you find?"

"I only have stocks on the NYSE, AMEX and NASDAQ. But I found only 360 growth companies and 222 dinosaurs, the rest were all stagnant according to my definition," I replied.

"How did you arrive at the twenty-five percent threshold?" he asked.

"Quite honestly, I guessed at that number," I said.

"Well, while your guess was reasonable for the current economic situation, it is not correct. That number must be a function of the 'bellwether-bond.' That is, the cost of money must be factored into your threshold. A good linear approximation is π times the prevailing rate of the bellwether-bond. That is, when the bellwether-bond yields seven percent, that threshold should be 21.99113%. Conversely, when the bellwether-bond is fifteen percent, that threshold should be 47.12385%. That's why in the 1976 to 1982 time frame companies could not survive. The cost of money was driving them into an untenable debt or into bankruptcy. These repercussions manifested themselves only much later or in 3 π years! Some of this fall-out you are experiencing now." Hermes paused.

"Very interesting," I said. Then I thought about it for a while and asked: "Why π, why not e or some other transcendental number?"

"Quite simple," he said, "π dominates all cycles. It is the basis which is most useful for cyclic representations. E dominates all accruals, hence e dominates all compounding effects. Thus e and π are critical in all market timing formulations. But you must also find the proper use of phi and gamma. Only then will you be able to formulate the market timing properly...

"Now, let me give you the next installment of history before we can tackle current events and how they affect the European Union. Let's call it 'The Plight of the Goths.'

"As I mentioned before, the Goths and Slavs merged in antiquity into one people. They did that by exchanging their Kings. From then on they were simply referred to as Goths. They were a numerous people, but they lived in small groups, each headed by a King. Herodotus called them Scythians, Amazons and so on. Strabo made a much finer differentiation identifying about 20 Gothic nations. Cassiodorus Senator also gave a good account of their multitude.

"The first recorded appearance of the Goths is in the Trojan War as recorded by Homer. They fought with the Trojans against the Achaean and Doric invaders. In fact, many other nations fought with the Trojans against the Achaeans: Celts, Etruscans, Ethiopians and others.

"When that war ended, the Goths and Ethiopians returned to their homelands. The Celts migrated along the Danube River and settled in Western Europe. Today, Ireland and Switzerland are populated by the descendants of the Celts.

"The Etruscans returned to their stamping ground, but a massive earthquake had devastated their land. They divided into two. One part stayed behind, while the other migrated to Italy. They established themselves in city-states in Northern Italy, to the north of present day Rome. Each city was governed by a King. They had mastered road-building, irrigation, sewers, farming and animal-husbandry. They also had a sacred text which they used to interpret the entrails in a sacrifice. They became the Roman Augurs. Julius Caesar had one, so had Augustus and so on...

"When Rome began to expand, the Etruscan cities became the first target of their destruction and conquest. In particular the Etruscan city Veii. It was the first city which was plundered and utterly destroyed by the Romans.

"When Hannibal invaded the Italian peninsula, he expected the Etruscans to rally to his cause since he saw that the days of the Etruscan cities-states were numbered. However, the Etruscans did not see it that way, leaving Hannibal no choice, but to march to 'Magna Grecia,' in Southern Italy, which was colonized by Greeks. From there he continued his war against Rome, but even though year after year Hannibal defeated the Roman army, the Romans had an endless supply of recruits while Hannibal's forces were steadily dwindling.

"When Hannibal invaded Italy, his army was 40,000 strong and he had 20 war-elephants. By the time he crossed the Alps, his army was reduced to 30,000 with 3 war-elephants remaining. One died, while another was limping and had to be destroyed. After 17 years in Italy, Scipio Africanus took the war to Africa. Hannibal was recalled from Italy and was defeated by Scipio at Zama. This war eliminated the Etruscans and the Phoenicians from the political scene in Europe.

"Shortly after the Etruscans colonized Northern Italy, the Macedonian Goths left their homeland at Lake Moesia (Azov Sea). They moved into an area in the Ukraine called today the 'Trypilian Area'..."

"Excuse me," I interrupted, "where is the Trypilian area?"

Hermes just looked at me. "Draw a line from Kiïv (Kiev) to Lviv (Lvov, Lwow or Lemberg). That is the diameter. Now draw a circle around it. Roughly speaking, that is the Trypilian area." Then, he continued.

"From there, they planned their conquest of Greece. At that time, the Persian Empire was at war with the Greek city-states. The Macedonians waited patiently until that war was over and then invaded Thrace. Meanwhile, Athens and Sparta fought for the hegemony of Greece. When they nearly destroyed each other, Alexander the Great conquered them.

"Shortly before that, Xenophon had returned from his Persian Expedition and wrote a book called 'Anabasis.' Alexander read it, and it became clear to him that Persia could be conquered. He hired 10,000 Greek mercenaries and integrated them into his army of 30,000. All the commanders of Alexander the Great were Goths; in particular his generals: Antiochus, Ptolemy and Seleucus.

"Alexander the Great conquered the Persian Empire, but while attempting to subdue India, he was wounded by a poisonous arrow which pierced his armor. Alexander never recovered from that wound and died at the age of 33. Upon his death, his loyal generals inherited his empire. Antiochus got Greece and Syria. Ptolemy got Egypt. And Seleucus got Persia.

"Cleopatra was a direct descendent of Ptolemy. She had an affair with Julius Caesar and had his child, a son named Caesarion. When Julius Caesar was assassinated in the Senate, Marc Anthony became governor of the Eastern Provinces of Rome. Cleopatra seduced Marc Anthony and they had two children. However, when Octavius -- later he was called Emperor Augustus-- came to Alexandria, he had Cleopatra's children killed. This eliminated all future contenders.

"The reason I mention all this is because: starting with Julius Caesar it was obvious that the location of Rome was badly suited to run the Roman Empire. Diocletian actually divided the Empire and Constantine moved the capital of the empire from Rome to Constantinople, former Byzantium.

"There was another compelling reason to change the capital of the Roman Empire. As soon as Christianity became the official religion of the Empire, the heathen temples were sacked and plundered. In that process the heathen priests and priestesses were slain. That is, Rome was burning. Her most valued treasures and her temples were utterly destroyed. Therefore, it was easier to build a new capital, with all the splendor it deserved, than to restore the old one." Hermes paused for a moment. Then, he continued.

"The Gothic general Odin was a contemporary of Julius Caesar. In Ukrainian, his name means 'One' or 'The Only One.' Well, Odin raised an army in the Ukraine and solidified the Gothic realm. He marched along the river Danube to the river Elbe. There, he turned north. He established the Gothic Kingdoms for the Wends, Sassons, Angles and Jütes (Jutes). He entered present day Denmark and conquered the northern lands: Denmark, Norway and Sweden. He settled on an island off Sweden and called it: Gothland (Gotland). Thus, the Gothic realm stretched from the river Elbe to the Ural mountains, and from the Danube to the Baltic Sea and beyond to the north in the Scandinavian countries.

"When Emperor Augustus conducted a census, the Goths made one also. The results were that the Roman Empire had 5.4 million souls while the Goths had 5.6 million. This was reported by Strabo and Cassiodorus Senator. To this point there were no major confrontations between the Romans and the Goths. Only one Gothic nation had moved into the German lands -- the Suevi. To this day, you can see the noticeable difference of body-types. The Suevi are often red-headed and green-eyed.

"The Germans occupied the land between the rivers Rhine and Elbe and from the river Danube to the Atlantic Ocean to the North. Just to give you a perspective.

"When Emperor Constantine made Christianity the main religion in his Empire, even though it was the Arian Faith, the Goths were at a loss. They gathered their sages and sent a delegation to Constantinople where they were received and treated royally. Both Emperor Constantine and Patriarch Arius spent much time with them.

"The Gothic leader was Ulfilas, and for the next ten years the Goths studied the new faith and translated the Old and New Testaments into their language, which was Runic. Parts of their translation are still prominently displayed at the University of Uppsala. When the sages completed their texts they returned to their homeland and became Christian missionaries -- albeit Arian Christian missionaries. They converted entire Gothic nations to this new faith. At that time, one strong Gothic King tried to form a more centralized government: Ermanric.

"Keep in mind, I am giving you their Latin names. So, as you 'stumble' across their names, don't be surprised if they are spelled differently. I will point out some of the nuances as me go along, but before I come to the major event, so to speak--let me explain a fundamental difference in rule between the Roman and Gothic models.

"Rome evolved from a Republic into an Imperial state. Her Emperors, ruled nearly in a totalitarian manner. Yes, they had a Senate, but for all practical purposes the Senate sided with the Emperor.

"In the Gothic model, their King was primarily the Chief Judge. Their laws were not codified -- neither were the Roman laws at that time -- but the Gothic Kings were raised with special sages who taught them the laws of the land. There were only a few Royal families. They identified themselves by appending a specific ending to their name -- ric, rik, ryc or rix; mir or mer; veche or veg and much later -- slav or laus, mir and polk. This told the other Goths from their name alone whether or not they were of royal lineage and whether or not they were well versed in the laws of the Goths. Furthermore, the ending identified which 'school of law' they practiced. In your country this would be like identifying whether they were Democrats, Republicans or Independents.

"They had a three tier justice system. First, the Princely court. There, the King or Prince presided over a council and they made a collective decision. The next level was a Veche or Thing-- a court of peers. Finally, there was a Sbor or Allthing. This is when all the Goths gathered, usually in the Trypilian area, and matters were brought up for their collective judgement and ratification.

"Women had the same rights as men. They could own property and they could initiate a divorce. The Goths had no slaves and no serfs. These institutions were introduced later into their system when they were ruled by non-Goths or converts." Hermes paused and started to stretch his legs.

"As I said before, as Ermanric was forging a unified Gothic state the unthinkable happened. The Huns invaded Europe. The Gothic Alans were routed. Then, a second Gothic army was defeated and the Goths started leaving their homelands in panic. Over 2.5 million Goths were on the move with all their possessions in wagons, on horseback and on foot. One contingent, about 1 million strong, reached the Danube river and asked for sanctuary in the Roman Empire. They were all Christian Goths, albeit Arian.

"The new Roman Emperor was Valens. A few years earlier, he had converted to a new brand of Christianity: Orthodoxy, and Arianism was now a heresy in his Empire. Reluctantly, Emperor Valens granted them asylum, but only after they gave up their arms and their children as hostages. In return, they were promised a rich and fertile region in the Empire where they could settle and build a homestead. The desperate Goths, with the Huns at their heels, agreed. About 1 million Goths were ferried across the Danube river...

"Meanwhile, the other contingent of Goths pressed on. They came to the Rhine river and crossed into Gaul. Many settled near Orleans, Rochelle and Bordeaux, but many others continued into Spain. Some even made it into North Africa and settled near Carthage.

"By the time Valens ruled the Roman Empire, the Western provinces had been abandoned: Britain, Gaul, Spain and North Africa. This was so because, while administratively Christianity was a God-send, militarily it was a disaster. It was more prudent to save the soul, rather than the body, according to the Christian faith. Why? Because, the 'Second Coming' was imminent.

"When Constantine fought for his supremacy, 52 Roman legions were strategically dispersed throughout the Empire. Together with their 'Federati' or allies, over 100 legions could be put into action in a short time. By the time Valens was Emperor, there were less than 10 legions in the entire Empire, mostly led and staffed by mercenaries. Thus, the first ones to feel the pinch of the shrinking military were the remote western provinces because they were, by and large, poor. The military might of Rome was concentrated in the East because it was rich and the primary source of revenue. This situation got progressively worse.

"The Goths who entered the Roman Empire under Emperor Valens, however, were mistreated. To begin with, their children were butchered because they refused to change from Arianism to Orthodoxy. The Goths were settled into the most arid piece of land in the Empire: Thrace. No matter how hard they worked the land, the crops were meager. When they discovered their children had been butchered, they sent messengers to their kinfolk with an appeal to be rescued.

"The Goths in their homeland gathered for an Allthing in the Trypilian area and elected Alaric as their joint military leader. Alaric raised an army and invaded the Roman Empire. He liberated the Goths and proceeded to conquer the rest of the Balkans. However, Alaric could not take Constantinople. Her walls and fortifications were too much for the Goths, enforcing a sort-of stalemate. The Goths controlled the hinterlands, while the new Emperor Arcadius, was confined in Constantinople. A truce was reached whereby Alaric was given the highest military rank in the Roman Empire: Master of The Horse. This gave Alaric control of the military supplies of the Roman Empire. He armed his Goths with the best and latest armor, weapons and horses.

"It was clear to everyone that Alaric and his Goths would never meld with the Roman Empire, the massacre of their children being too fresh on their minds. In a collective meeting, they decided to leave the Balkans, provided the Emperor grant them the right to settle someplace else in the Roman Empire. The Emperor agreed: any Province in the West, including Italy was available for them. In addition, the Emperor promised safe passage through his realm. With this agreement, the Goths gathered their belongings and left for Italy.

"As soon as the Goths left, however, the Emperor ordered Stilicho -- an Alan general in the employ of the Emperor -- to assail and destroy the Goths. While the Goths were crossing into Italy, Stilicho attacked them, but when he realized that he was attacking fellow Goths he stopped. Stilicho made a deal with Alaric and allowed Alaric's army to descend into Italy unmolested -- towards Rome. With Rome in sight, the Goths wanted revenge. They attacked and took Rome. Alaric allowed his army 3 days of looting -- which, by the standards of his time -- was very mild. All churches and their attendants, however, were off-limits. (In 1455, the Duke of Milan allowed his soldiers 9 months for raping and looting.)

"Then the Goths moved south and at the southern tip of Italy, Alaric died. The Goths buried him and his treasure in the Busento river and elected a new leader. That new leader had other plans. He wanted to link-up with the Goths in Gaul. The entire expedition then turned around and marched north. When they reached Rome, they decided to sack it again. This time their looting lasted 7 days -- also a very mild measure for that time. After that, the Goths left and joined up with their kinfolk in

Gaul and Spain.

"Meanwhile, the Huns settled in the Roman Province of Pannonia (Hungary). From there, they raided the Roman Empire incessantly. In 452, Attila became leader of the Huns and decided to conquer Gaul. He raised a huge Hun army and augmented it with his subjects: Burgundians, Germans and Eastern Goths -- the ones who had stayed behind. Your historians call them Ostrogoths. With that huge army, Attila invaded Gaul. Attila's army was unstoppable.They took every city in their path and ravaged the countryside. By the time they approached Orleans, the resident Goths of Gaul took up arms against them and the two armies met at Chalons-sur-Marne...

"Ares advised Attila. Ares had surveyed the opposing Goths and came up with a great battle-plan. On the right wing, he wanted the Ostrogoths because they were superb horsemen. In the center, Ares wanted the Germans and the Burgundians, because they were mostly foot soldiers. On the left wing he wanted Attila and his horsemen, but Attila refused. He wanted the center and the Germans and Burgundians on his left flank. Ares got so upset, he left Attila to his own fate and left the battlefield... .

"Meanwhile, Athena and Apollo surveyed the Hun army and they came to the conclusion that Attila would take the center. To make sure that he did, they sent Hubris to fortify Attila's resolve. They also formulated a great battle-strategy. They let the Alans take the center and instructed them to fall back as soon as Attila attacked. This would give the appearance that the center had collapsed...

"Meanwhile, a short distance behind them, they built horse-traps -- huge ditches with spikes in them. Behind these ditches the Alans would regroup and hack-away at the Huns.

"Theodoric -- the King of the Goths -- and his cavalry was placed on the left wing to take care of the Ostrogoths, their kinfolk, and just in the nick of time, Aetius arrived with the Scythians who had travelled all the way in from the Ukraine. They would be pitted against the Germans and Burgundians. There was no doubt that their cavalry would make mince-meat of their opponents.

"Aetius was the only Roman in this battle, a good general but a devout follower of the Bishop of Rome. Theodoric agreed to the plan immediately. It was an epic battle with over 1 million combatants on each side. When the battle ended, nearly 500,000 had lost their lives. It would take nearly 1500 years before a battle of this magnitude would be fought again (at Kursk, during World War II, in 1943 between the Germans and the Soviets.)

"As the battle unfolded the next day, it went just as Apollo and Athene expected. Attila charged, the Alans fell back and the Huns were trapped. Theodoric routed the Ostrogoths and the Scythians routed the Germans and Burgundians. Now the Huns were surrounded and were slaughtered mercilessly. Attila managed to escape. He raced to his camp, gathered the saddles, shields and spears into a huge pile and set it on fire. He knew that the battle was lost and that his camp was not defensible. He chose to destroy his weapons and kill his servants himself, but the victorious Goths did not come...

"What happened?

"Theodoric was mortally wounded in the battle. One of his sons was with him. The other son had been left behind to defend Bordeaux. But Ares had sent Eris to Aetius to sow the seed of discord. When Theodoric died, Aetius decided that the victorious Goths would be a bigger menace to Rome than the Huns. Thus, he used a ruse to divert the Goths from completing their job.

"Aetius went to Theodoric's son and told him: 'Now that your father is dead -- your brother will claim the throne. Why don't you go back with your victorious army and claim the throne for yourself,' and the inexperienced youth listened to Aetius, rather than Apollo. He took the army of Goths and returned to Bordeaux.

"Attila waited all night for the Goths. In the morning, when he realized they were not coming, he broke camp and took his remaining Huns to Pannonia. The Ostrogoths were badly mauled. They returned to their homeland with Attila. The Germans and Burgundians had likewise been decimated. As soon as Attila arrived in Pannonia, he prepared for a new expedition. This time into Italy.

"The next year, Attila ravaged Northern Italy. He plundered the big cities and decimated the population. Everything in his path was utterly destroyed. Thus, Italy paid for the folly of Aetius.

"Eventually Attila reached Rome. The citizens were trembling. There was no defense against Attila. Rome had a tiny militia which was no match for Attila's army. The city seemed to be doomed. As the Huns prepared for the siege of Rome, the Papa of Rome, Leo II, decided to visit Attila personally and somehow sway his mind. I counselled Leo. I told Leo to promise Attila the most beautiful Princess in marriage. This Leo did and Attila accepted.

"When Attila turned back, Leo II made arrangements for a young and beautiful Burgundian Princess to marry Attila. By the time Attila arrived in Pannonia, the Princess was there. They were married and on their wedding night Attila's main artery burst and he died in a pool of blood in his wedding bed.

"Attila had three grown sons. Each one of them was counselled by a Catholic and Orthodox legate, and, for the first time, both faiths saw an opportunity to rid themselves of the Huns. They encouraged each son to claim succession fomenting a civil war among the Huns, resulting in the near eradication of each other. When they stopped, they were only a shadow of their recent past. But, even that shadow was too strong for Rome or Constantinople to tackle...

"This is when the Emperor from Constantinople stepped in. He hired the Gothic Gepids to annihilate the Huns. They were promised Pannonia and a large sum of money. Half of the money was paid to start the war and the other half was due upon completion -- as soon as the Huns were exterminated. The Gepids accepted the offer and destroyed the Huns, but when the Gepids claimed the balance, Constantinople balked resulting in raids by the Gepids on the Roman Empire...

"At that time, a new Mongolic nation appeared on the horizon of Europe: The Avars. Constantinople hired the Avars to destroy the Gepids. Again, they promised them Pannonia and a large sum of money. The Avars accepted and destroyed the Gepids, but Constantinople reneged on its promise and did not make the last payment. Now the Avars raided the Roman Empire.

"At that time, Constantinople instructed her historians not to mention the Goths by name. They were afraid of another 'Alaric-type' invasion of their Empire. Their historians had to come up with a new name, to cut the umbilical cord of the Goths already in the Empire and the other Goths outside of it. The new name the historians chose was: Slavs. Thus, from the 6th century on, the Goths were no longer mentioned; instead they were called Slavs.

"When the Avars moved from Asia into Europe, they displaced many smaller Gothic nations, notably the Bohemians and Moravians, who moved into Central Europe, and the Croats, Slovenes and Serbs who moved to the South along the Danubian border. The Southern Goths or Slavs moved into the Roman Empire, while the Bohemians and Moravians settled further West along the rivers by a similar name.

"As the Southern Goths or Slavs now became a threat to Constantinople they hired the Mongolic Bulgars to eradicate them. For a while, the Bulgars made war against the Southern Goths.

Eventually, however, they reached a truce and staked out their territorial boundaries. In the end, the Bulgars converted to Orthodoxy and accepted many of the Gothic-Slavic customs. At this point, the Balkans became known as 'Slav-land.' The Croats and Slovenes accepted the Roman Faith, while the Serbs accepted Orthodoxy.

"The Avars in Pannonia remained a real threat well into the 9th century. Charlemagne made war against them when the Bohemians and Moravians were allied with him. But the Avars remained too strong. In another attempt to rid the Empire of its enemies, Constantinople contracted another Mongolic nation, the Magyars, to take care of the Avars. The Magyars agreed, descended into Pannonia and eradicated the Avars. Again Constantinople did not fulfill her promise. As a consequence the Magyars raided the Roman Empire and the Holy Roman Empire indiscriminately. By then, the schism had occurred and the two Christian Empires dominated Europe. However, at Lechfeld, in 955, near Ulm, the Holy Roman Emperor Otto I defeated the Magyars and they accepted Christianity from Rome. From then on, they ceased to be a threat to the Holy Roman Empire..."

"Wait I minute," I interrupted, "did not the Ostrogoths rule in Italy with Theodoric?" I asked.

"Don't be impatient, I am getting to it." Hermes replied. Then he started:

"Let me step back in time a little bit, back to the 5th century. As soon as Attila was defeated, the German tribes began invading the Roman Empire, mostly into Gaul and Italy. Emperor Zeno, in an attempt to protect the empire, urged the Ostrogoths -- who had become Arian Christians -- to take Italy for their homeland and to settle there. The Ostrogoths called for a Sbor in the Trypilian area, in the end they agreed to settle in Italy. They elected a new King, Theodoric, and moved to Italy, making Ravenna their capital. Theodoric ruled for over 30 years, held the Germans in check and brought peace and prosperity to the Italian peninsula. He is called 'Theodoric the Great,' and as long as he ruled, both the Arian and Orthodox Christians seemed to tolerate each other. They even intermarried with the native population.

"When Theodoric died, the new Roman Emperor was Justinian. He had two great generals, Belisarius and Narses. Justinian decided to eliminate the Arian Christians in Italy and North Africa. Since the Roman Empire had no Roman legions by that time, they hired two legions of mercenaries and Belisarius was directed to recover the province of North Africa from the Goths. Belisarius defeated the Goths, but allowed them to rejoin their kinfolk in Spain, while the great treasures they had amassed were transported to Constantinople. Then the Christian Donatists and Manichaeans were exterminated. Justinian left the Christian Monophysites alone, because they filled the coffers of the Roman Empire...

"With North Africa secured, Justinian charged Belisarius and Narses to drive the Ostrogoths from Italy. The Bishop of Rome sided with Justinian, and started preaching against the Ostrogoths. He annulled their marriages and urged all natives to rise against them, starting a civil war that lasted nearly 40 years. Justinian promoted the Bishop of Rome to Patriarch for his role against the Goths. In the end all of Italy was devastated and ruined. The upshot was the Ostrogoths who refused to convert to the Roman faith were evicted and permitted to rejoin their kinfolk in Gaul and Spain. This is described in more detail by the historian Procopius.

"Shortly thereafter, the Northern Goths began to rumble. You call them Norsemen or Normans or Vikings. The word Viking, however, is not a noun. It is a verb, and it means 'to go on a raiding expedition.' Starting in the 7th century, they began raiding Scotland, England and Gaul, eventually settling there. They occupied the greater part of England and Scotland. In England only a small enclave remained for the Britons and Welsh. In Scotland only a few Picts and Scots survived. England was then ruled by the Danes, then by the Normans from Gaul until 1715, when Queen Anne died and the Germans took over.

"In Gaul, Rolf Gange led 600 Viking ships up the river Seine to Paris. They raided and plundered that enclave. In the end they hammered out a treaty whereby the Normans could settle in the Western provinces of Gaul. Today you call one of them: Normandy.

"In the 7th century, the Spanish Goths converted from their Arian faith to the Roman Faith, and, shortly thereafter, the Goths in Gaul also converted to the Roman Faith. Their rulers were called the Merovingians. This was derived from their founder's name: Meroveche, a Goth of royal lineage. But, because they were tolerant to the heretics in their realm -- Arians, Manichaeans and Jews -- they were dubbed the 'do-nothing Kings' by Rome and Western historians.

"The Norsemen continued pressing south. They reached Spain, then Italy and then Greece. When they reached Constantinople, the Emperor had good use for them. He hired many into his service. They became known as the 'Varangian Guard,' the body-guards of the Emperor. They were tall, blonde, blue-eyed, loyal and fierce fighters. In fact, their service in the Varangian Guards was so commonplace that the aspiring Princes of Norway, Denmark, Sweden and Ostrogoths often served as a leader of that guard. One such example was Harold, the future King of Norway and the son-in law of Yaroslav (Jaroslav) the Wise from Kiev. They served the Roman Empire in that capacity from the 9th century until 1204, or until Constantinople was conquered by the Franks in the 4th Crusade.

"What is important is that the Varangian guard replaced the Praetorian guard. But the Praetorian guard had the right to elevate a citizen to be Emperor. Much earlier in Rome's history, Claudius was elevated in this way despite his unwillingness. Only the Praetorian guard wanted him to be Emperor, expecting many favors. Claudius did not disappoint them. With the Varangians cast into this role, they elevated Goths to become Emperors when the opportunity arose. This started with the Macedonian dynasty...

"The 10th century marked the conversion of the Eastern Goths to the Roman and Orthodox faith. Poland became Catholic and Kiev Orthodox. Shortly before, Cyril and Methodius, two monks from Constantinople introduced the Cyrillic alphabet in the Balkans to the Eastern Goths. It was nothing more than the Greek alphabet which replaced their Runic symbols. But the Greek alphabet was insufficient to replace all of the Runic letters.

"Therefore, a few new symbols had to be introduced--mostly in the 'j' and 's' categories: ja, je, ji, ju; sch or sh, ch, and schch. In addition, the Runic had a 'softening' symbol which could be appended to practically every consonant. Most often it was used in conjunction with the letters l and n. However, this created a new problem.

"Most scribes came from the Balkans or Constantinople. There, the official language was Latin and the common language was Greek. Certain letters posed a conflict. For example: The Latin B was pronounced V in Greek. The Latin C stood for K, yet in Greek it was pronounced S. The Greek Γ served both the H and G sound, depending on which way it curled. The Latin H was pronounced N in Greek. The Greek letter P stood for the R sound. There was no letter in Greek which was equivalent to the Roman Q. The closest letter, sound-wise to that was K. And, the Runic had a letter for the sound Kh. For that the Latin letter X was chosen. Finally, the Latin letter Y was pronounced U in Greek. Thus, in many ways the Cyrillic alphabet was ill conceived and added only to the confusion. In part, this was by design. But, the Goths did not realize that until it was too late. These letters caused much of the confusion later-on. Here is how it affected the Goths.

"The Spanish Goths used the Roman letter J to produce the Kh sound, and the letter B is pronounced as the V sound. The softening sound is used as a 'tilde' over the letter n. And, the softening sound for the letter L is used by doubling that letter. Thus, many of the Runic sounds were preserved.

"In Latin and in Italian, for that matter, the letters K and W are not used at all. What remained of the Gothic influence is the conjugation of nouns, the diminutive and the colossal.

"In France and in England the language was purged periodically to eliminate all non-native words. For example, in the English language the word Earl was derived from the Gothic word Yarl and so on. In France, the Kh sound was replaced with Ch. And today, France is to purge all American words from their language. In particular, the American technology words appearing in: Computers, Wireless Communication and so on.

"When Francis I made the French concordat in the 16th century in 1515, France was on her way towards a national identity. In England, Henry VIII cut the umbilical cord with Rome. Shakespeare and the Elizabethan Era ushered in the English language. That's the 17th century.

"The German language is very new in Europe. It took Martin Luther 20 years to form a tiny dictionary to write the Catechism, but hardly anyone could read it. The German language was created by Goethe, Schiller and Lessing. That is, during the Napoleonic wars, in the 19th century. Thus, when Wagner created the 'Ring,' he took the Gothic mythology and made it German...

"What language did the Germans use? Well, depending on the area they lived in, they used different languages...

"In the Low Countries, they used Dutch. When Peter I from Muscovy, spent some time in the Low Countries to learn the art of shipbuilding, he was so impressed with that language that he wanted to change the language in his realm to their tongue and script. His advisors pointed out the folly of such action. If he did that, then they could not raid the endless wealth of literature, tradition and art of the Ukraine...

"Peter I therefore, picked only selected words, such as the word Ross or Horse, which he used to name his realm. His primary reason was to eliminate the stigma that his realm was Tartar or Mongolian. At that time, the entire region from the Urals to the Vistula river was called Tartary, and Moscow was just a small area, smack near the middle of it. Peter I set out to erase that stigma...

"In Austria, the official language was Latin and the common language Italian. Mozart, the greatest composer of all time, wrote most of his operas in Italian. Only in the last days of his life did he start writing in German.

"In Bavaria, the official language was Latin and the common language French. Bavarian Dukes emulated the French Kings. It was

Napoleon who made Bavaria a Kingdom.

"In Prussia, the official language was Latin and the common language French, right through the 18th century. Just read the personal letters of Frederick the Great to his Queen mother on the progress of the Seven-Year war. They were all written in French."

I was almost jumping for joy as Hermes made that explanation. Thus, I piped in: "I am so glad you mentioned this. Just recently I worked on a relatively large project. It was called 'Name Clearance.' There I stumbled onto some very interesting names. In the United States there is a fair sample of Spanish names. At first, they gave me a lot of trouble. Names like Puj, Muja and so on. Then, I realized that the j had to be pronounced as kh for Spanish names. When I did that -- purely Ukrainian names popped out: Puj becomes Pukh, which means 'down' or feathers in a pillow; Muja becomes Mukha or fly, the insect. Then, I started to look at other names: Perez means pepper; Martinez means laundryman; Tesla means table-maker and so on. There is an endless number of names I found which correspond directly with Ukrainian words."

"Do you know why?" Hermes asked. But there I was at a loss.

"The Spanish Goths were conquered by the Moors. And, when the Moors were evicted from Spain in the 15th century, the New Spain did not have the time to purge their language and names. Many of the pre-Moorish names remained intact right into your era. The Spanish in turn colonized Latin America and these names migrated, so to speak, from Spain to Latin America. The same is true for Portuguese names. Try it sometimes..." Hermes looked at me with a big grin. Then, he resumed.

"Let me finish this segment until we come to Napoleon, because he still dominates the political scene in Continental Europe. As far as I am concerned, you are still living in the Napoleonic Era. The American Era has only begun, and if you are not careful it may not be as spectacular as it could be." He paused and drew some figures on the ground with his umbrella. When he finished, I recognized the contours of Europe. Then he stopped and said:

"On second thought, let me continue on our break, when we come back to this spot. Is that ok with you?" He asked.

I only nodded my head in agreement.

"Hold on to my rod." Like magic, the umbrella became a rod. I held on to it and we were off.

The next thing I knew we were sitting in a limousine, speeding along a highway. My back was turned in the direction the limousine was travelling. I was facing a beautiful female. This gorgeous creature sat directly in front of me. Her legs were crossed. Her kneecaps almost touched mine. My first impression was: Slender, long legs and an athletic body to boot. She wore a business outfit. A red jacket, a ruffled beige blouse and a green skirt. Her white legs exuded from that green skirt. She could not be older than twenty-five, I thought. Next, I noticed her hair: Dark blonde with a reddish hue. The hair was loose and untamed, yet very stylish. Her hair sloped gently around her head and fell below her neck-line. Her face had a slight tan, almost in direct contrast to her endless legs. Her face was oval and her long neck ended with an exquisite gold choker. Her eyebrows were black and natural. A tiny nose with two tiny nostrils pointed directly at me. A gently curved mouth with full, red lips gave her a very friendly appearance. But, there was a gentle fire in her green eyes which were surrounded by long eye-lashes. A real beauty, I thought.

"I am Artemis," I heard her say in a soft voice. "My realm is the hunt. In the past I was worshipped in a literal sense. I used to be pictured with a bow and arrow. But now that many forests are extinct my responsibilities include patents, copyrights and new products. This includes computers and weapons systems. I am usually the first on the scene when they are stress-tested. Now-a-days I am bogged down in a lot of paperwork and preliminary research. I do a lot of reading on my trips," and she pointed at a stack of files on the floor of the limousine.

She continued: "Today I am on my way to Boston. Actually, it is a small place near Boston. They developed a new submarine war game there, and I decided to take a look at it. Many noise problems of hydrophones seem to be resolved in that system, and if that system performs even close to the specs I have read-- we could have a break-through. The potential applications of that technology are endless," she paused.

"Why do you travel by car?" I asked.

"I don't do it very often," she explained. "Sometimes I want to see first hand and close-up the damage to my realm. Today is such a day. Then, I can reflect and seek out alternatives. With time passing and each alternative being perverted -- I see only drastic solutions on the horizon," she said softly.

"Is this a universal problem?" I asked.

"Yes, very much so. Once Washington DC was a sleepy village. Now it is a mass of concrete and steel. Once cities in the United States were self-contained. Now this mass of concrete and steel has oozed from Washington DC, right into Boston and beyond. Just like an endless stream of lava spreading south and north. All life in this way was raped and mutilated. Now this disease is spreading west. I am not so sure for how long the oceans will withhold this plague..."

"I see the same in Paris and in Rome, in Bonn, in Hamburg, in Munich, in Frankfurt and Berlin. Now that German re-unification is achieved, I see the same process in Leipzig, Dresden and Stettin. I see it in Tokyo, Hong Kong and Seoul. Yes, the problem is universal," she said sadly.

"Humanity is growing every year. How do we provide shelter, access roads, highways and a work-place for our citizens?" I asked.

"Partially that is the problem, but only partially," she said. Then she continued: "There is no plan, no purpose in your madness. The short term economic gains are sensationalized and the long term impact is diluted. The harmony is disturbed. You can not grow by leaps and bounds forever! Eventually you build your own black hole," she paused.

"Your work ethic begins with the axiom of mutual mistrust. Management mistrusts its workers, and in return the workers mistrust management. The only remedy you can see is presence. Therefore, presence on the job becomes the dominant criterion. Not skill, not intellect, not productivity, not even ethics are valued more than presence. Find a way to turn this axiom around and this abuse will cease," she said.

"But not all jobs are suited for this mode of work. Some jobs require presence," I said.

She looked at me and said: "Of course, some jobs require presence. But the majority of jobs do not, at least not all the time. Not if you use computers, not if you schedule and monitor the work. The United States ceased to be an agrarian nation or manufacturing nation a long time ago. It is now mostly a nation of service industries. The majority of jobs do not require presence but skill and performance. The skill must be taught and the performance can be monitored. Look at the countless energy which can be saved. Time, money, gasoline, all different forms of energy. The need for new roads, the need for new office space and so on would be significantly reduced," she said.

She resumed again: "The human race likes to build monuments to compensate for its mortality. In Egypt they build pyramids. In the United States they are building skyscrapers. In Egypt they glorified their ruler. In America they glorify the corporations. But the effect is the same. An endless stream of humanity moves to this focal point like locusts. Day in and day out, until it destroys itself and everything in its way. This is a major cause of your own destruction," she said.

"How about wars?" I asked.

"Wars are, of course, the other major cause. But wars are external forces of destruction. Because of their intensity, wars are always short and are binary in nature. There is the victor and the vanquished. Your quest for immortality is the internal force of destruction. It has a much longer time horizon. The impact is not seen as readily as in a war. Therefore, its impact emerges gradually. By the time the impact is recognized, the situation is usually irreversible. Yet, as you can see, each problem has its dual aspects. The key to a solution is always harmony," she paused.

"By the way," Artemis began,"...your patent keeps popping up each time I do a patent search on software. Give me a brief rundown..."

I think I started to blush all over. I mustered all my courage and replied: "Be glad to. I am flattered you recognized my name. The reason it pops up so often is, it was the first software patent ever issued. Once it was issued, it became the basis for all other software patents. I've been trying to get another patent using a different approach to patent software, but the patent office is reluctant. They want software to be closely tied to hardware and that, in my view, is a serious restriction on software..."

"In other words, you want it to be more universal, to stand on its own merits..."

"Exactly," I replied.

"Why don't you use copyrights?" She opined.

"As a matter of fact, I use copyrights and I find them to be more useful. When I developed QUEST (that's the name of the patented software,) I worked for BNL (Brookhaven National Laboratory.) Since they are funded by NASA, it became US Government property. In the process, BNL made a bundle by selling it to Control Data. Quest extended the useful-life of their hardware by about 10 years, so they made money. Then, it was used by TANDEM to build fail-safe computers. All I got out of it was a few articles in the Newspapers and a few 'thank-you' notes. On the other hand, I also developed ASSIST, CBM and RAM. Assist is a universal financial language, while CBM and RAM are trade based bond-pricing and risk analysis models. I made CBM a subset of RAM, for which I have a copyright. By not disclosing the technical details -- which is not required for a copyright --they remain my property. And, whenever the bond market goes into a tailspin I have many candidates who want to install and use my system. Indirectly, CBM and RAM have been very profitable for me. Besides a patent is only good for 17 years, while a copyright is good for 'life plus 50 years'..."

"I have used ASSIST. It is very good and easy to use. Give me a feature which makes it unique," Artemis asked.

"Aside from being an 'algebraic language,' which has every known financial term at its disposal which link it to the required database and a myriad of super-utilities, it is 'idiot-proof' for the user. Recursive expressions are trapped at execution time and the recursive linkage is identified for correction..."

"Yes," Artemis interrupted me, "...that is an outstanding feature. I wish they could transplant that technology to other compilers. What about a key feature in your RAM model?"

"The main strength of the RAM model is that it is trade driven, not 'Guru' driven. Gurus have a way of biasing their models to the portfolios they manage. Again, aside from a huge variety of financial functions, it has the capability to maintain a series of historical models which can be compressed or decompressed to adjust for the current market. The feature, which stuns most portfolio managers, is a command I call: FUTURE. There you provide a date and three points for the treasury curve -- as you perceive it to be on that date -- and the model finds the best historical model to use, makes the necessary adjustments and -- presto! -- you are at that date with a valid model..."

"A virtual time-machine? Didn't you also respond to NASA's RFP for hardware acquisition?" she asked.

"Yes, I did the technical response, programmed each kernel problem they posed and gave them the run-time timing formulas for each subset they requested..."

"Yes, I read your response. It was very good. In fact, I recommended that you get first prize when they evaluated the responses for completeness and accuracy, and NASA agreed..."

Hermes was nudging me with his darn umbrella. I wanted to continue. I did not want to leave this beauty. Another question, I thought. All I need is to pose another question, I thought. Artemis was so gentle and so kind in her way with me; I felt I could talk to her forever...

The scene faded, darkened, then lit up.

9

Apollo

We had returned to our familiar place in the valley. Hermes inspected his drawing and started:

"Let's turn our attention to the East," as he pointed squarely to Eastern Europe "... and step back in time a little bit to see how it evolved...

"As soon as the Huns were defeated by the Gepids, the Ostrogoths began rebuilding their realm. This is when the Roman Emperor Zeno contacted them with his offer to rule in Italy. The Goths assembled in the Trypilian area and debated that question. In the end, it was decided to accept Zeno's offer. Thus, a call went out for volunteers. And, many volunteered. Then, they elected a King, Theodoric, and departed their homeland. Of course, many more remained. They had a formidable job ahead of them. Their cities had to be rebuilt, their schools had to be re-opened and their land needed to be cultivated. Some Goths preferred to remain in smaller groups, notably the Bohemians, Moravians, Poles, Pomeranians and Prussians. The remaining Ostrogoths agreed to rebuild their country.

"The most important item on their agenda was to rebuild their cities and give them a 'Charter.' In today's terms, you call this a 'Bill of Rights' for the city dwellers. The Charter guaranteed each citizen a fair trial by the Princely Court and recourse in a Veche or Sbor. The realm was subdivided into 'Principalities.' Their ruler would rule from Kiev, his successor would rule from Novhorod (Novgorod) and so on. They started out with 12 cities or so, but, in time this grew to more than 200 cities. Each time a new city was founded, it got a Charter. In fact, I know of no city which they founded which did not have a Charter...

"When Theodoric left with his volunteers to settle Italy, they came to a grim realization. All their Kings had left the country over the last few centuries. Remember, their Kings were primarily Judges, and, without a trained Judge and trained Princes, the entire rebuilding process would not work. To consult on this problem, they gathered their sages in Kiev and charged them to come up with a solution...

"The solution the sages came up with was, to send a delegation empowered to find a royal family and to invite that family to rule their realm.

"Of course, this was easier said than done. There were Royal families in Spain, in France, in England and in the Scandinavian countries. But, in Spain, France and England they were Catholic. They had converted to the Roman Faith, while many Ostrogoths were of Arian faith. To avoid a religious clash, they preferred heathens. The only heathen Goths left lived in Norway -- they were called Varangians by the Ostrogoths, and so they sent their delegation to the Varangians..."

"Wait a minute," I interrupted. "The Kievan Chronicle states clearly that the delegation was sent to the Rus!" I exclaimed.

Hermes stopped for a minute. Then, he looked at me, almost in contempt and explained:

"I am surprised at you. We just discussed how the Greek and Latin letters played havoc with their words. Yes, in the Kievan Chronicle it spells the word 'PYC' or 'RUS' in Latin, but, by the time that Chronicle was written, most scribes came from Constantinople. Note too that the earliest version of that Chronicle comes from the 15th century when it was discovered by a farmer buried on his farm. How do you know it was genuine?

"Nevertheless, in Constantinople, Latin was the official language and Greek or 'Cyrillic' was the common vernacular. They often used the Roman letters for the Cyrillic counterparts. Thus, they meant to write 'RIK' in Cyrillic or 'PYC.' That is, the first letter is Greek and the next two letters are Latin. This type of error was common at that time. For example: the Latin name Barbara is pronounced Varvara in Cyrillic. The city of Tirene was spelled Tyrine or Tirine and so on." With that explanation, Hermes continued.

"The delegation went to the Varangians and found a Royal family who was willing to take up that offer: Ruryc (Rurik or Ruric). They took their entire family and sailed to Novhorod (Novgorod). There, Vadim had seized power. Ruryc defeated him and sent his younger brother Ihor (Igor) with his trusted general

Oleh (Oleg) to Kïiv (Kiev). Oleh was to rule as regent in Kïiv until Ihor reached maturity.

"When Oleh arrived in Kiev, he found two Vikings running the city -- Askold and Dir. They were deposed and Oleh ruled from Kiev. When Ihor reached maturity, he ruled from Kiev, but because his 'legal' training was incomplete, he would not append the letters 'ric,' 'mir,' 'slav' or 'polk' to his name. The subsequent rulers of the Goths were properly trained and appended either the letters 'ric,' 'slav,' 'mir' or 'polk' to their name in the tradition of the former Goths.

"By the end of the 10th century, Volodimir ruled in Kiev (Vladimir in Russian). He accepted Christianity from Constantinople, and was made hereditary King by Basil II, the Roman Emperor. To secure his loyalty, Basil gave his sister Anna in marriage to Volodimir. This is the only time in the History of the Roman Empire that an outsider married into the Imperial family. In addition, Kiev was made a Patriarchate for his realm and a Patriarch was installed there. This propelled Kiev to be the sixth most important city in the Roman Empire:Constantinople, Jerusalem, Alexandria, Rome, Antioch and Kiev...

"By the time King Yaroslav ruled, future European heirs stood in line to marry a Kievan Princess. Yaroslav's daughter Anna was married to the dauphin of France, Henry I. His other daughter married Harold, the future King of Norway. And Florence became the 'Sister-City' of Kiev.

"During the reign of King Yaroslav the Wise in Kiev, a scribe called Hipativ in Ukrainian, (Ipatiev in Russian) named the principalities of the Ostrogoths. He did that in accordance with the 'governing' or principal cities. The land governed from Kiev, Chernihiv and Pereyaslav he called: Ukraine. The land governed by the Prince of Novhorod was called Novhorod. The land governed by the Prince of Minsk, was called: Belarus (White Russia) and so on.

"By far the largest principality was the Ukraine. It stretched from Bratislava in Slovakia in the West, to the Don and Kuban rivers in the East. Bratislava was founded and Chartered in the 10th century by Sviatoslav, the King of Kiev. The Ukraine alone was larger than Spain, Gaul or England. But over time, the Ukrainian lands were taken away by her neighbors. Bratislava was annexed by Austria in the 17th century. In 1926, the Don and Kuban were forcibly annexed into the Russian Republic by the Soviets...

"The decline of their realm began in the 12th century. This was because their trade declined between Kiev and Constantinople.

And, with the sack of Constantinople in 1204 by the Franks, Kiev's trade with Constantinople became a trickle. This reduced her wealth and with it, her influence. Meanwhile, the Principality of Volodimir began to rise in wealth and power. They had developed their own trade with Persia. That trade made the city strong and powerful. What ensued was a struggle for supremacy between Volodimir and Kiev. In the process they made war on each other and both cities were sacked during that period.

"Be that as it may, the House of Ruryc ruled the Ostrogoths who were now called Slavs. In 1239, a new disaster destroyed their realm: the Invasion of the Tartars or Mongols.

"Shortly before that date, Genghis Khan and his Mongols had conquered China, a nation of 100 million people with many cities considered to be impregnable.His grandson Batu set out to conquer Europe. To him, the great cities in Europe were not an obstacle. In their war with China they had mastered the art of taking walled cities. Batu assembled a great army including many of the generals who had fought successfully for his grandfather. He called this army: 'The Golden Horde.' And they invaded Europe...

"When word reached Kiev of the Tartar invasion, they were not overly concerned. They had a great army and great walled cities. Little did they know that the same Mongols had conquered China only a few decades before. The Ostrogoths dispatched an army to drive out the invader. They met at Kalka in 1238. There, the Ostrogoths built a fort and repulsed the progress of the Tartars.

"The Tartars in turn, resorted to a ruse. They sent messengers to the Ostrogoths who told them that the Tartars decided to return to their homeland. Sure enough, the next day the Tartars were gone. The Ostrogoth army decided to return home and broke camp. Then, seemingly out of now-where, the Tartars fell on them and shattered the army. As an example of Mongol cruelty, captives were taken to the Tartar camp where they were told to cut down some trees and build a platform. When the platform was built, the prisoners were told to lift it. And, when they lifted it, the Tartars leaped on it and danced crushing the prisoners to death.

"A few prisoners were spared on purpose to watch that spectacle. They were then released to spread the word of the Tartar cruelty. The spectacle had been designed to spread fear, panic and discontent among the Ostrogoths. Among the prisoners was Danielo (Daniel), the young Prince from Lviv (Lvov), Galicia -- which is part of the Ukraine. When he arrived in Kiev and told his story, the Ostrogoths were not impressed. They still counted on their walled cities and their remaining army.

"What they did not know at that time was that one of their Princes had sided with the Tartars and led them to the key cities to be conquered. His name was Alexander Nevsky. Thus, with Alexander's help and the Tartar experience, all the great cities of the Ostrogoths fell one by one like dominoes. All except one, Novhorod, which survived because the spring thaw had begun and the Tartars were unable to transport their heavy siege engines to that city...

"In 1240, the Tartars reached Kiev and it was sacked and utterly destroyed.

"When the Tartars reached Galicia, Danielo went to see the Pope and asked for a Crusade against the Tartars. The Pope agreed, but first Danielo had to accept the Roman Faith. To this Danielo agreed. When the Tartars turned back to Sarai, Danielo converted his Principality to the Roman Faith,called Eastern Rite and was crowned King of Galicia by the Roman Church in Lviv. Despite this, the Pope failed to call for a Crusade against the Tartars, all promises notwithstanding. Thus, Danielo was tricked into accepting the Roman Faith.

"Batu went on to conquer Moldovia, Hungary, Poland, Bohemia, Moravia, and moved south into the Roman Empire. At the siege of Adrianople, a messenger arrived, requesting Batu to return to the homeland for the election of a new Chief Khan. Ugudai (Ogodei), the previous Chief Khan of the Tartars had been poisoned by a jealous concubine. Batu wheeled his army around and took it to Sarai (near Moscow) and set up a great tent city. Batu went to the election. When he was passed over as Chief Khan, Batu returned to Sarai where he decided not to continue his conquest but to live off the countries he had subjugated." Hermes pointed his umbrella to a spot in his map which I figured to be the location of Sarai. Then, he started again.

"Let me explain briefly how Alexander Nevsky became an ally of the Tartars. Alexander was a Prince and successor to the throne in Kiev. In that capacity he ruled in Novhorod. One day, a small group of Swedish missionaries arrived at the gates of Novhorod and made a nuisance of themselves. They were led by Jarl Birger, a Catholic. The city elders asked Alexander to chase these missionaries away. Alexander took his companions (he called them his 'Druzhina') and chased the missionaries to the river Neva, where he slaughtered them. This is how he got his name. When the details became known, the elders of Novhorod put him on notice. They considered his action despicable.

"As word reached Novhorod that the Tartars were on the move into Europe, Alexander Nevsky urged the Novhorodians to side with the Tartars. At that point, the city elders had enough of him, and banished him from Novhorod.

"Hence, Alexander Nevsky became the first Prince who was banished and who was without a Principality. By then, a watering hole called Moscow harbored a few renegades. Alexander Nevsky accepted when they asked him to rule in Moscow. Moscow was not a Chartered city. It was ruled in an absolute fashion, unabridged by any civilized law, and this suited Alexander Nevsky just fine.

"When the Tartars defeated the Ostrogoth army at Kalka, Alexander Nevsky offered his services to Batu. Thus, they became allies.

"In their conquest of China, the Tartar had learned that to get the most tribute from a country, it was best to let the local hierarchy administer a former Principality. They called it Yarlic. It was also best to keep their army intact, and pounce on any dissident or rebel and destroy them. Here again, Alexander Nevsky advised the Tartars of the Principality structure of the Ostrogoths, and, because he served them so well, Nevsky was given a Yarlic of his choice.

"He chose Volodimir, for it included Moscow. The Tartars then invited the former Princes to Sarai to bid for the Yarlic of their choice, auctioning off each Principality to the highest bidder of tribute. All the conquered lands of Batu were thereby 'redistributed.' Not only the land of the Ostrogoths, but also Poland, Hungary, Bohemia, Moravia and many more regions in Europe.

"Volodimir proved to be unsuitable for Alexander Nevsky, and his successors moved to Moscow with Ivan I Kalita or Money-Bags. From there, unrestrained by any civilized law, they could rule absolutely, and, as devout advocates of the Tartars, they became enforcers to collect the taxes. Of course, a portion of the tribute they kept for themselves and bought more Yarlics when they became available. Moreover, when the ruler of Moscow wanted a Yarlic, he just drummed up a charge, took it to the Tartars and together they pounced on the unsuspecting Principality. In this way, Moscow grew by leaps and bounds at the expense of her kinfolk. Eventually, the rulers of Moscow became stronger than the Tartars, especially when the Tartars divided into four Khanates in 1430: Crimea, Kazan, Astrakhan and Sibir...

"Many of the clergymen in Kiev came from Greece, and, when the city Volodimir was founded, a great cathedral was built there. When Alexander Nevsky started his rule in Volodimir, he invited the Patriarch from Kiev and his staff to move to

Volodimir. This would give Alexander the legitimacy he was seeking. At first they refused, but in the end the Patriarch moved from Kiev to Volodimir with his staff. This was done in order to avoid the incessant raids by the Tartars since the ruler in Volodimir or Moscow could offer better protection against them. The Patriarchate, however, remained in Kiev. A Patriarchate can only be moved or created by the Roman Emperor or in his absence, if three other Patriarchs consent.

"A Patriarch without a Patriarchate, however, is like a chariot without horses, and, since it takes three Patriarchs to establish a Patriarchate, neither Volodimir nor Moscow were made a Patriarchate. Thus was spawned the second branch of Orthodoxy in the East: A Patriarch without a Patriarchate. It is called Raskol or the break-up of the Orthodox Church. This issue became one of the concerns during the rule of Peter I. What you had was the legitimate Patriarch in Kiev and a roaming Bishop who claimed to be a Patriarch in Moscow.

"Ivan the Terrible decided to make war against the Tartars, but his army was defeated and this led to the destruction and depopulation of Muscovy. When Ivan died, a Tartar became Czar of Muscovy: Boris Godunov. Ivan the Terrible was the last descendent from the House of Ruryc, albeit from the Alexander Nevsky line."

"How did Boris Godunov come to power?" I asked.

"To begin with, Ivan tortured and killed his son and successor. This left Muscovy without a legitimate heir. Next, Ivan conquered the Tartar Khanate of Kazan and the Tartar Khanate of Astrakhan surrendered in horror at his butchery. The Crimean Tartars could not let that go unpunished. They invaded Muscovy, routed Ivan's army and took every non-Tartar prisoner. Then, they drove over 1 million prisoners, like cattle, to their slave markets in the Crimea. This is how Muscovy was depopulated of Goths and the Tartars became the majority there. They in turn elected Boris Godunov as their ruler."

"Did not the Tartars and Ottomans try to take Vienna." I asked.

"Yes, they tried. Let me describe one particular circumstance. Over the next few centuries, the 'western-most' Yarlics, Poland, Hungary and so on shed the Tartar rule. It was not until 1475,that the Crimean Tartars were conquered by the Ottoman Turks and, they in turn, pressed into Western Europe. In 1683,the Ottoman Turks and Tartars laid siege to Vienna.The siege was broken by Ukrainian Cossacks and the Polish army led by King Sobieski (who called himself the last Goth). However, the ungrateful Viennese refused to offer food or shelter to their saviors.

"Now, let me briefly describe what happened to the Western Principalities of the Ostrogoths or Kievan-Rus.

"As soon as the Ostrogoths were defeated by the Tartars, the Lithuanians started to rumble. They set themselves up as protectors of the Ostrogoths in the countries that are called Byelorussia and Ukraine. They just moved in, set up garrisons and the population welcomed them, even though they were heathens. They took on the Crimean Tartars in 1390 and vanquished them. Then, they bested the Teutonic Knights in 1410, and made them sign a treaty whereby the Knights would give up their expansion beyond the river Vistula. The Grandmaster of the Knights went to the Pope who disbanded the Teutonic Knights and chartered a new Teutonic order called 'The Knights of the Sword,' with the same Grandmaster and the same surviving members of the Teutonic Knights. Thus, in the end, their expansion continued unabated in the East.

"When Jagiello, (the Grand Duke of Lithuania), married Princess Hedzwiga in 1386, and accepted the Roman Faith in 1387 the Polish Barons swept into Byelorussia and the Ukraine in 1440, they demanded conversion to the Roman Faith. Widespread unrest was the result (1444). For nearly 200 years the Lithuanians administered the Ukraine and there was no major incident. But only 4 years of Polish administration provoked massive uprisings. In addition, of course, the Polish Barons brought with them a new brand of Catholicism -- the Roman Faith as opposed to the Roman Rite which already existed in Lviv and Galicia. The Ukraine now had two brands of Orthodoxy and two brands of Catholicism. That is, a religious goulash was steaming in the Ukraine. Therefore, the Cossack movement evolved in the Ukraine in 1444. While the Cossacks were mainly Orthodox, they accepted anyone who valued freedom, protected the Ukraine and became part of their brotherhood. (One Hetman was a Karaim Jew.)

"They banded together, built a fort which they called: Sich. In the Sich they built a long-house -- their meeting place. They next built a library and quarters for themselves. They tilled the surrounding area of the Sich where they could keep a family. They plowed the land with a saber on their side and a musket on their back, against Tartar raiders. There were four main Siches which sprang up in short order. In the Ukraine there were three: The Zaporozhian, Danubian and Don Sich. When Ivan the Terrible conquered Novhorod in 1570, just before he was annihilated by the Crimean Tartars in 1571, he butchered many and he forced the rest to flee to the Urals. There, they formed the Ural Sich. Their rule and government was democratic. Most were Orthodox, but that was not a requirement, love of freedom was. They embraced Catholics, Jews, heretics and heathens. They elected a leader when the need arose. They called him Hetman. Their 'brotherhood' had two main purposes, to protect and rescue

Christians from slavery, and to protect the Ukraine from Tartars or religious injustice. Their main targets were the slave markets in the Crimea, in the Ottoman Empire and in Czarhorod (Tsarhorod) the former Constantinople which was then ruled by the Ottoman Turks in 1453.

"They adapted the Viking ships for their region. They called them 'Chaika,' and, when they went on an expedition, they would chant: 'We are going to smudge the walls of Czarhorod.' Their Viking ships were unique in that, when they reached their destination and made landfall, they could attach a set of wheels to their ships, hoist a sail and scoot along the shoreline to the amazement and horror of the natives. This way they could be at the gates of the targeted town before a messenger could run the same distance. Then, they liberated all Christian slaves regardless of denomination, looted the city and sailed back home.

"Their presence terrified the Ottoman Empire. The sighting of a single Chaika would cause panic throughout the realm. The Sultan would then dispatch a few galleons to take care of the Cossacks. But, more often than not, the galleons were captured by the Cossacks, looted and burned. Once, the Sultan wrote them a letter requesting a truce with them. The Cossacks met and debated that issue and drafted the following reply: 'The moon shines on you and on us. Therefore, kiss our ass.'

"When Boris Godunov, a Tartar, became ruler in Moscow the Cossacks took action. The idea was simple and based on their tradition. They would call for a Sbor in Moscow, and then the collective body of all Ostrogoths and Tartars would decide who was to rule there. In order to do that, however, Moscow had to be conquered or liberated from the ruling Tartars. The Zaporozhian, Danubian and Don Siches combined thereupon and attacked Moscow in 1611. The Tartars were defeated and the Cossacks called for a Sbor in 1612. Their call was answered by a great multitude who came from all parts of their land. They came from Minsk and Novhorod; they came from Kiev, Chernihiv, Pereyaslav and Lviv; they came from Pskov, Suzdal and Tver and so on. When they arrived, a Sbor was held. It was decided that Tartars could not rule their land. A few candidates were nominated and Michael Romanov was elected Czar of Muscovy in 1613. By the way, the word Czar is a legitimate title for a ruler of the Goths. It was used by the Alans. (Michael Romanov was a descendant of the Prussian-Goths and Ivan's first wife was a Romanov).

"With their mission accomplished, the Cossacks and others all returned home, but, even though they changed the rulers in Moscow, they could not change the population, which was mostly Tartar in Muscovy.

"From 1618 to 1648, the 30 Year War raged in central Europe. It pitted the Catholics against the Protestants. At about the same time in England, Cromwell made war against the Monarchy. Again, the Protestants were pitted against the Catholics. And, in the Ukraine, the Cossacks made war against the Polish Barons. This pitted Orthodoxy against the Catholics. The Cossack leader, Bohdan Khmelnitzky (1648-57), defeated the Polish Barons and evicted them from the Ukraine. Knowing that the Ukraine could not survive without a strong supporter or ally, he sent out delegations to Moscow, Stockholm and Constantinople asking for an alliance.

"Why Constantinople which was ruled by the Islamic Ottoman Turks? The answer is not simple, but France had survived the fury of the Holy Roman Empire with her alliance with the Ottoman Turks. And, what was good for France, had to be good enough for the Ukraine. That was their reasoning.

"Why Sweden? They were kinfolk and at that time the mightiest power in Europe. They had saved the Protestants in Continental Europe (Gustavus Adolphus).

"Why Moscow? They were Orthodox, and only a few decades before the Ukrainian Cossacks had saved Moscow from Tartar domination and rule.

"Why not Spain, France or England? Their population was mostly Goths. When we spoke to Khmelnitzky, he realized that in Spain and France, the Goths had become religious zealots -- Catholics. Thus, they were eliminated right away.

"Khmelnitzky toyed with the idea of asking the English Goths for their protection. But, he soon realized that they were mostly Normans who were Catholics or French Goths. His experience with Poland had taught him not to trust the Catholics in a vital alliance. Thus, he rejected that idea.

"Moscow was the first to respond. Their delegation assured Khmelnitzky that the Ukraine would be autonomous and independent. All the Czar asked for in return was the right to ratify the Hetman after an election. This was presented as a rubber stamp affair.

"Khmelnitzky believed them and called his Cossacks to a Veche in Pereyaslav (1654). There, Khmelnitzky made a passionate speech about the necessity to ratify the treaty with Moscow. The Cossacks responded with a vote for ratification. Following this most Cossacks were disbanded.

"Khmelnitzky died shortly thereafter, and, when the next Hetman was elected and his name was sent in for ratification to

Moscow, the Czar's response was: "The Czar does not take orders from his subjects."

"The cat was out of the bag, but, before the Cossacks could act, Moscow regulars occupied the Ukraine. They then created more Cossack outposts in key cities who had to swear allegiance to the Czar,and the existing Siches were reduced to 8,000 Cossacks each. A multitude of Hetmans was now created, but their forces were significantly reduced and were nearly impotent. This historical period in the Ukraine is called 'Hetmanshina.' It pitted the Cossacks against each other by manipulating the various Hetmans. This created disunity in purpose and action...

"Meanwhile, the Czar made a treaty with Poland (Andrusovo in 1667), whereby half of the Ukraine and all of Byelorussia was given to Poland in exchange for a vague military alliance. Khmelnitzky's worst fears materialized from the best alliance he had in mind.

"Once again, the Polish Barons descended into the Ukraine and exacted terrible retribution on the population. The new Cossack Hetman became Ivan Mazepa (1687-1709). The ruler of Moscow was Peter I (1682-1725), and, in Sweden a boy-King of 16, Charles XII (1697-18), had just ascended the throne.

"Peter I decided this was a unique opportunity to take some real-estate away from the Swedes. Peter took the initiative and attacked Narva, a Swedish seaport. Narva held and sent messengers to their King to relieve the city.

"Charles XII assembled 12,000 Swedes and sailed for Narva. He arrived just in the nick of time as a blizzard was beginning to rage. Undaunted, he unloaded his soldiers, his light artillery and gave Peter a lesson in the use of light artillery. His 12,000 Swedes routed Peter's army of more than 80,000. Peter had to abandon his munitions and his artillery and fled to Moscow. There, he confiscated all church-bells and had new cannons cast...

"Charles XII decided to clear the Baltic coast of Polish expansion, and then to take up the matter of the Ukrainian alliance. But it took him over 8 years to do so. In 1709, Charles XII was ready to take up the Ukrainian matter. All this time, while he was in Poland, Charles XII kept in touch with Mazepa, and each time Mazepa urged Charles XII to come to the Ukraine and liberate it from Polish-Moscow oppression. Mazepa promised to raise 40,000 Cossacks for the cause. By then, the Swedish army had swelled to 44,000, but Mazepa could guarantee only 8,000 Cossacks which was all the Zaporozhian Sich was allowed to keep that time.

"Mazepa could not share his plans with the other Hetmans for fear they might tell Peter and spoil his plans. Thus, their arrangements were done in total secrecy. What Mazepa hoped for was that most of the Hetmans would rally to his cause. Finally, in the summer, Charles XII moved his army into the Ukraine...

"The Swedish army in the field needed to be re-supplied. A supply column, sent to meet with Charles XII in the Ukraine was attacked and captured by Peter's forces. Mazepa led Charles XII to Poltava, which was well supplied, but the garrison would not join Mazepa, as Peter was racing with his army to meet Charles and Mazepa...

"A battle ensued at Poltava in 1709. In the first artillery volley Charles XII was wounded. He was put on a stretcher and carried from battle scene to battle scene. The end-result was Charles XII and Mazepa were defeated. With only a small team left, they fled. They headed to the Zaporozhian Sich with Peter in hot pursuit. They crossed the Dnieper and fled to the Ottoman Turks, with Peter on their heels...

"The Sultan received the two fugitives and readied an army to greet Peter. When Peter entered their territory, he was surrounded by the Ottoman army and his main force was captured. Thus, Peter ended up in the captivity of the Sultan. Your history calls this 'The Prut (Pruth) Campaign (1710).'

"Not far behind the main body of Peter's army was the supply train and the camp-followers. In it was Catherine, a young Lithuanian mistress Peter had received as a gift from his friend Menshikov.

"Menshikov was a slave trader of sorts. He gifted Pushkin's grandfather, a pitch black Negro from the Sudan, to Peter I, and he was used in state functions to stun and dazzle the audience. When Peter sent his wife into the nunnery for life because she was sexually inadequate for him, Menshikov introduced him to Catherine (his personal sex slave), whom he had just bought for debt payments from her parents.

"Peter liked her right away and Menshikov gave her to Peter. Of course, directly or indirectly, Peter repaid each and every favor. In this way, Menshikov became not only Peter's confidant, but Peter heaped every post in his realm on him...

"When Catherine found out that Peter was captured by the Sultan, she sent a messenger to him offering to ransom Peter's freedom with her jewels. The Sultan accepted and Peter was ransomed and released. Next, Peter made an offer to the Sultan to ransom his entire army with uncut diamonds. Again, the Sultan agreed.

"However, the Sultan now demanded Peter sign a treaty with the Ottoman Empire, whereby Peter would give up the recently conquered fortress of Azov, the presence of Peter's navy in the Black Sea and the promise not to take any military action below a specified latitude -- which protected the Ukraine. It also stipulated that Peter was allowed to govern the Ukraine. To this Peter agreed. There were a few additional points which are of little importance...

"Peter sent Catherine to Moscow to fetch the uncut diamonds when the final agreement was reached. She returned with the gems and Peter's army was ransomed. A grateful Peter returned to St. Petersburg -- the city he was building -- and married Catherine. From then on and until his death, Peter continued his wars, but only in the North -- against Sweden.

"In a fit of vengeance, Peter instructed his administrators in the Ukraine to ravage the population, take her art treasures and steal her literature. From then on, and until the collapse of the Romanov dynasty -- with the exception of Elizabeth -- the Ukraine was mercilessly looted and exploited by the Romanovs.

"During Peter's rule, the Ukraine was depopulated to build his city of St. Petersburg in the Northern swamps of the Baltic Sea. Ukrainians were brutally forced into work gangs to drain the swamps under inhuman conditions and millions died there. The average survival rate was less than 3 months. It is said that St. Petersburg was built on the bones of the Cossacks and the Ukrainians. Furthermore, it can be said that Peter created the first 'Concentration Camps' in Europe and practiced genocide...

"Just like Ivan the Terrible, Peter I had tortured and killed his son and successor Alexis. On his second trip to Western Europe, to France, Peter contracted syphilis. He was treated with sulphur -- which did not improve his lot. He died in agony, and his latter descendants, including Peter III, were idiots.

"Upon his death, another succession crisis was created, similar to the period after the death of Ivan the Terrible. Your historians call this 'The Time of Troubles.' By the way, Peter was an admirer of Ivan the Terrible, and just like Ivan, Peter instituted many reforms.

"To begin with, Peter named his realm Rossija, 'The Land of Horses' from the Dutch word Ross, which means horse. That name is used to this day by the natives. Just look at their current postage stamps.

"Second, Peter is credited with creating the 'Table of Ranks,' which were given to him by Leibnitz. Thus, purely German words appeared in their dictionary: Ober-, Unter-, Prokuror, Fedwebel and so on.

"Third, he invented a third branch of Orthodoxy. He created a 'Holy Synod' which the Czar controlled, and which replaced the Patriarch in Moscow. The new title became Metropolitan of Moscow. Now Peter and his successors ruled without any moral authority, for they controlled the Metropolitan. The Ukraine had now three brands of Orthodoxy and two brands of the Roman Faith...

"Fourth, Peter is credited with creating the Rossijan language. Actually, Peter wanted to use Dutch, but his advisors argued against that. Instead he took the Ukrainian alphabet, crossed out a few letters and that became the new Rossijan alphabet. For example, some of the crossed out letters are: H, I and ї (ji).

"The French had convinced him that the letter H could be dropped -- because it was a silent letter, or it could be pronounced as a G. Now I ask you to pronounce Hermes or Honorarium, pronouncing the H as a G. Sounds like a disease doesn't it?

"Fifth, he introduced the Gregorian Calendar and changed the names of the months. This did not go over too well. The Calendar differed by 13 days. That's why the October Revolution was celebrated on November 7 and so on..."

"Please tell me about the calendar," I asked.

Hermes looked at me. "Be glad too. Here is the gist of it. After accepting Christianity from Constantinople, the Ostrogoths refused to glorify the heathen gods. They preferred words which reflected the seasons, but with Rome at the helm of Christianity, the Roman calendar became popular in the West. It glorifies the Roman gods...

"For example: January is derived from Janus, the four faced god of war. February is derived from Februs, the god of death. March is derived from Mars, the god of mindless war, Ares in Greek. April is derived from the muse. May is derived from Maya, the Egyptian goddess of the Earth. June comes from Juno (Hera), the wife of Jupiter (Zeus). July comes from Julius Caesar the dictator, who was deified. August comes from Augustus Caesar the Roman Emperor, who was also deified. The rest of the months were not assigned, but because they originated in Egypt and Egypt used only 10 months, they were numbered 7 through 10. Thus, the seventh month became September and so on. The last month, December comes from the number 10.

"Now, let me ask you this. Do you think it is fair that only Roman and Egyptian gods should be glorified in Europe? What about us, the Olympians?" It seemed to me that Hermes was notably upset. But after a brief pause, he continued on.

"Lastly, Peter created the draft: 40 years in the army or militia. Rossija now became an armed camp. In the Ukraine it was Catherine II, 'The Great,' who enforced this particular law which had a devastating effect on the Ukraine. A once Patriarchal society became Matriarchal, because once a couple got married, the husband was hauled off into the army -- and, when he returned, if he ever did, he was an old man. This is documented in the novel called: 'The Quiet Don.'

"Who paid for all these reforms? The Ukrainian farmers, of course. Direct taxes were increased to 60% and indirect taxes added another 30%, which included housing, food and expenses for the militia and army.

"I am not going to mention every Czar or Czarina but only the ones who shaped the future evolution of Rossija. Is that ok with you?"

I only nodded my head in agreement, "Yes, yes..."

"Peter died in 1725 without a will and his wife Catherine I (1725-27) became ruler. But for all practical purposes, Menshikov -- her former master and lover -- ruled Rossija. Catherine did complete all the works Peter had initiated. To illustrate: she opened the doors of the best University Europe had to offer -- in St. Petersburg, and she hired the best minds Peter had recruited: Daniel Bernoulli got the Chair in Mathematics; Euler got the Chair in Medicine and later in Mathematics and so on.

"But the German element among Peter's advisors had her eliminated. And, thus a another 'Time of Troubles' was ushered in.

"When,Peter II (1727-30) died at age 15 (the son of Alexis), Ivan V's oldest daughter Anna (1730-1740) became Czarina. She had been groomed for Kurland (Estonia, Latvia and Lithuania). Upon her assumption of the throne, she came with her German entourage, and they ruled. Anna was incompetent, leaving her advisor, Biron the German, in charge. Anna was succeeded by Ivan VI (1740-41) the grandson of Ivan V, but he was a babe and the Russian gentry imprisoned him at Schüsselberg. Keep in mind that Ivan V and Peter I were co-rulers and since there was no will, a committee had to decide the succession. In any event, this propelled Elizabeth (1741-1762), the younger daughter of Peter and Catherine I to power, and even though Elizabeth was a good ruler, she is chastised by Rossijan historians. Here is why...

"Elizabeth was a devout Orthodox Christian who, while in church, heard the 'angelic' voice of Alexey Rozumovsky (Razumovsky) who sang in the choir. She fell madly in love with him and married him. But Alexey was a descendent of a long line of Cossack Hetmans from the Zaporozhian Sich, and this is why the Rossijan historians will not forgive her. Rossijan historians stonewall his very existence. He is hardly ever mentioned. In addition, Elizabeth and their daughter Elizabeth (Tarakanova) are vilified.

"Elizabeth heaped every honor on Alexey. Yet Alexey refused to be drawn into politics. He only wanted to continue his singing. He had a brother Cyril, however, whom the Zaporozhian Cossacks had sent to study abroad -- which was their custom. The Zaporozhians waited patiently until Cyril returned and then elected him Hetman. Elizabeth not only ratified him immediately, she also made him Field-Marshal in her army. Once again the star of the Zaporozhian Sich was rising...

"During this time, Voltaire, the French playwright and historian heard the story of Charles XII, the Swedish King, and wrote a historical novel about him. This story became a 'best-seller' in Paris and then in Europe. After Elizabeth read that story, she hired Voltaire to write a eulogy to her father, Peter I. Voltaire, of course, agreed to this immediately. Elizabeth had all the records collected and sent them to Voltaire.

"The last of Peter's descendants was Peter III. He was a certified idiot, but when he had reached the age when men should be married, Elizabeth started to shop around for a suitable bride for him. (By the way, according to some historians, Peter III was not next in line but Elizabeth's daughter Elizabeth, known as Tarakanova. Once again, the Russian gentry changed the succession when Catherine's coup was successful and Tarakanova had to flee for her life when Catherine II took over.Catherine's agents located her in Ragusa Italy and Orlov brought her back. She was imprisoned in Schüsselberg until she died. Since Peter III was an idiot, Czarina Elizabeth never imagined that the Russian gentry would rob her daughter of succession.)

"A bit earlier, Leibnitz had shown Peter how succession and lineage worked in the Holy Roman Empire. What mattered most was to be married into a line of contenders for the German Concordat. Shortly before, Leibnitz had argued in the Imperial court that the Hanoverians were the legitimate successors to the English throne with James I. Peter was intrigued by the idea of taking over the Holy Roman Empire by marrying into the ruling line. He instructed that henceforth, all male heirs and potential successors must be married to such a line of Germans. That is, to a German Princess from that line. But how could such a line be found?

"Fortuna and Nemesis created this opportunity, and Frederick the Great identified that line. Near the town of Hannover there was just such a family which was related to the Hohenstaufen's. They had fallen on bad times and were running an inn. They had a daughter who worked as a barmaid. Her name was Catherine..."

"Excuse me," I interrupted, "was that her real name?" I asked.

"Actually, it was not. That became her assumed name, after she was Russified. I don't want to clutter your mind with unimportant names. That's all.

"She was 14 and quite suitable to be married to Peter III. A delegation was sent there, checked out her lineage and arranged her marriage with Peter III.

"Thereupon, Elizabeth sent Catherine a generous travel allowance and Catherine arrived in St. Petersburg with her mother, her Chamberlain and her maid. First, Catherine was 'Russified.' She had to accept Orthodoxy,learn the Rossijan language, customs, politics and take a Rossijan name: Catherine. Then, she was married to Peter III.

"However, Peter III had his own mistresses and never consummated the marriage. Yet each time Catherine had a child, he would exclaim: "Another immaculate conception," and despite it all, he would acknowledge each child his. Catherine had a son, Paul, a product between her and her German Chamberlain, even though most Russian historians claim that Sergei Saltykov was his biological father and three additional children, the product of her and Orlov, the commander of the 'Preobrazhensky Regiment.' This regiment was one of the two regiments which served the Czars as bodyguards. She never married Orlov.Later-on, she took another lover, Prince Grigori Potemkin, and when he lost his luster, he picked the best 'studs' for her.

"Word leaked out that Voltaire was writing a eulogy about Peter I. Frederick the Great openly chastised that endeavour, enraging Elizabeth. When the 7-Year War broke out between Prussia and France who was allied with Austria, Elizabeth joined the fray against Frederick. In quick succession the Eastern Provinces of Prussia (East Prussia and Pomerania) were captured and occupied by Rossijans who then brought the war to Prussia itself.

"This war allowed the Zaporozhian Cossacks to redeem themselves. At Kunersdorf, Frederick was defeated and Prussia was facing total ruin. Berlin was raided by the Cossacks (1762) and panic struck Frederick's realm. His letters to his mother attest to that. Frederick writes to his Queen mother: "All is lost..."

But then,the unthinkable happened: Frederick's provinces were restored, the Rossijan forces withdrawn and a peace conference was called for in Paris (1763). What happened?"

I did not answer this. I knew it was a rhetorical question. After a brief pause, Hermes continued.

"Well, the Germans, still entrenched from the days of Biron, eliminated Czarina Elizabeth. She died under mysterious circumstances. With Peter III slated for the throne, Catherine was facing a solitary life in the nunnery, just like Peter I's wife. To forestall this happenstance, she recruited Orlov, and together they staged a coup. Peter's forces were defeated and he was taken to prison where he was tortured and killed, while Tarakanova fled. With a handful of loyal supporters, Catherine ascended the throne as Catherine II, and, once she was in power, she stopped the war against Frederick the Great. (She also restored Biron in Kurland).

"Earlier, Frederick the Great had done a few favors for her family. Now, she was ready to repay him -- big time. Not only did she stop the war, she returned all the occupied provinces to him -- without any compensation. She then arranged the peace negotiations in Paris (1763). There, she had Prussia resurrected and Frederick the Great came out stronger than before the 7-Year War. Historians hail Frederick the Great for his great victories over the French, Austrians and Rossijans, while his defeats are swept under the rug. Later in history, as Hitler was facing utter defeat, he pinned his last hopes on a similar Rossijan miracle which never materialized...

"Catherine's rule was marred by constant revolts, which she suppressed ruthlessly. Many historians say: 'No wonder, she had no claim to the throne what-so-ever.' At one point Cossacks tried to rescue Ivan VI from Schlüsselberg, but the guards killed him (1764).

"One of the most important uprisings was led by the Cossack Hetman from the Don Sich: Puhachov or Pugachev in Rossijan. He started out with a few Cossacks and vowed to put Catherine into a nunnery. He mimicked her court, and as his ranks swelled, he took over the countryside. With his growing army he took a few important cities, and prevailed against an army of regulars. However, Catherine had many loyal and competent generals, and they defeated Puhachov in the end who fled to the Ural Sich. Why?"

I did not say a word. I wanted Hermes to continue. He did.

"Shortly before, the Don Cossack Hetman Stenka Razin staged a popular revolt. He too, was defeated in the end, and fled to the Don Sich. The Rossijan army descended to the Don and demanded his release, and Stenka Razin was turned over to them. When Puhachov was defeated, he knew he would not find sanctuary in the Don Sich leading him to flee to the Ural Sich.

"Catherine appointed her most competent general, Suvorov, to a task force to bring Puhachov back in a cage, but not to harm him in any other way. Suvorov chased Puhachov in the Ural region, caught up with him, put him into a cage as ordered, and brought him to St. Petersburg. There, Puhachov was tried by a kangaroo court and sentenced to death -- all the while, being caged like a wild animal. He was not allowed to shave, not to clean himself or not to relieve himself in private. This was the kind of spectacle Catherine cherished. For better or worse, the Nürnberg trials in Bavaria after World War II are perceived by many to be a similar spectacle, in particular by the Germans...

"Later, Pushkin came upon his story and wrote a book about it, for it epitomized the quest of a man in search of his liberties and freedom. The censors, however, would not allow that version to be published, so Pushkin rewrote the story and called the new version: 'The Captain's Daughter,' where he glorified the Czarist regime.

"Once Catherine II restored the semblance of order at home she branched out on three missions. First, the destruction of Poland; second, the total enslavement of the Ukraine, and third, the conquest of the Crimean Tartars.

"She made an alliance with Austria and Prussia and orchestrated the destruction of Poland. This is called the 'Three Partitions of Poland.' In the first partition she took back the lands which were turned over to Poland in the treaty of Andrusovo. That is, the Western Ukraine and Byelorussia, while Prussia and Austria got only a few border provinces. In the second partition, most of Poland was gobbled up by the Robber Barons: Austria, Prussia and Rossija, and, in the third partition Poland ceased to exist on the map of Europe. Catherine, of course, took the lion's share of the Polish lands.

"During the second partition, a young Polish woman, Countess Walewska by name, moved to Paris to escape the Rossijan oppression. There, she opened a salon, met Napoleon Bonaparte and became his mistress. She and Napoleon had children together, but Napoleon would not acknowledge them. He had grander aspirations.

"He did, however, promote their children to rank, and since that day they have served France in the Chamber of Deputies. Of course, their political ambitions favored Poland and undermined the Ukraine. Eventually, this led to the resurrection of the Polish state during Napoleon's rule and after World War I.

"Once Poland was out of the way, the Ukraine was ravaged and most Ukrainian farmers became serfs to the Rossijan overlords. It became a crime to speak Ukrainian, and it became an even greater crime to write or publish in Ukrainian. Shevchenko, a Ukrainian Poet and writer was repeatedly sent to Siberia for his folly.This pleased the Rossijan intelligentsia who hailed Catherine II and put her on a par with Peter I. She enforced and strengthened the programs Peter I had outlined for the enslavement of Poland and the Ukraine.

"During her reign, every Sich was razed (1774). The Cossacks were imprisoned and sent to Siberia. The fame of the Cossacks, however, had to be harnessed and made Rossijan. From then on, army regulars were called Cossacks. Of course, they had nothing in common with the original Cossacks. In fact, the 'new Cossack units' distinguished themselves by their singular brutality.

"The original Cossacks were fiercely democratic while the 'new Cossacks' were completely autocratic. The original Cossacks wore colorful clothes: red, yellow and blue 'sharavary' or baggy pants, a colorful shirt, a 'kuzhukh' or fur coat and a fur hat. Their head was shaven, except for a long pony-tail lock of hair. They sported a long mustache, called an 'oceledez' or 'herring.' This was done on purpose -- to proclaim their free spirit and to distinguish them from the Tartars. They flaunted the fact that they belonged to the 'Brotherhood of Free Men,' while the 'new Cossack' regiments wore black and brandished a 'knut' or whip. That is, not only their appearance was different but their mind-set as well. The original Cossacks valued liberty most, while the 'new Cossacks' valued total obedience. In particular, their kind of obedience. When they were resisted, their brutality knew no bounds. Here is a good example of the 'dark side' of Russification..."

"Excuse me," I interrupted, "explain Russification to me."

Hermes just looked at me, as if in stupor. Then he started: "Actually, it is a program of disinformation, to deprive a people or nation of her identity, traditions, language, history, culture and literature. This includes all aspects...

"It started in Egypt. Your historians say it began with Ramses II. He was a great conqueror. Each time he defeated a nation, he brought them to Egypt as slaves. Then, he erected an obelisk describing his victory over them. Those nations who fought valiantly were awarded a 'penis' in his text. Those who fought like cowards were awarded a 'vagina.' His successors envied his exploits, so they changed his 'cartouche' to theirs. This way, they immortalized themselves on his glory. In a way, his method evolved into the rating systems you use in your country. One star to five stars...

"In Greece it was a little different. Homer needed to meld the history of the Achaeans into the history of the Doric invaders -- the Hellenes -- to blend and legitimize the elusive 'Sea People,' with the prior civilization in Greece. This he did in his Iliad. Later-on, the Macedonian Goths, were 'Hellenized' in a similar fashion by your historians. That is, they were not counted as Goths but as Hellenes. Of course, there is not a speck of truth to that.

"The Greeks would not intermarry with foreigners -- even though many did, like Herodotus, who married the Gothic woman Melpomene. But in the end he left her and their children. That was the 'right thing' to do in accordance with Greek tradition. However, when Alexander the Great demanded that his soldiers intermarry with the Persians, the Greek mercenaries in his army refused. Alexander had to punish them. Only then did the remainder follow his orders...

"In Rome the situation was a little different. Northern Italy was colonized by the Etruscans, while Southern Italy and Sicily were colonized by the Greeks. The original settlers of Rome were bandits, robbers and outcasts. Rome was situated in the no-man's land between the Etruscans and the Greeks. There they built a city with a great wall and organized. Then they systematically eradicated the Etruscans and evicted the Greeks. When Hannibal invaded Rome, he counted on the support of the Etruscan city states, but they refused to join him. Therefore, he had no choice. He moved to Southern Italy where he got support from the Greek colonists. But because the Roman system was better and already established, Hannibal had no chance of winning the war. In the end his expedition failed. The Etruscans and then the Greeks were eliminated and all of Italy and Sicily became eventually Roman.

"In the process all vestiges of Etruscan culture were eradicated. However, the Romans were not able to read or interpret the 'Sacred Books' of the Etruscans. Therefore, they kept a few Etruscan 'Augres' to read and interpret them. This way, every Roman Emperor, including Marcus Aurelius had an Etruscan Augre who read the text and interpreted the sacrifices, directed the layouts of a city, the construction of roads, aqueducts, canals and sewers. And after the Greeks were conquered, the Greek literature was 'Romanized' by changing the Greek names to corresponding Roman names or by appending a Roman ending. I should know. I am called Hermes by the Greeks and Mercury by the Romans...

"This trend continued unabated to the present day. For example, when Mussolini got a piece of Tyrol in the Versailles Treaty, he formed a 'Tomb Squad.' Their mission was to read the tombstones in Tyrol, identify the obvious non-Italian names and change them to Italian names...

"Spain was an altogether different situation. The Goths, after accepting the Roman Faith in the 7th century, Latinized their words from their original runic using the Roman alphabet. But Spain was conquered by the Moors and their names took on a Moorish flavor. In the 15th century, Spain was reconquered and the latinized names became prevalent again. Then they became Roman Catholic zealots. The Inquisition originated there and spread through the rest of Europe. It had one sole purpose, to cleanse Europe of all infidels, heretics, gnostics and non-believers. The existing laws were brushed aside. All that was needed were two accusers and the Inquisition took over. Then they tortured the accused until a confession was extracted. In this way, nearly half of Western Europe perished -- Catholics, heretics, gnostics and Jews. The Inquisition was exported to the New World and entire nations were exterminated...

"The French experience was also different. Until the 4th century France was broken up into a number of Roman provinces. Their totality was called Gaul. Then, the Goths moved in and for all practical purposes it became a Gothic country. In the 8th century more Goths moved in. They were called Normans. It was not until Francis I struck the French Concordat with the Pope in the 16th century that an effective program was begun to rid France of all 'foreign perversions.' Once the French King was able to install French Bishops, the language and history were 'cleansed' of all Gothic influences. All that remains are the Gothic Cathedrals. From then on and to this day, they remove from their language and history all foreign 'subversion.' Today they are trying to eliminate from the French language all American words and notions.

"In England it was also different. In the 4th century Britain was abandoned by the Roman Empire. This allowed the Goths to move in. Then the Normans came and ruled England followed by the Danes. But along the way, Henry VIII broke with the Pope but not with the Holy Roman Emperor. This came to a head with his successor, Elizabeth I, and the disaster of the Spanish Armada. From then on, England freed herself of all Gothic and Norman words. And what best way was there then to 'create' a new author with a new language. That was Shakespeare. Thus, the best minds of England wrote the best plays, and this collected work was published under the name of Shakespeare. Instantly, England became the haven for intellectuals in Europe. Next England tried to resurrect her past. Thus, many English Kings were either found or invented such as Arthur and Alfred and so on. The curious part was their names started with the letter 'A.' Why?"

I did not say a word, so Hermes continued.

"A new text of knowledge had been created. It was called an Encyclopedia. And, in the early stages it was perceived that it was crucial that all the English Kings had to appear in the first volume, because very few readers, if any, ever got beyond the first volume. Of course, that proved to be unwarranted and was relaxed later-on. But then, the Germans came and took over the rule in England. Once again, history was changed to suit her new German rulers. By then, England was already a great colonial Empire -- in particular in America. Thus, when the Revolutionary war started in the American colonies, the blame had to be shifted from England to some non-existent entity. A 'Hessian Propaganda' was created and it worked perfectly. Despite the fact that England was the only country in Europe which consistently tried to subjugate America, Americans feel kinship with her to this day. What remains of the Gothic influence is the 'Gothic novel.'

"Therefore, when Muscovy started to claim to be a European nation, they had many methods and precedents to draw on. They started their claim by calling themselves 'The Third Rome,' starting with Ivan III who married Zoe, the niece of the last Roman Emperor. In many ways, their claim was well conceived but unfounded. Moscow started out as a refuge of bandits and outcasts, just like Rome. When the Greek monks came to Kiev, their primary mission was to cut the umbilical cord between the Goths and the Slavs just like the Roman monks did in Gaul. They cut the umbilical cord of the Goths and promoted the German converts. Mind you, the Merovingians had already changed to the Roman Faith, but they were tolerant to heathens, infidels and heretics. Therefore, the Roman Bishops and the Pope called them 'do-nothing Kings.' This is how the Carolingians moved in and took over. Once the break in the Christian Church occurred in 800, pitting Orthodoxy against the Roman Faith the real Roman Empire was dubbed the 'Byzantine Empire' by your historians...

"Once Muscovy called herself the 'Third Rome,' the Ukraine was cast into the role of the Etruscans. That is, they had to be eliminated, their language had to be perverted, their literature had to be erased, their history had to be transferred to Muscovy and so on. Moscow established 'Moscow Parity:' no title could exceed the title in Moscow. The Kievan Kings became Princes and Kievan Patriarchs became Metropolitans. Even Anna, the daughter of King Yaroslav the Wise who married Henry I of France is called Anna of Russia. What an abomination! Then, major works such as 'The Lay of Ihor,' which precedes the 'Song of Roland' by almost 100 years, was made 'Russian.' Then, there was an endless repertoire of short stories, sayings and so on. They were called 'Byliny,' the stories and ballads of their past and they are called 'Russian.' Yet the word Russia was coined by Voltaire in the 18th century or 600 years later, while the natives call themselves Rossjians to this day.

"Ivan the Terrible went one step further; he wanted Moscow to be made into a Patriarchate. So, he invited the Patriarch of Jerusalem. His intent was to have the Patriarch of Jerusalem pronounce Moscow a Patriarchate, but the Patriarch of Jerusalem refused. Why? Because Kiev was the only legitimate Patriarchate for that region. Even if he wanted to create a new Patriarchate, he could not. Only the Roman Emperor could create one. Instead, he pointed out a few inconsistencies in their liturgy. What followed was a 'Raskol,' a division between the two branches of Orthodoxy: Kiev and Moscow.

"Ukrainian literature had to be destroyed or better yet 'Russified.' The first thing that was done was all references to the Goths were eliminated. The Goths were cast into a Germanic role. The second thing that was done was to give all stories a Christian flavor. Third, Muscovy made claims that this treasure trove belonged to them.This is why Peter I embarked on a program to eradicate the Ukraine. Catherine II nearly completed it.

"Yet, almost miraculously, the Ukraine survived and many of her writers wrote in Ukrainian at great personal risk. While others wrote in Russian to get published, writers and poets like Shevchenko, Franko and Lesya Ukrainka wrote in Ukrainian and suffered accordingly. Hohol (Gogol), Chekhov and others wrote in Russian. They got published and have a world-wide audience. Shevchenko loved America. In his writings he would often exlcaim: "When will the Ukraine have her George Washington!..."

"Stalin persecuted the Ukraine even worse than the Czars did. While the Ukraine appears to be free today in a bean counting sense, it is not. The same Old Soviet Guard is still in power. They are not about to lose control any time soon. Let me give you a case in point. The President of the Ukraine is Kuchma. At a recent state function, an all-Ukrainian affair, his wife spoke only in Russian. Kuchma was asked why his wife did not speak Ukrainian. Do you know what he replied? "She does not want to pollute her Russian language. This is not some 'Joe Blow' talking. This is the wife of the Ukrainian President. What do you think?"

I said nothing, I wanted to hear his conclusion.

"Germany was a late comer to the scene of falsification. In the 16th century, Martin Luther spent 20 years of his life compiling a brief dictionary of the German language to write his Catechism. By then, the Jews in Germany had a German-type language of their own, called Yiddish. In fact, it had existed since before the First Crusade, in the town of Speyer. How do we know? Because, before the Crusaders left for the Crusade, they sacked the Jewish community first. This was the first pogrom of sorts...

"Another 300 years passed before there was an effort to form the German language. It was not until Goethe, Schiller and Lessing got into the act. That period was called 'Sturm und Drang.' That is, a mad rush to steal, divert and rewrite the history of the Goths into German. Wagner was the culminating point. Hitler took it to its logical conclusion. He called it 'Kulturkampf.' Their method of Germanization was simple. Declare it to be German and go from there.

"For example, after the German Empire was declared in 1871, by declaration in the Hall of Mirrors in Versailles, and German historians found tidbits of historical information, such as the defeat of Varus some place in Germany, action had to be taken. First, that 'some place' was narrowed down to the Teutoburger Wald (forest). But the Teutoburger Wald was situated in the area the Suevi occupied. By all accounts, the Suevi were Goths. Nevertheless, the Suevi were declared to be German. Their German name was declared to be Schwaben. In the same breath, of course, the Goths were declared to be a 'Germanic' people, which contradicts every ancient historian of repute. Next, a commission was formed to search that forest for a suitable battle-site. A ravine was found which seemed to fit the historical description. The commission declared that site to be the 'infamous' battle scene where the Suevi under Arminius, defeated the two Roman legions led by Varus in 6 AD. A monument was promptly erected there. Meanwhile, nearly 1900 years had elapsed. The battle took place in 6 AD, and the monument was erected in 1905!

"What do all these cases have in common? Except for France, all the other countries were ruled by Germans. England by Hanoverians, Austria by Habsburgs, Italy by Habsburgs, Spain by Habsburgs, Germany by Hohenzollerns, Russia by Romanovs who were German after Catherine II. And what was their policy of falsification? In England, Geopolitics; in Austria, Ausgleich; in Germany, Kulturkampf (Germanization, Sturm und Drang); and in Russia, Russification. That is, the same school of falsification spread systematic disinformation by a different name...

"In the Ukraine, I blame the clergy for allowing Russification to spread and to destroy it. To begin with, they accepted the Greek thesis that the Goths and the Slavs were distinct people as soon as they accepted Orthodoxy from Constantinople. As I pointed out they were not. In fact, as late as the 18th century, the Swedes considered the Ukraine, Belarus and Novhorod their original homeland. That's why Charles XII from Sweden took up their cause in the Ukraine. Orthodoxy put blinders on them after the defeat by the Tartars. The clergy championed an Orthodox alliance at all costs. They urged an alliance with Moscow, even though Muscovy was entirely Tartar after Moscow was sacked towards the end of the rule of Ivan the Terrible. Their mind-sets were entirely different. Muscovy was autocratic while the Ukraine was democratic. Muscovy wanted to exploit, while the Ukraine wanted to live in peace. Hetman Khmelnitzky listened to the clergy and thus brought on the demise of the Ukraine. Once he accepted the rhetoric of the clergy, he was able to sway the Ukraine into that miserable alliance...

"Real-Estate in Europe is extremely valuable. It is not measured in money. It is valued in human lives. I would say," as Hermes rolled his eyes and looked up to the sky, "it is worth at least one human life for every square inch of soil!

"Let me resume with Catherine II. Once she established herself, she invited the German writers to descend into the Ukraine and raid the Ukrainian literary treasures, such as the 'Byliny.' Thus, the Brother's Grimm and others came and carted off many stories to Germany. Catherine II also invited German settlers to come and settle in the Ukraine and the hinterlands of Moscow, and many Germans came and took over the best land available. Later on, a German Republic was created on the river Volga. It was called 'Volga-Germany.' It preceded the German state by over 50 years, but when the Germans invaded the Soviet Union in 1941, that Republic was dissolved by Stalin and all traces of it were erased...

"Finally, once her realm was under firm control, she invaded the Crimea and conquered the Crimean Tartars. With the Tartars out of the way,she initiated the wars against the Ottoman Empire. Her designs were monumental to say the least. She wanted to liberate the Balkans, then the Caucasus, then to annex Persia and lastly to annex parts of India. Concurrently, she hired German explorers who mapped Siberia, the Pacific Ocean, and she pressed on to conquer the rest of Siberia. Eventually, Rossijan colonists reached Alaska and moved South on the American continent. They came as far as San Francisco. A Russian Fort and a Russian River, just to the North of San Francisco, attest to that expansion.

"During her reign she found out that Voltaire was writing a eulogy for Peter I. She decided to 'upgrade' his task. She asked Voltaire to write the definitive history of Rossija instead. Voltaire was contacted and agreed to take on the new project. Her counsellors and advisors gathered records and made up a history they wanted to see published. Her loyal servant Shuvalov was selected to deliver that material to Voltaire. Of course, Voltaire was promised a King's Ransom if his work was satisfactory to Catherine II. Half was paid in advance, the other half was to be paid upon completion.

"Voltaire therefore, wrote a Rossijan history from the specifications provided. Diderot delivered the final installment and collected the last payment. Catherine II and her advisors were more than pleased adding a generous bonus to Voltaire. In homage to Voltaire, a library was dedicated to him. A statue of him was carved from the most exquisite marble, which is prominently displayed to this day in the Hermitage, in St. Petersburg. And, ever since then, every Rossijan historian of name has a dedication to Voltaire in his history. But Voltaire did not like the word Rossija. He liked the word RUS. Voltaire renamed Catherine's realm Russe in French or Russia in the Anglo-Saxon world, while the natives call it Rossija to this day.

"The history of the Kievan-Rus belongs to Kiev and the Ukraine, not to Rossija, as Voltaire claimed. This is not a technicality. It is a fundamental difference. The history of the Cossacks belongs to the Ukraine, yet Catherine perverted that word to mean oppression and brutality as were many other words such as Boyars, Duma and so on. Originally, the word 'Boyar' meant a career soldier, the equivalent of a Knight in Western Europe. However, in Muscovy the word Boyar was used for tax-collectors. Thus, most of them were Tartars. They dressed like Tartars and they acted like Tartars. The word became synonymous with oppression.

"The word Cossack was chosen when free men formed a Sich in the Ukraine. Today, even the word Cossack has been perverted. I would like to suggest that you use different spellings of that word to accentuate the difference. For example, spell it Kozaks for the period until the last Sich was destroyed by Catherine II in 1774. Thereafter spell it Cossacks, to identify the army regulars created by Catherine II." As Hermes turned to me.

"That is a good point." I exclaimed. "I'll make a note of it."

"Originally, the word 'Duma' meant the Princely Council in a principality. That word deteriorated into an impotent assembly. Therefore, the Kozaks used the word 'Rada,' and, to this day, they use the word Rada for a council. The words that were changed in meaning are far too numerous to mention today. Just be aware that many of the original words were perverted on purpose. Many of them now have a new and different meaning.

"As I have shown, the Rossijans are the descendent of Tartars or Mongols, while the Ukrainians are the descendants of the Goths. This manifests itself in the following way. The Ukraine is intensely democratic while the Rossijans are intensely autocratic. That is, their mind sets are totally different. A Ukrainian will die for his liberties; this they have demonstrated throughout their history. A Rossijan wants a strong and absolute ruler. A Ukrainian will roll up his sleeves and tackle any job, while a Rossijan will live off the labor of others, just as the Tartars did for over 500 years.

"Don't you think this is a serious infringement on the history of the Kievan-Rus and the Ukraine?" He only looked at me. I knew it was a rhetorical question. So, I said nothing.

"Just look at the Tartar history. They lived off the tribute they collected from the vanquished Yarlics, and when they needed extra cash, they raided the countryside and carried off everyone in their way to the slave markets in the Crimea. That is, they lived off tribute, enslavement and slave trading. They lived in the Crimea over 700 years, from 1240 to 1945, and in all these years they created nothing: no art, no literature, no science and so on. In fact they were most proud to be parasites. In 1945, Stalin exiled the Tartars to Siberia for collaborating with the Germans during World War II, without any prospect of reclaiming their land, and in 1954, Khrushchev gifted the Crimea to the Ukraine for its 300 year alliance with Muscovy. But then, Khrushchev was a Ukrainian 'Kukuruznik' anyway.

"Now, let's get back to Voltaire. You can see, money changes not only the character of man but alters the recorded history to suit and please the rulers. Voltaire was not the only historian who wrote to specifications. Practically every historian until Niebuhr wrote history that way. Including Gibbon." Hermes got up, stretched his legs and arms. Then, he continued again.

"As I see it, there are a number of forces which favor the European union and there are a few forces which will undermine it. The forces are: Religion, Ethnicity and Economics...

"Ever since Christianity became the dominant religion in Europe, only one denomination was tolerated, while all others were exterminated. For example: the change from Arianism to Orthodoxy. An alternate to Orthodoxy was created to satisfy the ambitions of Rome: the Roman Faith (Catholicism).When enlightenment swept Europe, the Protestants won the right of existence through prolonged religious wars.This is the clay and steel which will not mix.This has continued to this day.Somewhat reluctantly, three branches of Christianity have found acceptance in Europe: Catholics, Orthodox and Protestants: Lutherans and Calvinists. All others are considered to be Jewish sects. They may be tolerated today because your country still wields a big stick in Europe, but as soon as the Europeans have it their way, all the sects, heathens and infidels will be either converted, evicted or destroyed. This has been the history of Europe for the last 1700 years. Why should it change now? Religion is what polarizes Europe, and the Pope holds the spark which can turn this into a holy war. The German Concordat is alive and well. It is only dormant awaiting resurrection..."

I could not help it. At this point I just piped in, "What is your definition of a Christian?"

"Let me answer this on our next break. Is that ok?"

"Yes, yes, ... of course." I answered.

Hermes just shoved his umbrella, his caduceus, into my hand and we were off, travelling through space. We came to an abrupt halt. We were standing in a bright spacious office. It was a modern office. All around us was glass. Dark natural wood made up the office furniture. Antique fabric, gleamed from the couches, sofas and chairs. A deep golden carpet engulfed the entire setting. The office was furnished exquisitely. Two large windows invited the sunshine into the office. Directly in front of us was a large wooden executive desk. The rest of the office was furnished with matching furniture. A large credenza stretched from one window to the next and a sitting area was on my left. The office was neat and clean. Behind the desk sat a handsome man in his mid-thirties. He was blonde and wore a blue business suit. Only his profile was visible to me. On the desk, to our left side was a terminal. A pair of cables were conspicuously visible. The man seemed to be meditating or thinking about something. He was facing the sitting area. Two chairs were in front of the desk. Without looking at us, the man motioned us to sit down. We did. Still facing the sitting area, he made a motion for us to speak. Hermes took the initiative:

"Good morning, Apollo," I heard him say.

"Good morning," I heard myself repeating.

A nod from Apollo was his only response.

Hermes turned to me and said: "This is your opportunity to ask questions. Ever since Franklin stole thunder and lightning from him and discovered the nature of electricity, Apollo turned introvert. He will only respond in key-words. I will interpret them for you if you need an interpretation," he said.

I was in a spot. I was not prepared to ask any questions. Where should I start? Let me begin with some notions I had worked out first, I thought.

"How are stocks related to the bond market?" I asked.

"Implied parity..." I heard faintly.

"What are the key variables in the bond market?" I asked.

"Bellwether... Quality... Coupon... Maturity... Provisions... Volume... Sentiment... ... ...," he whispered softly. But I could not make out the last few terms.

I looked to Hermes for an interpretation. Hermes had almost a grin on his face as he said: "The variables are in the order of their significance. The ones you did not hear are the ones you are not ready to tackle. Don't worry about them for now. When you get further along in your work we will have another meeting."

I thought for a moment and asked Hermes: "Does Apollo mean quality or rating?"

Hermes had almost a frown on his face as he replied: "Of course he means quality. A rating is only an artificial ordering. It is a loose coupling of price and quality or yield and quality. Naturally, price and yield are directly coupled. They allow no degrees of freedom. They allow no alternatives. However, by the time the ratings are produced and available they are obsolete in the critical cases..."

"But,... " I interrupted, "this implies that the solution for the linear system for yields or prices depends on yet another linear system which characterizes qualities."

"Of course," Hermes replied.

I still was not finished with Hermes. I asked him again: "When Apollo said 'provisions' did he mean all the provisions attached to a bond? There is a multitude of provisions and for some the data was never collected."

"Of course," Hermes replied. "The provisions are very important. They are the market differentia for each issue. If the provisions did not exist the solution space would be completely homogeneous. Then, the solution alternatives would be almost trivial. And, real problems do not have purely linear solutions."

I turned to Apollo and asked: "Is there a hierarchy in the provisions?"

"Taxes..., Call..., Sinking Fund..., Refunding..., Variable Coupons..., Guarantee..., ..., ..., ..., ...," I heard faintly.

I looked at Hermes. He anticipated the questions in my mind. He started to explain: "Naturally, the tax implication is the most dominant provision. The debt market is even segregated along these lines. For example: The corporate bond market and the municipal bond market. If it were not for taxes the two markets would behave exactly the same way. The tax implications have yet another impact. This is clearly visible in the convexity of a given yield surface. That is, the tax implications define not only different markets but also influence each market on the coupon axis. Conversely then, one solution method is equally valid for corporates and municipals. In fact, when a good solution method is found for the corporates, that same solution method will yield even better results for the municipals. This of course, should be obvious. Yet the converse is not true."

He paused for a while as if he was sorting out my mind for additional questions. He went on: "I will skip the intervening provisions. While they may pose technical difficulties, they pose few conceptual difficulties. Let us look at the guarantee provision instead. Clearly, when an issue is guaranteed by the government, that issue will command a very high rating. In the United States, the hierarchy is: Government bonds, Agencies and then issues guaranteed by the US Government. However, it does not end there. An issuer may have a multitude of issues which are guaranteed with some asset while others are not. We simply say, some are 'secured' and other unsecured. Paradoxically, the strongest provision is good faith. Only when good faith and prior performance are violated or abused is a collateral required. Naturally, the unsecured issues are of the lowest quality for an issuer within the spectrum of secured issues. However, the type of 'security' forms a hierarchy within itself. That is, the rating scheme in use, does not reflect the quality in use. This is because, at different times, different 'securities' are perceived to be of different strength. And, this influences the sentiment..."

"You mean the rating scale should be two-dimensional in nature," I replied.

"At least that," Hermes responded.

Hermes paused for a while and then said: "When we saw Poseidon, he demonstrated fractals to you. Well, you can observe the occurrence of fractals here also. You will have an idea as to their nature when you consider the trade volume. To make the analogy somewhat simplistic, consider a unit trade and a myriad of units traded at one time. Fortunately, you do not trade in fractional units of an issue. Very seldom do you trade in blocks larger than one myriad. Therefore, a unit and a myriad are reasonable boundary conditions when we speak of volume in the bond market for one trade. That is, a simple trade and a block trade. Then, your logic demands, according to the demand-supply axiom, that there must be a continuous variation in price within this trade range. This variation in price is a fractal differential. Because your currency has a lower bound, a nominal unit, this fractal variation can not be observed in your currency when a trade occurs. What you do observe are 'step-functions' or fractal differences in price for trade volume fluctuations. That is, the block trade must be lower in price than the unit trade when a well informed buyer buys from a well informed seller. There could be anomalies, but as a rule you can use near certainty to this principle," Hermes seemed to have finished with his interpretation.

I pondered my next question. As far as I was concerned, I wanted to get more information about market timing. So I asked: "What are the dominant variables which influence the stock market?"

"Economy..., ..., News..., ..., Option Spreads, ..., Earnings, Alpha..., ..., HPR..., ..., Dividends..., Cycles..., ..., Liquidity..., ..., Sentiment..., Fundamental Beta, ..., Latent Volatility..., ..., Signature..., ..., Leverage..., Implied Volatility..., ..., Fungibility..., Channels..., ..., Parity..., ..., Trend..., Momentum..., ..., Support..., Resistance..., Historical Beta, ..., Volume..., Close..., Value, High..., Low..., ..."

I looked at Hermes to interpret the variables. Hermes was almost amused as he began: "Needless to say, the economy is the most dominant variable. In fact, modern portfolio theory and modern selection theory divides the market attributes into macro-economic variables (which affect all issues across the board), and micro-economic variables (which affect only a segment of a market or only specific issues). Markowitz developed a few procedures along these lines. Thus, the economy and news are of the macro-economic variety,..." he paused.

"Is the bellwether bond a reasonable proxy for the economy?" I asked.

He continued: "Actually, a good proxy would be a model to forecast the actions of the FED. That model would be dominated by the M2 at this time -- but that emphasis changes from time to time and includes many other variables. The bellwether bond, is a consequence of the actions of the FED, therefore it is a reasonable proxy, but it is not a primary leading indicator. Actually, that model should include: M1, M2, M3 and the monetary policy of the major trade partners or G7's. Of course, in the absence of this model the bellwether bond is a necessity," he paused again.

Then he continued: "Of course, if you could interpret the shape of the government characteristic curves correctly for the G7's, then you should be able to use that quantification as an even better proxy. The bellwether bond by itself is necessary but not sufficient," he said. After a pause, he continued: "The news acts more as a fractal variable and the contrarian aspect of the news is usually more important. Of course, certain news items are acted upon immediately, such as acquisitions, takeovers, dividend changes, earnings changes and so on. This is why news and dividends are so high in the hierarchy," he said.

"Could you give me a contrarian example for the news impact?" I asked.

"Certainly. I will also demonstrate this effect and its interpretation.

"In mid 1991, Lockheed was awarded a massive contract by the military. In fact, the contract was so large that it dwarfed the company's market value. After the announcement was made, practically everybody bought call options to capitalize on the good fortunes of Lockheed. So, what happened? Over the next trading month the stock value of Lockheed declined and all call buyers were stranded! Why? The market was already positioned for Lockheed to win the contract. Therefore, when the news broke, it had a negative effect on the stock. Of course, the market has a cliche for this effect. It is called: 'Buy on rumors and sell on facts.' The only problem with that cliche is that there are just too many unsubstantiated rumors floating around, hence the cliche is worthless in most instances. On the other hand, that very same effect was visible three months before in the option calendar-spread. And everybody who bought then, and sold after the news, made a tidy profit," he looked expectantly at me.

"How does one model the news?" I asked.

"That is a major problem today," Hermes said. "News acts like a delta function on an otherwise stable system. Each delta function could be quantified and its dominant effect could be measured. Fortunately, most news items have little impact. We are generally insensitive to news. Therefore, we rationalize that the market already discounted the news. Only massive, unexpected news changes affect the market's direction. Expected news changes favor the contrarian view. Otherwise the situation would be very difficult indeed.

"Option spreads have many components. First, the obvious components for one issue: Bull-spread, bear-spread and calendar-spread correlations. Since the price motion obeys a log-normal price distribution for stocks to be optionable in the first place, anomalies in their density function are valid directional indicators. The key, of course, is to filter out the noise which is inherent in the density function to begin with,..." he paused again.

Then he continued: "Of course, you should go one step further and determine the rational relationships between the issue and the industry leader. Between them and the characteristic index. And, all three of them with respect to the dominant exchange. While the secondary exchange will act as leading indicator of impending volatility, the dominant exchange will often act as a market maker. Then, even the put-call ratio will provide a kind of delta function for a trend reversal. But, the market's significance is important. For now, you could use the CBOE to indicate market reversals. The open interest is very important at that time.

"Actually, we touched on alphas when we discussed the effect of the economic variable. While the economic variable is global, the alpha of a stock is that issue's attribute which the market prefers at a particular time. Naturally, that preference can change as economic conditions change. A reasonable proxy for alphas is to solve the major market index for alphas and then one can infer the particular market preference at that time.Thus, the alphas form a sub-system within the entire system. The reason the major market index is such a good proxy is because there are only 30 issues in that index and the linear system will be sufficiently small to provide a solution..."

"That need not be entirely true," I interrupted. "Such a system would require 30 independent variables and only a small subset of which can be solved for. This is because some of the eigenvalues will tend to zero and will veil the succeeding eigenvalue of the system which could be significant," I said.

"Of course." Hermes replied. "I take it for granted that the singularities of the system have been removed before the final determination is made. If they are not removed, they create a black hole in the system and any solution near that black hole will diverge. Actually, as the solution passes the black hole, the subsequent eigenvalues will be out of phase with the principle branch of the incident space. Euler demonstrated this for simple complex function and Jacobi demonstrated this when solving for the eigenvalues and the implied stability of a linear system," he said.

"HPR, of course, is the holding period return. The advantage of HPR over say, a trend analysis, is that it includes the earnings estimates of an issue. Therefore, HPR is more significant than technical charts. However, the principle is almost the same. Notice the dimensional compatibility of the factors involved for HPR in terms of percentages:

$$HPR = \frac{PE * EPS + DIV}{\text{Current Price}} * 100$$

"Then, if the current, historical minimum and historical maximum are applied to that formula for PE, (for a range of 1 to three years you get a minimum and a maximum,) one obtains a reasonable projection for the variation of the projected annual return for HPR for the period in question. That is, HPR is evaluated twice, once for the minimum PE and another time for the maximum PE for that period. EPS are the currently projected earning. The factor 100 is used to produce a percentage result. And Current Price, is the current close price.

"First, you can see the dimensional compatibility: PE= PRICE/EARNINGS, EPS= EARNINGS/SHARE. Thus, the numerator becomes price and the denominator becomes shares. Therefore, the end-product is price per share. Of course, we must adjust that price by the known dividend and the formula is essentially correct.

"Second, the HPR formula includes earnings estimates for the immediate future. Then, if we have the variation of the PE's and future earnings estimates, we can estimate the expected future price of the stock in terms of percent upside and percent downside or a 'trade channel'..."

"But that price estimate may vary by more than 100%," I interrupted. "How is a 100% variation an admissible solution?" I asked.

"Well, ..." he thought for a moment and then he continued: "We established before that an analytic solution may not be possible. However, in the HPR formulation the historical PE's act as statistical inferences which are modified by the future earnings. Their product yields an adjusted price with reasonable certainty for the new earnings. Therefore, we expect that the future minimum and maximum are reasonable bounds for the future. The time horizon being the min/max PE's used. Thus we have an expected trade band for the future time horizon..."

"Ok,..." I interrupted again. "Look at IBM and it's present price range, at it's historical PE's and the future earnings estimates. Do you really think that IBM will trade again at the PE multiples of the past?" I asked.

"You are right," Hermes said. "IBM is a special situation. Here is a company which provided technical excellence until 1964. Then, it became a marketing company. From then on, they lost touch with technology, practicing predatory tactics in the industry. The PC industry is now clearly outperforming IBM's mid-range main-frames at a small fraction of their price. IBM is in a tailspin, losing its installed client base, and there is nothing IBM can do about it. If they introduce PC's just as powerful as the competition, these PC's will displace their installed base and significantly reduce their earnings. If they try to keep their installed customer base, the competition will replace IBM altogether and IBM will cease to exist as we know it. This poses a real dilemma for IBM. They will have to branch out into other fields: Wireless, consulting and so on. They will survive for quite a while because they have a huge client base: Corporate America..."

"Funny, you put it this way," I interrupted Hermes. "I just read an article in Business Week in the March 17, 2003 issue. It tried to find positive aspects in IBM's gradual demise. It flaunted IBM's new buzzword: E-Business on Demand. Is that what you mean?" I asked.

"Of course. But what that article did not say was that IBM is poised to take Corporate America to the cleaners, as you say in your country. They have established themselves as the super-consultants. Yet their personnel are not qualified to attack vertical problems. That is, they are 'jacks of all trades and masters of none.' This re-alignment is doomed to failure.

"Besides," Hermes continued, "there are two developments which will hurt their image. The first is, there is a book out which details IBM's complicity in the last Holocaust. It is highly provocative and emotionally charged. It is called: 'IBM and the Holocaust.' Second, as the accounting scandals expand after the Enron debacle, IBM will be taken to the carpet for their questionable accounting practices for 2000 and 2001. It will be interesting to see what comes of it. Now let us get back to the HPR formulation...

"As you pointed out, the earnings projections are probably still overinflated. Thus, quarter by quarter IBM will reach new plateaus on the down-side, until it will cease to exist as we know it today. The PE multiple is also reflected in the sentiment. Therefore, after a while that sentiment will be reflected in the new PE's. Then, if you adjust for these two factors using other statistical inferences, the HPR estimate will still be very reasonable," he said.

Hermes thought for a while and continued: "Liquidity is very important. And, as you pointed out in your book, for all practical purposes only optionable stocks are liquid. This restricts the choices a great deal. But the results could be made rational. If the results are made rational, they could be repeated time and again when a similar situation arises.

"Look at the sentiment as a self-fulfilling attribute of the market. Whenever the sentiment is completely one-sided it will overpower everything in its way. Normally this will last only for a short time. Then, the price reaches a new plateau level, and the sentiment becomes divided. The first to capitalize on that reversal are the market makers for that issue. Since you will not know who is selling and who is buying, a reasonable proxy can be the volume. But a better proxy is the anomaly, if any, in the calendar-spread of the issue.

"Latent volatility, implied volatility, fungibility and trade channels are closely related. Of these only trade channels are attributes of stocks. The others are really measures for options. Since stocks and options interact very strongly, these variables are important. Trade channels tend to expand and contract in a regular manner. Look at their density function and the changing slope over the normal life of an option. Again, you will be able to develop statistical measures which will be useful. Latent volatility is only a phase shift of implied volatility. Therefore, latent volatility is more important. That is, latent volatility is the volatility to come or to be expected. Whereas implied volatility is the historical volatility, or that what transpired in the past. Accordingly, the implied volatility is often called the 'combat' premium. Of course fungibility or the ability to change from a put writer position to a call writer position. This contributes directly to the volume of the stock market. Fungibility 'feeds' off the stock market causing its volume to explode. A great deal of the increased stock volume is due to fungibility. Very soon, the stock volume due to option activity will overshadow the actual stock market activity of its own. Right now we have passed this break-even point. Therefore, market timing of options is clearly more important than the market timing of stocks. This is why leverage becomes so important in a rational model," he paused again.

Hermes reflected for a moment and continued: "The signature of an issue is overpowered only by the leverage components of an issue. That is, the signature of an issue is so low in the hierarchy because the option components have inherent multipliers. Otherwise, for stocks without listed options, the signature is substantially more important than in the hierarchy provided. The reason the signature is so important is, because it provides a cycle norm. Anomalies are highly visible and can be used and readily tracked.

"The remaining variables are of much lower importance. Parity describes two aspects. The first is usually called the monotone increase characteristics of the stock market. A reasonable up-trend is in the order of three to four percent compounded semiannually. Of course, when the bond market exceeds this growth expectation in a substantial manner, the stock market reacts violently. It collapses back to a normal yield expectation level and the trend begins to stabilize. This occurs when the bond market or the dominant force in bond market reaches a yield level in excess of ten percent. The trend and momentum are standard industry tools. You should not expect to get much new information from them. Support and resistance levels are also much overworked basic tools. All four exhibit interesting dualities which can cause many misinterpretations. The actual prices are the least important variables, because they do not reflect the center of gravity of the trade activity during the course of a day or week or month. Much less so when they are used in the course of a year," Hermes seemed to be finished.

"What happened to 'Value?'" I piped in.

"The value of a stock is a very ambiguous term. Practically ever trader, investor and portfolio manager has a different definition for it. We discussed it briefly when I pointed out that the stock price or the value of a stock is the present value of all its future earnings. In practical terms, this is extrapolated to about 20 years. However, there are other measures which are quite suitable. For example, consider the class of stocks which are interest sensitive, pay dividends and the dividends are supported by the earnings. That is, the dividends are legitimate. Entire Industry Groups of stocks fall into this category: Utilities, Banks, Financial Institutions and others; some even include Convertibles -- even though they have a dual behavior and need to be compared with Bonds when they trade below their conversion value -- then, default is their greatest risk.

"One can divide that set into three subsets. First, the class of stocks which pay less than the historical current yield or: (Annual Dividend) divided by the (Current Price) times 100; this equals the Current Yield in percent -- they are called 'Overvalued.' Second, the class of stocks which pay the historical prevailing current yield, they are often called 'trading at par.' Thirdly the stocks which pay more than the prevailing current yield -- they are normally called 'Undervalued.'

"All that remains is to compute the historical current yields, compute the thresholds for each class and voila -- you have a means of selecting stocks which are overvalued and undervalued and, you can proceed from there...

"When you couple these stocks with the notion that 'sooner or later' stocks should be trading at par -- in terms of their current dividend yield -- then it stands to reason that overvalued stock should decline and undervalued stocks should increase in price.

"Historically, the stock market's current dividend yield has been in the range of 2% to 6%, when the Bellwether Bond is below 8%. Now it is up to your risk tolerance to set the thresholds. If you call all stocks which yield more than 5% undervalued and all stock with less that 2.5% overvalued, you should come up with only a handful of stocks which are your prime candidates -- when no other key factors are dominating.

"Finally, in this scenario it should be quite obvious why money switches from stocks to bonds once the Bellwether Bond yields more than 8%. As you can see, investors begin to switch from stocks to bonds at about 8.5%. At 10% percent and over that switch becomes a stampede, as savvy investors try to lock-in high yields. Conversely, when the Bellwether Bond falls below 8.5%, investors begin to switch from bonds to stocks and at 6% that switch becomes a stampede...

Aha, I thought, a whole branch of analysis was left out. I turned to Hermes and said: "All these variables are technical variables. Are the fundamental variables not important for market timing?" I asked.

"Of course they are important," Hermes said. "They are the differentia for the investment horizon. But you choose not to listen to Apollo as he enumerated them. Therefore, I felt no need to explain them to you at this time."

"But you have not explained cycles and the two types of betas," I countered.

"You are right. Let us discuss the betas first..."

"Before you continue," I interrupted, "... can the association between the dividend in the stock market and the coupon in the bond market be made?"

"Of course it can be made." Hermes replied. "But then, the duration formulas must be adjusted to permit the changing nature of the dividend and the future value of the stock price must be adjusted to compensate for the redemption value of the bond. Once this is done properly, the techniques from the bond market carry over to the stock market," he replied.

I was very excited. I asked: "You mean to tell me that stock portfolios could be immunized? That duration windows could be computed and stocks could be used instead of bonds?"

"Yes, but you must keep in mind that many of the formulations of Bierwag, Fong and other must be adjusted for the variability of dividends and the redemption value of the issue...

"You pointed out that the historical betas are of little value even though they are used quite extensively by portfolio managers. Thus, a historical beta is that linear system which correlates an issue with an index. The fundamental betas are different. Suppose for one moment the historical beta could be solved for the alphas within the historical betas. If such a solution exists, that solution is called the fundamental beta."

"Why do you say 'if such a solution exists'?" I asked him.

"Actually,that's quite simple. The historical beta is solved with respect to a basket of stocks. With respect to an index. Some indexes are small. Then, the alphas can be readily solved for. But some indexes are very large as the Wilshire 5000. Some are even larger. Then, for all practical purposes the composition of the fundamental beta can not be solved for, simply because there are not enough independent variables in the system...

"In a way I did not want to go into cycles. Partially, because they may leave you with the impression that after all these discussions of rational behavior of attributes I would throw in a cosmic variable and render your approach useless. Let me demonstrate that this is not what Apollo implied. For example, Kondratieff (Kondratiev) demonstrated a 54 year economic cycle for the United States. This cycle was developed at the turn of last century and was dismissed by the industry. In the last 30 years it found limited acceptance. According to that cycle, a major upturn in the United States was to occur in 1994, and it did...

"But there are still other cycles. You pointed out in your book that futures in general, and commodity futures in particular dwarf the stock market. Let us look at the commodities for a moment.We know that sun-spots or their absence directly influence the harvest and growth of all life on earth.

"Does it not stand to reason that when commodities are plentiful, they depress the commodities market? This in turn affects the stock market. However, the sun-cycle is approximately 22 years. That is, roughly π times 7, the moon cycle. Remember how Archimedes approximated π? Twenty-two divided by seven...

"Thus, a half-cycle is roughly 11 years. Notice that major economic cycles have a peak or valley roughly every 11 years. I only bring this up because you asked for it. If you were to be serious about this kind of a model you would have to include many more planets, comets and other cosmic forces. I really don't think that you or your clients are ready to pursue this matter at this time..."

I had the distinct feeling that my session with Apollo was over. Oh, how many more questions I could ask, I thought. Why could I not control myself. Hubris got me...

Sure enough, Apollo waved his hand gently. I knew we were dismissed.

The next thing I know, we were travelling through space to our familiar place for another rendezvous.

10

Athene

We came to a rest in our familiar place in the valley. As soon as Hermes got seated on the rock, he started.

"Let me pick up with your last question: 'What defines a Christian?

"I think there are three events which define a Christian: the proclamation in Antioch by the Church Elders after the fall of Jerusalem in 70; the proclamation by Constantine, called the Edict of Milan in 313, and the Council of Nicaea in 325. All other proclamations were only nuances, imposed by the Christian hierarchy in power. They were done for purely selfish reasons.

"In Antioch, the Jewish dietary laws, rituals and the Old Testament were discarded. This included circumcision. I consider circumcision to be an act against nature. It serves no purpose whatsoever. In fact, circumcision is harmful to both body and soul. Regardless whether it is performed on a man or woman.

"Here's how it came about. After Christ was crucified, his followers dispersed and the Romans started to hunt for the Apostles. Peter was well known, so he became the prime target. Therefore, Peter had to leave Jerusalem. He appointed James, the brother of Jesus, to lead that congregation while Peter left. Paul began preaching to the Gentiles, and right from the very beginning, three separate branches of Christ's teaching evolved. Paul and James were at the extremes, while Peter was somewhere in the middle. The issue was this. If a gentile converted, did he or she have to become a Jew first?

"James insisted that to be a follower of Christ, the Jewish traditions had to be followed. He and his flock continued to practice Jewish dietary laws, circumcision, study the Old Testament and the New Testament. Paul argued that Gentiles did not have to obey any of the Jewish traditions and became followers of Jesus by reading and practicing only the New Testament. Peter was somewhere in the middle. While there are no documented writings of Peter's beliefs, his attempts to reconcile James and Paul suggest his position.

"In Antioch, the Church Elders accepted Paul's teachings, and it is there that they were called Christians for the first time, thereby distinguishing Christians from the Jews.

"Despite this delineation, the followers of James and Peter continued to preach their way. Therefore, while Paul's teaching became the mainstream, the others became sects of Christianity.

"The Edict of Milan was an 'Edict of Tolerance.' All religions had the right to exist and had to tolerate each other. This is not possible in a Theocracy, no matter by what name you call it. The Roman Empire had the right idea. The Pontifex Maximus, or supreme religious leader, was the Emperor -- for all religions. He had not only the right, but also the obligation to appoint Church leaders who suited him. Why? Very simple. All priests were his employees, and when they are supported by 'contributions,' it means the Emperor allowed the diversion of taxes to that religion. This was only another form of compensation by the Emperor. Your country has taken this idea one step further. You call it: 'Separation of Church and State.'

"The Council of Nicaea defined Christian belief. The text is called: 'The Creed.' Now, keep the following in mind. Emperor Constantine presided over that council and approved the text -- yet he was a heathen. Of the 600 Bishops or so in attendance, more than 400 were Arian Christians, and less than 20 were Orthodox. The rest were other denominations. (The Roman Faith did not exist at that time. It emerged in 800 with the German Concordat.) Both Arius and Athanasius agreed to the text, yet shortly thereafter the holy wars began and have continued to this day. In my view, these three events define a Christian..."

"I love your definition," I exclaimed. "It legitimizes most Christian branches in America, and since there are more than 6,000 of them, I like it even more. Now there are more than 6,000 ways to reach salvation and go to Heaven, and no single branch of Christianity has a monopoly any more..."

"Heaven and Hell," Hermes interrupted, "are concepts you have created to browbeat the congregation into submission. They are a 'sales-gimmick' which every religion uses to exploit their flock...

"We divided the earth into three regions: Upper Hemisphere, which was ruled by Poseidon; Lower Hemisphere, which was ruled by Hades and the Center, which was ruled by Zeus. I am both messenger and herald of Zeus, my father. The dividing line is the 30th parallel. Homer called Hades the ruler of the 'Underworld' and Dante called his realm 'Hell.' Meanwhile, Homer called Poseidon's realm the 'Clouds' or 'Sky,' while Dante took it beyond the stratosphere and called it 'Heaven.' But, as you can see Heaven and Hell are right here on earth." Hermes paused briefly.

"Nationalism is a new phenomenon in Europe. Its present form was created by Napoleon. However, ethnicity is not a new phenomenon. It has been smoldering in Europe since the first city state was established in Greece.They coined the word 'Barbarian,' which separated them from all other ethnic groups. The Greeks believed their culture was best, yet Kingship came to them from Egypt and Phoenicia, with Cadmus. And the Athenian democracy, which your country cherishes so much, destroyed the Greek city-states. Democracy in its purest form is not workable. No government can be run by a mob for long. Every notable Athenian was ostracized and either killed himself like Socrates or took refuge among his enemies, like Alcibiades, Themistocles and so on...

"The Roman model was much better. It is called a 'Republic.' It had some checks and balances, the Emperor and the Senate...

"The Gothic model was even better. It had a three tier justice system, and it had a 'Duma' or the equivalent of the Roman Senate. The Duma had more power than the Senate. No Senate ever banished a ruler. Yet, I described to you how the Novhorodians banished Alexander Nevsky, but because the Gothic writings were destroyed, their ways and deeds were suppressed until they ended up in oblivion...

"Your form of Government is even better. The President has the power, yet the Senate doles out the money for his programs. You have the House of Representatives, which speaks for the people, and last but not least, you have an independent Judiciary which reviews and corrects the law of the land...

"If history is any indication: the Greek system lasted barely 300 years -- from about 600 BC to 300 BC. The Roman system lasted more than 2100 years -- from about 700 BC to 1453 AD, when Constantinople fell to the Ottoman Turks. Your system therefore should last at least 2100 years...

"Now, let us look at the ethnic make-up in Europe. The Goths dominate the ethnic scene in Spain, Portugal, France and England; the Scandinavian Countries: Denmark, Iceland, Norway and Sweden;

the Balkans: Bosnia, Croatia, Macedonia, Montenegro, Serbia and Slovenia; Central Europe: Czechia, Poland, Slovakia and Moldovia; Eastern Europe: Byelorussia and Ukraine. The next largest ethnic group are of Mongolian or Tartar descent:Bulgaria, Finland, Hungary and Russia. All others are minorities in Europe: Basques, Belgae, Britons, Etruscans, Frisians, Celts, Gaels, Greeks, Germans, Latins, Picts, Scots, Walloons and so on. But the minorities rule Europe, and this is a paradox. Again, here is more clay which will not mix with steel...

"Each nation, each state and each community wants to enjoy American luxuries. This 'Drang to Possess Plenty' overshadows their differences for the time being. Therein lies the paradox. It is the nature of man that once a certain amount of wealth is acquired the other forces spring to the foreground. The European Union faces this dilemma. In order to be competitive with America they have to unite. But, as soon as they reach a certain standard of living they will be at each other's throats." Hermes leaned toward me pensively. The next thing I heard was:

"Let's be on our way. I made another appointment for today." With that he shoved his rod into my hand and we were on our way.

Then, I felt vibrations as though I was in an airplane. I opened my eyes and sure enough we were in a small jet cruising through the sky. Hermes was not at my side. I thought I had lost him. Another look and I noticed him in a window seat a few rows behind me. I was sitting on the aisle. Seated next to me was the most ravishing creature I had ever seen. She radiated beauty...

She turned to me and simply said: "Hi, I am Athene."

"I ...." was the only word I could get of my mouth.

She continued in a very gentle manner: "My realm is Justice and crafty warfare. I am on my way to Washington. The Pentagon requires some restructuring. Now that the cold war is over..."

I could not hear the rest. The airplane was drowning out her speech. I had to bend down a little bit and stare at the floor in order to hear her at all. I just nodded my head, trying to covey to her that I understood what she was saying to me.

"... layers ... reconcile ... balance ... equilibrium ..." she continued.

How could I convey to her that I heard only fragments without offending her, I thought. There was no way I was going to offend her. I was not going to commit Hubris again. I just kept nodding my head gently, hoping she would continue. Her presence next to me made me euphoric. I heard her lilting voice in sporadic bursts.

"...social justice ... natural justice ... harmony ...," she said.

And again I nodded my head without catching the gist of her conversation. I felt frustrated in one sense but elated and almost jubilant.

"... creative ... parity ... continuity ... humanity ... women ...," I heard her say.

I noticed how she moved closer to me. Her head hovered right next to mine as the started again:

"Technology has changed the old world... The new struggle for dominance will be fought in the economic battlefield.... Those who adapt will prosper and survive, those who do not will be swept away.... Worse of all, many will be enslaved by the new masters of finance and economy... Money will rule the new world order more than ever before... "

At last. I could hear whole sentences, not only fragments as before. I forced myself to ask a question:

"You mean technology will dominate the future?"

"Not at all. The disposition of capital will dominate the future... Trade alliances must be not only made but properly capitalized... Real trade partners have to be groomed, not exploited... Understanding the economic forces must become the major agenda for your schools..."

Now she moved closer still. We were nearly cheek to cheek.

"Do you know what precipitated Japan's near takeover of America's industries in the 1980's?" She asked.

"They built a better and cheaper product and nearly took over the American market..." I started rather meekly.

Athene cut me off. "Not at all. Japan's money supply was growing nearly 10 times faster than America's because of incompatible reserve requirements. That's all. Once that was corrected America recovered and has outperformed Japan ever since...

"Here's how it evolved. In the old days gold was used to back the money supply. But, when America found herself in a bind, having less than 3.5% of her money supply covered by gold in Fort Knox, a new standard had to be developed. Because all the gold on this earth was not enough to cover the money supply America needed in order to continue to grow. And within a decade or so, all the gold in your galaxy will not be enough. The new means to control the money supply became the 'reserve requirements' for banks. It needed to be flexible, so a norm was established ranging from 10% to 17%. As soon as America got off the gold standard most European nations followed suit -- except for the Swiss.

"In a small country like Switzerland that's ok. It has the following advantages: inflation is checked at home and the purchasing power is increased abroad...

"Japan, maintained a much lower reserve requirement, about 2%, the reason being that America was effectively at 3.5% when it switched. Japan switched later, so they just extrapolated America's gold reserves and pegged their reserve requirements that way. Nobody paid much attention to this imbalance until about 1980. This is when Japan unleashed her products on America. In particular her cars. They were fuel efficient and caught the fancy of Americans. Now the reserve requirements showed the horrible inequity. Each time a Toyota was sold at say, $10,000, it increased Japan's money supply by $500,000. Because, the money supply increases inversely with the percent reserve. That is, 1 divided by .02 produces a factor of 50...

"Meanwhile, when an American car was sold, say at $10,000 it increased her money supply by as little as $60,000 or at most by $100,000. Because, 1 divided by 17% produces a factor of 6 and 1 divided by 10% produces a factor of 10. Therefore, under the best conditions for America, her money supply was growing at 20% of Japan's rate. And, under the worst of conditions, America's money supply was increasing by as little as 12% as compared to Japan! Consequently, Japan very quickly built up a huge monetary surplus and started to buy out the best properties in America: Rockefeller Center in New York City, the best hotels in Hawaii, the choicest properties in California and so on.

"With America seemingly in the bag, Japan turned her attention to Europe, but Europe had huge trade barriers with Japan to protect their local industries. They had a number of meetings where Japan asked for the easing or even the abolition of these trade barriers. In one of the meetings, the Swiss countered that Japan fall in line with the European reserve requirements. Japan agreed.

"As soon as Japan complied with the European reserve requirements money became tight, then extremely tight. In fact, it became so tight that stocks had to be sold to maintain the properties bought in America and other places. Ever since then, Japan's money supply has been dwindling, her financial markets declining and one political crisis followed another. Today, they are roughly at the 8% level, that is still far away from the other industrialized nations but falling in line...

"This entire sequence forced the issue to be resolved at Maastricht and then came the formation of the G7. Now, with the collapse of the Soviet Union, it is called the G8, which includes Russia.

"Do you see how a seemingly insignificant change in one economic variable changes the entire world picture?" She asked calmly.

"Amazing,..." was all I could utter. "Truly amazing..." I repeated myself. After a pause I asked Athene.

"What prevents this from happening again?"

"Well, once you understand the cause and effect, there are many things that can be done. One can prevent trade when such an inequity exists. Another is to create trade barriers, tariffs, taxes and so on. Practically anything will work which makes it prohibitive to trade with a partner who is highly leveraged against you. But, the critical thing is to understand the cause and effect. Only then can you impose the proper counter measures.

"In many ways this situation was unique, yet it took 22 years to play out the full cycle..."

"When America abandoned the gold standard, there were many voices who predicted that America was flirting with disaster. Practically everybody in the financial community predicted inflation, which is the primary cause when there are no reserves or no reserve requirements. You can see this quite easily. When the reserve requirement is zero you have an infinite money supply and results in a hyperinflation such as in Germany in 1923 and in Hungary in 1946. This was the first experiment with 'soft controls' to control the money supply. By and large it works..."

"Are there other surprises lurking in the future?" I asked.

"Quite frankly nobody know for sure. That's why financial analysis is so important. Not only for the nation but also for the individual. A seemingly insignificant change or accommodation can have colossal impact downstream."

"Is the Nikkei a good source to find bear-spreads?" I asked.

"The best you'll ever find. But you will have to make many adjustments, because their data is collected on a somewhat different basis..."

She leaned back somewhat and started again:

"Economic.... Warfare.... Reserve Requirements.... Survival.... ....," she said.

I could not make out her sentences at all.

Then silence.

I overslept again. It was nearly six o'clock in the morning. I could see Marinella. She was getting up herself. That's unusual I thought, she was getting up ahead of me. Quickly I jumped out of bed, grabbed my things and made a dash into the kitchen...

11

Ares

One moment my head was on my pillow, the next I was at our familiar meeting place. I was standing next to Hermes. He wore the same suit as from the day before, and was evidently expecting me.

"Well?" is all I heard him say.

"Can I apologize to you for my behavior yesterday?" I asked.

"We resent being entrapped," he replied. "I understand that you were focusing on the technical aspects of the problem. This means in turn that you were not ready to be enlightened to the other aspects. Do not shift the blame to others. We generally do not differentiate for the intent. However, I will accept your apology and I will pass it on to all involved.

"Do you want a review of yesterday?" he asked.

"Please explain to me what transpired. I will try not to repeat my mistakes," I said.

"Artemis is very close to the problem. She takes many excesses personally. But her concerns are justified...

"Apollo tries to perfect artificial intelligence. He relishes deep-rooted problems. In the past he kept a resident sibyl who interpreted his form of communication. But in our modern society this would be highly frowned upon. So, I interpret his messages...

"Quite frankly, it was Athene who was upset with you most. You just nodded to everything she said. Had you not tried to entrap me with the fundamental variables, we would have had the conversation with Athene in her office. Since you cut the meeting short with Apollo, I took you right away to her, while she was still in flight," he explained.

I started to say, "I was deeply impressed with your understanding of the nature of the problem. It took me nearly twenty years and many models to arrive at the point where I understood what Apollo was saying and you interpreting...," when he interrupted me:

"Ha! Twenty years is nothing on our time scale. A good problem does not even reach maturity until it is two-hundred and eighty eight years old. At least twenty-six hundred myriads of man-years should be devoted to it before we even consider the first interview. This should tell you how important the solution to the problem is for us. Yet while the solution is important, we want you to maintain its holistic impact. This is why we made an exception with you and started to interview you so early in the development cycle," he paused and looked at me with a smile.

I was thrilled. I felt I had redeemed myself for the night before.

"Meanwhile, how are your models coming along?" he asked me.

"Today I tried a new approach. Instead of the traditional method to solve the cause and effect problem for each time frame using multivariate regression analysis, I time-lagged the effect against the cause and then I solved the system ..."

"That's very interesting," I heard Hermes say. "Why did I not think of that ..." I heard him say very pensively. I had the distinct feeling that he was solving the system in his head.

He squinted his eyes, tilted his head back a little bit and seemed to look in the direction of some far away object. His barely visible eye-balls were rolling back and forth as he concentrated. I had the distinct feeling that he was actually iterating through the multivariate regression process. But how could he do that? I asked myself. He had no idea what vector space I used and he could not possibly know which variables were annihilated in the process and which remained. He just stood there, rolling his eye-balls and focusing on this distant object. Then, he opened his eyes, looked at me and exclaimed: "Well,... What did you find?"

"I found a very curious phenomenon," I said. "Independently of the time lag, the retro-fitted results were excellent, somewhere on the order of 99 plus percent. But depending on the time lag, the future projections were only of the order of 80 percent or even less," I said.

"Of course, that's perfectly normal," he said. "What you observed was the interference of the alphas for the future projections," he continued.

"But then, how come the retro-fitted results are so good?" I asked.

"Look, that's simple," he started to explain. "The future projections are influenced by the newly changing alphas. Since the forward sample is necessarily small, their influence is pronounced. However, when you solve the system, you must necessarily use many more incident points. Therefore, you will mute the effect of the past alpha changes and you obtain an excellent fit. Thus, the historical alphas are muted and the future alphas are overemphasized," he stopped and seemed to meditate again. He turned to me and asked: "Did you solve for the eigenvalues of the system first?"

"Actually, no. Not because I did not try. I did. But I used Jacobi's method to solve for the eigenvalues and as you know that method requires precise sines and cosines to annihilate the off-diagonal elements. So, I changed that module to double precision to maintain the required accuracy. When I did that, all hell broke loose. My results were unadulterated garbage. It took me nearly the rest of the day to find the problem. Do you know what it was?" I asked.

He just looked at me and raised his head: "Well, ... tell me already."

"The double precision divide in the Microsoft's Quick Basic compiler has a bug. I actually isolated the statement which caused this havoc. Naturally, I had to back out the double precision code and replace it with single precision. But, then the error in the annihilation process becomes too large and the results are nearly useless," I lamented.

"Good try," he told me. "Keep on this track. I think you will find an excellent measure for latent volatility. Then, if you compare this with the implied volatility and the dominant option spreads, you will improve your projections," he said.

I could sense that Hermes did not want to get entangled in operational problems.

"How about the historical aspects I talked about," Hermes continued. "... did you check them out?"

"Yes I did, but I ran into a curious phenomenon. I have six Encyclopedias at home. They are in: English, (the Britannica); in American, (the Americana); in German, (Brockhaus); in French, (Larousse); in Russian, (Verman); and in Ukrainian, (Hrinchenko) and I have over 200 history books in these languages. Here is what I found: The Encyclopedias agree, by and large, with what you said, but the history books do not agree at all. In fact, more often than not, they simply omit a particular topic or event."

Hermes was chuckling, "I told you time and again -- history was written not as an objective account of an event, but to suit or to glorify a nation or a ruler. By definition, therefore, anything that might be considered to be unpleasant or derogatory for one ruler was changed or simply omitted. While Encyclopedias have short accounts of historical facts, they are usually not interpreted. They tend to be more factual. The problem is reconciling the two. Then you need a hook, a specific event or name to look it up in an Encyclopedia. History is what a ruler wants his subjects to know, while an Encyclopedia contains the facts for the select few who write and interpret history..."

"You mean to say that history is written for the masses?" I piped in.

"Of course. If you want to put it that way." Hermes replied. Then, after a brief pause he started again.

"However, I noticed that you have a huge gap in your library. You have no Encyclopedias in Latin and Greek. That you must remedy." He urged.

"I have many translations...," I started, but Hermes cut me short.

"That is not good enough. You must refer to the original text in the original language. A translation is often far removed from the real facts. Nevertheless, I am glad you checked out what I said." He stated. "Now, let me continue with the events that followed and impact the European Union...

"Starting with Charlemagne (Karl der Grosse), Western Europe was unified. His realm stretched from Spain to Germany. From the river Ebro to the river Elbe. He had one son. But, Charlemagne's son had three sons. According to Carolingian tradition the empire was divided amongst them. Lothar (Lothair), the eldest, got the central portion, while the other two, Charles and Louis got Gaul and Germany respectively. Naturally, Charles and Louis made war on Lothar, defeated him, and divided his realm (Treaty of Verdun). This is when the baton of the German Concordat passed to 'Louis the German.' Ever since then Gaul and Germany were at war with each other.

"Charlemagne made war against the Avars in Pannonia. At that time he extended the realm of the Germans beyond the river Elbe. Eventually, a 'Mark' was created once the Goths there were defeated. The Mark is a 'militarized' zone. It was called Brandenburg. From there, the Germans expanded further East. They conquered the Gothic Prussians. They exterminated them and took their name. Thus, Prussia was created.

"The Teutonic Knights or Knights of the Sword expanded further East. They conquered the Goths in Pomerania and moved into the Baltic States. Pomerania was annexed to Prussia. Eventually, the Baltic States were conquered and called Kurland. Poland was spared, but only because she had converted to the Roman Faith. All other nations not of the Roman Faith, were ruthlessly annihilated, their land seized and German overlords placed in control. These overlords called themselves 'Junkers.'

"Meanwhile, the baton of the German Concordat passed to the Habsburgs in Austria, and they in turn, started to nibble away at the Ottoman Empire. They reconquered Hungary and annexed it to their Crown. They conquered Bohemia and Moravia and divided that land with the Prussians. They then swept through Croatia and Slovenia and made them Austrian 'Crown-Lands.' Spain was reconquered (under Ferdinand and Isabella) from the Moors. By Napoleon's time, all of Europe was ruled by the Germans except for France and the Scandinavian countries.

"In England, the Hanoverians have ruled since 1715. In Russia, Catherine II and her offspring have ruled since 1762, while the rest of Europe was controlled either by the Habsburgs, Hohenstaufens, Hohenzollerns or Wittelsbachs.

"During the reign of Francis I, the name of Gaul was changed to France, and to avoid the fate of all other 'nations' in Europe, France made an alliance with the Ottoman Empire. This alliance saved France from German rule, but, from then on, France was pitted against constant German encroachment.

"Starting with Louis XIII in 1610, France began to expand into German territory to the north, but the incessant wars left France depopulated and economically ruined by the time Louis XIV died in 1715. France needed reforms, but her monarchy refused to accede, resulting in the inevitable revolution of 1789.

"The revolution in France propelled Napoleon Bonaparte to supreme rule. The intent of the revolution was to sweep away all vestiges of monarchy and religion. Therefore, as soon as the revolution was successful in Paris, all priests and Bishops were deposed and a prostitute was promoted to the 'goddess of reason' in Notre Dame Cathedral: Marianne. Of course, that too was an abomination. Today she is portrayed as a bare-breasted woman leading French patriots to victory.

"The greatest travesty in a monarchy is the fact that it is based on hereditary succession, not competence, ability nor concern. Centuries of inbreeding has transformed them into a race of degenerates. Deformity, hereditary disease and insanity are the norm, not the exception among the 'royals.' Just read 'Royal Babylon' some day. To this the Church adds 'by the grace of God' and all faults are swept away. Consequently, incompetent rulers dominate the landscape. What is needed is a system of checks, balances and consent. Even today there are not many countries who have these safety valves in place to keep their governments in line." Hermes took a short pause.

"As the revolution was unfolding, France's neighbors seized that opportunity to take some real-estate away from her. Napoleon was brought in to save the 'Convention' from the mob, which he did. This pleased the Convention and he was promoted to save France's eastern border. He was pitted against the Austrians, and he defeated them. This propelled Napoleon to be 'First Consul' of the Republic. He defeated all invaders and took the wars to their land. In quick order he conquered all of Europe, except for England, Russia and the Ottoman Empire.

"Napoleon planned to conquer England and to collect the bounty from the Pope, but Horatio Nelson foiled that attempt. He imposed the 'Continental Blockade,' to starve England into submission. It nearly worked, but Portugal, Sweden and Russia defied the blockade and England escaped his attempt at conquest.

"Napoleon's stellar success on the battlefield gave him a new idea. He installed his brothers as Kings throughout Europe. In this way, he raised his own prospect of becoming Emperor himself and taking the baton away from the Germans. He carved up Germany into three Kingdoms: Bavaria, Würtemberg or Nassau and Prussia (Hannover was given to the Prussians for their support of Napoleon). This tactic eliminated some 20,000 German Dukes and reduced the number of nobles to less than 20 powerful Princes, and paved the way for a German State. To please his new-found lover, Countess Maria Walewska, he created the Kingdom of Poland, a small enclave around Warsaw. With these moves he was ready to legitimize his Empire, but in order to do that, he first had to perform a number of vital tasks.

"Initially, he had to re-instate the Catholic Faith in his realm and recognize the Pope. Which he did.

"Second, make himself Emperor. He did this in 1804, but during the coronation, Napoleon took the crown from the Pope and crowned himself. A symbolic gesture that he was in power and not the Pope.

"Third, he had to marry into the Habsburgs. He discarded his longtime lover and wife Josephine and married Marie-Louise from Austria. The Pope, of course, acquisced and annulled his marriage to Josephine.

"Finally, to earn the baton, he had to conquer Russia and install the Roman Faith there. This of course was a bit of a problem. Accordingly, Napoleon proceeded cautiously." Hermes got up from the rock and stretched his arms.

This was a good time to pose a question. So, I asked, "Didn't you say before that the German Concordat was irrevocable. How could Napoleon take the baton away from the Germans?"

Hermes continued with his exercise as if he was ignoring what I said. When he was finished, he replied.

"The Franks and Allemani were a coalition of tribes. These coalitions were dominated by the Germans but included many other ethnic groups. In fact, among the Franks the German element was in the minority, yet they ruled in Gaul. Charlemagne was a Carolingian. His son partitioned the empire and his sons made war on each other. Therefore, as far as the Pope was concerned regarding ethnicity, the baton remained among the Germans even if it was taken over by the French."

After a brief pause, Hermes resumed, "Let me continue with Napoleon...

"Napoleon called for a conference with Czar Alexander, the grandson of Catherine II. They met at the river Niemen, near Tilsit in 1806, on a barge midway in the river. Their assessment was that the 'sick man of Europe' was the Ottoman Empire, and they sort of agreed to dismember it. They parted with a 'non-aggression' pact between themselves and a new map of Europe, wherein they had staked out their claims and future expansion. Both returned to their camp fully satisfied, Alexander in the belief that peace was made with Napoleon, and Napoleon with the assurance that Alexander had no plans to make war against his Empire. This peace gave Napoleon all the time he needed to to complete his conquest of Germany, assemble the greatest army Europe had seen for a long time, and plan his invasion of Russia.

"Alexander returned to St. Petersburg and stepped up his wars in the Balkans, Caucasus and Siberia and made plans to conquer Persia. Napoleon returned home, completed the conquest of Germany and assembled a French army of about 400,000 to which he added some 250,000 confederates from Spain, Italy, the Low

Countries, Austria, Bavaria, Würtemberg, Prussia and Poland. Napoleon prepared Western Europe for a crusade, and on June 22, 1812, Napoleon's army invaded Russia. The Russian writer Tolstoy has a good account of that war in his book 'War and Peace.'

"On the eve of the invasion," Hermes continued pensively, "I visited him in his sleep. I heard about the invasion plan from Ares. I was not actively on Napoleon's side, only Ares, Aphrodite and Artemis were. In all fairness, however, I sympathized with him. Ares had formulated a great plan. Take Vilna, Vitebsk and Smolensk and then take the Kaluga road right to Moscow. Next, take Kazan and then Astrakhan. After that, the Czar would be hemmed in -- in Siberia. Three forts and a Limes-type wall would keep him there forever. Napoleon could then proclaim victory and rule over all of European Russia. With that his mission would be accomplished and the baton of the German Concordat would pass to France and Napoleon. Needless to say, Napoleon loved his plan, but, I had my reservations about it.

"Aphrodite loved the 'salon scene' in Paris and opened her own boudoir. Artemis was with Napoleon because the former Goths of Russia had forsaken her sacred animal, the Unicorn. And, practically all the tapestry of it was now in France. Only Poseidon and Athene were on Russia's side. Poseidon loved the Ukraine, because they still preserved his trident on their flag, and he had sided earlier with England against Napoleon. Athene despised Fouche, Napoleon's Chief of Police. He had turned France into a virtual Police-State. The rest of us were neutral, some leaning towards Napoleon, like me.

"So, on this fatal night I visited him and I proposed an alternate plan. I told him: Take Vilna, Minsk and Kiev. Then, Kharkiv and Rostiv. These are all areas oppressed by the Czar. They will rally to your cause. They will treat you as a liberator. This way you will neutralize their armed camp.

"Napoleon only looked at me. Then, he screamed at me, 'Are you crazy? I am about to conquer all of Russia. I have the greatest army in the world. Do I need allies? I have no plans to liberate anybody.' With that outburst, I left him to his fate...

"Next day, Napoleon unleashed his army and invaded Russia. He took Vilna, Vitebsk and then Smolensk easily, but on September 7, a contingent of the Russian army engaged him at Borodino. The battle lasted three days resulting in a draw. Athene advised Kutuzov, the Russian general, to withdraw, to save his army and wait for more reinforcements to arrive from Bessarabia and the Caucasus. With them he could annihilate Napoleon altogether. At first, Kutuzov balked: 'These reinforcements will not reach me until late Fall -- not until

November or December. By then, we could have 3 or 4 feet of snow on the ground.' To this Athene said: 'This is precisely my point. Let Napoleon roam. Let him ravish Moscow. You stay on his heels and when the reinforcements arrive and the seasons change you tear his heart out.' Kutuzov saw the light. He exclaimed: 'I love your plan.' He gave her a bear-hug which nearly crushed her bones. Before dawn, Kutuzov ordered his army to withdraw.

"On September 14, Napoleon entered Moscow unopposed. The Czar had fled and with him was an endless column of the well to do. All the commoners stayed behind. Napoleon entered the city and requested the Czar to appear, to sign a formal surrender. When he was told that the city had been abandoned by the Czar and all officials, he would not believe it. That night, Ares paid him a visit and told him: 'We have some unfinished business. Take your army. Let's take Kazan and Astrakhan and complete my plan.' Napoleon shrieked: 'Are you crazy? I am over 3,000 leagues away from Paris. You want me to move another 1,000 leagues? That's madness. Not one foot beyond Moscow will I go!'

"This outburst offended Ares so much that he left Napoleon to the Fates. And, when Ares left, so did Aphrodite and Artemis. Next morning Moscow was on fire...

"Napoleon wasted more than one month doing nothing in Moscow. He only sulked. He did not move beyond the city. He did not prepare for winter. He did not prepare for a defense and he made no effort to keep his army well supplied. On October 17, he had enough. He issued orders for a general retreat to begin October 19...

"Meanwhile, Kutuzov stayed on the heels of Napoleon, almost within sight of his army. When Napoleon occupied Moscow, Kutuzov wept and when Moscow burned, he wept some more. He picked a fort, Malo-Yaroslavets, which was well fortified to smoke out the intruder. From there he harassed the French rear guard day and night. Additionally, practically every day, large columns of reinforcements arrived from the many parts of Czar Alexander's realm. By the time Napoleon decided to retreat, Kutuzov had numerical superiority over the French, with each man itching to fight the invader. When Kutuzov learned that Napoleon was retreating, he fell to the ground in prayer and thanked the Lord...

"As he made preparations for attack Athene paid him a visit. She told him: 'Don't be a fool. Don't attack him, pulverize him.' 'And how do I do that?' Kutuzov asked. Athene said, 'Now you are stronger than his army. Force him to retreat along the path he came, right to the bridgeheads he still holds. Set up your artillery at the bridgeheads and pulverize them as they cross. Kutuzov fell on his knees, he clutched her legs and kissed them.

Then, he got up and exclaimed: 'Athene, you are the greatest! How can I ever thank you?' Athene left, afraid his bear-hug would injure her, but she was very pleased...

"And so, right from the start, two columns of Kutuzov's army flanked Napoleon's retreat. Neither column would yield an inch to the path ravaged by Napoleon's invasion. On the third day snow began to fall. Kutuzov thanked the Lord and his guardian angel for their aid. He ordered all horses to be re-hoofed for the winter. The snow rendered the French cavalry impotent, while Kutuzov's cavalry could punish them each day...

"Under normal conditions, Smolensk was only a 10 day's march away. There Napoleon kept a garrison and plenty of supplies for his army. But because of the constant harassment by Kutuzov's army and the inclement weather, the retreat took nearly 30 days. By the time they arrived, the garrison had been plundered by the advance units and there was no relief in sight. The highly disciplined army of the French turned into a mob. At the river Berezina, Kutuzov's artillery pounded the invaders, but many made it across. At the Niemen river, on December 14, 1812 the French invaders were pulverized again. This time only a handful escaped. In all, from Napoleon's Grand Army of over 600,000, only 5,000 or so reached Paris to tell the tale...

"Napoleon left his army on December 5, leaving Murat in charge. He raced to Paris to raise another army. Now, his alliances in Europe began disintegrating. Prussia and Austria joined Czar Alexander. In fact, all of Europe rose up against Napoleon: Italy, Spain, the Low Countries and so on. At Leipzig, the new army of Napoleon was defeated again. Once more Napoleon left his defeated army, raced to Paris to raise still another army. Now the Russians were at the gates of Paris and Paris finally refused to continue with Napoleon's folly. Thus, Napoleon abdicated and Czar Alexander and his army occupied Paris on April 6, 1813...

"Napoleon was exiled to Elba, where he was allowed to rule. Abandoned by his friends, and his wife Marie-Louise -- who got herself a lover and refused to bring their son to him -- Napoleon wasted away on Elba. Only his Polish love, Countess Maria Walewska, would bring their son and stay with him for a time. I think her sign was Scorpio. They are very loyal, you know," as Hermes added pensively.

"Meanwhile, Czar Alexander was the talk of Paris. His army was on its best behavior. Many were quartered in Paris. They loved the attention they got: the Parisian women, the salons and the night life...

"Czar Alexander restored the prior monarchies in Europe in the Congress of Vienna. He then proposed a 'Holy Alliance,' which was to include all monarchs but reduced the Pope, to an advisory capacity of sorts. (Eventually, this led to the 'League of Nations,' and then to the formation of the UN.)

"With Europe seemingly secured, Czar Alexander took his army and returned to Russia, June 3, 1814...

"On March 1, 1815, Napoleon escaped from Elba, landed in France and marched with a handful of supporters on Paris. Louis XVII fled and Napoleon was received jubilantly. His supporters felt they could raise an army of 750,000 for his cause. All Napoleon needed was time, and everybody knew it.

"In Russia, Czar Alexander commandeered 450,000 men and marched on France. Prussia raised 150,000 and gave the command to Blücher. Austria raised 80,000 and they were to link up with the Prussians. England contributed 28,000 plus 80,000 Hanoverians from King George III's restored Duchy of Hannover. All of Europe raced toward Paris to stop Napoleon in his tracks before he could build up his forces...

"The Prussians, Hanoverians and Britons were the first to arrive. Like it or not, Napoleon had to take the initiative. He mustered an army of about 150,000 and advanced against the Prussians at Legny. Wellington was in command of the English and Hanoverians. Here, Napoleon committed the cardinal sin of warfare. He split his forces. The main force engaged the Prussians, while he and a much smaller force engaged Wellington. The Prussians escaped defeat and swarmed onto Napoleon as he was trying to take Waterloo. Waterloo thereby became the last battle for Napoleon, which he lost...

"As you can see, England contributed the least to defeat Napoleon, yet she claimed the 'Lion's Share'. Ever since then, this became the policy of the English. This is why the Battle of Waterloo is so important to them. It is the watershed of English foreign policy...

"Napoleon surrendered to the English. This time he was exiled to St. Helena, where he was kept prisoner and was slowly poisoned with vintage wine. He died May 5, 1821. His body was returned to France in 1840...

"Napoleon overshadows French history. While Louis XIII and Louis XIV fought all their lives, they fought for the survival of France. Napoleon, on the other hand, fought for and gained the dominance of Europe. Indirectly, the Pope brought him down when he requested the last challenge, to conquer Russia and to install the Roman Faith. Had Napoleon dismissed that challenge, Western

Europe would be speaking French today." Hermes got up from the rock and stretched his legs. After a while, he sat down again.

"Although Napoleon ruled for a short time and was constantly at war, he introduced many reforms which are still widespread in Europe. He changed the weights and measures to kilos, liters and meters. That is, he introduced the 'Metric System.' He also defined the current map of Europe. The 'Curzon-Line,' still separates the West from the East. In law, the 'Napoleonic Code' still dominates many European nations, and so on. But, most importantly, Napoleon raised 'national consciousness' in Europe; in particular with Garibaldi in Italy and Goethe in Germany, where they clamored for a national state...

"However, the introduction of the metric system, while convenient in a sense, perverted our code in the great effigies in the civilized world we had left behind. Thus, our messages have been lost." Hermes paused briefly.

"How did Napoleon raise nationalism in Europe?" I asked.

"The most important commodity in the Roman Empire was to be a citizen. A Roman citizen could only be tried in Rome and only by a Roman court. In time a system of patronage evolved. The ruling class were the patricians who represented their constituents, the plebeians. In theory, patricians protected the rights of their constituents, doled out favors, land and pensions, nominated officials and in return the constituents were expected to vote for their candidates, because the Roman Empire had many elective offices...

"When the Holy Roman Empire was created, the elected offices had to go, otherwise the Goths, who were in the majority in Gaul would swamp them. A new system of patronage was created. Your historians call it the 'Feudal' system. An overlord was designated and he doled out the favors. He in turn demanded loyalty or an oath of 'fealty.' This way all underlings were directly responsible to him. In this way 'families' ruled the Holy Roman Empire. Eventually, the major ones being the Borgias and Medici in Italy; Hohenstaufens, Hohenzollerns and Wittelsbachs in Germany; Bourbons and Valois in France; Habsburgs in Austria and Spain, and the Romanovs in Russia. In Western Europe, this began with the Electors and Dukes set up by Charlemagne which evolved into these families. In Russia, Catherine II seized power. Starting with her and to the last Romanov, the rulers did not have a single drop of the Romanov's blood in them, yet that's what they called themselves...

"Initially, there were seven electors who elected the Emperor. Their title was hereditary. The title Elector, therefore was more important than that of a King. For example, in France, Spain, Portugal and England Kings ruled, but they had no say in the election of the Emperor, even though England, Portugal and Spain paid tribute to the Emperor.

"There were seven original Electors. Three Archbishops from Cologne, Mainz and Trier, and four Dukes or Kings from Bavaria / Palatine, Bohemia, Brandenburg and Saxony. This was extended to 9 in 1692, including Brunswick and Palatine. This way the Germans managed to corner the election of the Emperor and the Italians-- the Borgias and Medici -- controlled the election of the Pope. By the way, the Borgias were from the Spanish-German branch.

"Napoleon dismantled this arrangement. And, just prior to Napoleon, the French Revolution initiated general elections. This led to 'Nationalism.'

"Once Napoleon was eliminated, the German Dukedoms which Napoleon promoted to Kingdoms moved toward the formation of a German State, and the Italian City-States moved towards Italian unification. In 1865 Italy was forged. And, in 1871 Germany was proclaimed an Empire after a successful Franco-Prussian war. It should be noted that Belgium, Netherlands, Luxembourg and Austria rejected being part of the German Empire, even though they were invited to join." Hermes paused. Then he turned to me and asked:

"Have you noticed that the flags of Imperial Germany and Belgium have the same colors: Black, red and gold?"

I nodded my head. Hermes continued.

"Nationalism, however, created an entirely new problem in Europe. The newly formed nations Germany, Italy and Belgium had no colonies. The agenda to conquer and colonize the world was orchestrated by the Pope and the Emperor of the Holy Roman Empire. Germany was charged to colonize Eastern Europe. That's why the Teutonic Knights and then the Knights of the Cross were formed by the Pope in the first place. Austria was to eradicate the Goths in Central Europe and annex their land. Belgium came into existence when the Low Counties were permanently divided by Napoleon.

"In the Treaty of Tordesillas (1494), Portugal was given the Eastern hemisphere to colonize while Spain got the Western hemisphere.

"This is when England, France and the Dutch played the roles of spoilers. They sent out their own explorers anyway. They sailed the oceans and claimed their discoveries. Each one of them used a slightly different tactic...

"The English concentrated on intercepting the Spanish ships which sailed from the New World to Spain filled with gold, silver and precious stones. England engaged deliberately in open-sea piracy. You have romanticized this in your country. When piracy was no longer profitable, England switched to the slave trade. This was the 'Black Gold' which filled England's coffers. They even fought wars in Europe to get the monopoly for the slave trade, resulting in the Treaty of Westphalia of 1648 and 1704.

"Very often, other nationals brought colonists to America under the English flag. For example:Giovanni Cabotti, an Italian, brought colonists to New England, but before he sailed from England he had to change his name to John Cabot...

"While Portugal and Spain concentrated on bringing the spices and gold home, England, France and the Dutch focused on staking out as many regions of the New World as they could for themselves. On occasion, they would swap the real-estate among themselves to streamline their administration and exploitation.

"The slave trade was immensely profitable for England. Shortly after the Napoleonic wars, Cecil Rhodes began colonizing Africa systematically. This gave England an endless pool of slaves to sell in the New World. From Africa they branched out to India and from India to China. But, the Chinese refused to deal with the 'Western Devils.' So, England introduced opium into China, shelled Shanghai and the 'Opium Wars' ensued, (1840 and 1841.) After 1860, England groomed Japan to police the Pacific for her. England saw a great similarity between herself and Japan -- an island nation,surrounded by much larger continental powers.

"After Napoleon was eliminated, two new ideas began to evolve in England: Propaganda and Geopolitics. To serve the propaganda line, a school was set up in England by Cecil Rhodes to train devout Anglophiles. In this way, a program was created which brainwashed promising future politicians for the 'English Cause.' The students were called: 'Rhodes Scholars.'

"In America this took on the form of the 'Hessian Propaganda.' In other words, the loyal soldiers of George III from Hannover were dubbed Hessian mercenaries, even though there was no such country in Germany. Thus the Germans in America did not protest. A province by that name was established after World War II, which England occupied: the British Occupation Zone was dubbed Hessen.

"Propaganda of this sort alienated the Americans from the Germans and allowed the English to dictate foreign policy for their own benefit, despite the fact that the only European nation which tried to subjugate America time and again was England. For example, during the Revolutionary war in 1776 and right after the

Civil War in 1866, when the Russians aided America's cause against the English...

"Geopolitics was a program designed to pin-point the potential future economic competitors of England and to surround them with English allies. Thus, they could be choked off readily. In this area, England identified two potential future threats: Russia and the United States. To contain Russia, a policy was implemented which 'encircled Russia,' and denied her access to the sea -- to a warm water port. Keep in mind that once the monarchies were restored in Europe, Germans ruled all of Europe, except for Switzerland and the Scandinavian countries. To keep Russia in line, Germany had to be made sufficiently strong, and, to choke off Russia in the Pacific, Japan had to be modernized and groomed to serve England.

"By the end of the 19th Century, the United States emerged as an economic power which the British felt had to be contained. Initially, this was done with 'Disinformation,' such as the 'Hessian Propaganda.' Then, Canada, Mexico and Japan became England's targets to contain the United States. For example: The Great Depression in the United States was a direct cause of that encirclement. Yet, each time England's Geopolitics would turn against her, she had no problem whatsoever recruiting the United States as her ally. This situation is alive and well to this day.

"Let's step back in time a little bit. When Germany and Italy were at last ready to colonize, most of the New World was already spoken for. Italy chose Libya, Somalia and Ethiopia as potential colonies and Germany cleaned up all the 'left-overs' in Africa, Asia and the Pacific Ocean. Belgium took the Congo..."

"Excuse me," I asked. "Why was slavery abolished?"

"By 1840 the Age of Industrialization swept though Europe and the United States. It was no longer economical or prudent to keep slaves. And, about that time, colossal projects were conceived: the Suez Canal, the Panama Canal, the Transcontinental Railways in America and Siberia and others. All these projects required an endless amount of workers at the lowest possible wage so that industrial barons could make a hefty profit. Former serfs, slaves and coolies from America, Europe, India and China were imported to perform that work. This need prompted the emancipation of the slaves and serfs -- nothing else.

"During this period, Germany began to undermine England's influence. Bismarck advocated a permanent alliance with Russia. He reasoned that France was the 'eternal enemy of Germany' and to avoid a war on two fronts, Russia had to be allied with Germany. Germany also befriended the Ottoman Empire, and decided to build a railroad from Baghdad to Berlin. This project, once completed, would threaten ruin to the English trade monopoly. Europe began arming herself and struck a whole new set of alliances. Essentially, this boiled down to two camps: England and France on one side and Germany, Austria, Russia and the Ottoman Empire on the other side. However, when Bismarck died, the German Kaiser did not renew his alliance with Russia. France jumped at this opportunity and struck an alliance with Russia. Therefore, from 1910 on, Europe became a powder-keg ready to explode. The slightest incident could unleash a global war between the 'super-alliances.'

"The spark which ignited this war came from Sarajevo in Bosnia-Herzegovina, in the Balkans. The Archduke of Austria was assassinated by a Serbian national. Austria demanded satisfaction and issued an ultimatum. But in all fairness, Russia had no time to respond to the ultimatum, while Prussia supported Austria. By then, Russia had taken on the role of the protector of Orthodoxy in the Balkans. Russia balked and mobilized. This ignited World War I in 1914. Germany invaded Belgium and France. This brought England into the war.

"Keep in mind, this war started out as a family affair, so to speak. The Kaiser, Wilhelm I from Germany; King George V from England and the Czar Nicholas II from Russia were cousins. They were directly related to Queen Victoria. They looked like identical twins. Just look at their photographs without the head-gear and the military trappings. Add to this the new military technology -- dynamite and the machine gun -- and this war promised to be very short. All experts predicted that the war would last no more than 3 months. It was hailed as the 'war to end all wars.' What nobody counted on was that nationalism in Europe allowed their leaders to draw on millions of recruits. Russia alone could send over 10 million soldiers to the battlefield, if only she could arm and equip them. The numbers of soldiers in this war were staggering and so were the losses...

"After a few military successes by the Germans, a trench-war ensued in the West. The Germans came to within 30 miles of Paris. This is when the Parisian Taxi drivers stepped in and ferried fresh recruits to the front to hold the German advance. It is still called 'The Taxi Defense of Paris.' Meanwhile, England urged America to enter the war on her side. But, America refused. The Senate did not want to get involved in this European morass.

"The Senate did grant financial and economic credits to both combatants. The Lion's share of that credit, however, went to England. In the end, America had no choice but to enter the war on England's side to protect her financial interest. Italy was also averse to entering the war. Eventually she did, on the side of the allies. Bulgaria joined Germany and the Axis

Powers to win back some territories she had lost earlier to Serbia, and the Ottoman Empire joined the Axis Powers. They wanted the Berlin-Baghdad railroad completed, which promised immense riches in the trade with Europe, and Russia was seen as the arch-enemy. Japan joined the allied camp, because she was so induced by England. German presence in the Orient and the Pacific was puny. This meant Japan could take the German colonies for herself. The war was world-wide indeed." Hermes paused. He looked to the ground and mumbled, "I am getting ahead of myself." Then, he resumed again.

"I'll continue on our next break..."

Before I could respond or utter a sentence, Hermes shoved his umbrella into my hand and we were off.

We landed in an open market. Around us were vendors selling fruits, carpets, trinkets, strange vegetables, dates and olives. A regular bazaar, I thought. As if it was lifted right out of the movie Ali Baba, a movie I saw many years ago.

Next to us stood a giant of a man. He was dressed in a turban. A loose garment fluttered in the soft breeze. He was so tall I could barely make out his features. His feet and his boots were enormous.

"Hello, Ares," I heard Hermes say.

"Hello, there," I heard a deep voice reply. It was like the rumble of thunder. The air reverberated when he spoke.

"I relish wars. I thrive on them. The art of war is a problem all its own. There is no other problem more important than war. Homer described my ways in poetry. Von Clausewitz described my actions in prose. The Teutonic tribes use my method consistently. Look at my success..."

"My solution to a problem is simple. I see the situation. I determine the center of gravity of the problem. And then, I attack the center with all my might. I was at Alexander's side when he destroyed Darius...

"War is a numbers game. Whoever has the greatest number of soldiers left at day's end is the victor for that day. That's why I attack the center...

"A long time ago I set myself a goal for war. A myriad of my enemies each day. That is my self-imposed quota. It is a noble goal and I try hard, each day, to meet my quota...

"My ways are immortalized in games. Go and checkers are good examples. Games prepare the mind to reduce problems to their simplest form," I heard him thunder. Then, silence. Only the noise of the market could be heard. There had to be more to it, I thought. It just could not be this simple, I thought.

"What about tactics?" I asked.

"More often than not, tactics work against you in more than one way. Tactics prolong the agony too long. The most effective way is: 'Size up the beast and decapitate its head.' That is the only proven tactic..."

"What about Hannibal and Cannae? His tactic worked that day," I said.

"I was with Hannibal that day! I say his plan worked because he concentrated his strike at one critical point. The fact that he used a diversion to conceal his intent was immaterial. My plan would have worked without the diversion..."

"What about Hannibal and the battle at Zama?" I asked.

He seemed to smile as he continued: "By then I left Hannibal. When Hannibal refused to sack Rome and cash in on my labor, I left him to his fate. And, what happened? He encamped, he feasted on the land. His soldiers lost the spark for battle. Thereafter Hannibal had no stunning victories..."

"What about Napoleon?" I asked.

"Well, what about Napoleon?" he thundered. "I was with Napoleon until we captured Moscow. Was that not a glorious time! We raced from one battle to the next. Each battle became a victory. Each battle brought more glory. The culminating orgy was Austerlitz. What a battle and what a victory!" I was nearly deafened as he all but laughed out loud.

"What about Borodino?" I asked.

"Well, what about Borodino?" he roared again. "Did we not hold the field? Did not the Russians retreat? I must say, had Napoleon listened to me and released his guard, the victory would have been complete. At Borodino, Napoleon lost his nerve. He tried to compensate for his fear with tactics. Was tactics not his undoing in the end?...

"When we captured Moscow, Napoleon turned into a coward. I pleaded with him to do away -- to annihilate -- that tiny Russian fortress at Malo-Yaroslavets. He would not hear of it: 'Not one French soldier should be wasted' he said. I remember this distinctly. So I left him to his fate. I went to Aphrodite and we celebrated my victories..."

"What happened at Verdun during World War I?" I asked.

"The Bavarian prince offended me. Hubris ruled that battle. I only watched as two headless armies ground themselves to earth. Oh what a victory it could have been!

"Enough of this, enough! I have to go to Samarkand," I heard him thunder.

"May I ask how this affects market timing?" I asked timidly.

"Now that is simple. I have five cardinal rules. All my rules are based on buying low and selling dear.

"My first rule is: buy industry leaders when their price is depressed. My second rule is: buy new issues with products of great potential in the 'Cinderella' industries. Third: buy issues which are in bankruptcy but received major financing. Fourth: buy issues with massive insider trade action on the upside. My fifth rule is: buy commodities at the bottom of their cosmic cycle," and he paused.

"Does this mean you are a buyer of IBM right now?" I asked.

"By Zeus! Do you think I am stupid?" he roared. "I have been shorting IBM since 1989 each time they reach a local high! IBM ceased to be a technology leader in 1969. From 1969 to 1989 they concentrated on marketing and not on technological excellence. Since then they put all their eggs into marketing, not into new technology. The new leader is Microsoft. IBM lost the PC market, the Wireless market and so on. They have become a consulting dinosaur because of their installed base, but that base is eroding. The dinosaurs have been defeated by the ants. Eons ago the dinosaurs vanished from this earth. Now it is time for corporate dinosaurs to vanish. Can you imagine producing computers which require more plumbers than systems architects? Ecologically this is not feasible for any length of time," and he started to laugh.

"Besides, ... " he continued, "... I gave you my preferences in the reverse order of my hierarchy. Thus, IBM is on the bottom of my list of my concerns right now. Today, the real opportunities are in former East Germany, China, Hungary, Poland, Czechoslovakia, Russia, Mexico, Vietnam and the Ukraine," he paused again.

"When do you sell?" I asked.

"I am glad you asked. You know, selling is much harder than buying. Greed and Hubris have sweet talked me many times into a folly. Then, paper profits turn into cash losses. So, I have set myself three cardinal rules to sell: I sell as soon as the issue approaches cyclic tops. I sell when my investment horizon has been reached. I also sell when I observe cosmic cycle reversals," he replied.

"Do you apply these rules uniformly to all instruments?" I asked.

"Of course not!" he exclaimed. "For options I use primarily an investment horizon. Then, I sell my calls or puts one month before their expiration for American options. Of course, European options are different so this rule does not apply. For commodities, currencies and bonds I use cosmic cycles -- they are most reliable. For stocks I use mainly cyclic tops or bottoms to determine my entry and exit points. Convertibles I don't use at all, they get convoluted when they trade near or above their conversion privilege," as he looked at me.

"How do you determine cosmic cycles?" I asked.

"Ha, ha, ha ...," he started laughing. "Your species is preoccupied with the rational method. You have been perverted by Newton and Dedekind. You have dismissed quantum arithmetic. We taught you quantum arithmetic because we wanted you to solve the cosmic n-body problem so you could begin to understand us. So you could understand how we created harmony in the cosmos. What have you done? There is not even one reference to quantum arithmetic in your entire educational system. We introduced it some 3000 years ago. You have purposely deleted it from your pool of knowledge...

"Instead you mention Fibonacci and his useless series. This series should be called the Pythagorean series if anything, and the quantum numbers the Pythagorean numbers. These numbers come in fours and in powers of fours for each higher order. Thus, the linear set has four numbers with 'Fibonacci' properties. The quadratic requires 16 quantum numbers, then you can solve the problems inherent in ellipses and so on. The cubic has 64 quantum numbers and so on. Kepler found some of these relationships. Konig and Gauss found others. But, as soon as education became institutionalized their usefulness was first muted and then silenced altogether. How do you hope to understand our ways?" he roared.

At this point Hermes was nudging me with his rod. He shoved the rod into my hand and we floated away.

12

Aphrodite

We were back in our familiar valley in no time at all. It seemed that our return trip was much quicker. Maybe my mind was preoccupied with the notions we discussed. As soon as we landed Hermes made himself comfortable on the rock.

"I am ready to continue where we left off." I heard him say.

"I am ready," I replied.

"Let me discuss the progress on the Western Front first. Then, I'll explain the details separately, when I discuss Russia. The developments there are more complex. I will only outline what happened there for now. Is that ok?" he asked me.

I nodded my head, "Yes, of course..."

"In August 1914, the Russians suffered a major defeat, and by 1917 they sued for peace. This is when the minorities in Russia, including the Ukraine, tried to work out a peace treaty independently with Germany. In fact, the Ukraine sued for a separate peace which the Germans were stalling. They had much better prospects in mind. In the Treaty of Brest-Litovsk, Russia signed a peace treaty with Germany and the Ukraine was given to Germany as reparation for the war. The freed-up German army units were transferred to the Western front and occupation units were sent in to clean the Ukraine out of grain and livestock. These units took everything that was not 'nailed down' and carted it off to Germany...

"As the carnage of the war increased, President Woodrow Wilson proposed 14 points to settle the war between the combatants in the West. In the 14 points, Germany was to keep her pre-war borders and her colonies, but pay reparations to France, England and Russia. While border adjustments were called for and many minorities would be freed, the German leadership felt they could live with that. The 14 points promised an honorable exit from the war for Germany. There was one pre-condition, however: Germany had to lay down her arms and surrender unconditionally.

"One last German offensive was launched, strengthened by the soldiers from the Eastern front. That offensive bogged down because America had entered the war on the allied side. America's army stopped the German offensive in its tracks, all with fresh troops. Germany capitulated and accepted Wilson's 14 points as a pre-condition for surrender. As soon as Germany surrendered, however, Wilson's 14 points were brushed aside by France and England, and they dictated their own terms...

"Germany, Austria, Russia and the Ottoman Empire were dismembered. Germany's colonies were taken away and the once mighty Ottoman Empire became a multitude of small colonies: Syria, Egypt, Iraq, Kuwait, Bahrain, Aden and so on.

"A feeble attempt was made to conquer Turkey but it failed, only because the allied powers were salivating with the victory they had achieved and were ready to exploit...

"Statistically speaking, since bean counting is so popular in your country, England got over 70% of the booty for hardly participating in the war; France got 26% -- they suffered less than Russia in the war, but France was the major combatant in the West; 1% went to Serbia, at the expense of Austria and Bulgaria, presumably for having started the war; 2% went to Japan, for her alliance with England -- Japan had less than 300 reported casualties when they took the German colonies in the Pacific and China; less than 1% went to Italy, because they waited too long to join the allies. Russia, their major ally, lost Finland; Estonia, Latvia, Lithuania, Poland and parts of the Ukraine. America got to pay the war costs -- her credits were never repaid and she never got a word of thanks for saving France and England. Instead, England coined the title: Bubus Americanus...

"Germany, an industrial giant before the war, was wrecked. When France and England demanded Germany pay monetary damages in addition to the lost territories, a hyper-inflation wrecked Germany's financial system and beggared her currency. Within four years the Mark dropped by 10 billion to 1.

"That is, a loaf of bread, worth 1 Mark right after the war in 1919, was worth 10 billion Marks by the end of 1923. This ushered in massive unemployment and discontent in Germany.

"Germany felt betrayed. First and foremost by America. Wilson's 14 points became known as an English ruse, tricking Germany into a disgraceful peace. And, since America is considered to be a Jewish State in Europe -- the entire fiasco was perceived to be a Jewish plot to destroy Germany. Second, Germany felt betrayed by her own leadership, because -- right up to the unconditional surrender by Germany -- Germany was winning the war by all accounts. Victory was imminent, according to every newspaper of repute. That was the propaganda in Germany. And then, seemingly out of no-where, the German army surrendered. This could not be! Therefore, as soon as the gravity of their lot became apparent, revanche was on their mind, and this revanche came sooner than expected -- with Hitler.

"In the German mind-set, Hitler equalized this dishonor when he defeated England at Dunkerque in 1940 and seized all of France. Hitler forced Marshal Petain to sign a similar treaty with Germany, in the same rail-road car near Versailles, just like the original treaty was signed. Germany was thereby vindicated and von Clausewitz's axioms were satisfied."

"You mean von Clausewitz who wrote 'On War'?" I asked.

"Of course," Hermes replied. "Von Clausewitz used statistical inferences for battles, for offense, for retreat and so on. That is, on war in general. There, he detailed the differences in strategy and tactics. His model was based on Napoleon and his wars. However, he had to sweep Napoleon's disaster in Russia under the rug. It defied his model. So, he simply ridiculed it. But his book is still the 'Holy Writ' on warfare to this day -- even in your country. Of course, his 'leitmotif' is European in nature. It is based on revanche, on surprise attack, on the assumption that there are arch-enemies and how to mislead the opposition. For Hitler, this book became his 'bible.'

"Before Petain capitulated, he sent his favorite general DeGaulle to England to rally for France on the allied side. In this way, no matter who won the war, in the end, France would survive. Petain and DeGaulle had made a pact. One of them would carry on, ensuring that France would survive...

"Of course, DeGaulle was convicted in absentia for treason in France when the Germans took over. When the victorious Allied forces came to France and all war criminals were tried, Petain was pardoned by DeGaulle. As you can see, France survived. No matter how devious the plan of Petain and DeGaulle was, it saved France just as they expected.

"Before I touch on Russia, let me explain how the United States became such an important power in such a short time.

"As soon as Columbus returned and demonstrated the riches he had found the scramble was on in Europe to stake out territories for themselves. The Treaty of Tordesillas was sort of brushed aside and the seafaring nations of Europe took to the sea.

"France sent an expedition under Cartier. He explored Canada. Then, LaSalle explored the Mississippi valley. Eventually, the Cities of St. Louis and New Orleans sprung up there.

"The Dutch sent out colonists, settlers and all their religious dissidents. The Amish and Quakers sailed to what is today Philadelphia and settled in Pennsylvania. They are still called the Pennsylvania Dutch. The Dutch also bought the island of Manhattan from the Indians for $25 in trinkets and founded the City of New Amsterdam, which became known as the principal borough of New York City -- Manhattan Island.

"The English settled along the Eastern Seaboard, from Maine to Georgia, and the English pirates built strongholds in the Caribbean sea from where they harassed the Spanish fleet on their return voyage.

"Of course, Portugal's charter in the Treaty of Tordesillas was to explore the Eastern hemisphere. But, the way the world was divided by the Pope and the Emperor, it left Brazil for the Portuguese to colonize, which they did.

"Amerigo Vespucci mapped the New World and discovered that it was a continent, which blocked Europe from a shorter trip to the Orient. Spain dominated that continent from about the 30th parallel in the North to the Southern tip.

"Above the 30th parallel, England, France and the Dutch settled the East Coast where 13 English colonies were established. France concentrated in the central area which became known as Louisiana. Spain colonized the western portion: California, Texas, New Mexico, Arizona, Nevada plus Florida in the East. Most of Florida is below the 30th parallel. Russia encroached on America from the North, from Alaska and along the Pacific shoreline to San Francisco.

"As France was staking out Canada, the English began to intervene. French and English interests began to clash. They recruited the native Indians to fight the war for them. This resulted in decimation of the Indian population...

"The English began to impose heavy taxes on their colonists. This led to the 'Boston Tea Party' and to the Revolutionary War as the predominantly English colonies rose up against England. To the amazement and total disbelief of Europe, the colonists won that war and proclaimed a Republic in 1776. France recognized the new republic and gave it legitimacy.

"By the time Napoleon came to power the United States of America was still an insiqnificant speck on the American continent. The French and English wars in America were draining Napoleon's resources. Therefore, he decided to sell the Louisiana Territory to the USA. The deal was made and overnight the USA more than doubled in size. From there, American settlers pressed further West to Oregon and Washington, leaving only the Spanish possessions in the way of a super-state. As Europe continued to ferment with revolutionary upheavals, American settlers moved into the Spanish territories in Texas and California. This led to the Spanish-American war with the upshot that California, Texas, New Mexico, Arizona and Nevada became American territories. In 1848, these possessions became part of America in the Treaty of Guadalupe with Mexico...

"It should be noted that, while most of Europe's powers converged in America, there was a conspicuous absence of German and Italian colonies. The main reason being that neither of them was yet a nation. As I mentioned before, Italy became a nation in 1865 and Germany in 1871. By then, America was well formed and the new borders were well defined. This is not to say that Italians and Germans were not present at that time in America. They were, but they acted under the control and direction of the other nations.

"When Alaska was sold to America by Czar Alexander II in 1867, America had the potential to became the most powerful nation in the world. All that, within less than 100 years of her existence. And, within a span of another 50 years, the United States of America became the richest and most powerful nation on earth. Here's how that happened.

"When the age of industrialization was ushered in, America was in the forefront. The North industrialized, while the South remained agrarian. Cotton was King in the South, while steel and coal fueled the new age in the North. This polarized the South and the North. In the South slaves were needed to harvest the crop, while in the North cheap labor was needed to harvest the coal and to produce the steel. This led to the Civil War, pitting the agrarian South against the industrial North. Of course, the agrarian South had no chance in that war. It was outgunned and outnumbered.

"President Lincoln fought the war to preserve the Union. Then, as the war came to the inevitable end, President Lincoln decided to emancipate the slaves in the South. This increased the pool of humanity for the industrial pool beyond its capacity. Huge projects were needed and were undertaken. The Transcontinental Railroad was built, the Panama Canal was dug, Telegraph wires were installed, crisscrossing the country and so on.

"From then on, and to this day, America has led the process of improving the lot of humanity: electrification, electric stoves, plumbing, bathtubs and water-toilets for every home, sewers, refrigerators, steel bridges, steel ships, cars, skyscrapers, airplanes, telephones, super-highways, computers, lasers, wireless satellite communication and much more.

"Of course, all these technologies and innovations produced industrial barons, and many of the barons exploited the workers. Many abuses were tolerated, but in the end the job got done. The workers earned a living wage, enough to buy a home, enough to feed and raise a family and it was said throughout the world that the 'streets of America were paved with gold.' From then on all Europeans, in particular the religious oppressed and financially destitute, tried to come to America to improve their lot, and, for the most part, America welcomed them all.

"Let me demonstrate this process with electrification, the telephone and a few other 'toys.' Ben Franklin discovered the nature of electricity, and Edison developed the idea with direct current and worked on a light bulb. By then, a Serb of Ukrainian descent came to America from Serbia: Nikolai Tesla. He discovered how to transform direct current into alternating current and put it to general use. This allowed electricity to be used on a grand scale.

"Just at that time, at the turn of the century, America prepared for a World Fair in 1893, in Chicago. Both Tesla and Edison bid on the contract to 'light up' the fair. Of course, Tesla won the contract but, Edison provided the light bulbs. Thus, the Fair became a spectacular which baffled and amazed all visitors, including the Europeans. Within a mere 10 years most of America was electrified. When Edison died, America wanted to pay him a tribute by turning off all the lights for 3 minutes, but they could not do it, because America had become so dependent on electricity.

"At the same time, most of Europe, from London to Moscow was lighting their homes with candles, oil lamps or gas. Romantic? Maybe. But, efficient? No way. Tesla's technology, created the industrial giants: Westinghouse and General Electric, specializing in turbines and generators. What did Tesla get out of it? Very little. He sold his patent to work on bigger and better things, allowing Edison to wire New York City. And, when Westinghouse was squeezed in the financial markets, Tesla gave up his royalties for the sake of progress in America..."

"Does this make him a patriot?" I asked

"I should hope so," Hermes replied. Then he resumed.

"By the time World War I started, practically every home in America had running water, a bath-tub and a water-toilet. At the same time in Europe, from London to Moscow, communal out-houses and communal bath-houses were still the mainstay of their everyday life. In Germany, the communal bath-house ceased to exist about 10 years after World War II or 1955. In Russia, it is still popular to this day...

"In fact, technology moved so fast in America that even Americans were often dumfounded by it. A good example is the telephone. By the time the telephone was invented, Western Union had wired most of America for the telegraph. However, the Federal Government wanted the telephone installed, partially for its own uses and partially because they recognized its future potential. Federal representatives approached the board members of Western Union and asked them to install the telephone throughout America with installation cost to be subsidized by the Federal Government. The Board of Directors met and rejected the idea. In their opinion, 'that toy would never work.'

"Thus, the Federal Government funded a new company called AT&T, (American Telephone and Telegraph.) And, AT&T became not only much larger than Western Union, but nearly as large as the Federal Government itself. Within 75 years AT&T had to be broken up to allow competition...

"First generation Americans, however, were often exploited. More often than not because of their lack of the English language. Today, every immigrant living in America, who intends to benefit from America's opportunities must learn American, not English. Unfortunately, many are taken in by their ethnicity and insist on preserving their language and customs. To them I can offer only one word of advice. Preserve your language and ethnicity, if you must, in your home, but as soon as you cross the threshold of your front door to the outside world -- become a native; become an American. If you resist, you will be part of the unemployed. The best you can ever hope for, will be to land a minimum wage job. Then, America may seem to be a land of misery...

"Take the case of Enrico Fermi. He invented and built the Atom Bomb practically singlehandedly. He started in Italy. He founded Quantum Mechanics, a new branch of Physics and Mathematics. At that time, Hitler and Mussolini became allies, and when the Germans entered Italy in 1938, they started persecuting the Jews in Italy. Since Fermi's wife was Jewish, when he was selected for the Nobel Prize for his work, he took his entire family to Stockholm, from there to Oslo. After he received the Nobel Prize, he went to America where he continued his work at Columbia University. The facilities there were too small so he and his staff were transferred to Chicago. In December 1944, Fermi demonstrated a controlled, sustained nuclear reaction in Chicago. What remained to be done was to 'miniaturize' that bomb to be practical. Meanwhile, the DuPont Corporation was given the right to build nuclear reactors while a special team was formed and sent to Los Alamos. The administrative leader of that team was Robert Oppenheimer, and the entire team was dubbed 'The Bomb Makers.' By June, the miniaturization and detonation problems were resolved by Fermi. In August 1945, an Atom Bomb was dropped on Hiroshima and then on Nagasaki in Japan. Japan surrendered unconditionally...

"Of course, what nobody knew at that time, was that the harmful effects of radiation and the associated problem of the waste disposal would become a serious issue. Because Fermi was at the forefront of each experiment, he died of radiation poisoning. Technically, the Federal Government owes the Fermi Family the royalties from the reactors built and installed, because much of it was patented before Fermi came to America. Instead, the Fermi family had to accept a small amount as compensation and his work is down-played in America. But I am getting ahead of myself again." Hermes paused, got off the rock and stretched again. Then, he resumed.

"When America entered World War I on the side of England and France, she was stronger than Germany and France combined, but her strength was not understood in Europe. Writers like Karl May still portrayed America as the 'reckless, ignorant, gun-slinging cowboy.'

"This sentiment is still prevalent in Europe. It vents their anger and frustration at the opportunities offered in America to this day. Sir Arthur Conan Doyle created the image of the bumbling American idiot-reporter, who, by his ignorance and rashness, prevents Sherlock Holmes from catching the arch-villain Moriatrity. Yet despite that negativity, Sherlock Holmes is very popular in America.Don't you think it is time to shed the English coat-tails?" Hermes asked me.

"Oh, I could not agree with you more. It starts with the language. It is called English, yet it is distinctly American. When I correspond with foreigners in 'English,' I have to tell them up-front that I write in American, not English. This alerts them to our dictionary, our spelling and our grammar." I replied.

With that Hermes shoved his caduceus into my hands. Instinctively I held on and we were off again. This time the journey seemed endless. I tried to digest what Ares had told me, but I could not. I was preoccupied with the journey. It seemed to last forever.

Finally, I found myself in a lavish boudoir. My impression was 'baroque.' Drapes, curtains, sofas, chairs, recliners, footstools, lamps, desks and statues took up all empty space. No room to walk around, I thought. All that paraphernalia of the idle rich, I thought. Too many things in one room, I thought. Yet each piece was ornate and probably worth a small fortune.

A door opened and a beautiful female floated towards us. She was blonde and tall. About six feet tall, I thought. She wore a lot of makeup: Powder, rouge, lip-stick, eye-liner and sparklers on her face. Despite the makeup, she was beautiful.

"Am I late? How is my Ares? How are you darlings?" she flirted out with a seductive voice.

She moved closer and reposed in a recliner close to us. She motioned us to come closer and to sit down in the chairs next to her. Her pose was provocative, I thought. Two full breasts were staring at me. The nipples protruded from her garments as if they wanted to be freed from her clothes.

I was speechless. I could not utter a sound. I only thought of concentrating on the subject. I was not about to miss a thing she said, I thought.

"No Aphrodite, you are not late. Ares is in good spirits and we are fine," I heard Hermes say.

"Love is what binds the cosmos and produces harmony," I heard her say seductively.

"Boundless love generates more love...

"Unselfish love creates more love...

"Even selfish love produces some redeeming aspects...

"All forms of love generate positive energy," I heard her say seductively.

"What is love?" I asked.

"My darling, love is the divine spark of giving," I heard her say. "To love is to give of yourself, my darling."

"What about motive?" I asked her.

"Motive is a human attribute, my darling. Thus, motive is what perverts love. The parity of love is more love, not a reward! The harmony of love is more love, not some fractal ratio of love and hate. Hades has bound these frightful aspects for us immortals. Your race must still subdue these dragons of your mind," I heard her say seductively.

A pause, and she continued: "We have revealed this mystery to man so many times. In so many different ways. By now this aspect should be clear to man. Yet each time man stretches our intent to the limit and finds a perversion. This, with his limited and restricted mind. Man finds a fractal inconsistency in his mind and what is the result? A war, a strife, a feud..." she said seductively.

"How does this aspect apply to market timing?" I asked.

"Simple. First must be the love to the problem. Then, there must be endless love to find the solution,..."

Whenever Aphrodite spoke, her body quivered with each sound. Her bosom moved in rhythmic motion. Her nipples oscillated through her clothes. I could not concentrate at all.

Why did I ask that last question? All of a sudden my feeling was: Our session was over.

I was right. Hermes had shoved his rod into my hand and we were gone.

13

Hades

We landed in our familiar spot. Hermes started right away even before he got seated on the rock.

"Now, let me catch up with the events in Russia..." Hermes began.

"After the crushing defeat of Napoleon by Russia, Czar Alexander restored the monarchies in Europe. At the Treaty of Vienna, Alexander wielded the 'big stick.' Russia had finally gained full recognition in Europe, but Alexander's ideas were politely rebuffed. The 'Holy Alliance' he advocated never materialized. However, Poland was annexed by Russia again. Alexander returned to Russia and then he disappeared in 1825.

"Legends began to circulate that he went into hibernation in Siberia, to return when Russia needed him again. In reality, he caught a cold, went to the Crimea to recuperate, and died there. Officially, it is said that he abdicated. In any event, his brother Nicholas I, another grandson of Catherine II, succeeded him. He too was married to a German Princess.

"Czar Nicholas I, vigorously pursued the destruction of the Ottoman Empire along his borders. He made war with Persia and gained much of the coastline of the Black Sea, and using the French model established by Fouche, he created the 'Third Department.' This turned Russia into a police state. The purpose of the Third Department was not only to keep track of every citizen and to terrorize them, but also to single out the Jews and suppress them.

"Some Jews were left behind in Russia when Poland was partitioned, while others lived in Poland, which was now a province of Russia. To keep the Jews at bay, he orchestrated pogroms. Since the majority of Jews had settled in the Ukraine when they served the Polish Barons, most of the pogroms were staged in the Ukraine. This accomplished two things. The Ukraine was vilified in world opinion, while Nicholas terrorized his realm at will. More specifically, he directed his terror on three minorities in Russia: Ukrainians, Poles and Jews. Russians relished his iron rule, however, and dubbed him 'The Iron Czar.'

"As Czar Nicholas started to gain ground in the Balkans, he invited the European Powers -- England, France, Austria and Prussia -- to liberate the Balkans from the Ottoman Turks. This was politely rejected.

"Then, because his secretary was a Greek, the Czar proposed to liberate Greece. To this England and France agreed. In 1827, Russia, England and France liberated Greece and Nicholas's secretary, Capodistrias, became President of the Greek Republic. However, this violated the German Concordat. Thus, the Greek President was deposed in 1832, and a German Monarch was installed -- Otto I, from Bavaria...

"Czar Nicholas I pressed on to liberate the Balkans on his own. By now, France had expanded into North Africa. Algeria, Tunisia and Morocco became known as the 'Garden of France.' England subjugated India. The Mediterranean Sea became very important to both countries. When Czar Nicholas launched another offensive into the Balkans, they decided to take action.

"A fleet was sent to aid the Ottoman Turks, but by the time the fleet arrived, Czar Nicholas's forces had been defeated and returned to their border. However, since the fleet was on a mission, the commanders decided to teach Russia a lesson anyway. They sailed into the Black Sea and landed in the Crimea in 1853 launching the Crimean War...

"This war in and of itself was not very important. What was important is the fact that the Crimea is virtually inaccessible from the mainland. It was therefore difficult for the Russians to get there in sufficient numbers to oust the invaders. To the English and French it was important because, for the first time, foreign nationals could be tested under real battle conditions. France had brought in many French speaking Arabs, while England brought in mostly Indians, from India. The battles were fought halfheartedly. For the most part the Russians built redoubts and the Indians charged for the glory of England, while their high command stood on the hills watching them being slaughtered. The English Poet Alfred, Lord Tennyson wrote a heroic poem about one such battle: 'The Charge of the Light Brigade,' but what he failed to mention was that the brigade consisted of Indians, not Englishmen...

"In most aspects, the war was a disaster for all concerned. The only shining light was Florence Nightingale. She tended to the sick and nursed the wounded. Nursing thereafter became an honorable profession for women...

"Meanwhile, a revolutionary movement sprung up in Russia against Czar Nicholas I. Their goal was to abolish the Czar, free the serfs and slaves, divide the land and re-distribute it among the peasants. The 'Decembrists' staged a badly conceived coup and were mercilessly eradicated by Czar Nicholas I, yet the revolutionary movement continued.

"In 1855, Czar Nicholas died and Italy -- that is, Savoy under Cavour -- entered the fray on the English side. The new Czar, Alexander II, decided to resolve the Crimean War with a peace in Paris in 1856. Russia made a few concessions and Czar Alexander II could now embark on his own agenda...

"Many historians call him an 'enlightened' Czar. This was on account of three main programs: Emancipation of the serfs and slaves, aiding America and liberating the Balkans. He began his rule by easing the repressive programs of Czar Nicholas I. In particular, the role of the 'Third Department' was slightly reduced. On the top of his list was to free the serfs and slaves, not for humanitarian but for economic reasons. Russia had to be industrialized, and, to accomplish that, a bottomless pool of cheap labor and lots of money was needed. Plus, the Trans-Siberian railroad had to be built and so on. Thus, in 1861, Czar Alexander II freed the serfs and slaves in Russia.

"In 1866, a delegation from America asked for his help. England took the opportunity after the American Civil War to attempt to -- retake the colonies. They initiated a blockade. Czar Alexander II, sent two fleets, one to New York City, the other to San Francisco and lifted the blockade, a major confrontation with England was averted. He then sold Alaska to the USA in 1867...

"Next, he embarked on a program to evict the Turks from the Balkans and Europe. While the Germans engaged the French in the Franco-Prussian War, Czar Alexander II made his move to liberate the Balkans. First, national consciousness was raised in Bulgaria, Serbia, Macedonia, Bosnia and Rumania. Greece and Montenegro joined the cause, and with Russia's military muscle, the Ottomans were evicted from Europe, and Russia occupied Constantinople. Czar Alexander II brought the liberated nations of the Balkans together in San Stefano in 1878, and a joint treaty was hammered out in accordance with the ethnic distribution of the population in the Balkans. That treaty was ratified and promised peace in that area. That is, everybody immediately concerned was satisfied...

"But as soon as that treaty was ratified in San Stefano, England, Austria and Germany intervened. They met in Berlin in 1878, the same year. They redrew the map of the Balkans, brought back the Ottomans and imposed their treaty on the liberated nations. Czar Alexander II did not want to start a global war and simply withdrew. Left to the mercy of the European powers, the liberated nations of the Balkans had no choice but to consent to the Berlin boundaries. Austria got Bosnia as a protectorate--which was later annexed and called Bosnia-Herzegovina. The borders of Serbia were reduced for the benefit of Croatia, Slovenia and Bosnia, while the Ottomans got Constantinople and the surrounding area which was called Rumelia. From then on, and to this day, the Balkans became a powder-keg as each nation tried to reclaim the original borders as mutually agreed to in the Treaty of San Stefano."

"Excuse, me..." I interrupted, "What prompted this re-alignment?"

"Well, think about it." Hermes started pensively. When I did not respond, he continued.

"There is the 'official reason' and then, there is the 'real reason.' Let me start with the official reason.

"English Geopolitics targeted Russia as the prime 'colonial contender' to England. And, to contain Russia, she had to be denied access to warm water ports. In particular, access to the Mediterranean. Russia also had to be evicted from Constantinople. As Serbia was labelled a protege of Russia, Serbia likewise had to be denied access to the Mediterranean. Thus, the borders of Croatia and Slovenia, who were already under Austrian control and Catholic, were extended to land-lock Serbia. To keep everybody else equally dissatisfied, Bulgaria -- which is not Catholic--had to be cut down in size. Ergo, Rumelia was created and given to the Ottomans. This policy was already practiced by Austria. It was called 'Ausgleich.'

"When Metternich was asked what 'Ausgleich' meant, he replied: 'A policy of maximum discontent among the foreigners, short of insurrection.' Therefore, Geopolitics and Ausgleich dictated the realignment of the borders in the Balkans.

"Now, let me touch on the real reason. By the 19th century, the Ottoman Empire could have been expelled from Europe, starting with Napoleon Bonaparte. The reason it was not expelled but only gradually reduced in size was that they were the guardians of the 'Sarcophagus of Claims' in Europe. There are two aspects to that: legitimacy of Religion -- Orthodoxy versus Catholicism -- and the legitimacy to rule Europe: the Electors and their descendants versus the descendants of the Emperors of the Roman Empire.

"Remember, Constantinople was the legitimate capital of the Roman Empire. Her rulers and descendants have a legitimate claim to rule all of Europe.This legitimacy was usurped by Pope Leo III when he made Charlemagne an Emperor and promoted himself to Pope. Who has the legitimate claim to rule Europe? To begin with, in the Ukraine. King Volodimir had married the sister of Emperor Basil II, but that line may be extinct. Later on, Czar Ivan III married the niece of the last Emperor. From then on, Moscow claimed to be the 'Third Rome,' meaning that the Czar of Russia could become a serious, legitimate contender to rule Europe. This is why the Ukraine has been mercilessly suppressed by Moscow and could not find an ally in the West. While in the West, Otto I married a distant cousin of the Roman Emperor. Therefore, in the scheme of things, as far as lineage is concerned, who has the best claim?

"Now, let's look at religion. Emperor Constantine created the first Patriarch and the first Patriarchate in Constantinople. That is, the supreme Christian authority rests in Constantinople. Emperor Valens added new Patriarchs and Patriarchates: Jerusalem, Alexandria and Antioch. Jerusalem, because this was the cradle of Christianity. Alexandria, because Athanasius exposed the Arian heresy. And Antioch, because it delineated Christians from the Jews..."

"Could you be more specific on the division between the Jews and Christians," I asked.

"Here's what happened in Antioch. After Christ died on the cross, the Apostles, especially Peter, were hunted by the Romans. Thus, Peter left James, Christ's brother, in charge of the congregation in Jerusalem, while Peter went into hiding. The Apostle Paul started preaching to the Gentiles. When the Gentiles began converting, the following question arose: Did a Gentile convert have to become a Jew first or could he directly become a Christian? This issue was resolved in Antioch. That is, in order to become a Christian, it was no longer necessary to become a Jew first. Thus, the dietary laws, circumcision and the Old Testament were cast aside as prerequisites to become a Christian. It was replaced with 'baptism.' That is, the old jealous God Jahweh was replaced with the merciful Christ. This dispute lasted for over 30 years and nearly destroyed the early Church. James spoke against it. Paul for it. And Peter? We don't know for sure, but it is assumed that he was somewhere in the middle.

"Now, let's get back to the Patriarchs. At the time of Emperor Valens, there was only a Bishop in Rome. He was subject, so to speak, to the Patriarch of Constantinople. The Emperor Justinian made Rome a Patriarchate, because the Bishop of Rome helped him evict the Ostrogoths. In the hierarchy of Patriarchs, Rome was on the bottom of that list. Later on, two more

Patriarchates were created: Armenia and Ethiopia for the Coptic Church. By the way, this is why Mussolini targeted Ethiopia and the Western powers consented to his conquest. But that get's me ahead of what I have to say...

"As soon as Rome was made a Patriarchate, the Roman Patriarch claimed to be 'Primus inter Pares,' or first among equals. This claim, however, was rejected by all other Patriarchs. Consequently, the Patriarch of Rome wanted to elevate himself over the Christian Church, and there was only one way to accomplish this...

"With the help of Charlemagne in 800, the Patriarch of Rome proclaimed the supremacy of the Roman Church, calling himself Pope. He got away with this claim only because Constantinople was too weak to intervene. It was surrounded by the Arab Muslims. Kiev then became a Patriarchate. This added yet another reason for Moscow to repress the Ukraine, and another reason in the West, not to help the Ukraine.

"In fact, when Mazepa had the Patriarch of Jerusalem confirm Kiev as a Patriarchate, Peter I unleashed his fury on the Ukraine. This was his primary reason to sidestep that issue, creating the 'Holy Synod' and a third branch of Orthodoxy.

"These eight Patriarchates are still symbolized with the eight-ended cross and with eight-ended decorations in the Orthodox Churches to this day: two overlapping squares.

"Step by step, the Pope took away the powers inherent with the Roman title 'Augustus' or Emperor in the West -- in particular, the title of 'Pontifex Maximus.' By 1100, that title belonged to the Pope. Your historians call that struggle 'Investiture,' to veil the real issue. That title, and the powers that go with it, belongs only to the Roman Emperor.

"In this way the Roman Emperor could control the many religions in his empire. Only the Roman Emperor could create a new Patriarchate, and install or depose a Patriarch or Bishop. Once a Patriarchate existed, however, the local clergy may elect a new Patriarch for the existing Patriarchate when the prior Patriarch died or was taken into captivity. The Patriarchate was consequently perpetual and unmovable, except by the Roman Emperor. Today there are still eight Patriarchs, but seven of them are impotent in terms of military power. Some of them reside outside their Patriarchate: Constantinople, which is in Turkey and is called Istanbul; Antioch, which is in Syria; Alexandria, which is in Egypt. This leaves Jerusalem, Armenia, Ethiopia, Kiev and Rome. Of these, only Rome is strong and powerful. The others barely exist.

"Now, imagine this for a moment: Russia establishes herself in Constantinople, installs a Patriarch of her choice and begins to make her claims to rule Europe; for example, install a legitimate Patriarch in Rome. This would undermine the authority of the Pope and expose the German Concordat. This would also eliminate the powers of the Electors, and Russia could then make the claim that they were the sole protector of Christendom and the only legitimate successor to the Roman Emperor. The very thought of this possibility sent shudders to the Pope, the Habsburgs and the Hanoverians. That is, to the Pope, to Austria, to Germany and to England. Therefore, they had to act immediately -- and they did. That's why the Treaty of Berlin was imposed in the Balkans."

"But wait" I interrupted, "why do Western and Eastern historians claim that Moscow was a Patriarchate, confirmed by Constantinople?"

"That was just an unfounded claim which was started by Ivan III, called 'The Great.' He married Zoe or Sofia, the niece of the last Roman Emperor. And, since the Tartars had made him 'Prince of all of Russia,' this included Kiev. Thus, he transferred the Patriarch to Moscow from Volodimir. He labored under the delusion that transferring the Patriarch to Moscow also transferred the Patriarchate, which is not so.

"Earlier, some of the Greek clergy, including the Patriarch, accepted the protection offered by Muscovy from Tartar raids. But the mere fact that a Patriarch resided outside his Patriarchate does not establish legitimacy there. The custom had become to confirm a new Patriarch outside his Patriarchate by three other Patriarchs in the absence of the Roman Emperor, and none of the Patriarchs ever confirmed Moscow. It was this issue which Peter I tried to resolve when he stopped naming a new Patriarch and established the 'Holy Synod;' but as soon as he did that, the leader of the Orthodox Church in Moscow could only be called a Metropolitan.

"However, it takes only one Patriarch to reconfirm an existing Patriarchate. This is why Mazepa invited the Patriarch from Jerusalem and had Kiev reconfirmed, and ever since then Russia saw Constantinople as the only solution to gain leadership over Orthodoxy and Christian Faiths. When Czar Alexander II returned to Russia from the Balkans, all of Russia was near rebellion. He was blamed for selling out the Balkans to the Pope and to the Germans, and in 1881, he was assassinated...

"His son, Czar Alexander III, vented his anger on the revolutionaries, the Jews, the Ukraine, Finland and Poland. He imposed a harsher police state than Czar Nicholas I, if that can be imagined. Whoever could, fled Russia. This is when many Jews and Ukrainians from Galicia came to America.

"He enforced a program called 'Russification.' All minorities in Russia, were forbidden to speak their native language, observe their customs or to practice their religion at the expense of death or permanent exile to Siberia. He demanded all his subjects be counted as Russians. In the process original native names and history were changed and made Russian. Russian became the only language of his realm. This was resented in the Ukraine, Poland, Byelorussia and among the Jews, and all four became his prime targets of repression. He died in 1894 and hardly anyone shed a tear except in Moscow and St. Petersburg.

"It was the same tactic used by the Germans in Austria and Germany to create a fictitious history, language, mythology and so on. The German rulers in England, Germany, Russia and in the rest of Europe used pretty much the same technique to spread disinformation world wide. Consequently, even today, you admire German culture and downplay the others. This is particularly true in your country, in America.

"The last Czar, the last Romanov, (who did not have a single drop of the Romanov's blood in him) Nicholas II, came to power. Shortly before, in 1891, he was prepared for his rule with a grand tour of the world. A steamer took him from St. Petersburg to Copenhagen, Morocco, Madagascar, India, and Vladivostok. By then, the Trans-Siberian railroad was nearly completed, and, by that railroad he and his entourage travelled across Siberia to Moscow and then to St.Petersburg. Along the way, he was briefed on the geopolitical significance of the world to Russia and her rival England.

"About the same time, the English took the Crown Prince of Japan on a similar tour.

"Earlier, Bismarck had hammered out a treaty with Russia in 1870 which expired in 1901. When Germany did not renew that treaty, France jumped at the opportunity and cemented a Franco-Russian Alliance in 1902, while England entered the Anglo-Japanese Entente.

"Aided by the English, Japan attacked Russia. To counter this thrust, in 1905, a Russian Fleet was dispatched from the Baltic Sea and steamed for Japan. By the time it arrived the war had shifted from the coastline to Manchuria and Siberia, and, as the fleet approached the Sea of Japan, it was ambushed and destroyed by the Japanese. Japan imposed a harsh treaty, which was moderated by England, repeating the San Stefano fiasco in the Orient. This alienated Japan from England, but they remained in the Anglo-Japanese Entente.

"In Russia, the defeat by Japan resulted in open rebellion and revolution which was repressed mercilessly, but it was clear to all intellectuals that the oppressive, corrupt and incompetent Czarist regime had to go. Various parties sprung up. Most wanted peaceful reform, in particular, the Social Democrats.Many others, primarily the Bolsheviks, wanted nothing short of violent overthrow. This is when Lenin, Stalin and Trotzky appeared on the radical left.

"Practically every reformer, dissident or revolutionary was imprisoned, tried and then sent to Siberia. Lenin and Trotzky were sent to Siberia repeatedly. Each time, however, they escaped and went to the West. Lenin to Switzerland and Trotzky to England.

"In Switzerland, Lenin met with the leading revolutionaries of Europe, and it was there that he was exposed to Gustave LeBon's book 'The Psychology of a Revolution,' which documented all the errors of the failed revolutions of the 1840's and 1850's. It provided a virtual blueprint for a successful revolution. Gustave LeBon and his book became the 'bible' for Lenin. What makes a successful revolution? Money. Lots of money...

"In London, Trotzky met a few financiers. They opened the doors for him to the American financiers. In particular to the people depicted in the book 'Our Crowd;' the Rothschilds, Seligmans and so on. He went to America by way of Cuba and met the financiers in New York in 1917. Later on, he visited them again, and at the most critical time they provided the money to keep the revolution going. There were strings attached. Oil-rights to the financiers and the minorities had to be given a prominent role in the revolution, especially the Jews.

"Eventually, Lenin and Trotzky met, and, as far as the expected revolution in Russia was concerned, they were of the same mind.

"Meanwhile, Stalin 'operated' in Georgia. He was a divinity student who was expelled for his revolutionary activity. He joined the Bolsheviks, and, to raise money for his cause, he became the 'Jessie James' of Georgia.

"With a small band of followers he held up banks, robbed stagecoaches and seized a Czarist supply train. Once, he captured the entire payroll for the Czarist army in the Caucasus (Georgians are ethnically conscious people, being a minority in Russia.) His favorite book became 'The Prince' by Machiavelli."

"Excuse me," I piped in, "isn't 'Das Kapital' by Karl Marx the bible of the Communists?"

"It is," Hermes replied "to the rank and file -- to the masses. Each one of them read 'Das Kapital.' Each one of them was convinced of its eventual correctness, and each one of them used it as a tool to rise to power. But Marx does not provide the 'how to.' He only develops a theory, based on the industrial model Karl Marx found in England. That was his role model. He described something that might happen if conditions do not change and you take it to its ultimate, logical conclusion. But conditions change all the time, and this rendered his book useless. Just as Plato had found out more than 2500 years earlier.

"On the other hand, the other two books are very specific. One is a primer on how to conduct a successful revolution, while the other maps out, how to maintain the rule over diverse ethnic groups -- as Hannibal did. The intent of Machiavelli was to provide a blueprint for a Prince in Italy to seize power, take over the many city-states and form a unified nation. That blueprint was ideally suited for Stalin, especially in the years to come.

"Lenin was in Switzerland when World War I broke out. He seized the opportunity to contact the German high command, and told them that, if they funded him, he would start a revolution in Russia, depose the Czar and thus eliminate the Russian front. By the time his letter arrived, Samsonov and his Second Russian Army was defeated, but despite that defeat the war in Russia dragged on. Therefore, starting in 1915, the German high command contacted him and started negotiating, so to speak, how much was needed to eliminate the Russian front.

"Lenin was a good lawyer. He got his law degree from St. Petersburg University, and he was a great orator. But he was a lousy mathematician. He could not pinpoint the exact amount he needed for the revolution. Thus, one night I visited him and we discussed that issue.

"First, I asked him how long it would take to complete the revolution? He replied, 'One year.' I told him double or, better yet, triple that. Then, I asked him 'How many men will you employ?' He replied, 'Ten thousand.' I told him, 'Make that 300,000.' And, finally I asked him, 'On average, how much will you pay them each week?' He replied, 'Ten Rubles.' I told him, 'Make that 75 Rubles.'

"Now it was easy to estimate what he needed, 300,000 times 75 Rubles per week, times 156 weeks or 3.5 billion Rubles. Then, I told him that he had to ask for at least twice that much. And he had to justify that figure to the Germans in terms they could readily understand. When he stared at me, I told him to estimate what it would cost Germany to bring Russia to her knees...

"I then asked Lenin, 'How many German soldiers are needed to defeat Russia?' He replied, 'One million.' Then, I asked him 'How long will it take?' He replied 'Four years.' That was 208 weeks. Then, I asked him 'What is their average pay?' He answered, 'Four hundred Marks per month.' This was about 100 Marks per week. This added up to 20 billion Marks: 1,000,000 times 208 times 100.

"Finally, I told Lenin, 'Now stress the fact that 20 billion Marks is only the tip of the iceberg. It does not include munitions, clothing, rifles, armor plus the support services. The total will easily triple that estimate.' That is, 'Ask for 60 billion Marks,' I said. 'And if they give you only 5 billion Marks, you will have more than you need by your estimate, for the revolution...' because the Mark and the Ruble, at the beginning of the war, were near parity.

"Then, to cement my point, I told him to stress the fact that 'If the Germans give you anything less, the revolution will fail and their investment will be wasted. But, if they give you the full amount or more, you will sign a treaty whereby the Germans could recoup their investment. Promise them a few provinces as reparation...'

"Thus, 60 billion Marks was what Lenin asked from the Germans to take Russia out of the war. Of course, there was no doubt that in the end, Germany would be defeated by France and England once America joined the conflict on their side. Germany's victory would therefore be short-lived, because the allies would restore the provinces to Russia. In the end, it was Germany who funded the revolution in Russia and no one else.

"The defeat of Samsonov's army on the Eastern Front had another effect in Russia. Czar Nicholas II, took over the command of the army. This was, of course, a blunder of the first order. This did not endear him to his subjects at all, because at the front, it exposed the incompetence and nepotism of the leadership. In St. Petersburg, the monk Rasputin took over. He had gained the undivided devotion of the Czarina because her son and heir was a hemophiliac, and only Rasputin could stop his suffering. Rasputin in turn, started to sell every post imaginable to the highest bidder.

"For example, the German national, Stürmer, became Minister of War in Russia. Then, Russian industrialists began producing shoddy products: defective bullets, defective armor and so on.

"First, there was the munitions scandal, then the armament and clothing scandals. Then, Russia began to starve.

"By 1916, entire regiments were sent to the front with a single day's ration, without boots, without an overcoat, without bullets, equipped with wooden rifles. The lucky ones who were 'well equipped,' got a rifle and two bullets, and, while this wretchedness grew only worse by the day, the Czarina sent care-packages to her German relatives in Germany.

"By mid-1916, mutiny, desertion and disorder became the rule at the front, not the exception. The common soldier now realized that he was led to slaughter by his Czar, and that the war had deteriorated to freak notions of honor among the German rulers in Russia, Austria, Germany and England. A grotesque family squabble brought misery to millions of Russians.

"All you had to do was to ask a Russian soldier, 'What are you fighting for?' Nobody had an answer...

"On March 5, 1917, the Czar abdicated. A new provisional government was formed under Kerensky, but he continued the war.

"By the end of 1916, the Germans 'bought' Lenin's numbers. They outfitted a special train, loaded up an entire rail-car with German Marks, Rubles and other currencies. They put Lenin on that train, escorted him past the German and Russian front until he had clear passage to St. Petersburg. Of course in his haste, Lenin never counted the money. German sources claimed they gave him as much as 10 billion Marks, while Lenin never acknowledged more than 2 billion Marks. However, nobody mentions the Rubles and other currencies...

"Lenin arrived on April 16, 1917 in St. Petersburg, Russia, and instantly became the most popular man in town. I wonder why?" Hermes mused. He got up and stretched his legs for a while. Then, he continued.

"Lenin was the ideal choice to lead the revolution. His father, Ulyanov, was of Tartar descent. His mother was German: Blum. He was fluent in Russian, German and a few Tartar dialects. In St. Petersburg, Lenin appointed Trotzky as War Minister and Stalin as Minister of Internal affairs, dealing with the minorities in Russia.

"On November 7, 1917 the revolution became a reality. Lenin and his revolutionaries hijacked the government in St. Petersburg. Lenin created the Cheka, a secret police under Dzerzhinsky.

"Later on they were renamed -- NKWD, KGB, they are all the same to me. They are all carved from the same 'apple tree,' whether you call them KGB or Gestapo. They were all mentally depraved hoodlums. Then, Lenin appointed Trotzky to form the Red

Army. On March 13, 1918 Lenin was able to repay the Germans in the Treaty of Brest-Litovsk.

"Trotzky headed the negotiations for Lenin. As war reparations, Germany got Poland, Byelorussia and the Ukraine, while the minorities in Russia labored under the belief that they had been liberated by Germany. Especially in the Ukraine.

"Meanwhile, Russia was still an armed camp. Large army units were still stationed throughout the Russian Empire.In Bessarabia, in the Caucasus, in Siberia and in the north, near Murmansk, and most of them rejected the Brest-Litovsk treaty. Instead, they were determined to crush Lenin's government in St. Petersburg and resume the policy of the Czar and Kerensky. Huge army units began to move on St. Petersburg, but their actions were uncoordinated, and the newly formed Red Army led by Trotzky defeated them one by one: Generals Yudenich, Wrangel, Denikin and Kolchak.

"A vicious Civil War ensued which pitted the Reds or revolutionaries, against the Whites or the supporters of the Czar. Most of this action took place in the Ukraine, ravaging and depopulating it as the Ukraine became the battleground of these opposing factions.

"However, as soon as the treaty of Brest-Litovsk was ratified, the Germans annexed part of Poland into Germany, armed the rest of Poland and unleashed them into the Ukraine -- into Podolia. Austria occupied Galicia and Germany the rest of the Ukraine and Byelorussia (it was called White Russia at that time). Thus, Lenin paid more than he had bargained for, and the burden of war reparations was pawned off to the Ukraine. Therefore, the Ukraine was ravished in the process by Poland, Austria and Germany.

"The ratification of the Brest-Litovsk treaty forced the allied forces to intervene. The United States sent General Miller and an expeditionary force to Murmansk, while England, France and Italy sent armies to the Crimea to support Denikin and Wrangel. Within a few months after the signing of the treaty, five foreign armies operated in Russia and over a dozen White armies tried to dispose of Lenin's forces. The objective of the allied intervention was to keep Russia in the war and prevent Germany from reinforcing her forces in France. However, their efforts failed, and, in the long run all of them were expelled.

"In November 1918, Germany surrendered to the allied forces and the Treaty of Versailles was imposed on Germany while the Civil War escalated in Russia. With that treaty, Germany and Austria were dislodged from the Ukraine while Poland held on to some prime Ukrainian lands.

"The Treaty of Versailles created a number of new nations in Eastern Europe: Czechoslovakia, Hungary, Poland, Estonia, Finland, Latvia and Lithuania, Byelorussia and Ukraine. Now, they entered the fray in Russia. A Czechoslovakian army was sent to liberate the Czar, a Hungarian army moved into Western Ukraine, and a Romanian army moved into South-Western Ukraine and into Moldovia.

"This incessant intervention by foreign powers led to the notion of 'War Communism.' That is, in order for Communism to survive, it had to be in a perpetual state of war. Therefore, Russia's economy had to be changed to a war-economy to match. However, the Civil War had drained all its resources. Thus, starting in 1920/21 Lenin introduced 'NEP' or the 'New Economic Program.' This encouraged private enterprise, to get the economy going again and deferred, for the time being, the plunge into a war-economy. Many Communists, however, perceived it to be a retreat to the capitalist system.

"By 1920, the funds provided by the Germans were nearly depleted, primarily because of the inflation in Germany. Trotzky stepped in and got more money from the American financiers. This kept the revolution well-oiled and well-supplied.

"The Civil War and foreign intervention resulted in economic and financial ruin. Despite it, the Red Army prevailed. They expelled and/or defeated the foreigners and the Whites. In 1923, the remnants of Denikin's and Wrangel's armies were evacuated by the allied fleet to Yugoslavia. From there many moved to Western Europe: France, Germany, Italy and Spain. By 1934, America recognized the Soviet regime and established its legitimacy.

"In 1922, Stalin became Secretary General of the Party, putting control of the entire Bolshevik apparatus in his hands. In 1923, Lenin got sick became paralyzed and died in 1924. Stalin seized control of the party. Trotzky was exiled to Central Asia in 1927 and deported in 1929 to Turkey. Eventually, Trotzky was killed in Mexico in 1940 as he was writing his memoirs on 'Stalin's School of Falsification.'

"In 1923, the Union of Soviet Socialist Republics was formed. It created 21 republics which comprised the Soviet Union, but the Civil War was still simmering. It was not over until 1933, but the Red Army was now in control, and the formation of the Republics promised broad local authority which the minorities were yearning for. Of course, this was nothing but a huge propaganda ploy to draw them into the Communist orbit and then to repress them as never before.

"In 1928, Stalin abolished NEP and replaced it with his '5 Year Plans.

"By 1934, the Civil War, (which was now in its 17th year) was practically over. In the process, Chechnya was integrated into the Russian Republic as was the Ukrainian Don and Kuban area. Then, Stalin began his 'Great Purges.' They lasted from 1934 to 1939. Every perceived enemy to Stalin, real or imaginary, was tried and killed. This way the military leadership was decapitated. Over 90% of the officer's corps was eliminated.

"Just for one moment look at it this way. The Civil War in America lasted 4 years. It was fought only between the Union and Confederate armies. Yet look at the devastation it caused in the South. In total there were about 600,000 casualties. About 300,000 of them in the South.

"Now multiply that by 4 to account for the additional years, then multiply this by 8, to account for the additional soldiers and military actions by armies in the Ukraine. Then, multiply this by 2 to account for the ferocity, as each force decimated the property, people and produce. That is, multiply the effect of the American Civil War by 64 to give you a perspective of the devastation it caused in the Ukraine. In terms of casualties, over 12 million perished in the Ukraine alone and some historians claim that it was much higher...

"Stalin next focused on collectivizing the farms, the majority of which were in the Ukraine. Everybody who resented his 'Collectivization Program' was ruthlessly deported to Siberia or starved to death. In the Ukraine, the Kulaks, as they were called, were his first targets. They were mostly small property owners who responded to the NEP initiative. Most of them were taxed out of existence and many perished in Siberia.

"However, when the Ukrainian farmers still refused to join Stalin's collectivization program, Stalin engineered an inconceivably brutal program to starve them to death. The larger cities and communities were cordoned off, while the farmers were forced to stay out. Then, systematically, all the foodstuffs and farm animals were confiscated, including the seed for the next crop. Within six months the farmers were starving. This way, in a span of less than 2 years, nearly 9 million farmers were starved to death in the Ukraine...

"Thus, Stalin's rule proved to be more repressive than the Czars, in particular in the Ukraine. It is no wonder, therefore that when the opportunity came to rise against him, many took it.

"In 1939, Hitler had absolute power in Germany and was ready to embark on the conquest of Europe. In order to secure his Eastern border while he conquered Western Europe, Stalin was offered a Non-Aggression pact with Hitler. This suited Stalin just fine, and the two greatest tyrants Europe had ever seen met and reshaped their border. Poland was divided, and some of the provinces lost during World War I by Russia, were turned over to the Soviet Union. Napoleon's Curzon Line was alive and well again.

"What is curious is that neither Napoleon, nor Hitler, nor Stalin were natives of the country they ruled. Napoleon was a Corsican; Hitler a Bohemian and Stalin a Georgian. Yet, they are labelled: French, German and Russian respectively."

After a while he changed topics, "I will cover the modern era next time. I have scheduled another appointment for today..." With that he got up and shoved his rod into my hands and we were off.

Again we were floating through space. But this time it was different from all other times. Total darkness engulfed our flight. My eyes were wide open, yet I could not see anything at all. I closed my eyes again. What was the use of trying to see in total darkness, I thought. So I tried to relax.

We landed unexpectedly. In front of us were thirty two steps leading to a landing. On the landing was a huge chair. In the chair sat a figure of a man. He was dressed in dark purple, crimson and black.

Three lights illuminated the landing. Eleven lights illuminated the stairs. On the stairs stood figures in two columns. They were dressed in long robes of different colors. On the bottom of the stairs, to my left, the figure was dressed in a robe of crimson. On top of the stairs, on my left, the figure was dressed in a robe of dark purple. The figures in between, to my left, wore long robes in different hues from crimson to dark purple. To my right were also figures on the stairs. They also wore long robes, but the colors were exactly reversed. On the bottom, to my right, the figure wore dark purple and on the top of the stairs, the figure wore crimson. Behind the figures on the stairs were tall torches. The torches were lit and cast eerie shadows on the stairs. The figures formed two widening lines, from the chair to the first step. At the first step the figures were far apart, about twenty two feet, I thought. Together they formed an equilateral triangle, I thought.

The figure in the chair motioned us to approach. We began to walk up the stairs. The steps were made of cut gray polished granite. I could clearly see small pieces of crystals in them. The imbedded crystals shined brightly when the light from the torches fell on them and formed the right angle. As soon as I moved even a little bit, the shining crystals were no longer visible, but other crystals flickered just ahead.

We reached the top of the landing and I heard Hermes say: "Greetings to Hades and his court!"

"Welcome to my realm," Hades said softly.

Then, after a pause, Hades started: "I am the reason and the cause for the reflection principle, the symmetry principle and the duality principle...

"I felt like demonstrating these principles to you," and he looked at me.

"Chaos and hierarchy, death and life, male and female...

"They are the dual aspects of a higher purpose. Neither dominates the other and neither casts an inference on the other. Yet, both must exist in order to form harmony and continuity. These are the two rows of figures you can see...

"While each row may exhibit continuity, the two rows need not be reflexive nor symmetric. This is because each row can be defined by me, according to my rule...

"Yet your species observes the color, observes the steps and implies that it found all attributes of my ordering. This vanity of yours, to presume to know my ordering, leads you astray. Why can you not accept what is?

"Can you not see that you use only artificial attributes to satisfy your vanity? Can you tell me which member judges life? Can you tell me which member is a female? Can you tell me in what sense these members are symmetric or reflexive to each other? Of course you can't," he stated.

I was not about to contradict what Hades said. I only stood there in silence.

Hades continued: "Let's say the figures that you see are truths. Let's say each truth has a duality at each step. Let's say I veiled each truth in one color. Let's say your quest for knowledge are these steps. Then, as you stood at the bottom of the stairs no members flanked your sides. You saw a void on that level of reality. You phantom chaos. But you could see the ordering ahead. As you moved up in your reality with each step, the dualities moved closer and appeared to be less diverse. Midway, the dualities were nearly the same. Yet when you reached the top, the dualities were closer, more pronounced and more diverse than on the first step. Yet you learned nothing of the nature of each truth!" he said.

"Now, let us say the two rows are religion and science. Let's say to believe is to ascend the stairs along one file of truths. Let's say to be scientific is to ascend along the other side. Then, the believing soul walks closer to one file and the rational mind walks closer to the other.

"Let's say we take two souls and let them make this journey. Let's say that, at each step they shout to each other as to what they see. Do you think, they could ever have the same answer? Do you think one answer is more true than the other?"

"Of course not, you have a multitude of variations at your disposal," I said.

"Why then do you kill each other in the name of truth?" he answered.

Then, silence for a while. Hades resumed again: "I made my case so simple that even you could grasp it. Now..., do you think I have but thirty-two members in my realm? Of course not..., I have myriads of myriads of legions in my realm to serve my purpose. Then, each file could become a legion, could they not? Suppose I placed a legion on each side. Do you suppose I could be restricted in any way to change their hue? Do you suppose I would be restricted in any way to show their truths? Of course not!"

Hades seemed to wait for me. I was not about to ask anything. Not at this time. I felt there was more to come.

After a pause, Hades continued: "You understand..., my example is not limited to religion or science. It applies to any prevailing but opposing truths at each particular level. It applies for one religion against another. It applies for one science against another. It applies for one prevailing truth against another..."

"But..., is that not chaos?" I asked.

"Chaos and order are intertwined. Each order has chaos within its order. Each chaos can be ordered. The problem is, an ordering is a finite, artificial presentation. However, chaos is an infinite presence. Thus, each finite presentation has infinite variations. The infinite variation we call the fractal difference..." he paused.

"You heard of Zeno and Dedekind? I revealed this mystery to them. Zeno tried to explain this with numbers for a long, long time. When he could not explain its nature, he gave you paradoxes in its place. Since then, your race entangled itself with endless paradoxes of the infinite. You circumvented many problems of the past. When Euler found their nature, he defined it rigorously. Once that was done, you were ready to re-discover this mystery again. But from another step, from another level, with Dedekind. The nature of the infinite has not changed and you still have no answers. Have you made progress? No..., not in the explanation of the nature of the infinite. I have only seen new entanglements. All you have done is created more confusion," he paused again.

"What is the fallacy in our logic?" I asked.

"You demonstrate correctly that the infinite has no representation; no value can be assigned to it. But as soon as you do that, you give it a name and symbol. Once you give it a symbol, you have given it a representation. Thus, you violated your initial premise. Once you violate that initial premise you create the paradoxes which go with it." I had a feeling he was waiting for me to ask a question. So, I inquired.

"You mean to tell me that there are as many whole numbers as real numbers?" I asked.

"Of course, ..." he replied. "Can you not see that?"

"I have been taught that there is no one-to-one correspondence between the whole numbers and the real numbers. We have proven that this is true. How can it be false?" I asked.

"You see, the fallacy lies in the first step. Once you assign a representation for the infinite for the whole numbers, you then simply demonstrate that this particular representation is not sufficient to account for the admissible variations for real numbers. Hence, you conclude there are degrees of the infinite. And, to veil your initial folly you call it 'cardinality.' Let me give you a counter example. You have been programming for a long time. Have you not used arrays to hold related data?" he asked me.

"Of course I have. Fortran, Quick Basic, C, Algol, PL1, Pascal even Cobol have means of representing data with arrays," I answered.

"Well, ..." he resumed. "Did you not have occasions to index an n-dimensional array with a single variable?" he asked.

"Of course, I do it very often. Especially in Fortran," I replied.

"Then, is there not a unique map which maps n-dimensional cells into linear cells?" he asked.

"Of course there is. The maximum of each dimension is needed to construct the linear index," I replied.

"You see, ..." Hades resumed. "Once the infinite is assigned a value, cardinality is created artificially. And, to resolve this artificial cardinality, infinity is needed to produce a linear map. I rest my case," and Hades was smiling.

After a while, he added: "In addition, you used the reflection principle and compounded the problem. Then, you used the symmetry principle and compounded it again. Now, you try to solve a myriad of problems instead of one. You try to solve one problem and determine its nature. You apply this principle to the next problem and so on. You form a class of problems and solve that class of problems in that sense. But, the classes of problems are infinite. So..., what is left when you reduce the infinite by a handful of solutions?" he asked.

I was silent, but he could read my mind. He said: "Of course, the remainder is still infinite. Your whole approach must take on a new direction. You must begin to tackle problems for what they are. Solutions to linear problems are of little interest to me. They have little to do with reality and truth. They are restricted idealizations of cases which are not real. They are figments of your desires. The real truth is different. It is changing, yet remains the same. It is not linear. You make it linear. You wish to see it in a linear way. That does not make it linear!" he paused.

"Does this mean that problems should be solved within a certainty allowing for uncertainty?" I asked.

"Of course," he said. "All problems have potential solutions. But, the solutions are only valid to within a degree of certainty within the axioms and the solution space. Solution are only possible when all three are in harmony. Change the axioms and you have a new solution space, hence new solutions. The new solutions are just as valid as the ones before, they only adapt to the changed axioms. And, further still, change the solution space and you have new solutions within the same axioms. That is, the simplest problem has three variations, not two: The certainty of a solution, the axioms of the problem and the admissible solution space of the problem. These three are intertwined. Change one and you will change the others. Change two and you will change the third. Change all three and the solution will change again. This is the class of problems you should be concentrating on."

"Is market timing of that class?" I asked.

"Of course it is." He said.

I was searching my mind for another question to ask. Finally, I came up with: "Is your realm structured?"

"Of course it is. There are many misconceptions as to how we are organized. So, let me explain. There are twelve Olympians plus Demeter and me. Poseidon, Hera and I are siblings. Poseidon rules the sea, Hera rules the home and I rule over the souls. The rest of the Olympians are sons and daughters of Zeus. Since I am too preoccupied, I have appointed Hestia to take may place on Mt. Olympus. Demeter is the daughter of Chronos and Ghea (also known as Rhea.) She is of a prior generation of immortals. She rules the seasons, but her work keeps her from Mt. Olympus too. Therefore, she appointed Bacchus in her place.

"We are the rulers of all the primal and benevolent aspects of your race and ours. We live primarily in the 6th dimension. Occasionally, we materialize in the third dimension, then you can interact with us and we can interact with you. We have reserved the 4th and 5th dimension as a fire-wall, so to speak, between your race and ours. However, we have imprinted your soul to recognize the 6th dimension so that it can easily find its home when your body turns to dust. Your soul is immortal..."

I got scared. The first thing that came to my mind was, "What if someone wakes me while I am with you?" I asked timidly.

"Don't worry about it." Hades replied, then he continued: "Before you can blink your eye, your soul will be with you. Hypnos makes sure that nothing can interfere with that."

That was a relief. Hades continued.

"We have a number of gates through which your soul can enter my realm when your body dies. They are only visible in the 6th dimension, when Thantos guides your soul to the main gate..."

"What if the soul refuses to enter. Is that possible?" I asked.

"That's entirely possible. These creatures you call ghosts. They only linger until there is closure, but eventually they all leave and arrive at the main gate with Thantos. There the soul is checked by Cerberus, my three-headed dog. He makes sure that only dead souls enter my realm..."

"How did I get here?" I asked nervously.

"Don't be concerned. Hermes has special privileges. He can bypass my safety-net and bring any soul before me whenever he chooses..."

What a relief, I thought.

"Once Cerberus admits a soul, it is led to the river Styx. Then Charon takes charge. He ferries the souls across to the Elysian fields. From there the soul is taken to Minos. He is the keeper of the 'Book of Life' for each soul. When your soul is with Minos, he reviews the deeds and misdeeds of each soul. When the misdeeds are capital offenses, then the soul is judged by a panel of peers, and when they find the soul to be incorrigible it is sent to Tartarus, to be chained and released no more. Only a few souls fail to get past the judgement of her peers, statistically speaking, less than .5%. These are the 'rotten apples' of your race. They must be chained and not allowed to re-enter your world again. This way I purge your world of habitual criminals, rapists and murderers.

"The rest are led to the river Lethe, from which they drink and thereby loose their memory. From there they go to the Island of the Blessed and await their return into your world..."

"Wait!" I exclaimed, "My faith does not admit reincarnation. I am a Christian," I exclaimed.

Hades only smiled at me. "What makes you think Christianity does not admit reincarnation? The early Christians all believed in reincarnation in the form I just described to you. They may have changed the names of the aspects but that was all. Ok, replace Island of the Blessed with Paradise; replace Elysian fields with Purgatory; replace Tartarus with Hell and you have exactly what the Roman Faith teaches today. Does it not?" Now Hades leaned forward and looked me straight in the eyes.

"I am not a Catholic..." I started as Hades interrupted me.

"Ok. Replace Thantos with the Angel of Death; replace Hypnos with your Guardian Angel; replace Minos with St. Peter; replace Charon with Angel of Mercy and replace Cerberus with the Guardian Angel to Eden. Are we now talking about the same Underworld?"

"My Church teaches resurrection..." I started.

"Well, are we not talking about the same thing!" Hades bellowed. Then he continued. "The early Christians, the Arians and Manichaens taught reincarnation exactly as I have explained to you. In fact, many of the Christian sects today still teach reincarnation the way I outlined it to you. Of course, they use different names for the aspects, but otherwise they are the same. I gave you the Greek version which was derived from the Egyptian version, which was derived from the Mesopotamian, which was based on the Hindu version. The Roman version was not as colorful, but was essentially the same as the Greek."

"Were not the Arian and Manichaen Christians exterminated by the Orthodox and Catholic Christians?" I asked.

"To a large extent, yes. But, many survived to this day. What do you think gave the Reformation the base on which to build on? Just because your historians were mum about it does not mean it did not happen. But then, you use Catholic Bishop historians who have a vested interest in protecting their position, income and power. How can you possibly get at the truth this way? Today, many of the atrocities are gradually coming to light -- such as the Crusades."

"You mean the 7 major Crusades into the Holy land?" I asked.

"Let me explain something to you. There were not 7 Crusades -- there were closer to 700 Crusades. Most of them were 'internal' Crusades to annihilate the Gnostics, Arians, Manichaens and Jews. But once the rampages started even the Catholics who were in the majority in those areas were not spared.

"In Southern France there was a nation: Languedoc, also known as the Albi. Their capital was Toulouse. They were peace-loving, frugal and very prosperous. Then, in 1002, a zealot monk called them heretics. He called them Cathars, because Catholics, Arians, Manichaens, Gnostics and Jews lived side by side and worked together. From then on and until 1271 -- that's 269 years -- the Pope called for one Crusade after another to destroy that nation, to kill her population, to burn their cities and to devastate their land. In the end, the nation was destroyed. Her cities were razed. Her rich land was ravaged and thousands upon thousands were burned at the stake. Utter mayhem was the result. Is this what Christianity is all about? Is this something for which the Papacy should be praised?"

I said nothing. I knew I had no defense to argue for the Pope.

"Now consider this. A Crusade into the Holy land absolved the Crusader of all legal and financial obligations for one year. An internal Crusade, however, absolved the Crusader for 40 days. That is, to sustain an internal Crusade for one year, 9 Crusades were called for.

"Therefore, to maintain an internal Crusade for 269 years, 2421 Crusades are called for. I claim there were at least 200 Crusades called by various Popes to obliterate the Albi, but Languedoc was not the only country. The first invasion by the Crusaders into Languedoc started in 1209 when the city of Bezier was sacked. The last invasion into Languedoc was in 1244 when Montsegur was sacked. That is a span of 35 years...

"Therefore, 315 Crusades were needed. I rest my case. The persecution of Christians by Catholic Popes was brutal and relentless, but that was not all...." Hades paused briefly.

"There was Provence, Bordeaux, Rochelle in Gaul; Lombardy, Tuscany and Venetia in Italy; Spain, Portugal and the Low Countries; Bohemia, Moravia, Hungary and Poland. I am not including the Balkans and Eastern Europe, and I am not including the Inquisition. All I can say is, the Crusades and the Inquisition were an abomination to humanity..."

I knew I had to try a different topic. I was upsetting him. So I began anew: "We have unlocked the DNA chains. There are about 3 billion DNA components, yet our world has more than 4 billion people. Does this mean there are some individuals which are exactly alike?" I asked.

Hades leaned back and started to laugh. When he finished, he looked at me again and answered: "You will never exhaust the permutations possible. That's for starters. But if you do, then you have to take into account the mutations of each DNA. There are 2 π mutations possible. Therefore, the total possible outcomes are 2 π raised to the permutation of 3.6 billion--since there are 3.6 billion DNA's in each chain. That is a really big number, even for me to accommodate. In fact, that is the physical limit of my database Apollo is working on. However," Hades continued, "this only accentuates one of the problems we have today. Do you know how many 'royals' have defective DNA's?"

"You mean present monarchs, rulers and princes?" I asked.

"Of course. The situation is so bad that about 95% of all royals can not be reincarnated. And, we try very hard to reincarnate each soul. Centuries of inbreeding have made the royals insane, diseased, imbecilic, deformed and warped. Some have turned into murderers and rapists and defy each and every civilized law. They have become a downright a menace not only to themselves but to the entire human race. I am curious how long it will take before humanity recognizes this..."

"Does this include the Hanoverians?" I asked.

"Especially the Hanoverians. All the Georges and Edwards were insane. Some were hauled off in straight-jackets from their office. On Elizabeth II, the data is still sealed. It will not be available until she dies. Look at Prince Charles and Diana..."

I woke up. It was pitch black in our bedroom. Not a light was visible. How strange, I thought, even the moon was hiding. I got up. I felt for my things. I found them. I took them and left the bedroom to make coffee...

14

Bacchus

I stood in front of Hermes. He was apparently not expecting me. He was in his casual attire. The suit and umbrella were shed for more comfortable clothes. He was drawing pictures in the dirt with his rod.

"Oh, it's you," I heard him say. Then, he added: "How time flies. I was just optimizing our travel arrangements for today.

"Well, what do think of yesterday?" he asked.

"Very interesting." I said.

"Do you want a brief review?" he asked.

"Yes, please." I said.

"Ares hangs out where he expects the next major military action to occur. This is why he was in Baghdad and plans to move to Samarkand. He is the primal force of confrontation. His methods are not elegant, but sometimes very effective -- in a limited sense, of course.

"Unfortunately, his way leaves many issues unresolved and we have to restore harmony by other means. This is a lengthy process. It's like the eighty-twenty rule. It takes twenty percent of the time to arrive at an eighty percent solution. The remaining eighty percent of the time are needed to improve the solution to within ninety-nine percent or better," he paused again.

Then he continued: "Generally, we frown on his methods. But because the human race worships him so much he is strong and powerful. If we could only enlighten humanity of his futile ways we could make him much less dominant in our hierarchy and yours...

"Aphrodite is the oldest aspect of our race. She even precedes Zeus (by some historians), his bothers and sister. Her ways are primal in many ways. Yet, because her ways are essential for the human race, she will always remain beautiful and desirable.

"Hades, of course, will also remain powerful and strong. In fact, his power has only increased with time and will continue to do so for the duration of the human race. Most of your intellectuals are preoccupied with Hades and expand his domain. Accordingly, his powers expand. Realistically, this need not be the case. Originally, we used Hades to guard the destructive aspects of the cosmos. He still does. But your race gave him many new aspects which he has to manage. Of all the principles, the reflection principle expanded his domain the most. Now his powers nearly equal those of his brother Zeus...

"I think it is a fatal mistake of humanity to grant him so much power. The Pope, the clergy and the ministries stress his powers needlessly in order to secure their own jobs. His powers are perverted in order that the human intelligentsia expands its own influence...

"So far our generation has been holding his expansion in check. His parties are hardly attended by the Olympians. But little by little he has convinced some to attend. Poseidon, Demeter, Bacchus and even Artemis have attended his parties. Then, almost inevitably, great calamities have occurred in the harmony of nature." he finished.

"I liked his analogies," I said.

"Yes, he has a good way of demonstrating his points. However, be careful -- he always promotes his ways," Hermes said. "How was your day?" he continued.

"Today I finished the graphic parts for technical displays," I said.

"Are they in color?" he asked.

"Not only are they in color, I allow the user to rotate colors for optimum visualization ..."

"Oh, that's very good. You know, eons ago we used to be colorblind. Some of us still have difficulties with certain colors, so color rotation is a nice feature, but..."

"How about the technical aspects?" he inquired further.

"I am very excited, ... " I blurted out "... I think I have found market timing classes which are very well defined and I believe that each class has its particular market timing formulation which is very accurate!" I added.

"Well, let's hear of your classes and the market timing algorithms," Hermes said.

"The classes I defined, which are all well behaved within each group are: The top class of the growth stocks, the worst of the dinosaurs, and the center of the dormant class. That is, the upper one third of the best class, the lower one third of the worst stocks and middle one third of the dormant class. In addition I found a special class which I call 'physical market timing stocks.'

"The best of the growth stocks actually defy market timing. They grow exponentially in time and market timing does not apply to them at all. These are stocks that should be bought whenever an investor has excess cash, regardless of their current price as long as the P/E ratio is less than fourth power of π. I have noticed occasional pull-backs on these stocks, but they are insignificant with respect to the over-all growth of the stock. These stocks can be characterized in the following way: Annual increase in sales and earnings in excess of π squared times the bellwether-bond!

"Conversely, when a stock exhibits negative earning and pays no dividend it should be sold or shorted mercilessly. In some respect short-selling presents a paradox of sorts because generally short-selling is viewed by many as a 'bullish' action -- simply because 'eventually' the stock needs to be bought back. Thus, short upside rallies are possible in a declining stock. But these up-side rallies should be used to sell the stock short again and again until the dinosaur is extinct.

"The last case is actually the best suited for market timing. I call this case 'technical market timing.' I started with Demeter's formulation which I modified. The results are best observed in the following way: Pick two weighted moving averages whose ratio is π (I used 10 and 32) -- where the short moving average is no longer than four π but greater than two π. Then their respective difference in amplitude can be looked as an 'oscillator.' If we map the graph of this oscillator on a compressed time axis, the optimum exit point for the stock is one divided by 2 π with respect to its maximum amplitude! That is nearly a perfect Fibonacci ratio.

"Right now, these three cases form my kernel market timing process. What is interesting, is that of the remaining cases, actually the three higher and the three lower cases are best 'market-timed' with the 'holding period return' or 'fundamental' market-timing process, where the reference space is the EPS variation over the last three years and one year of projected earnings. Then, the 2 π ratio on the low end forms a buy signal and the 2 π ratio on the top end forms the sell signal. Therefore, the complete model consists of four market timing algorithms which blend into each other as the financial, fundamental or technical data changes. Only one transition zone is not properly described at this time -- the transition from fundamental to exponential. That is, how the 'fundamental' market timing changes to an exponential growth or decline process," I said.

Hermes just kept looking at me in amazement. Then, he started to roll his eyes, shift his head and I could see how he was digesting these statements in his head. Finally, he stopped, turned towards me and said: "I don't believe you! You modified Demeter's model. I detected a number of other cases which do not obey your algorithms," he said.

"Okey, ... " I answered and dared him: "Name one," I said.

Again, he rolled his eyes, looked up to the sky and I could see how he was trying to find a company which violated my modelled behavior. Then he stopped and said: "Kelly Oil."

"Great!" I exclaimed, "... I forgot to mention the exceptional case to you. That case I call 'physical market timing.' In that case known physical events drive the market action.

"Normally, these cases involve oil and gas exploration companies. However, some financial situations can be included also. For example, a company in bankruptcy which is restructured and obtains new credit or financing. And, as a generic case, the oil and gas exploration companies. Thus, the oil and gas exploration companies form the 'regular case' for these special cases," I said.

"Alright," Hermes said. "Describe physical market timing to me as a regular case."

So I began: "The cycle in a 'physical market timing' situation is usually very long, about two years or so. Most of the time the company explores areas where it makes sense to drill for oil and gas, based on geological data. Once a site is located the company tries to get financing and so on. During that time the stock trades at a 'baseline price.' However, once financing is obtained the stock shifts gradually to a premium of the baseline price. Let us call this: the stock basis. From then on, actual events must take place before the stock moves upwards, based on pure speculation. These events are: when drilling begins -- the 'hype' in the market starts and rumors abound that the company is about to discover massive oil or gas reserves whichever the case may be. Based on these rumors the stock begins to rise in value. This rise culminates when 'something' comes out of the ground.

"However, since statistically less than one percent of oil and gas explorations are a success, the 'smart money' sells their stock as soon as they get word that 'something' comes out of the ground. The remainder lingers on and waits for the results and the potentially huge profits. The analysis determines whether or not it is profitable to pump oil from the well. As mentioned before, statistically, less than one percent of the oil wells are commercially feasible to exploit. Thus, in the great majority of cases as soon as the results are in, and they are usually negative, the well needs to be capped and is not profitable. Thus the stock plummets back to its 'baseline' price. Therefore, these stocks are not dependent on the economy, the fundamental or technical data but only on physical events to take place. Hence, they form a special class which can not be mixed with the regular cases."

Hermes listened to me intently, then said: "That's very good, but I think I can find a few other cases which will violate your model."

I could see how he was trying to find another case, but he could not. Then he turned to me and said: "Let's summarize your findings. You have three major classes aside from your 'physical market timing' case: growth, dormant and dinosaurs. Each class has three sub-classes, let's call then high-medium-low. Then technical market timing applies to the dormant-medium class, fundamental market timing applies to growth-low, dormant-high, dormant-low and dinosaurs-low. The extremes are dominated by exponential behavior and the two transition zones for which you have no good solutions at this time are exponential-medium for growth and dinosaurs, is that correct?"

"Essentially, yes. Technical market timing applies best in the dormant-medium range. That is, the results are better than fundamental market timing in that region, although the fundamental method can be used there. However, the fundamental method is much better in the next two adjacent zones and breaks down on the exponential side. Therefore, there must be at least one method left which forms the transition to the exponential behavior," I explained.

"That's very good. I like your approach," I heard Hermes say. Then, after a pause, he started again.

"Any questions on the history I covered?"

"Oh,..." I exclaimed. "I made a long list of them. But I left that list on my desk."

"In that case, let me resume where we left off. When I finish, you will have a much better perspective of what faces the European Union. Let me start with the allied powers first.

"Even though America was the decisive factor in winning the war in France, President Wilson's 14 points were dismissed at the conference table in Versailles. The following paradox evolved: at home the returning American soldiers were given a hero's welcome. However, in Europe they were seen as bumbling idiots, because they did not ravish the land, rape the women and take the treasures with them. In Europe, these were the standard rewards for a victorious army. In political circles the contemptuousness was even worse. Thus, England and France brushed Wilson's 14 points aside and dictated their own terms. Consequently, America turned introvert. However, her economic might did not go unnoticed. America was seen as a trade competitor to England. Thus, England encircled America economically which led to the 'Great Depression.' Her industrial output was boycotted, her factories started to shut down and massive unemployment set in. The stock market crash was the ultimate manifestation.

"France and England tore Germany, Austria and the Ottoman Empire apart and gorged themselves with their possessions. Oil was the new 'Black Gold.' It fueled the industrial complexes. France and England entered a 'Digestive Period' of about 20 years, from 1919 to 1938. During that time they concentrated on exploiting their gains and did not monitor the developments in Germany and Russia at all. Their intervention in Russia was half-hearted and uncoordinated. Their attempt to stop Hitler was mere 'appeasement.' When they woke up in 1939, it was too late.

"Germany had leapfrogged ahead industrially and forged new alliances with Austria, whom they annexed, and Italy, who was pushed into Hitler's lap. Japan turned on her benefactor England because she needed oil, and Stalin was used as a security blanket by Hitler to complete the first stage of his plan, i.e., avenge the Versailles Treaty.

"Mussolini was outraged when he got only a piece of Tyrol and a piece of the Dalmatian coast from Austria at the Versailles Treaty. Italy's losses were greater than England's and Italy received no colonies at all, just a small enclave in Tripoli.

Mussolini was the reason Italy declared war on Austria in 1915.

"He formed a unit called the 'Black Shirts' and marched on Rome in 1922. The Senate fled and King Victor Emmanuel III asked Mussolini to form a government. Mussolini became 'Il Duce,' the leader of the Italian People.

"While England and France sat by, Mussolini tried to take Corfu in 1923. In 1927, he made a pact with the Albanian royalists and occupied Albania. In 1929, Mussolini proclaimed himself protector of Islam, so that Turkey would guard the 'Sarcophagus of Claims' in Istanbul. The same year he resolved the issue with the Pope. Thus, the Italian Concordat was formed and the Vatican established. This endeared Mussolini to the Pope and the Italian people...

"King Victor Emmanuel III was still the head of state, but by 1930 Mussolini held the executive and legislative powers of the government and was the virtual dictator of Italy.

"In 1935, Mussolini invaded Ethiopia, Libya and Somalia. Neither England, nor France, nor the League of Nations raised a finger to stop him. While economic sanctions were imposed, nobody blinked an eye to stop the genocide in Ethiopia. By 1936, Mussolini's conquest of Ethiopia was complete and he proclaimed Victor Emmanuel III Emperor of Ethiopia.

"In 1937, Mussolini tried to make Austria an Italian protectorate, but Hitler had other plans. When Mussolini backed off, Hitler annexed Austria to Germany in 1938. This was called 'Anschluss,' the unification of the two German States.

"Mussolini's expansionist policy finally cornered him into Hitler's camp. In 1939, Hitler and Mussolini signed a military alliance. With that, all future policy matters were dictated from Berlin.

"From then on, Italian military matters started to go downhill. When Hitler unleashed his war on France, Mussolini was on his side. In 1940, Mussolini attacked France, but was decisively beaten back. In 1941, Mussolini tried to take Greece, but he was beaten back again. Hitler had to delay his invasion of the Soviet Union and mop up the Balkans. By 1941, Mussolini's armies were melting away in Africa, compelling Hitler to send Rommel with his 'Afrika Corps' -- one beefed up division -- to prevent the total collapse of the Italian African armies. The same year Mussolini provided Hitler with two armies for the conquest of the Soviet Union.

"Finally in 1943, after America had invaded North Africa and was in Sicily, King Victor Emmanuel III found enough courage to form a new Senate. Mussolini was deposed, imprisoned and taken to a mountain fortress; however, a daring rescue by Hitler freed Mussolini. In the end, Mussolini was captured and killed by Italian resistance fighters in 1945...

"Geopolitically speaking, Mussolini's military expeditions made no sense. If looked at it in terms of faith-politics, his wars and proclamations made a lot of sense. His declaration to be the protector of Islam brought the Patriarchates of Alexandria, Antioch, Armenia, Constantinople and Jerusalem into his sphere of influence.

"The conquest of Ethiopia gave him control of the Ethiopian Patriarchate. The war against Greece was to capture the Patriarchs outside of their Patriarchates. His support of Hitler promised to bring in the last outstanding Patriarchate in Kiev, and potentially capture the Patriarch himself. In this sense, he conducted a Holy War which was orchestrated by the Pope." Hermes stopped for a moment.

I said nothing. I wanted Hermes to continue. After a short pause he did.

"Now let us look at Hitler. In many ways Mussolini was his role model. Instead of the Black-Shirts, he created the 'Brown-Shirts,' and Mussolini's march on Rome became his march on Berlin. Actually, it was a 'Putsch,' an attempt to seize the government in 1923, but it failed. Hitler was captured, tried, convicted and sent to prison.

"Many Germans remained sympathetic to his cause, including the court that tried him. There, Hitler mesmerized the attendees with his speech and his mission. He got 5 years, but was eligible for parole in 9 months. When he was released he vowed to take over the government by legitimate means...

"The prison, however, was more of a retreat than punishment. He was allowed every conceivable privilege. Hitler turned it into his office and wrote 'Mein Kampf.' There he outlined his policy for the entire world to see. Initially his book did not sell well at all, about 5,000 copies. It became a best-seller when he came to power. Even today, his book sells reasonably well...

"In 1928, Hitler's party, the NSDAP became a permanent fixture when they won a few seats.

"Hitler's party got about 30% of the vote in 1933, and was a major force in the Reichstag. From then on Hitler muscled-in on the government of Hindenburg, he became Chancellor and when Hindenburg died in 1934, Hitler appointed himself Chancellor and President for life and became the undisputed dictator of Germany.

Then, he had the German army swear a personal oath to him. That is, the army owed him personal loyalty from then on...

"Contrary to popular belief, Hitler's great innovations were copied from abroad: Mussolini (Brown-Shirts, Neoclassical buildings etc.), Churchill (concentration camps in the Boer war), Rhodes (white supremacy) and Roosevelt (massive work programs like the TVA), and so on.

"Hitler knew that England and France were trying to live off the gains of World War I. Viewing this as a weakness, he started testing their resolve.

"In 1935, he defied the provision of the Versailles treaty which limited the size of his army, and started to build a powerful 'Wehrmacht.' The Saar left France for Germany in 1935. In 1936, he flagrantly sent his army into the Rhineland again violating the Treaty of Versailles and neither France nor England intervened.

"In 1938, he had Dollfuss, the President of Austria assassinated and brought his successor Schuschnigg to Germany. There, he dictated his terms for an 'Anschluss' (unification). Later that year, he made claims on Czechoslovakia. Hitler staked out an area he called 'Sudetenland.' He claimed the Germans there were repressed. Chamberlain, the British Prime Minister went to Munich and 'sold' Czechoslovakia to Hitler 'to buy a peace in our time.' When Chamberlain returned to London, he waved that treaty for all folks to see. However, Hitler moved in, took over Czechoslovakia, and called that land Bohemia and Moravia, a protectorate of Germany.

"Now Hitler was ready to expand his horizon. To secure the rear, he offered a 'Non-Aggression Pact' to Stalin, and, even though they were mortal enemies politically, Stalin accepted in 1939. Thereupon, Hitler sent his troops to the free city of Danzig, annexed her to Germany, and evicted the Poles. From there he planned his conquest of Poland.

"On September 1, 1939 Hitler invaded Poland from the West, while Stalin moved the Red Army in from the East. Within 18 days the conquest of Poland was completed, and, once again Poland ceased to exist on the map of Europe, while Russia was once more on the Curzon Line. At this point England and France declared war on Germany, but not on the Soviet Union. This started World War II.

"The original Non-Aggression pact was modified slightly in 1939. Stalin got the Baltic states and parts of Finland. Estonia, Latvia and Lithuania were ceded to Stalin. However, Finland balked. Stalin then invaded Finland, Hitler launched a paratroop invasion of Norway and also occupied Denmark. While the rulers of Norway fled to London, Quisling rallied the Norwegians for Hitler's cause on April 9, 1940.

"On May 10, 1940 Hitler began his conquest of the Low Countries with about 90 divisions. Luxembourg fell in 1 day, the Netherlands in 5 days, Belgium in 18 days. On May 10, Chamberlain was replaced by Churchill as Prime Minister in London...

"On June 4, 1940 the combined forces of Britain, France and the remnants of the Belgian army were decisively beaten at Dunkerque. They abandoned their armor and fled for the coastline. At this point Hitler could have annihilated some 30 divisions, but he committed Hubris, his first mistake in the war. Meanwhile, England launched one of the greatest rescue efforts in history to save the stranded soldiers on the coast at Dunkerque. Every floatable craft was requisitioned to save the soldiers, while Göring promised to show off his air wing and pulverize the rescuers and the rescued. Göring unleashed his Luftwaffe while the Wehrmacht watched. The result was not exactly what Hitler had expected. While some boats and ships were sunk and many soldiers killed, most made it across to safety. After the abortive spectacle, the Wehrmacht resumed her lightning strikes into France. On June 14, they were in Paris...

"Just before the Germans entered Paris, DeGaulle and Petain made their infamous pact. DeGaulle went to London, while Petain remained. Once defeated, France was divided into two zones. One administered by Petain from Vichy, while the 'Northern Zone' was administered by Germany. Petain was then forced to sign a treaty with Germany in the same location and the same railroad car Germany had signed the Versailles Treaty in 1919. In 35 days France was conquered, but, much more than this, France became an ally of Germany. Her navy and her colonies were now run from Berlin.

"Franco, the Generalissimo in Spain and Mussolini in Italy were already allies of Germany. Germany was, therefore, in control from Gibraltar to the Vistula river. Only England, Portugal, Switzerland, Sweden the Balkans and the Soviet Union remained outside her control. To further secure his gains, Hitler forged an alliance with Italy and Japan. They became known as the Axis-Powers. With continental Europe secured, Hitler now focused his attention on England.

"First, Hitler tried to negotiate with Churchill. His terms were: 'Restore our colonies and renounce England's influence on continental Europe.' Churchill refused. So, in September 1940, Hitler assembled an army to assault England. To soften-up the beach-heads, Göring's Luftwaffe had to gain air superiority; 'the Battle of Britain' ensued. After a month of sporadic aerial fighting, Göring could not subdue the Royal Air Force (RAF). It should be noted that even at that time America made the difference. They trained and equipped the RAF pilots in Florida!

"Meanwhile, three events changed Hitler's focus. First, he was told that the Duke of Windsor was ready to cooperate with him. This obviated the invasion of England. From then on, Britain was shelled with V1, then with V2 rockets.

"Second, Mussolini started a war with Greece, which led nowhere.

"Third, Stalin expanded his claims. He annexed Estonia, Latvia and Lithuania into the Soviet Union as Soviet Republics. He also made claims on Bukovina and overtures to Rumania, Hungary, Bulgaria, Turkey and the Dardanelles.

"This led to Hitler's second mistake. Instead of negotiating with Stalin, Hitler appeased him while he planned an invasion of the Soviet Union. On December 5, 1940, Hitler issued a directive to have the invasion forces ready by May 15, 1941. It was dubbed: Operation Barbarossa." Hermes paused for a while as if to collect his thoughts.

"Of course, before Hitler could embark on the conquest of the Soviet Union, he had to secure the Balkans and sway Rumania, Hungary, Bulgaria and Turkey to his side. The oil-fields in Rumania were of vital importance to him.

"Hungary and Rumania joined Hitler while Bulgaria and Turkey tried to maintain neutrality. However, Bulgaria agreed to allow Hitler's troops to pass through her territory to aid Italy against Greece. German troops moved in, in February 1941, and Bulgaria was taken over. A new government was installed and they joined the Axis on March 1, 1941. Yugoslavia was given an ultimatum to join the Axis by March 23, 1941. Yugoslavia agreed to join the Axis on March 25. The next day, however, on March 26 1941, the Serbs revolted. On April 6, German bombers struck Belgrade. Within 11 days, the Germans were in control in Yugoslavia. Now only Greece was left. The Germans moved in and Athens fell April 27, 1941.

"Technically, Hitler could have launched his invasion into the Soviet Union on May 15. He had more than 140 divisions ready and waiting, but the logistics of bringing the 22 armored divisions back from Yugoslavia and Greece, and replacing them with occupation troops proved to take longer than expected. Many historians claim today that: 'Had Hitler been able to launch his invasion on May 15, he would have conquered the Soviet Union.' To this I say: Bunk!"

"The delay was the best thing that happened to Hitler. Had he invaded on May 15, his armor would have been stuck in the mud. There is one season of the year when it is virtually impossible to conduct military operations in Russia: the spring thaw. It lasts from March until mid June. On the other hand, the most advantageous season for warfare is the winter, because the many rivers which crisscross the European part of Russia are all frozen. This was the lesson Countess Maria Walewska taught Napoleon. Thus, by sheer accident Hitler launched his invasion at the earliest time possible: June 21, 1941.

"Actually, it was the influence of Ares, to synchronize the seasons for Hitler. He liked the Panzers so much, he was itching to start a mad dash across Russia's plain. He wanted to be in Moscow by August 17 and in Astrakhan by September 13. Then, he could lock up Stalin beyond the Ural mountains. Remember, Napoleon reached Moscow September 14, and his army was not motorized. They walked on foot the entire distance. Napoleon fought just as many battles along the Kaluga road as the German Army Group North did under von Manstein. And, proportionately speaking, Napoleon faced greater numbers of dedicated patriots than Hitler ever did in his entire campaign. Hitler had two additional advantages over Napoleon.

"First, Stalin's army had abandoned their defenses when they marched into Poland, where they had made no attempts to set up defenses. This was true along the entire Curzon line.

"Second, even though the Ukraine was repressed by the Czar, she rallied to his cause to expel the French invader. When Hitler invaded, all of Russia was in near-revolt against Stalin. His rule was much worse than the Czars. All minorities in Russia were eager to join Hitler and drive Stalin out of Russia. So, what happened?" Hermes asked, as he turned to me pensively.

I was not about to answer his rhetoric. He continued.

"The first phase of Hitler's attack was countered by a comedy of errors. Stalin was caught completely off guard. When word reached him in the Kremlin that Germany had attacked, Stalin issued orders not to fight them. According to Stalin: 'The Germans had initiated large scale maneuvers and the Red Army was not to interfere with their exercise...'

"It took several weeks, for Stalin to realize that Hitler was really invading the Soviet Union; then he isolated and chastised himself for having made such a cardinal blunder. When he emerged, he had a new program in mind. He called for all Russians to rise to the occasion. He called it 'The Great Patriotic War of Russia.'

"Some Communist ideas were scrapped. The Churches were allowed to reopen. Some of the clergy were released from Siberia. Even some political dissidents were allowed to leave their prisons. By then, no less than four Red Armies had surrendered and the German Panzers were deep inside Russia.

"Keep in mind, when Hitler launched the invasion, he started with about 160 armored divisions. As he advanced, more European countries rallied to his side, while others waited patiently in the wings for the right moment to join him. Italy, Rumania and Hungary joined right away. They declared war on the Soviet Union on June 22, 1941. Spain, France and The Netherlands joined a few days later and sent legions to assist Hitler without declaring war. Croatia, Slovenia and Bulgaria joined a few days later. Finland, Estonia, Latvia and Lithuania waited for the Wehrmacht to get closer. Norway sent an army to Finland to help them against Stalin, to take Moscow. Consequently, within a few weeks of the invasion, over 100 allied divisions either joined or were waiting orders to join Hitler. With each division averaging 20,000 men, over 5 million soldiers were on Hitler's side, marching into Russia. And, with 1.5 million Soviet front-line soldiers already in German captivity, who could stop the German onslaught?

"Byelorussia, Ukraine and the Tartars in the Crimea wanted to join Hitler, but they were rebuffed. Why? Hitler had all the allies he needed and he had no intention of sharing his glory with anyone else but those who were already on his side.

"In Western Ukraine, the situation was slightly different. A nationalist leader rose, Bandera. He tried to rally the Ukraine against Hitler and Stalin, and, to a large extent he succeeded. He broke up his army into regimental size units and they waged war against Hitler. They became known as the original Partisans. His army was called the Ukrainian National Army or UNA for short. He started operating just before Tito in Yugoslavia.

"Bandera fought the Germans from the day they invaded to the day they were expelled from the Ukraine, but then, the Red Army moved in and he fought the Soviets until 1953, the year Stalin died. By then, his army, once over 1 million strong, was reduced to less than 50,000. They made their way into Bavaria and surrendered to the Americans. They received sanctuary and were allowed to emigrate to America, Canada, Argentina and so on. Bandera stayed in Germany, in Munich. In 1960, however, he was assassinated by the Soviets. But, I am getting ahead of myself." Hermes said.

"Let's look at the progress of the Wehrmacht, the German army. They were organized in three Army Groups: North, led by von Leeb; Center, led by von Bock; and South, led by von

Rundstedt. The overall command was directed by Hitler. Each army group was supported by Panzer (tank) Groups and an air-fleet (Luftwaffe).

"Army Group North had two armies. They were led by: von Manstein and von Reinhardt. It had one Panzer Group led by Keller and one air-fleet.

"By September 8, von Manstein cut off Leningrad, (formerly St. Petersburg.) He left the capture of Leningrad to the rear units and the Axis allies from France and Spain. By September 5, his advance units came to within 30 miles of Moscow. Now, Estonian, Latvian and Lithuanian units joined his ranks, while Finland and Norway launched an offensive on Moscow.

"Stalin and his high command were near panic. They began to evacuate Moscow.

"During Stalin's purges only a minimum of top officers had been spared: Vlasov, Zhukov, Koniev, Vatutin, Rokossovsky, Timoshenko and a few others. Stalin's favorite, by a longshot, was Vlasov.

"When Stalin took up an active defense, these generals started to take on a more prominent role because their defensive strategies worked better in their sectors.

"As von Manstein was approaching Moscow with his Panzers, Stalin called Vlasov and told him to organize a counter-offensive. There was only one problem -- Soviet forces were spread very thin along a huge front of nearly 1500 miles and nobody could be diverted for the offensive. That is, in your terms, a solid front roughly from Boston to Miami...

"There was a large Siberian army, but it would take months before they could be pressed into action in Europe. Vlasov suggested that Stalin free all prisoners and press them into action. This way, they could 'redeem themselves under fire.' To Vlasov's amazement, Stalin agreed.

"Vlasov took the prisoners, and everybody else he could muster including single women, and pressed them into action. On November 7, many of them paraded for the October revolution in Red Square and from there they were sent directly to the front. With this new-found mass of humanity, Vlasov was able to beef up the entire front, shift army units and get ready for the counter-offensive.

"Meanwhile, new weapons were rolling off the assembly line from the Urals and Siberia: T34 tanks, mobile Katjusha rocket launchers, airplanes and a light sub-machine gun.

"Many historians are taken in by German technological superiority, especially over Russia. Don't believe it. While across the broad spectrum of technological trinkets that may be true as a generality, especially when it came to consumer goods -- this was not true on the weapon-system side.

"Beginning with 'War-Communism,' the Soviet Union placed great emphasis on new and effective weapons. In this category, in terms of effectiveness, the T34, the Katjusha (little Cathy) rocket launcher and the light sub-machine gun became the nemeses of the German army.

"The Katjusha rocket launcher was duplicated by German technicians, but it was never successfully replicated. The German version never worked, while the Soviet version spread chills and horror through them. It was dubbed by the Germans: 'Stalinorgel,' (Stalin-Pipe-Organ.)

"While the light sub-machine gun was not a precision weapon over a long distance -- over 200 feet -- it was deadly at closer range. Just imagine for a moment that practically every soldier by the Soviets was equipped with a portable machine gun pitted against a German with a rifle.

"Last, but not least, the Soviets were the first to produce 'Tank Killer Planes,' helicopters and much more. Sikorsky was a product of that era. He escaped to America and his helicopters are still a major weapon in the American war-arsenal to this day. The aircraft developed for special purpose action by the Russians did not take a back-seat to the German Luftwaffe.

"In the early stages of the German invasion, the T34 was misused. It was used as a 'single fortress,' while the Germans operated in a 'wolf-pack.' This was rectified by Vlasov as large numbers of T34-s became available. Tank for tank, the T34 proved to be far superior to any tank the Germans were able to throw at them, including their later models in 1943: Tigers and Leopards.

"On December 6, 1941, one day before Pearl Harbor, Vlasov unleashed a counter-offensive along the entire front. It caught the Germans totally off guard. To begin with, it was inconceivable to the German high command how large numbers of Soviet soldiers could materialize after the many prisoners they had already captured. They labored under the impression that the worst was over and the Soviet Union could not have more than 100 divisions left. And, of course, it came to them at the worst possible time. Their lines were overextended.

"In addition, they were still laboring under the 'Roman War-Fare Style.' During the days of the Roman Empire, warfare began in March when the gates to the temples of Mars and Janus were opened and ended in December when they were closed. Then, the army rested and took up winter quarters. Thus, as the Germans were getting ready to hibernate, Vlasov unleashed his offensive.

"The result was panic along the entire front as the Germans were pushed back, on average, 175 miles. That is, nearly the distance from New York City to Washington DC. Visions of a Napoleonic disaster were on their minds, and, had it not been for Hitler's personal intervention during those panic-stricken days, the German front would have collapsed totally. In February the Soviet counter-offensive bogged down as each German soldier became personally accountable to Hitler. In March, the 'Great Thaw' and sheer exhaustion on both sides saved the German Wehrmacht. In the north, Vlasov came to within a few miles of Leningrad, and took up quarters in Volkov, about 75 miles away.

"While Stalin was elated with Vlasov's success, he started to have second thoughts about the released political prisoners. He sent out the KGB to 'cleanse' the army, and, when Vlasov found out the KGB was looking for him, he knew his days were numbered. He took his staff and crossed over to the Germans who captured him. Vlasov was interrogated and imprisoned. When word got out in Russia that Vlasov had defected, over 1 million Soviet soldiers defected to the Germans before military action was resumed that year. All these defectors were devout followers of Vlasov. He treated his soldiers well and they responded in kind...

"Vlasov wanted to cut a deal with Hitler. He offered to take the Russian soldiers in German captivity and lead them against Stalin. In return, he wanted an alliance with Hitler. Vlasov felt he could raise as many as 30 million soldiers to take up the cause. But Hitler vacillated for a long time, and in the end, kept Vlasov and his followers in prison. Hitler had all the allies he needed and was not about to share his glory with anyone. Despite that, a Vlasov movement emerged which reached its peak in 1942. A new leader was identified who was willing and able to take up the cause against Stalin. All that was needed was to convince Hitler...

"In 1944, Vlasov and his soldiers were armed, outfitted and released by Hitler to fight the Soviets. By then, it was too late. Vlasov was defeated. Vlasov tried to surrender to General Patton, but General Eisenhower would not allow Patton to accept his surrender. Instead, Vlasov was forced to surrender to the British, who brought in the Soviets. Vlasov was forced to dismiss his army, while the Soviets were in ambush and, as soon as they were dismissed, they were hunted down by the Soviets. All officers who were caught, were lined up and shot. Vlasov and his adjutant were whisked to Moscow where they were hanged in Red Square. The rest of his army went on a Siberian vacation: ten years of hard labor and loss of all human rights. Eligible for repatriation only after 20 years...

"Be that as it may, the fact remains that the Soviet victory over the German army was unique. For the first time a German army was defeated in the field on a grand scale. German invincibility became a myth, and German losses were staggering. Over one-half million German soldiers were killed or maimed, taking them out of the war. In addition, much needed war materiel was abandoned or turned into 'Schrott.' From then on, German Army Group North, ceased to be a major factor in the war...

"From Stalin's perspective, however, that victory could not be credited to Vlasov. He was erased from the history books. His credits were (later-on) heaped on Zhukov. And the mass of humanity Vlasov rallied to accomplish the feat became known as the elusive Siberian soldiers...

"With America's entry into the war, Churchill urged President Roosevelt to supply Stalin with all the war materiel he needed. So, Stalin was given a shopping list of items to choose from. On top of Stalin's list was: Spam and other canned food items, Jeeps, trucks, tires and other consumer items. Conspicuously absent were munitions, rifles, artillery pieces, tanks, airplanes and other weaponry. However, Stalin accepted a few American production experts to help him streamline his production facilities, and construct a new factory to build a replica of the American Jeep. From then on, Soviet and Russian historians have claimed that 'While the Soviets paid for the war with lives, America paid for it with Spam.'

"Of course, supplying the Soviet Union with the items Stalin needed was another problem. The Crimea and the Ukraine were in German hands. The only other available Soviet ports which could handle America's aid were Murmansk and Archangel on the White Sea. Therefore, American 'Liberty Ships' had to run the gauntlet from England to Murmansk,while under constant attack from the Norwegians and German U-Boats.

"During the spring thaw, Hitler reorganized the entire invasion force. First, he gave von Manstein a tongue lashing for being indecisive. He reamed out all the other generals and reshuffled their responsibilities. On May 8, 1942, the Wehrmacht was regrouped for a new objective -- to encircle and to annihilate the Kursk salient. Here's the situation he faced:

"In the 1941 offensive, Army Group North and South made good advances, while Army Group Center got stuck near Kursk. Vlasov's counter-offensive pushed back the entire German front some 175 miles. A huge salient developed around Kursk, about 400 miles long -- from Kholm to Kharkiv, protruding by about 200 miles into the German line, roughly from Moscow to Smolensk.

"Hitler wanted that salient amputated. As far as Hitler was concerned this was the last major concentration of Soviet forces, but instead of confronting it head-on, he wanted Army Group South to penetrate to the Volga, turn north to encircle that entire area from the rear, and then annihilate it. Army Group South was to be 'the Hammer,' and Army Group Center, 'the Anvil.' It was a grandiose plan doomed to failure. But the generals were meek from the tongue-lashing they got so they agreed to Hitler's plan.

"There was only one little problem. A small city, originally called Tsaritsyn, then called Stalingrad, had to be taken. That city became, so to speak, the anchor of the entire operation. This is when Ares left them to the Fates...

"The new German General of Army Group South, became von Paulus. The Soviets started the offensive on May 12, 1942, but von Paulus crushed it, and secured the sector from Voronez to Rostiv, both on the Don river. There he made his fatal mistake. He separated his Panzers from his main force. Kleist was given 17 armored divisions and moved south to the Caucasus. His new objective became to secure the oil-fields at Baku, while von Paulus was ready to take on Stalingrad. Why did he do that?

"To begin with, the German offensive in 1942 was very successful and von Paulus did not anticipate many problems. Peeling off 17 armored divisions from the 75 or so he commanded did not appear to be significant at that time. Besides, Army Group Center, which was to act as the anvil in this operation was now more than 120 divisions strong and was ready to support him. Thus, Kleist went to the green lush hills, while von Paulus marched into the light brown yonder...

"Von Paulus reached Stalingrad virtually unopposed, and, on August 9, 1942 he stood in front of that city. It was shelled into the ground and the Germans moved in. They expected little if any resistance, but what ensued was the fiercest resistance they had encountered thus far. Practically out of no-where, out of the ruins of the town, Soviets appeared and counterattacked. What followed was a door to door, ruin to ruin, battle for every square inch of the town. By November 18, von Paulus controlled most of the city. What remained was a tiny sector which would not quit. What was so eerie to von Paulus was that no matter how many Soviets were killed during the day, next morning they were again at full strength, attacking every corner of his positions. His Panzers were immobilized, his artillery was dwindling and the only shelter he an his troops could find were rickety cellars, holes in the ground and abandoned shelters.

"Von Paulus was drawn into a brawl from which he could not extricate himself or his army. Of course, Hitler did not help his situation at all. To Hitler it became a symbolic battle of Fascism over Communism, of Hitler versus Stalin. And Hitler had to have that victory at all costs...

"As soon as von Paulus started shelling, the Soviets dug in. The town lies on the western bank of the Volga river. Stalin had put Zhukov in charge of the defense of Stalingrad and Zhukov needed time before Siberian reinforcements could arrive. Zhukov controlled the east bank of the Volga. Thus, all the reserves were kept on the east bank of the Volga while only small fighting contingents were kept in the town. That is, Zhukov's plan was to create a 'Thermopylae' where the German armor was ineffective and a small band of defenders could paralyze an entire army. At night they took the wounded and dead out and ferried fresh reinforcements into the town. Thus, the number of defenders never dwindled, while the number of attackers took a terrible toll, especially their armor...

"There was one case worth mentioning. One commander of about 20 squads devised a scheme to beat Zhukov's system. He was nearly court-martialed for his action, but Zhukov was quick to grasp his motive and made him a hero. At night, when the messenger came for the report, he would turn over the wounded but reported no deaths. This continued day after day and caught the attention of Zhukov. Thus one day, after nearly a month of combat, a special messenger was sent in, with orders from Zhukov to do an actual head-count. It turned out, that there were less than half of his contingent left. He was arrested and brought before Zhukov. When asked why he did such a stupid thing, the commander replied: 'to get extra rations of Vodka for my men.' From then on, the ration of Vodka was increased for all defenders in Stalingrad...

"By November 19, Zhukov amassed the armies he needed to crush not only von Paulus but all the support armies on his flanks, and launched the counter-attack. By January 13, von Paulus was encircled and four German support armies were smashed. Göring stepped into the picture promising that his Luftwaffe would provide all the supplies von Paulus needed. The upshot was, however, that the Luftwaffe was shot out of the sky. Less than 5% of the promised supplies reached the Germans. Once, a plane got through. The Germans rushed for the cargo: it was loaded with condoms...

"Then, in the 11th hour so to speak, von Manstein rushed to the rescue. He came to within 50 miles of Stalingrad. He urged von Paulus to break out and join him, but Hitler intervened. He demanded that von Paulus stay in Stalingrad and take the town. Thus, von Manstein's effort was in vain, but it is very doubtful that von Paulus could have escaped. That was the last and only opportunity he had.

"Von Manstein was beaten back. Now, a new problem emerged: Kleist and his army in the Caucasus. Here, even Hitler agreed that Kleist had to retreat with all speed in order not to be caught and destroyed in that huge encirclement around Stalingrad which expanded day by day. Von Paulus had to hold Stalingrad for Kleist to escape the noose.

"Von Paulus wanted to surrender, but Hitler promoted him to Field Marshal, with the message: 'No Field Marshal in German history ever surrendered to the enemy.'

"Despite these warm words from Hitler, von Paulus surrendered February 2, 1943 as soon as Kleist escaped the noose. The once mighty German 6th Army was reduced to 90,000 men who went on a Siberian vacation, while the Soviets mopped up another 25 German divisions or so. From then on, Army Group South played only a minor role until the end of the war. What was left of it were less than 12 divisions of battle-fatigued soldiers. In the end, less than 5,000 Germans returned home when the war was over from the Stalingrad fiasco...

"The Soviets now had the upper hand in that sector. They captured Kursk and Kharkiv, but Kharkiv was retaken by the Germans March 14. Thus ended the operations when the spring thaw set in. However, the Kursk salient was now more pronounced than ever before, stretching from Orel to Belgorod, a few miles shorter as the crow flies but deeper and more pronounced than before, spanning about 2,000 square miles. Picture a rectangle, from New York City to Cleveland and from New York City to Washington, D.C. That was the battle-scene to come.

"During the spring thaw, Hitler reshuffled his generals again. Von Manstein got the honors to eliminate the Kursk salient, while Zhukov received the task to defend it. It was clear to everyone that Kursk could not be postponed any more. Not by maneuver, not by encirclement or any other means. It was also quite obvious how the attack would begin. It had to come from Orel in the north and from Belgorod in the south. Probably at the same time. Why? For two years Army Group Center tried to eliminate that salient with a frontal attack in 1941 and 1942, but each time it got only larger. Much real-estate changed hands several times. By the time the spring thaw came, the Soviets ended up with more than they held before. Army Group Center had been held in check, some 120 division by 1943. All it needed was a few more divisions to tip the scales. This was the assessment of the German generals...

"Von Manstein waited for the new Panzers to arrive: Tigers and Leopards, while Zhukov laid mine-fields, beefed up the defenses, and saturated the area with artillery and Katjusha rocket-launchers.

"Just before the battle started, Hitler initiated a peace conference. Stalin sent Molotov. Hitler proposed to cease hostilities. Germany would keep the territories she occupied. Molotov insisted on the Curzon Line. That is, the borders before the war. They disagreed on the real-estate, but they agreed that the Battle of Kursk would settle that matter once and for all...

"Since Zhukov decided to wage a defensive battle, he waited for the Germans to begin. They started on July 5, 1943. Just as expected, the German Panzers hit simultaneously from Orel and Belgorod, and, by the end of the day, they were hopelessly stuck in the mine-fields. The artillery and Katjusha rockets finished them off. July 12, Zhukov counterattacked at Orel, at Belgorod and at Kharkiv. By the end of the year the Soviets had taken Poltava, Kiev and Zhitomir; Bryansk, Smolensk and Roslavl.Army Group Center was virtually annihilated. From the original 120 divisions, less than 50 were of any use. The loss of armor was immense. To all intents and purposes, the Panzer corps and the Luftwaffe were destroyed and the Germans were retreating along the entire front. This battle broke the backbone of the German Wehrmacht. From then on, Hitler was not able to launch another offensive in the East...

"This victory, got the attention of Churchill and Roosevelt. There was one thing they did not want Stalin to do -- to make peace with Hitler. So, they called for a Three Power Conference in Teheran, Nov. 28, 1943. They impressed on Stalin that he not make a separate peace with Hitler, while Stalin urged them to open a Western Front in Europe, 'or else,' threatening that if they did not, Stalin was prepared to take Italy, France and Spain, to repay them for their alliance with Hitler. This got the attention of Churchill and they agreed to meet again in Yalta, next year.

"By the time they met at Yalta, Feb.4, 1945, Italy had surrendered and a Communist regime was in power. Stalin promptly recognized them. It was headed by Badoglio. The Allied invasion of Normandy was completed. America liberated Paris and Americans were at the Rhine, while the Soviets had crossed the Vistula and were headed for the Oder. From the Oder, Berlin was only sixty miles away...

"At Yalta Stalin made it clear that he had carried the burden of the war and accordingly he wanted proper compensation. Germany and Austria had to be divided equally into three Zones: American, British and Soviet. Their capitals had to be divided into three sectors, Berlin and Vienna. In addition, Stalin demanded to administer Europe from the Elbe to the Urals. In particular, the Soviet Union wanted the Curzon Line as its western border, while the nations between the Elbe and the Curzon Line were to be in his sphere of influence. The Balkans were to be administered by Stalin. Eventually a compromise was reached. Greece and Finland, except for some minor adjustments, were to remain under Western control.

"When Poland came up, Churchill claimed that the legitimate Polish government was in London, to which Stalin replied that he had a new Polish government in place already, and that the Polish borders were still fluid, but shifted to the west. Finally, Stalin demanded the repatriation of all former Soviet citizens, from all parts of the world -- from Europe, America and Asia. This became known as the 'Keelhaul Agreement.' That is, anyone living in the Soviet Union after 1923, was subject to 'repatriation' -- twenty years in Siberia. A subtle distinction was made between an 'old immigrant,' the White Army remnants evacuated by England and France to Yugoslavia and the 'new immigrants,' those who fled the Soviet regime or were taken by the Germans. To this both Roosevelt and Churchill agreed. And, subsequently many were forcibly repatriated this way, even from America -- from Lakewood, New Jersey. But then, America stopped that practice and became the only sanctuary...

"Since Tito was already in charge in Yugoslavia and the Baltic states were already integrated into the Soviet Union, Churchill and Roosevelt agreed to his terms.

"However, they asked Stalin in turn, to declare war on Japan. To which Stalin agreed. However, Stalin's entry against Japan was deferred until the next conference to be held in Potsdam, after Germany was defeated. Thus, everybody was satisfied and appeased.

"The Potsdam conference took place on, July 17 and lasted until August 2, 1945. By then, the war in Europe was over, May 8, 1945. Churchill was not re-elected and was replaced by Clement Attlee. Roosevelt died on April 12, 1945 and President Harry S. Truman was in charge. Stalin had moved some of his armies to Manchuria, to begin the offensive against Japan. They were told to wait until Stalin gave his go-ahead.

"But, even before the conference was to start, DeGaulle was introduced. Stalin objected. As far as Stalin was concerned, France was an ally of Germany and DeGaulle a puppet of Petain. Reluctantly England and America excluded DeGaulle. Truman agreed to give parts of Germany to DeGaulle from the American share as the French Occupation Zone (Baden, Rhineland and Würtemberg).

"From the original deal-makers only Stalin was left, and he demanded the terms agreed to in Yalta. When Truman hinted that America had the Atom Bomb, Stalin was not very impressed. Why? Stalin had a nuclear program already. A few of Fermi's students had defected to the Soviet Union and a nuclear program was in full swing; but they did not have the bomb ready. Thus, Stalin took it more as a bluff rather than a reality. Even when Stalin was told a nuclear device had been exploded in America, he would not yield. Stalin had come to Potsdam to collect his promises and anything short of that was not acceptable. Therefore, Truman agreed to the terms of Yalta to draw Stalin into the war against Japan.

"As soon as Stalin was satisfied in Potsdam, he declared war on Japan and unleashed his army. The unbreachable defenses built up by Japan with German engineering were smashed. The Japanese defenders were routed and Soviet troops swarmed into Korea and to the sea. Thus, Stalin prepared for an invasion of Japan. But then, Japan surrendered on September 2, 1945. What happened?" Hermes looked at me.

I was not about to interrupt him. So, he continued.

"When Mussolini invaded Libya and targeted Ethiopia, Japan invaded Manchuria in 1932 and targeted China in 1937. When sanctions were imposed on Italy, they were also imposed on Japan. This drove Italy and Japan into the German alliance in 1939. The German alliance made Japan realize her dependance on oil. An industrial nation needed access to oil, and the nearest oil fields were in Dutch Indonesia. Thus, they changed the direction of their conquest from north to south. But, the south was dominated by the Dutch and the British. America held the Philippines...

"England felt betrayed. She had groomed Japan into an industrial power which now turned against her. Thus, England turned to America for help, and, obligingly, America helped.

"Meanwhile, the war had started in Europe. Roosevelt was sympathetic to the English cause, but the Senate would not let Roosevelt enter the war. Entering the European conflict was perceived to end up as a bigger fiasco than World War I.

"Therefore, Roosevelt embarked on a 'Lend-Lease' program to help England, but to deliver the promised goods to England a new fleet had to built. They were called 'Liberty Ships.' Thus, while America focused on Europe, Japan focused on expanding to the south of Asia and the Islands of the Pacific Ocean.

"Thus, gradually and inadvertently, America was drawn into the conflict in Asia. And, when negotiations failed, England and

America took a drastic step. They 'froze' Japan's assets. Japan was now forced into a binary decision, either abandon her imperial ambitions in Asia or to go to war against England and America. They chose to make war...

"On December 7, 1941 -- one day after Vlasov's counter-offensive at Moscow -- Japan attacked Pearl Harbor, to eliminate America's power in the Pacific, and Germany declared war on America. Thus, America was compelled into war.

"However, both Japan and Germany had underestimated the resolve, the industrial power, the ingenuity and the resources of America. At that time, America was not much larger population-wise than Japan, but on the West Coast were less than 15 million Americans. Thus, in a 'bean-counting scenario' Japan was pretty sure that she could handle America since most of her resources were committed to Europe.

"Therefore, while Japan thought that America was taken out of the Pacific theater, with her Pacific fleet defeated, America was not.

"The big ships, the carriers, were not in Pearl Harbor. Why? Because Pearl harbor was too shallow to accommodate them. They were at sea. While the rest of the fleet was crippled, it was not destroyed.

"Many malcontents claim that Roosevelt could have prevented the attack. Many go so far as to accuse him of allowing the attack to happen, to enter the war. Don't believe it. Roosevelt was a patriot. However, what that unprovoked attack accomplished was to rally all Americans behind his cause. America wanted revenge for the unprovoked attack and the Soviet union wanted revenge for the atrocities the Germans had committed in the Soviet Union.

"What was different between the Pacific and Europe was MacArthur, the ablest American general. He was put in charge in the Pacific (he was first in his class at West Point) while the worst American general was put in charge in Europe (Eisenhower was the third from the bottom in the same class at West Point). Why? Because, MacArthur was to be supreme commander in the Pacific and direct America's war -- no holes barred -- while Churchill was to handle the sensitive political situations in Europe and would not allow anyone else to meddle with his strategy. There was only one man who could sway Churchill -- and that was Roosevelt.

"When Eisenhower arrived in England, therefore, an English spy became his personal driver, personal secretary and lover. Thus, Churchill and Roosevelt knew not only what Eisenhower thought and planned but his every intent. As it turned out, both MacArthur and Eisenhower were ideally suited for the missions they were assigned.

"In the Pacific, America was totally unprepared for the war. Japan had 2.5 million soldiers, 3 million reserve, 7,500 planes and 230 warships. At the same time, the entire American forces were: 1.5 million soldiers, about 1,200 airplanes and 350 warships. But, America's commitments in Europe claimed much of her resources. American forces in the Pacific were at a great numerical and material disadvantage -- often as much as 10 to 1 and more, making initial Japanese successes unavoidable. MacArthur had to retreat, gather his forces and strike back...

"The turning point of the war in the Pacific was Midway, June 1942, about the same time von Paulus launched his offensive on Stalingrad. This was the first naval battle in history where the two opposing fleets did not see each other. All the commanders could go on was the feedback from their air-reconnaissance and gut feel. In the end the Japanese fleet was destroyed while the American flat-tops suffered only minor damage. The first allied victory, if the battle of Moscow is to be discounted, was achieved by the Americans at Midway, not as the British would like you to believe at El Alamein.

"Besides, I don't understand at all, why such a pimple of a battle as El Alamein is mentioned to begin with. All Rommel had was one beefed-up division called the Afrika Corps, and look how much havoc he caused the British. The reason Rommel and his small force was airlifted by way of Crete to Tripoli was to rescue the Italian army in Libya. This he did. But, his stunning success prompted Hitler to expand his mission to rescue the Italian prisoners in Egypt. The rescued Italians in Libya were of no help at all -- being demoralized, without armor, without arms, short on water and short on food. Of course, after the disaster at Dunkerque in 1940, the British needed an equalizer and since this was their only victory in the war, it has been magnified beyond all reasonable proportion. The war in the Pacific and in Europe ended up to be an American war for the western part of the alliance.

"Where were the British? After Dunkerque, the British refused to fight the Germans, unless they had an overwhelming advantage, and this became the rule in the Pacific also.

"Instead, they shipped in Indians from India to do battle for them. At El Alamein, there were more Indians than British. Even at Monte Cassino in Italy, it was the Indians and the Polish legions who fought and defeated the Germans.It became Churchill's policy to spare the British and let America, India, Canada and

Poland do battle for them.

"As soon as America entered the war, she had to fight on two fronts thousands of miles apart. In the Pacific MacArthur had to be strengthened. In Europe the Atlantic had to be cleared of German U-Boats; England became America's arsenal. From there, a second front against the Germans had to be established. But Churchill had different plans. He wanted the Soviets to take on the Germans while he secured the rest of Europe for England; restore Gibraltar, Malta, Crete and Cyprus; take out the French colonies of Morocco, Algiers and Tunisia; take Sicily and invade Italy; and, only as a last resort, establish a second front in Europe. In 1942, over 250 German divisions and her Axis allies were deployed on the Eastern front while less than 25 guarded France and Italy...

"Thus, on November 8, 1942, the Americans -- with only minor support from the British -- invaded North Africa. The Americans landed on three beaches near Casablanca and on three beaches near Oran, while a British task force landed near Algiers.Who defended the beach-heads at Casablanca, Oran and Algiers? The French, of course. But the Americans won a stunning victory and the French surrendered in North Africa, on February 14, 1943. Did the French in North Africa join the Americans and British? Not at all. They became neutral...

"Once the Americans recaptured Tunisia, they invaded Sicily on July 9, 1943 at a time when the Battle of Kursk began to unfold in the Soviet Union. By May 2, 1945 all of Italy was occupied by Americans. Churchill called this plan: 'attacking the soft underbelly of Europe.' It may have been soft for Britain but not for America...

"On D-day, June 6, 1944, America was assigned the most heavily fortified beach-heads in Normandy, while the British landed on beaches that were not defended at all. They just landed, sipped tea and bragged: 'Jolly good sports, our allies.'

"And later on, when the Germans launched the only counter-offensive in Western Europe with 10 armored divisions -- the Battle of the Bulge -- and the Americans were encircled at Bastogne, Montgomery, who led the British forces, refused to aid the Americans. Thus, in sleet and snow, General Patton pressed his men to the limit, from southern France across the Alps, to relieve Bastogne. If you don't believe me, just go there and see their graves at Bastogne, at Monte Cassino and Normandy...

"Where were the elusive 'Free French?' In the Soviet Union Frenchmen were fighting at Leningrad, Moscow, Stalingrad and Kursk against the Soviets. In North Africa they were fighting against the Americans and Britons. During D-Day there is no account of them. Not a single squad of Free French tried to liberate their country! Even on the march to Berlin, there is no account for them. How did they redeem themselves? With the highly elusive 'resistance fighters' created by Hollywood...

"Keep in mind, the entire Western Front had less than 50 German divisions by 1944, while even during the Battle of the Bulge, Germany had to maintain over 300 divisions in the East, in order not to be overrun by the Soviets. Each year Germany was required not only to replace her losses, but to put some 50 additional divisions in the field. And, as the war was coming to an end, German divisions were more than eager to surrender to the Americans rather than to the Soviets, because they knew the Soviets came with retribution on their minds...

"In the Pacific, MacArthur started his counter-offensive by island-hopping towards Japan: Tarawa, Guadacanal, Saipan, Guam, Iwo Jima and Okinawa. In October 1944, General Douglas MacArthur was back in the Philippines. Thus, at the time the Philippines were liberated by MacArthur, the conference in Potsdam took place and Fermi had the Atom Bomb ready for use.

"After the Potsdam conference, President Truman consulted with MacArthur. The invasion of Japan was imminent, but there were two problems. First, the Soviets were nearly ready to invade Japan. They were on the coast from Vladivostok to Wonsan and in Korea. Should America let them? MacArthur felt that America should finish the war in the Pacific.

"Second, Truman asked MacArthur, 'What are the expected American casualties if we invade?' To which MacArthur replied, 'About 1 million.'

"Thus, Truman made the decision to drop the Atom Bomb on Hiroshima, to save American lives and to prevent the Soviets from occupying Japan. But, before the bomb was dropped, Truman sent a message forewarning Japan of the impending destruction and asked for their surrender. The Japanese military refused to listen. Thus, Hiroshima was annihilated. Another message was sent. It was rebuffed again. Thus, perished Nagasaki. A third message was sent. The Japanese military still refused, but their Emperor stepped in and accepted the surrender on August 14, 1945. On September 2, 1945 it was formalized.

"While all this was going on, the Soviets took the southern part of Sakhalin Island, the Kuril Islands and were half-way in Korea. Keep in mind, Korea was occupied by Japan. But, when the surrender of Japan was announced, the Soviets stopped their conquest in the Pacific. Thus, the two Koreas emerged. The North, occupied by the Soviets and the South by Americans.

"What followed is the reconstruction era of Europe and Japan. By the end of the war America and the Soviet Union emerged as the only two undisputed super-powers. But Stalin was bent on reparations -- the traditional remedy imposed on the vanquished, while America wanted reconstruction -- a new approach. However, Great Britain and France were facing colonial disintegration.

"This was the main reason why Churchill was not re-elected in the first place...

"The crown jewel in the British Colonial Empire was India. Every Briton could take a boat to India, get a cushy job and return to England a wealthy person. The word 'POSH' came from that era. It is an acronym for: 'Port Out, Starboard Home.'

"But, to keep India in the war, Churchill had promised independence to Gandhi.

"French Indochina served a similar role for France. There, a national leader emerged, Ho Chi Minh, who wanted to free Indochina from French Colonial rule. When the Japanese occupied French Indochina, he started to fight the Japanese and the French. Since Indochina was under the thumb of the Vichy Government of Petain, both Churchill and Roosevelt promised the independence of Indochina to him.

"The Soviet Union was arm-twisted into the war against Japan. Thus, Stalin occupied Manchuria and from there Stalin supported the Mao Communist movement, eventually dislodging the regime of Sun Yat Sen and Chiang Kai Shek (the Nationalists) to Formosa (Taiwan.)

"And, last but not least, Churchill's plan to invade Europe by way of the 'soft underbelly of Europe,' caused the Americans to land in North Africa, raising hopes of independence for Morocco, Algeria and Tunisia, enabling the notion of national independence to cross over into Africa. Africans now began clamoring for independence, from Algeria to South Africa.

"Churchill's policy was diametrically opposed to British geopolitics. Therefore, Churchill had to go and Clement Attlee was elected to shore up the British Empire and reaffirm British geopolitics...

"In addition, Churchill's policy of avoiding battle with the Germans caused Rome to be liberated by the Americans; Paris to be liberated by the Americans and Berlin to be 'liberated' by the Soviets.

"In Paris, General Omar Bradley and his 28th division had liberated Paris, but, in a magnanimous gesture, DeGaulle was allowed to gather a handful of French and enter Paris first, with Bradley's units right behind him, August 25, 1944. Of course, everyone knew the Americans had liberated Paris, but DeGaulle's star was on the rise nevertheless...

"As soon as the war ended, Gandhi came to London to demand the British make good their promise to free India. He was rebuffed. He returned to India and embarked on a program of civil disobedience to drive the English from India. Eventually, he succeeded in 1947, but the cost was staggering. It pitted the Hindus against the Muslims. Gandhi was assassinated and India divided into two Muslim states -- Pakistan (East) and Bangladesh (West) -- and one Hindu state, India...

"Then, Ho Chi Minh came to London to make his claim. He was sent to Paris where DeGaulle rejected his plea, leaving Ho Chi Minh no choice but to return to Indochina and resume his war of liberation against France. Eventually, the French were defeated at Diem Bien Phu, but the Americans were drawn into this war to save French Indochina -- under the pretext of the 'Domino Theory' -- however, not before Cambodia and Laos were amputated from Indochina in 1951. Gradually, America was drawn deeper and deeper into Vietnam. Eventually, students in America began to protest and forced America to terminate that war. Then, Algeria, Morocco and Tunisia clamored for independence. They were repressed by DeGaulle but achieved independence anyway. At this point all of France rose up against DeGaulle. And so it went on and on as Africa and Asia gained independence from their colonial rulers, mostly England, France, Portugal and the Dutch...

"After the Potsdam Conference, Germany was officially divided into three Occupation Zones: American, English and Soviet. But, to appease DeGaulle, America gave him a piece of her share: Baden, Rhineland and Würtemberg; while America kept Bavaria.

"The English took Northern Germany and created the state of Hessen. This way, 250 years of English disinformation in America could be reconciled. That is, 'this' was the homeland of the elusive Hessian mercenaries who fought in the American Revolution.

"Stalin got East Germany: Brandenburg, Pomerania, Thuringia and Saxony. Everything from the river Elbe to the East or the original dividing line between the Germans and the Goths, now called Slavs.

"When Churchill was not re-elected in 1945, he realized the horrible mistake he had made, and, to prevent an even bigger one, he embarked on a course to alienate America from the Soviet

Union. If America and the Soviet Union, he reasoned, got together at that time, they were in a position to carve up the world for their purposes without regard for either England or France. Thus, in 1946, Churchill delivered his famous 'Iron Curtain' speech at Westminster College in Fulton, Mo. His intent was to drive a permanent wedge between America and the Soviet Union -- and he succeeded!

"In America, his speech was called 'controversial.' In the Soviet Union, Stalin was irate. In retaliation, he put pressure on Berlin, which was situated entirely in the Soviet Occupation Zone. America responded by moving a Strategic Air Command force to England, suggesting an Atom Bomb. For a while it seemed that a shooting war could start over Berlin as Soviet Mig fighters began buzzing the city. The Soviets then blockaded Berlin, cutting off all access to the rest of Germany. America responded with an Airlift, to supply the Berliners with food, fuel and consumer goods. Eventually, the blockade was lifted and all Berliners-- maybe the whole world -- breathed a sigh of relief. A war, possibly a nuclear war, had been averted, but the Cold War had started...

"Meanwhile, America and the Soviet Union had diametrically opposite plans of what to do with the 'Germanies' they occupied. Stalin annexed parts of Pomerania and all of East Prussia into the Soviet Union, and, when America refused to impose war reparations, Stalin imposed his own. Everything that was not 'nailed down' was carted off to the Soviet Union. Then, to render his part of Germany impotent, he introduced 'land-reforms.' That is, he changed a once thriving industrial area into a farming community, and the industrial workers into farmers. This was his way of making sure Germany would not be a threat to humanity. And, last but not least, Stalin imposed a Communist regime which was directed from Moscow.

"However, America had an entirely different plan. To begin with, Germany needed to be purged of her war criminals. In Europe this was an absurd idea. The victor got the spoils. The victor could rape, pillage and kill practically indiscriminately. This mode of operation was practiced for over 1500 years. Why should it change?

"When Stalin was asked what to do with the war criminals he replied: 'Shoot them.' But that is not the American way. First you convict them, then you shoot them. What Europeans did not know was that America had a precedent from its own Civil War of the 1860's. When the Civil War ended concentration camps were found where Union soldiers (prisoners of war) had been badly mistreated. The administrators and others responsible for these atrocities were brought to justice. They were tried and those who were convicted were punished accordingly.

"Thus began the Nürnberg trials in Bavaria, in the American Zone. To most Europeans this was nothing but a white-wash spectacle to establish a legal means to punish Germany's leaders and to impose American moral authority. European moral authority came from the Pope, Bishops or other Church leaders -- not from a court.

"During the proceedings, of course, the defense of the War Criminals was: 'We were only doing our duty and following orders.' While a handful of criminals were tried and found guilty, the real impact of the trial evolved later on: the complicity of the Pope, Bishops and Church leaders. From then on, the influence of the Church in general, and the Pope in particular, began to erode in Europe and throughout the world...

"This erosion began in Germany, spread to Italy and France. In Italy it was epitomized by a film, 'Don Camillo and Pepone,' the struggle for power between a priest and a communist mayor in a small town as the battleground for the mind of man. This contest endeared the communists in Western Europe, and, had it not been for America's economic incentives, the communists would have taken over...

"Once Germany was cleansed in Nürnberg, instead of imposing reparations on Germany, America offered the Marshall-Plan to rebuild and arm Germany again. For the British this was consistent with her geopolitics. This kept Germany relatively strong, in order to neutralize the Soviet Union. English geopolitics again prevailed: deny the Soviet Union access to a warm port at all cost. Keep the Soviet Union surrounded and encircled...

"The Soviet Union countered by exporting revolutions to Africa, Asia and to the rest of the world. In this way Cuba was drawn into the Soviet sphere of influence.

"In addition, England wanted to install monarchies in Europe wherever possible. Why? Because, by definition, all monarchs were Germans or of German lineage by that time. Keep in mind that, when the English monarchs changed their name from the House of Hannover to the House of Windsor, many other European dynasties followed suit. In Spain, the Habsburgs became the Bourbons and in Italy, the Habsburgs called themselves House of Savoy. However, that attempt was rebuffed in Greece, Italy, Spain, Portugal and France...

"America's policy was also consistent with the policy of France, because Germany would be a buffer against the Soviet Union in case of war, and the Reds would be kept out of the French colonies.

"America offered the Marshall-Plan to Czechoslovakia, Hungary and Poland, but Stalin would not permit them to participate. In Hungary a hyper-inflation followed which dwarfed the German hyper-inflation of 1923.

"By 1949, the Soviets had the Atom Bomb and a nuclear arms race ensued. Eventually, this led to a near-nuclear confrontation between America and the Soviet Union during the Cuban Missile Crisis in 1962. In the end the Soviet Union backed down and America embarked on a program to scrap and reduce the nuclear stockpiles to which the Soviet Union agreed. They became known as the 'Non-Proliferation Treaties.'

"That era, from 1949 to 1980 was dominated by MAD, or Mutual Assured Destruction. Movies like 'Dr. Strangelove,' 'Fail Safe' and 'War Games' depicted the madness humanity had arrived at.

"The scientific community started to point out the insanity of the program. Stockpiles of nuclear bombs had reached about 10,000 nuclear bombs on each side. It was pointed out that, even in a small nuclear exchange of say 200 nuclear bombs each, the end result would be a 'Nuclear Winter.' That is, the destruction of humanity in at least one hemisphere.

"President Ronald Reagan refused to accept MAD as the only alternative and embarked on a new program called 'Star Wars.' The economic resources of the Soviet Union were already strained to the limit, and, when yet another weapon system was perceived as a reality, a restructuring of her economy was in order. The Soviet leader was Gorbachev, from the former Ukrainian-Don area. He embarked on a program called 'Perestroika,' or the re-building of resources, you call it 'retro-fitting.' That rebuilding led to the collapse of the Soviet Union.

"Thus, America and America alone, was the direct cause of the Soviet Unions's demise. Of course there were contributing factors. The revolt in Hungary, then Czechoslovakia and then Poland. But these were manifestations of the root cause. In order to keep pace with the American weapon systems, the Soviet Union and her satellites had to sacrifice. But, decades of sacrifice had already produced nothing but poverty. The people simply rebelled...

"Thus evolved the Cold War, the industrial West pitted against the communist East, and, thus ended the Cold War, with the disintegration of the Soviet Union.

"This may have been a Pyrrhic victory for America, however, because now there are at least seven former Soviet Republics who are potentially an even greater threat to world peace than the Soviet Union ever was: Kazakhstan, Kirgizstan, Tadzhikistan,

Uzbekistan, Turkmenistan; Ukraine and Byelorussia. The Ukraine emerged as the third largest nuclear power after the break-up. Kazakhstan is the fourth largest nuclear power. The main problem is that the Siberian Republics, such as Kazakhstan, are Muslim." Hermes stopped, looked at the sky as if to check the time and changed topics.

"Ok, let's be on our way, I'll finish later..." I heard Hermes say.

We took off and started floating through endless space. The ride was very pleasant. I felt elated during the entire journey.

We came to a stop on a hill-side. We were surrounded with grape-vines dripping with clusters of ripe, red grapes. The whole hill-side was terraced with red grapes and vines. They were planted in neat rows very close to each other. Only a small passageway was left between succeeding landings. The dew was still clinging to the leaves, to the vines and to the clusters of grapes.

Slightly ahead of us was a group of human forms with their backs turned to us. They appeared to be inspecting the grapes. One of them turned towards us. He was not at all surprised by our presence. He said: "I am Bacchus. I am inspecting my crop. This will be a good year indeed..."

"Hello Bacchus," I heard Hermes say. "Is this the appointed place?" Hermes asked.

"It is, it is. This is the best place to show my aspects," Bacchus continued.

"In front of you, you see a full crop in my vineyard. Soon it will be harvested. The grapes will then be cut from the vines. The vines will wilt from the pain. The leaves will fall off by themselves, mourning the loss of the grapes. What will remain are the dried-up vines. This agony of the vine is endured for two seasons. In the early spring, the tasks must be completed. The dried up vines must be cut down to their stems to prepare them for the new growth. Only then is the vine ready to yield an abundant crop. These are the prerequisites of an abundant crop. This by itself, if followed to the letter, need not produce a crop like this. An element of chance is needed to produce the rest. The sun and rain, the wind and calm, the heat and cold must nurture the vines in the right proportion to yield abundance. That is, three aspects must be satisfied. They are: The vine, the maintenance of the vine and the elements of nature. Two of the three I leave up to you. The third, I lavish or withhold depending on the piety of man...

"This mystery is a universal truth. The element of chance, while it can be minimized, can not be eliminated. Within these boundaries of reality the best solution of the problem is in your hands...

"This mystery is also a universal aspect of each mythology and religion. I am this aspect for my generation. I die and then I am re-born to die again. This cycle of my birth and death are cosmic generative cycles. It is that cosmic spiral you were told before. Each time I am re-born I manifest myself in stronger ways so that this mystery is understood by man," he said.

"How do I use these aspect in my work?" I asked.

He looked at me and said: "Each market, every instrument, has three potential motions: Up, down and sideways. Each signal, to be used, needs at least two more independent confirmations," he said.

"What is an independent confirmation?" I asked.

"Your axioms define dependency. Therefore, obtain the independent confirmations with respect to your axioms. That is, each market has a set of axioms. Then, a pattern observed in one must coalesce with two other markets to improve certainty. But patterns from the same market will confirm nothing. This is because the base signal is only accentuated or muted with other signals from the same market.

"For example: Suppose we have a number of measures from the stock market for one issue. Let's say we have: Two moving averages, the oscillator, the summation index, the trade channels, the resistance and support levels and so on. These measures are expressions of the same thing. Therefore, they are not linearly independent. They only accentuate a given state within their inherent error. Thus inferences based on three dependent measures of the same class will be misleading," he paused.

"Why is that?" I asked.

"First, the inherent error for each measure changes over time. This allows a particular signal to dominate or stay dormant at different intervals. Therefore, the best of these measures is necessary to characterize the trend or state within that class. That measure dominates the current action. It dominates the first potential cause...

"Second, an independent class of measures must be used to confirm or reject the findings of the first. That is, another market must be valued for concurrence. Let's say we use the bond market to provide the next measure. Then, the characteristic government curve and its relationship to the stock provides a new measure. Let's call this the influence of the economy. Since the economy is from a different class of measures it is a valid differential. Then, trend and economy can form a strong confirmation. Again, their confirmation reflects only necessity...

"Third, the final differential must come from a market which measures volatility. Here valid measures are: Latent volatility, the spreads and implied volatility. Of course, implied volatility is the weakest of these measures. This is because it is a measure from the past where the future is inferred to repeat again, and to the same degree. Naturally, the error in this measure is the absence of the inherent error in that stipulation. The correlated spreads are better measures. Because, they are actual measures of the leverage into the future. That inherent influence and error can be computed quite accurately. Therefore, the distribution functions of the spreads and their implied leverage are better measures for the future...

"The best, of course, is latent volatility. It binds a multitude of variables and produces their combined residual error," he paused.

"Let me explain this with my grapes. Let's say we have three classes of measures: The vine, the leaves and the grapes...

"When the vine is dry, surely the grapes will be dry also. This is akin to the measure of the economy. Then, the most prudent action could be: to cut the vine and let the sap nurture the remaining stems. When the leaves are dry, this should alarm the keeper of a problem. That is, the first signal or a trend. And when the grapes are rotten or destroyed this signals yet another action. The grapes then, are a measure of the actual volatility of the plant or issue. The vineyard then, is a measure of the volatility of the entire system...

"That volatility of the system or of the issue begs for the proper action. A keeper might respond by adding water or fertilizer or a protective screen. That is, the best course of action becomes apparent to the keeper. The same is true for market timing. That is, a call, a put or pass," he seemed to be finished..."

"How does your aspect affect my generation?" I asked.

"My aspect is relatively new. It is rebirth as opposed to reincarnation. It was practiced first by the cult of Isis. Your Dollar bill still honors that cult: the seeing eye of Isis. But when Christianity became the sole religion in the Roman Empire, the cult of Isis was destroyed, her priests and priestesses killed, her temples plundered, desecrated and destroyed..."

"What is the difference between,..." I asked.

"In reincarnation the individual soul is lost. It enters a new body and becomes a new soul. In rebirth the individual soul stays the same and the body stays the same. The cult of Isis demonstrated this with her trinity: Isis (mother), Horus (son) and Osiris (husband) and the ever present evil force, Seth. Now, Seth wanted to be supreme ruler, so he tricked Osiris into a coffin, dismembered him and buried him in a giant Cedar tree in Lebanon. Isis found him and restored him to his glory. Yet the struggle between good and evil continued. This cult was dominant in Egypt. Therefore, when the Christians became dominant and Athanasius became Bishop of Alexandria and Arius the Patriarch of the Christian faith, they were at odds with each other over the nature of the Christian Trinity. Athanasius preached the 'Isis version' while Arius preached the 'Syrian version.' After much bloodshed, the Egyptian version prevailed..."

"Does this mean that the dead must be buried instead of cremated or burned?" I asked.

"Some Christian sects demand burial, but that is not necessary as long as the ashes are preserved in one place. Eventually the flesh and bones turn into ashes anyway, even if the body is buried whole...

"Let me explain the main religions of your day. I will count only those religions which have a myriad times a myriad members. Maybe then this notion will become clearer. You have 4 main religions left: Hinduism, Buddhism, Christianity and Islam. Christianity and Islam evolved from Judaism. Christianity with Jesus Christ and Islam with Ismail, the illegitimate son of Abraham. Eventually, Mohammed took up his cause and created Islam...

"The Hindu religion is the oldest. It pre-dates the great flood in your Bible. Some of your historians claim that Aphrodite was the founder of that religion (Istarte). That civilization flourished in the Indus Valley. They were conquered by the Aryans, who superimposed their cults. With that conquest many sects evolved, some superimposed ancestor worship. But their common thread is reincarnation which renders their religion introvert or peaceful..."

"Who were the Aryans?" I asked.

"That depends on the historian you ask. Some claim that they were Goths. The reason being that Amazons guarded their processions. And as you know, the Amazons were Goths. Others claim they were an extinct civilization...

"In any event, Buddhism was founded about 600 BC. They too teach reincarnation. But over the years ancestor worship was superimposed. Then, in China, Confucius added a way of administrative rules and they turned introvert also. Today China is mostly atheist. Therefore, they have become extrovert and are bent on expansion and conquest. Japan's version of Buddhism became extrovert with the European colonists. Since then they have become extrovert and cherish expansion and conquest..."

"Excuse me," I interrupted, "...did not the Chinese expand, at one time or another, South into Burma, Siam, Indochina and to the East, to Japan?" I asked.

"Yes, they did. But that was during a time when Mongols ruled China. The Mongols were very extrovert and bent on conquest and dominance. This was because their land was poor and the only way they could attain the 'good life' was by conquering rich civilizations." Bacchus answered. After a brief pause he continued.

"According to your calendar, the birth of Jesus marks the new era. But Christ began to teach when he was fully grown and crucified shortly thereafter. He preached rebirth or resurrection. His teachings were meant to be not only introvert but downright docile. However, once Christians were installed as administrators in the Roman Empire His teachings became eventually downright expansionist, intolerant and imperialistic. All this for the personal greed and the lust for power of the administrators..."

"Why were the Arians and Manichaens so mercilessly persecuted," I asked.

"The main reason, of course, was the insatiable avarice of the Christian administrators. Christianity offered for the first time a chance to establish a single, uniform religion in the entire Roman Empire. The Arians had the first shot at it. In that role they persecuted the nonbelievers and heretics, thereby setting the norm for future events. For the most part their teachings and writings are extinct; only fragments exist today. According to the fragments left the following picture emerges:

"They were the most extreme branch of Paul's teachings. They rejected not only Jewish dietary laws, Jewish traditions, circumcision and the Old Testament -- they called the Old Testament the 'works of the devil.' I'll give you a few specific examples from the Old Testament.

"First, according to the Old Testament human sacrifice was sanctioned. When Abraham was told by Jahweh to sacrifice his only son, Abraham thought nothing of it and took him to an altar he built for that purpose. This was perceived as an abomination in Christian teachings...

"Second, according to the Old Testament adultery was sanctioned. For example, when Abraham did not have a child by his wife Sarah, she gave him her 'hand-maiden' who bore Abraham a son called Ismail. This was also perceived to be an abomination in Christian teachings...

"Third, according to the Old Testament there was a multitude of gods or godly offspring. Just read Genesis Chapter 6. It talks about 'the sons of god taking earthling women for wives.' This was also perceived as anathema to Christian teachings...

"Fourth, according to the Old Testament human coexistence hinged not on the law of forgiveness -- as taught by Christ-- but on retribution, revanche and oneupmanship. An 'eye for an eye,' a 'tooth for a tooth' was preached, causing endless vendettas, wars and retribution. Yet we know that violence breeds only more violence. Again this was not Christian thought but the thoughts of a devious and malevolent god...

"Take the Ten Commandments. For each Commandment I can give you a specific example how Jahweh himself violated each Commandment and forced it to be violated by humanity...

"Therefore, they reasoned, the Old Testament was not the work of God but the work of the Devil. On the other hand, their missionaries and teachers took the oath of poverty, gave away all their earthly possessions, travelled in two's -- because Christ said; 'whenever there are two of you gathered in prayer, I am amongst you' -- they did good works, preached His gospel and were highly respected in their community. The case of the Albi demonstrates this. They were highly respected and revered, but because they were poor, pacifists and did not establish a powerful hierarchy, they could neither muster armies nor defend themselves properly once the Pope and the Inquisition was turned on them. Yet they survived the relentless persecution of the Catholic Church for over 500 years. That is, the early Christians in Rome -- the heretics at the time of the Roman Emperor Justinian and the heretics after the German Concordat -- are the true martyrs of the Christian Church..."

"During the reign of the Roman Emperor Valens, the Orthodox Bishops made the case that the Arians were too docile and thus not suited to administer his empire and he agreed with them. Therefore, the Arians were declared heretics and the Orthodox Bishops replaced them as administrators. This is when the first bloodbath occurred. Orthodox zealots massacred Arians and heathens alike. This became a model for the Catholic Church. They in turn, based their teachings on Peter, admitting the Old Testament for their clergy but not to their congregation as a whole -- it was forbidden to read the Old Testament by lay people. When they came to power in the West, they were even greater zealots than the Orthodox Christians. From then on, and until today, Christianity, in the form of the Roman Faith, has become downright militant when compared to any other form of Christianity, heresy or heathen belief. This led to the Reformation, the Counter-Reformation and with it the admission of the Old Testament. The paradox is: while Christianity is the most docile religion it was transformed into a very militant religion by her clergy, in particular by the Popes.

"About 600 AD, Mohammed and his followers used the Koran to spread the Islamic faith by war and conquest. They teach both rebirth and reincarnation, depending on the sect. When the Roman Emperor Heraclites tried to convert the Monophysistes -- the last large Christian group -- they converted to Islam. While the teachings of Islam are more militant than the teachings of Jesus, their teachings spread more rapidly than Christianity. Even though their teachings are downright oppressive to women, they embraced it nevertheless. They circumcise not only their men but also their women. Their spectrum of beliefs spans both militant and docile sects. At one time they were very powerful, in fact more powerful both militarily and economically than Europe-- from about 625 to 1919 or to the end of World War I. Then they were carved up by England and France into small insignificant colonies. With that their culture declined, their economy was ruined and their influence nearly eliminated.

"However, the industrial revolution in Europe required oil. Since most large oil deposits are in their lands -- from Saudi Arabia to Indonesia -- they reap the profits. Today they control the Oil Cartel and gradually raise the price to satisfy their greed. Huge investment and cash reserves -- managed mostly by England -- give them great economic power. And, with economic power comes military power. Thus, once again they are a dominant factor in your era. Not surprisingly, however, that wealth is concentrated in a few Arab families -- all supporters of England during World War I -- while the great majority of Arabs is desperately poor. To these destitute Arabs, Western Europe has a magnetic attraction for them as they try to improve their economic lot.

"There is great antagonism in Europe against Islam, especially in countries were they ruled before, mostly in the Balkans. The Ottoman Turks demanded not only tribute but a specific number of young boys between the ages of 8 to 10 who were taken away and trained as Janisaries. The Janisaries were the most ferocious fighters for Jihad or the conquest of the rest of the world by holy wars. When the required number was not provided -- and it hardly ever was -- they raided the towns and villages and took these boys away by force. This reign of terror is still remembered to this day. In the Balkans, the population will never forgive them for that. Therefore, as Muslims migrate to Europe to improve their lot, they migrate to the Western countries of Europe where they can easily brush aside these atrocities of the past..."

"You mentioned calendar before,..." I started.

"Oh, I am so glad you asked. As far as I am concerned, a calendar is the pinnacle of human knowledge because it requires precise knowledge of sidereal times, or precise eclipses of the planets. As far as I am concerned, the residual error in time tells me how advanced a civilization is or was.

"The Babylonians counted time according to their ruler as did the Egyptians -- which is not a very effective method. The problem with it is if you don't know all the rulers in the right sequence of their rule your calendar gets messed up.

"The Greeks improved that system. They counted time with their Olympiads. That, however, had two minor problems. First, during fierce wars Olympiads were not held. This created gaps in their calendar. In addition, Olympiads were held every four years. Therefore, in order to be specific one needed to include not only the last Olympiad but the year or years (displacement) away from that Olympiad.

"The Romans adopted the Egyptian calendar -- with Julius Caesar -- and started counting from the time Rome was founded according to Livy. That is, they created a calendar about 50 BC and retro-fitted it to 753 BC or so.

"When Christianity became the dominant religion of the Roman Empire, the baseline became the birth of Christ for calendars in Europe. Everything after his birth got the letters AD attached to it and everything before his birth got the letters BC attached to it. The problem with that is, however, nobody knew precisely when Christ was born. Therefore, there are inconsistencies from 3 to 7 years in the baseline and some historians claim much more.

"In addition, the Egyptian calendar or Julian Calendar had an error which was corrected by Pope Gregory -- an algorithm was introduced to account for the leap years which is very confusing to say the least. To add to this confusion different countries of Europe adopted Gregory's calendar at different times. In particular England and Russia.

"Therefore, when you read an account of the Spanish Armada in English, the dates don't match with the Spanish version and visa versa of course.

"In Russia, the Gregorian Calendar was introduced by Czar Peter I, and they are out of sync by 13 days with Western Europe. Therefore, the Soviets celebrated the October Revolution in November and so on.

"Then you have the Jewish calendar, it is described in the 'Apocrypha,' Nicodemus Chapter 22. It begins with Adam and the Garden of Eden. There, it is implied that from creation to Adam 500 years elapsed. From Adam to the flood took another 2212 years. From the flood to Abraham took 912 years. From Abraham to Moses 430 years elapsed. From Moses to David took 510 years. From David to the Babylonian Captivity you have 500 years. And, from the Babylonian captivity you have 400 years until the birth of Christ. That is, from creation to the birth of Christ 5,464 years elapsed..."

"At least we have a reference,..." I started when Bacchus interrupted me.

"Why don't you reconcile the Mayan calendar with yours and the Jewish calendar and come up with the right calendar to begin with?" He paused, sort of challenging my response.

I was not sure what he was getting at. Could it be Atlantis? Plato referred to Atlantis in his discourse in 'The Republic.' How did the Mayans create such a perfect calendar I asked myself?

Bacchus was reading my mind, he continued.

"The Mayan calendar is off by 1 day in 14,000 years. For the same period, the Gregorian Calendar is off by more than 4 days, and the Julian calendar is off by 113 days..."

"How did they arrive at such an accurate calendar," I asked.

"Well, nobody is sure, but there are many theories floating around. The one I like best is based on Plato's discussion. In effect, Plato said that a huge island existed where the Azores are located now. In his words, 'it was larger than Asia--meaning Asia Minor, and Libya combined.' Or roughly 400,000 square miles in size.

"In the north was a huge mountain range. The tallest mountain in that chain was called Mount Atlas -- it was a volcano. It was over 30,000 feet tall and was forever covered by large clouds. This gave the appearance that Mount Atlas was holding up the sky. Therefore the myth evolved that Atlas himself was holding up the sky and shielding the earth. Of course later historians said that Atlas was holding up the earth, which was more palatable to your race.

"In the south of the island was a huge plain. It was very fertile and supported a very large and highly advanced civilization -- more than 1 million souls.

"Since it was semi-tropical and was shielded from the north by the huge mountain chain, it produced many fruits unknown to Europe at that time, such as: bananas, mangos and much more.

"It stands to reason that this civilization colonized both America, Europe, Africa and Asia minor. This is how the Mayans got the calendar.

"Then, at 'time zero' according to the Mayan calendar, a terrible catastrophe occurred. A huge asteroid hit the Atlantic Ocean, just off the coast of Georgia in America. The impact was so great that it shifted the Tectonic Plates in the Atlantic Ocean which are riddled with submerged volcanos to begin with, separating the Tectonic Plates and causing the largest catastrophe ever experience by your planet Earth. A colossal volcanic eruption ensued spreading many billion tons of ash, and a huge flood -- nearly inundating the entire human race. The entire island of Atlantis disappeared from the surface of the Atlantic Ocean.

"This calamity explains many physical phenomena. To begin with; the fertile crescent. Which begins in Europe as a narrow band, becomes large in the Ukraine and much larger in China. That is, the jet-streams deposited that fertile soil a long time ago. Now it has turned into the 'black earth' which is as much as 6 feet deep throughout the fertile crescent. This also explains why for over 3,000 years thereafter the Atlantic Ocean was not navigable -- the ash turned into slush and was not absorbed by the waters of the Atlantic Ocean until about 5,000 BC. This is why Homer wrote the Odyssey: to show the known world that the Atlantic Ocean was again open for navigation...

"What was that 'zero base' of the Mayan calendar," I asked.

"June 1, 8498 BC" Bacchus answered...

Hermes turned to me and said: "This interview was meant to be short. We'll have another chance to talk to Bacchus. Let's be on our way, ..." as he extended his rod to me.

"Thank you Bacchus," I heard myself saying as I grabbed the rod. As soon as I did, we floated away into space to yet another destination.

15

Zeus

We were back in our familiar place in no time at all. 'How time flies' is all I thought. Hermes made himself comfortable on the rock and said:

"Let's resume the threads of history. Let me shift to America for a moment and then I'll bring the pieces together. Is that ok?" Hermes asked.

I only nodded my head.

"Despite the colossal commitments America made to rebuild Europe and Japan, America made even greater commitments at home for her returning GI's. It was called the GI-BILL: free education, free medicine, affordable housing, affordable household and convenience gadgets of all kinds. American genius worked overtime optimizing, minimizing, maximizing and miniaturizing.

"The 'All-American' dream became to own a home in suburbia; equip that home with the latest gadgets: refrigerator, stove and dishwasher; own a car, a radio, a telephone; praise the Lord and raise a family...

"Just like Henry Ford had made the Model T affordable to everyone in 1903, Levit made homes affordable to everyone in the 1950's. Levittown USA became the buzzword overnight. Every returning GI had a job waiting for him, and every job afforded the credit to buy a home, a car and all the luxuries.

"All that was needed was to upgrade America's highway system. Until then, 'The Lincoln Highway' was the main road which linked the West Coast with the East Coast. Most roads in America were paved Indian trails, such as US 1, US 17 and so on. The new cars coming off the assembly lines were bigger and better. They needed real highways, the kind the American GI's had found in Germany -- 'The Autobahn.'

"Thus, an entire modern highway system was constructed-- limited access roads called 'Interstate Highways:' from Miami to Maine, from Maine to Seattle, from Seattle to San Diego, and from San Diego to Florida and much more. Over the next 50 years, over 1 million miles of highways were added to America's grid.

"Then came new products: television, computers, microwave, laser and wireless-telephone. Airtravel became affordable as Americans travelled the world over. All this was done while new weapon-systems forced the Soviet Union to keep pace with the Cold War -- escalating until she was utterly exhausted and bankrupt.

"Of course, the cardinal mistake of the Soviet Union was her misuse of her most precious resource, her people. While Stalin manned his Gulags in Siberia, America harnessed her people in great industrial projects which provided consumer goods at home and exports for her partners aboard. An unprecedented wave of prosperity started in America which has continued to this day. Competition in America produced the most affordable products possible, starting with the Model T, to housing, to clothing, to food, to computers, to the 'Two Buck Chuck,' a vintage wine at $1.99 per bottle.

"However, while America basked in her wealth, the rest of the world began resenting America's genius, including her trade partners. They became jealous of her accomplishments-- especially in England and France. Once the Americans pulled out, their factories were neglected, their products became uncompetitive. France found an ally in Germany, but England, still clinging to her Colonial Empire, began to crumble. In England, more cities decayed due to the neglect and obsolescence of her factories than were damaged by German air-raids. Today, all the cost-effective colonies are gone. They all gained independence except for Canada and Australia. Most abandoned the Commonwealth altogether, and they are on the verge of losing Canada and Australia too. What will be left will be a Commonwealth of nearly deserted rocks that are nothing but a liability to Great Britain.

"The gradual erosion of British power manifests itself with the Pound Sterling. As late as the late 1960's it was $4.80 to the US Dollar. Now it is about $1.60. And, if that trend continues, it will be roughly $.45 by 2020. But it does not end there. This is only the beginning. The culprit is what you might call 'Reverse Migration.'

"The fruits of European Colonialism are coming home to roost. The former colonial powers have to support their colonial subjects instead of the other way around, but since each major European power administered her colonies somewhat differently, let's look at them from their perspective.

"Spain ceased to be a colonial power by 1899, leaving her hardly affected. Yet Muslims have moved into Spain. Today, 500 years after the Moors were evicted from Granada, a Mosque is being built there.

"In the British Commonwealth, all natives in the employment of the Crown became British subjects. That is, in India, Egypt, Pakistan, Bangladesh, Malaysia and so on. As these colonies gained independence, many of their subjects moved to England, and, from England, many moved to America.

"America's quota system makes it far easier to enter America from England than from their native land. America is much larger and much better equipped to absorb that migration. England, however, is not. Many of her new arrivals are Muslims. They started to build Mosques. By the late 1980's, many of the Muslims turned radical, while the Mosques expanded. By the end of 2003, there will be 1200 Mosques in Great Britain, with a fair number of them in London. And, if that trend continues, London could be called Londanabad by 2010...

"In France, the situation is much the same, even though her approach to colonial rule was slightly different. Many of the colonies are 'Departments' or extensions of France. Hence the population are French subjects. For example: Algeria, Morocco, Tunisia and so on. Many of these subjects moved to France once they gained independence, and many of them have settled in Paris. However, although they were not allowed to build Mosques, they too have a fair share of radicals. But France decided to 'outlaw' all sects and close down their centers of worship, for fear that Paris may be called Paristanbul...

"This of course affected not only the Muslims but all Christian sects, specifically the Baptists. Belgium and The Netherlands are also affected somewhat in between these two modes of reverse migration.

"In Germany the situation is entirely different. Germany lost her colonies after World War I, but the economic boom generated by the Marshall-Plan created many jobs that were not filled, especially in her transportation industry: street-cars, buses and so on. Thus, Germany began importing 'Gastarbeiters,' (guest workers) primarily from Turkey, Syria and Lebanon.

"Most of them are Muslims and many of them are radical. Until the collapse of the Soviet Union that was not a problem. There were plenty of jobs. But when East Germany became 'available,' West-Germany jumped at the opportunity to re-unite Germany at any cost. In the process they discovered that the West-German work ethic had been replaced with complacency and incompetence in East Germany. The entire generation of East-German workers had to be carried and retrained. Thus, the 'Gast-arbeiters' became a real drain on the German economy. However, because Germany had been brow-beaten into ethnic and religious tolerance with the 'Holocaust Scenario,' they let France do the bidding for them. All is now quiet in Germany on the surface, but the pot is near a boiling point, ready to explode. Germany's plan, is that, as the European Union will expand to the East, they will pawn off their problems there.

"To sum up the reverse-migration scenario, the radical Muslims have found a safe and wealthy sanctuary in Europe which they plan to saturate and take over. The major stumbling block for Europeans to take a more active role against that silent subversion is the American presence in Europe. Once America leaves Western Europe, the stage will be set for an ethnic and religious cleansing...

"By the way, Hitler's star is rising in Western Europe, particularly in the least expected country of all -- England. A number of Hitler-Historians have emerged. They claim that the holocaust never happened. Their main argument is that it takes 26 kilos of coal to burn one human body. Hence, Germany did not have the coal resources of coal to commit such wholesale atrocities...

"Now, let's look at the UN. The UN was conceived at the Yalta conference, by Roosevelt, Stalin and Churchill. I emphasize this hierarchy in accordance with their seating order. Roosevelt was seated in the center, hence he was the leader. Churchill was seated to his right but close by. While Stalin was seated to his left. Symbolically this suggested that Churchill was the right-hand-man of Roosevelt, while Stalin was an independent force.This is in accordance with military formations. At Yalta, protocol became important. Roosevelt gave the body its name: United Nations.

"In any event, prior to Yalta, two attempts were made to set up a world-governing body. Both times they failed miserably. The first attempt was Czar Alexander I's Holy Alliance, which deteriorated at the very beginning in Vienna.While the monarchies were restored and all monarchs agreed to join, it ended up consisting of only Austria, Prussia and Russia.

"The second attempt was the League of Nations. It was formed after World War I and had no teeth. Mussolini, Japan and Hitler violated its very charter while everybody else sat idly by. This time the 'Big Three' were going to do it right. But, from the very start they hit many roadblocks.

"It was agreed to establish a permanent Security Council. Furthermore, it was agreed that it should be headed by the Big Three and any action by the UN had to be agreed on unanimously by them. By then, the liberation of France was in progress and Churchill asked for the inclusion of France. Stalin rejected the idea and suggested the creation of a subordinate council of the 'Big Five.' This was to include France on Churchill's side and China on Stalin's side. However, Mao was not yet in control. Thus the Nationalists under Chang Kai Check got the 'seat.' Of course Stalin knew that very soon Mao would be in control and he fully expected that seat to go to Mao. So, he did not press that point.

"Next, it came to the eligible member nations. Churchill wanted all nations who had declared war on the Axis powers by March 1, 1945 to be eligible to join. Stalin wanted each Soviet Republic included, 16 of them. So, they haggled for a while. Stalin got concessions in Central Europe, which was under his control already and scaled down his request to include Byelorussia and the Ukraine. This made some 50 nations to be eligible for the UN to join. Thus, when Stalin walked away from Yalta he was left with the impression that the Security Council was to consist of the Big Three and some 50 eligible nations would form the General Assembly.

"The first meeting of the UN assembly was held in San Francisco, in the Opera House on April 25, 1945. There the final draft was hammered out. Roosevelt had died and President Truman attended the proceedings in his stead. But now the Security Council consisted of the Big Five instead of the Big Three. This became one major point of friction at the Potsdam Conference of the Big Three. In any event, the final Charter was signed on June 26, 1945. And, in America it was approved by the Senate by 89 to 2, on July 28, 1945. The UN officially opened on October 24, 1945.

"By the end of the year it became clear that the Opera House was not quite suitable for its operation. To begin with, the city wanted its Opera House back, UN or no-UN. The UN migrated East to New York City, but New York City was in a building boom and there was no suitable location available. For the next year or so, the UN met in an ad-hoc fashion in facilities in Flushing Meadows Park and Hunter College. However, in 1946, the John D. Rockefeller Foundation donated 6 blocks to the UN in New York City to establish permanent quarters.

"The UN consists of a General Assembly; 5 major councils: Security, Justice, Secretariat, Economic and Social, and

Trusteeship; and some 36 specialized agencies plus a host of other administrative bodies. The original idea of eligible members was scrapped by 1949. By then, all nations became eligible. Thus, as new nations emerged, mostly from colonial rule, they became eligible for the UN. And, in no time at all it became a forum dedicated to US bashing. This is akin to the cult of Ahura Mazda. Why worship the good deity, appease the devil...

"In any event, no sooner had the UN became established when two trouble spots developed in 1947: Kashmir and Palestine, and they have remained problems to this day.

"By 1950, the Nationalists in China had been defeated by Mao and moved to Taiwan. The Soviets demanded the seat for Mao. However, by then, the Cold War was in full swing, so the West refused to give up a valuable pro-western vote. The Soviets boycotted the UN and while they were absent, a vote was passed in the Security Council to launch a 'Police Action' in Korea...

"Of course, in America it is called the Korean War. However, the rest of the world calls it a UN Police Action. This was the last time the Soviets boycotted the UN by leaving the Security Council.

"As new nations became independent they joined the UN, changing the count from the original 50 to over 200 today. This body quickly deteriorated into 'Blocs.' The Western Bloc, the Soviet Bloc, the Non-Aligned Bloc, the Muslim Bloc, the African Bloc and so on. Tiny 'Banana Republics' began dominating the proceedings. By 1980, it was obvious that the original intent and purpose of the UN had been perverted. What was needed was a multi-tier system such as a Security Council, Senate and House. That is the Big Three, the mid-size Ten and the General Assembly. This prompted Ares to say that the gangs in the Bronx were better organized than the UN...

"Practically each year some UN Police action occurred in Africa or Asia. The larger ones were carried out mostly by the USA. But they did not serve America at all. They benefited either England as in Somalia and Kuwait or Germany as in Bosnia. The largest intervention being the war against Iraq in 1991.

"Since the UN ceased to be a forum for the major industrial powers to resolve issues, a new forum was created by America. Initially, it was called G7. After the Soviet Union disintegrated, it became known as G8, which included Russia.

"In time, the precedent evolved that America picked up the tab at the UN while everybody else pleaded poverty. Technically, each nation owes her fair share of the expenses authorized, but they quickly learned at the UN that the best way not to pay their share was to plead destitution. America always picked up the tab, but, as soon as each bill was paid by America, America was trashed in the UN. Keeping the peace at all cost, in a mob-like atmosphere at the present day UN, has become not only very expensive but highly counter-productive.

"This abuse has been going on for too long and America got tired of it. In 2003 a bill was introduced in America in the House to take America out of the UN and the UN out of America.

"Actually, this process is well underway. Some branches of the UN have moved to Geneva, Switzerland and Vienna, Austria already. What remains in New York City is the Security Council and the General Assembly. That is, the mob, which is bent on chastising America.

"Where would the UN move? The most obvious location will be Rome. Thus, the old capital of the Roman Empire will once again administer the New Order, but you can be assured that when they move they will restructure the General Assembly and the Security Council...

"Two other aspects are worth mentioning. The first is, subversive agents and the International Court.

"All members of the General Assembly and some members of their staff enjoy diplomatic immunity. This allows them to bring their most radical elements, spies, terrorists and other malcontents into America. Once they are there, they not only take the valuable parking spaces in New York City but they can pursue their sordid activity under the cloak of diplomatic immunity. This allows them to plot, plan and pursue the demise of America in the open and then flaunt it.

"From the inception of the UN, the International Court was delegated to The Hague, The Netherlands. For the next 30 years it was inactive, trying to 'define' its mission and purpose; but, as soon as the European Union became a reality, it has crystallized its purpose. Using the Nürnberg trials as their model, the International Court has embarked on a program to cleanse Germany and to punish America...

"Cleansing Germany takes on the form of identifying a culprit and then try him 'Nürnberg Style' for the alleged atrocities. Eventually, once enough culprits are tried and convicted, they will downplay the culpability of the Germans tried in Nürnberg. How do they identify a culprit? Simple. Any member nation of the UN can submit a 'candidate' of their wrath. In this way, a number of American names have been submitted already, but, for now, their charges have been dismissed. Thus, while Milosovich is tried by the court, Arial Sharon is under review. But, because America is drawn into every conflict the world over, it is only a matter of time before a prominent American will become a target...

"On September 11, 2001, America got a wake-up call. Four Arab suicide-commandos, mostly Saudi and Egyptians, attacked the World Trade Center in New York City and the Pentagon in Washington DC. One suicide-commando failed in its mission, presumably to attack the White House. It became known as 'Nine-Eleven.' These synchronized attacks changed the complacency of America, just like Pearl Harbor did in World War II. President George W Bush Jr., declared war on terrorism. Hot-beds of anti-American terrorism were identified and targeted: Afghanistan and the Axis of Evil -- Iraq, Iran and North Korea. A world-wide dragnet against terrorists was also initiated.

"Since America did not want to act unilaterally, she tried to use the available channels first. That is, the UN. While action against Afghanistan was ratified, action against Iraq met opposition. Thus, the battle-cry in America became: 'With the UN or without the UN.'

"Once again, America took the initiative. She warned her opposition, and, when they rebuffed America's demands, they were invaded and defeated. However, while America was swift in winning the war, she has now an even bigger task in front of her, in winning the peace...

"The main opposition to America's action came from France, with Germany not too far behind. Oh, how soon the French have forgotten that when her liberties were at stake, America came to her rescue in the last two wars. Had it not been for America, they would be sipping beer and eating Weisswurst and Sauerkraut today...

"Let's get back to Germany for a moment. Germany was rebuilt in 'waves,' beginning with the currency reform, followed by a building boom, an industrial boom and a global economy trade boom. Within less than 50 years after the war, Germany was again an industrial giant in Europe. Of course, the reasons were obvious. New, streamlined factories in Germany outperformed the old and dilapidated factories in England and France. While France lives under the illusion of being a great power, South Korea now has a greater GNP than France. And England is even worse off. Their major exports are the Beatles and now Harry Potter...

"Along the way, during the Chancellorship of Adenauer, Germany and France saw eye to eye on their future policy in Europe. This policy was consistent with Napoleon and Hitler. I.e, begin with a European Trade Alliance which would stimulate trade. Then, introduce a common currency, then a common defense strategy with a common army to match. This would create the Europe Napoleon had formed. Finally, sway the Eastern-Block countries to join that alliance until Hitler's abortive attempt at Kursk, to define the new borders of Western Europe will be accomplished. When Byelorussia and the Ukraine join that Union, Phase One of Hitler's back-up plan will have been accomplished. This would leave Russia on her own, and, given enough economic incentives, Russia herself will join that Union.

"Accordingly, European Trade Alliances were formed in 1956 and by 1973, 23 nations of Europe were part of that alliance, from Andorra to Yugoslavia. In 1990, the unthinkable happened. The mighty Soviet Empire collapsed. This opened the window for the Soviet Republics and satellites to declare independence and seek alliances with the European Union. East Germany, a satellite of the Soviet Union, was 'released' on October 3, 1990, and, in quick succession the other satellites followed: Albania, Bulgaria, Czechoslovakia, Hungary and Poland.

"Yugoslavia had left with Tito and was accepted into the European Union in 1969. While Turkey had joined the European Union in 1960 (Phase One, member of Europa).

"Meanwhile, Great Britain applied in 1961. But France held her acceptance back until her economic standards were brought up to par with the rest of the European Union. Finally, in June of 1971, Great Britain was accepted in their Phase One: economic alliance. Phase Two being a common currency on which Great Britain will vote in June of 2003.

"In 1991, the Soviet Union started to break up. In 1991, Estonia, Latvia and Lithuania broke away. In March 1992, Byelorussia, Ukraine and the other republics broke away from the Soviet Union.

"Now, the Russian Republic herself is on the verge of disintegrating. Starting with Chechnya and in the hinterlands in Siberia. In the end, what may be left of Russia is the old Duchy of Muscovy, prior to the rule of Ivan the Terrible."

"How can this possibly happen?" I interrupted Hermes. So he explained.

"On our visit with Hera, you chose to ignore her findings on migrations. So, I will give only a short version, as I know it from her. Here is the crux of the matter.

"When China introduced the 'one-child' policy to stem her growth, many Chinese started to migrate to Siberia to raise more children. Keep in mind, Russia's border with China is far greater than America's border with Mexico. Yet America is unable to stem the covert migration of Mexicans. Well, in a similar way, Russia is unable to stem the migration of the Chinese into Siberia.

"Siberia is now predominantly Chinese. But, very much like the Mexicans, they are not counted in the census. Thus, the census data for Siberia is grossly misleading.

"There are two forces at work in that area. First, within the next 20 years there will be a dire shortage of women in China. Why? Because, the 'one-child' policy favors male children to be kept and females to be aborted or given up for adoption. Thus, China is headed towards an 'all-male' society. This, of course is an absurdity, and, sooner or later, this will come to a violent climax...

"Second, the only remedy to this policy is to emigrate, but all doors are shut to the Chinese except for Siberia. Hence, they migrate to Siberia. Today they are illegal aliens. Tomorrow, however, they will be legal citizens for two reasons. Their children will be natives by virtue of birth, and Siberia needs the population to harvest her resources and bring them to market. Once they gain the vote, they will dominate policy in Siberia. But, their policy will be to link up with China, not Russia. Thus, eventually Siberia will be lost, leaving Russia only with the Moscow-St.Petersburg enclaves.

"That area is exceptionally poor in mineral resources and agricultural land, moving Russia towards a crisis of unparalleled proportions. Therefore, Russia is more than eager now, to strike a permanent deal to circumvent that entire issue.

"It was not until the 1990's that America started taking steps to create a market for herself outside of Europe. This is called the 'Free Trade Agreement.'

"The model for that market was Canada with whom America has had longstanding free trade, whereby duties and taxes on most products were eliminated, starting in the late 1950's. This program has benefited both Canada and America to the point that, for all practical purposes, the border between Canada and America has been eliminated. It exists only as an imaginary line. This arrangement stimulated not only free trade but tourism as well. So much so that many Canadians own summer homes 'South of the Border.' That is, in America, and, more specifically, in Florida, Texas, New Mexico and California.

"In the late 1970's, this was extended to the Caribbean Basin and Puerto Rico became the prime beneficiary of that program. Puerto Rico enhanced this program by offering tax shelters to American companies and they moved to Puerto Rico in droves.

"Starting in the 1990's, Mexico was offered the opportunity to participate in a similar fashion, and, after Mexico, all of Latin America was offered a similar program. America is now focusing on Brazil, the idea being that if Brazil signs a 'Free Trade Agreement' all other South American nations will follow suit.

"In the late 1990's, a similar program was initiated in the Pacific Rim basin, from Korea to Australia which many nations are considering quite seriously.

"Nine Eleven and its aftermath, America's targeting of Afganistan and Iraq for harboring terrorists and developing weapons of mass destruction, presented a unique opportunity for all supporters of America's Free Trade Agreement to shine. All they had to do was to support America's initiative at the UN to be counted alongside her. But, in that hour of need, very few of them supported America, in particular Mexico and Chile. Mexico, because she already is a member of America's Free Trade Agreement. And Chile, because she was about to join the Free Trade Agreement with America.

"Only Great Britain supported America in word and deed. Partially, this was expected because Iraq was a former oil-rich British colony.

"But a few countries deserve special mention: Poland and Singapore. Poland, because she might switch from the European Union in favor of an American Free Trade Agreement. This could unravel parts of the Curzon Line, especially with Byelorussia and the Ukraine, if they join America's Free Trade Agreement. Thus, when President George W. Bush Jr. made his tour of Europe to mend relations with France and exert more pressure for his 'Road Map for Peace' in the Middle East, he made a special stop in Poland. This stop could have significant implications in the future...

"Meanwhile, Singapore joined America's Free Trade Agreement shortly after the UN vote, where she supported America, and, instead of signing that Free Trade Agreement on the West Coast of America in May 2003, Prime Minister Goh Chok Tong was invited to the White House and the agreement was signed there. Chile, which joined the Free Trade Agreement on June 6, 2003, was delegated to Miami where Governor Jeb Bush, President Bush's brother attended the ceremonies." Hermes paused briefly.

"I find these events very encouraging. Maybe, just maybe America has cracked the code of France and Germany, and, if America plays her cards right in the next few months, she could stop that entire Franco-Teutonic menace altogether. In fact, I think I am going to visit President Bush on my next outing." Hermes said pensively. Then he continued:

"As you can see, the path to a European Union is not exactly smooth and is not yet cast in concrete, but now is the time to strike a deal with Russia. Remember, she is a consumer nation, not a producer nation, an ideal candidate America. And, at the same time America could torpedo a good part of the Franco-German agenda. America is under siege and bold action is required. America's Free Trade Agreement includes only six partners so far: Canada, Mexico, Chile, Singapore, Israel and Jordan. What do you think?" Hermes asked me.

"I think you hit the nail right on the head. I think it is high time for us to stake out our turf and cut the European Union down to size. To tell you the truth, I have been wondering when we will take the initiative. I am glad we finally have!" I exclaimed.

"Let me finish with this installment and then we will discuss the possibilities..."

As I nodded my head, Hermes got up and shoved his rod into my hand. I held on and we were off.

Our journey ended in front of a huge pagoda. In front of the pagoda was an endless staircase. At least 288 steps, I thought. On the third step stood an old man. His posture was that of an old man. He looked like a Buddhist priest, yet he was not. He wore a turban on his head and one eye was covered with a patch. He held a large shepherd's crook in his right hand.

"Your messenger Hermes salutes you," I heard Hermes exclaim.

This had to be Zeus, I thought. How different he looked from all the statues I have seen of him. This man had no hair at all. Not on his head. Not on his face and not on his arms or legs. The reality was not what I had expected.

The man turned towards me and asked: "So, what have you learned from the many aspects?"

"Market timing is a tough problem but history is worse. I hope I have the energy to tackle market timing correctly ..."

"Which aspect do you think is more important: Selection or portfolio management?" he asked me.

I was not ready for this question. Until now I was concentrating on selection. Portfolio management was far removed from my mind at this time. First, I needed models to make the best possible selection. Besides, there were some decent portfolio management techniques around: CAP, based on the capital asset pricing theory. APT, based on the arbitrage pricing theory.

Immunization techniques, based on the business needs and many more.

If I could pick a real winner with each selection, then portfolio management became redundant and management was greatly simplified. Each selection had an investment horizon. Hence, each selection had an implied redemption date. Portfolio management was reduced to an administrative task to execute the buy-sell alternatives.

"Quite truthfully," I said "... I had no time to worry about the portfolio management aspect of market timing."

"Is that because you think that selection in and of itself will circumvent the totality of the problem or is your presence premature?" he asked.

"There are many good portfolio management methods around. Most are widely accepted ..."

"Name me one," Zeus interrupted me.

"Ok," I started concentrating "... how about APT" I blurted out.

"That's only a theory. It has been applied only in an up-market. Even there, it's performance is not exactly anything to rave about. Marginal improvement yes. Systematic improvement is yet to be demonstrated. Plus, performance of this theory remains untested in a down-market. In other words; nothing concrete. Only speculations. Do you want to try another?" he asked me.

"How about immunization?" I asked.

"Well, what about immunization? True, Bierwag demonstrated correctly that any portfolio can be represented by two bonds, one with short the other with long maturity. Cast against this portfolio is an anticipated cash outflow. Then, immunization is the process to match the income or redemption stream against this cash outflow. What makes you think the required bonds exist in the universe of available bonds to suit this purpose?" he asked.

"If they don't exist we can use point by point dedication," I replied.

"Again, your method will only work if the required bonds exist. Otherwise, you are approximating and you introduce an error. Besides, how do you reconcile duration and market duration?" he asked.

"I know, I know ..." as I nodded my head, "call schedules are still a real problem. There is even a third type of duration. I call it optimum duration. But, that terminology has not yet found wide acceptance," I added.

"You see," Zeus continued, "... within this order and reason there is another multitude of choices. Which choices are better?" he asked me.

"Off hand, I would say that systematically better choices should produce better results in the end," I answered.

"Bravo. Spoken like a true futures trader. But then you should be concentrating on improving the APT theory and forego being a better stock picker," he replied.

"My experience, however, has shown that outstanding stock selections produce superior results," I answered back.

"Bravo again. Now, you seem to imply that portfolio management is the management of past errors in judgement rather than the deliberate structure of a portfolio to achieve a specific goal, ..."

"Oh no," I interrupted him " ... I did not mean that at all. I meant that opportunities to choose a stellar stock present themselves rarely. Meanwhile, a systematic optimum return is expected from a portfolio manager. Thus, a portfolio manger can not rely on the fact that a superior stock will be available for selection. And a portfolio manager may be constrained within the universe of stocks available to him for selection," I replied.

"You see, there are many other aspects to the problem. The totality of these aspects need to be addressed for a complete solution," Zeus replied. After a brief pause he started again.

"By and large the American investor has been sold on the premise that professional investment management is superior to personal money management. This is not the case. This concept has been sold in terms of a risk tolerance factor. Simply stated it says that risk tolerance decreases linearly with age. The standard formula advocated is:

percent risk tolerance = 100 - age

"This formula clearly favors the stock market, and this formula is false in many respects. First, let us look for investors approaching retirement. By definition, retirement is the age at which the investor gives up his regular job and lives of the fruits of his past labors. In America this age is 65 right now. This is because for most workers Social Security kicks in at that age.

"Then, according to this formula, market gurus suggest that: 35% should be invested in equities and 65% should be invested in fixed income securities. That is, in the stock market and in the bond market respectively. In the stock market, however, the down-side risk is 100%. That is, it is entirely possible to lose your entire investment. Therefore, the investor must not follow this formula blindly but ask the question: 'can I continue to live in the life-style I am accustomed to, if I loose 35% of my assets?' If the answer is yes I can, then by all means use that formula if that suits you. However, in most cases this is a resounding no, because periodically the market wipes out the euphoric investors. To demonstrate my case as just look at: 1929, 1941, 1962, 1986 and 2001.

"When the answer is no, however, the investor must find better uses for that portion of the money: pay off the credit card debt, pay off the mortgage and so on. This will directly increase the monthly income, if done properly. The key is, the investor must do what is best for him and not what is best for the market guru, he only tries to separate you from your money, if need be with a 'crow bar.' That is, with all the market razzle-dazzle in his repertoire. His number one weapon is to 'raise your greed level.' His number two weapon is to 'take that opportunity away.' This creates urgency and panic. Then the investor becomes prey.

"Now let's look at the fixed income portion of the portfolio, the other 65%. There, the primary goal should be preservation of capital or protection from default. The most secure bonds in that area are: Government bonds, bills or notes or bonds guaranteed by the US Government. The reason being: if the US Government defaults, all other bonds will default -- no matter what their rating..."

"Do you mean the rating system in place is no value at all?" I asked.

"The value of the ratings assigned to each issue serves Wall Street, not the investor. Just look at the ratings for 1976 to 1982 -- when interest rates were high. The original rating system as defined by Moody was: AAA, AA, A and BAA for investment grade bonds. It was changed to: AAA, AA1, AA2, AA3, A1, A2, A3 and BAA1, BAA2, BAA3. Doesn't this demonstrate that the original rating was false to begin with? What makes you think that the new ratings are any better? The only rating which is of only any value is a trade based market rating...

"Besides, when high grade companies were facing bankruptcy they were still touted to investors -- such as WOOPS and others.

Consequently, ratings have to be treated with great caution. They are at best an indicator. That's all..."

"But, our tax-structure favors Municipal bonds over Corporate bonds in certain situations," I said.

"That's all fine and good. All I am saying is, as far as safety is concerned, the US Government bonds, bills and notes are in a class by themselves. Everything else, as far as I am concerned, are 'Junk Bonds.'

"Keep in mind that long-term yields in excess of 8% are not sustainable by the stock market, even though many market gurus will claim that they consistently outperform the market and generate as much as 22%. This is possible only in very special situations and not in the long haul. My word of advise is don't become a victim of rogue companies..."

"You mean rogue brokers..." I piped in.

"No, I mean rogue companies, because the companies set the tone, they monitor their brokers and they should be held accountable. Putting the blame on the broker, is like blaming the janitor for 'Nine-Eleven.' Invariably, of course, the broker is blamed anyway, but the main culprit is the company which allows that broker to run amok.

"For example, in the 1990's, Prudential Financial sold limited partnerships under the guise of 'risk free' investments. Many fell for that ploy and those who did, lost their money. Eventually, Prudential Financial was made to reimburse the investors, which resulted with pennies to the dollar invested. But, that was such a blatant case of fraud that I am surprised Prudential Financial was allowed to remain in the financial industry at all.

"An investor who is careless will find himself separated from his money -- his capital. Some think they can re-enter the job market and make up their losses. This is much easier said than done. As a rule, once you retire and stay out of your profession for more than one year, kiss your job good-bye. America worships the 'youth-culture,' therefore after age 40 new jobs are hard to come by; after 50 you will be shunned like the plague and after 60 only the most menial jobs are available to you..."

"How about your own business..." I interjected.

"That will work, especially in America. That is the singular viable alternative, but only a few are equipped to pursue that alternative..."

"Are you suggesting that only 'mad-money' should be used in the stock-market and all other liquid investments be in US Government bonds, notes or bills?" I asked.

"If you want to enjoy your retirement, then this is what I am suggesting, yes. In fact, I am suggesting one more thing. When you invest in the stock market you must control that investment yourself. Here is the reason why:

"Portfolio managers have demonstrated time and again that they are not equipped to handle market down-turns. The reason is because they are evaluated themselves on a short-time basis by their bosses and when they don't meet the market expectations they are out of a job. In addition, because they handle large portfolios, they can not use short term 'protection strategies' like puts and calls when the situation arises.

"The reason they use 'diversification' is to hide their selection errors. Diversification works when there are minor downturns in market sectors. But it does not work at all when the market declines on a broad front.

"In an up-market it works for them -- but then any stock picked randomly works just as well if not better. In a down-market it works against them. That's why the 'random walk Theory' is so prevalent to this day. That is, the portfolio managers are muscle-bound by their portfolio. A much better strategy is to have reasonable diversification which can be covered with puts and calls when the market dictates such action. An individual investor can use these tools effectively without being whip-sawed by the market. Here is another reason why only optionable stocks are investment candidates..."

"But, then every investor must be a pro..." I piped in.

"That's why it is so important to become a financially astute investor. You have a saying in your country: 'if you can't take the heat in the kitchen, then get out'..."

"What about Mutual Funds?" I asked.

"Didn't I just cover that? Just look what happened in the last down-turn. Mutual Funds were the biggest losers...

"Now let's look at a young investor, say age 20. Then, the formula suggests to put 80% into the stock market and 20% into the bond market. Again this formula favors Wall Street. It depends what the risk-free rate is. If it is over 8%, all of the funds should go into bonds. If it is below 6% for the Bellwether bond, then the formula may apply with caution. I say with caution, because again the investor must invest according to his needs and what suits him best. The single biggest investment is to own a home. This need not be a house, it way well be a condo or co-op or some such thing. To begin with, we all need a roof over our head. In that respect, it is essential to make that the first order of business. Historically speaking, most investors in a home have done exceptionally well and to boot, their investment is highly leveraged. Therefore, at an early age instead of investing in the market, invest in your long-term needs -- a home. Only when that nut is covered consider putting money into the market. Again, the overriding factor should be what is best for the investors in the long term. Now, at age 20, 5 years could seem like a long term, but I mean at least 10 to 30 years. That should be the investment horizon..."

"Are mutual funds ok at that age?" I asked.

"Only if the investor is ready to relinquish the control of his capital. Then, any Mutual Fund with a guaranteed fixed return of 8% or more can be considered. Almost by definition such a fund would be 80% in bonds or more and the rest in stocks, probably in high dividend paying stocks..."

"What about low priced emerging companies? They have often spectacular performance results..." I piped in.

"That may be so. But their default rate is more than 90% and of the remaining 10%, 90% turn into dogs. That is, out of 100 stocks, only one may be a winner. I think that in the long haul, a good, steady return will beat practically every stock ever issued. In fact, it is safer to invest in puts and call than into low priced stocks..."

"How does this affect the global economy?" I inquired.

"There are three major trading exchange clusters: America, Pacific Rim and Europe. They are dominated by the NYSE in America, Nikkei in Japan and DAX in Germany. By and large, America sets the sentiment because it is the largest market. It is also the most sensitive.

"It is often said that corporations in America have no soul and are insensitive to socio-economic needs. This manifests itself in loss of facilities and outsourcing -- to use cheaper labor markets. This pressure comes from the investors. They demand improved earnings. The easiest way to improve earnings is to cut salaries, jobs or both. When that does not work, the entire company migrates to anther country. Once the trend begins, the entire industry follows suit. This way America has lost one company after another and one industry after another. And, with it the jobs.

"The underlying economic theory being that jobs which are menial can be shifted to countries with a much lower minimum wage. This in turn suggests that better jobs are kept and the minimum wage increases. In particular, labor intensive jobs can be shifted to other countries outside of America. In the end, marginal production facilities are shut down and employees lose their jobs. Of course, this is only a theory and more often than not it results in massive unemployment and discontent. But, because America has been at the forefront of technological innovations this theory, by and large finds many supporters.

"This insensitive job slashing and industry migration technique is claimed to be the only way to keep America's market efficient. Again, this is an underlying Theory. This Theory suggests that a range of 2% to 6% of unemployment can be managed this way. With 2% being pegged as 'full employment,' which is inflationary and 6% and over as a recession.

"Japan follows a different model. Companies in Japan hire workers for life. This builds strong company loyalty. Until the 'reserve requirements' were revised to match the Western model, Japan had a great amount of excess cash and was ready to 'buy up the world.' However, as soon as she agreed to conform 'gradually' to the Western model, that excess cash vanished. This put pressure on the Nikkei to come up with the cash to maintain Japan's obligations abroad -- creating more sellers than buyers. Therefore the market (Nikkei) began to decline. This decline will continue until the 'reserve requirements' fall in line with the Western countries: America, Canada, France, Germany, Great Britain, Italy and Switzerland.

"During this market decline the companies did not hire new workers -- on the whole -- but they did not lay off anybody either. Therefore, the manufacturing sector kept producing at the old rate. The result was an oversupply of products which could not be absorbed in her retailers. So, they began cutting the price of their products. This resulted in a 'two-tier' retailer market: discount and regular. The discount retailers swamped the regular retailers and forced them out of business. This had an 'avalanche effect' as one retailer after another started to close down creating unemployment in their business sector: retail.

"Therefore, while Japan protected her skilled workers, the oversupply caused wide-spread unemployment in the retail sector. The worst is not over, but if Japan continues at the rate she is going she will achieve parity in the next few years. By then, however, her unemployment rate may be as high as 8% -- which is extremely high for modern Japan. Right there you can observe the two tactics at work. Which one is better? On the surface, the American model is better..."

"How does the unemployment rate affect the economy?" I asked.

"Let me first finish, then I'll discuss the unemployment figures," Zeus retorted. Then he continued:

"Western Europe falls somewhat in between the American model and Japanese system. By end large, they hire their employees for life, especially skilled workers. That's why they import Gastarbeiters for menial or semi-skilled jobs. This gives them a valve to control their changing economies and their unemployment rate.

"By contrast, in America only the most menial jobs are farmed out to foreigners. You call them 'migrant workers.' Their work conditions are appalling but everybody shuts their eyes to their plight. The claim, of course, is that without the migrant workers the price of produce -- especially fruits and vegetables would increase substantially.

"The key in this whole scenario is: each country has carved out a nitch of the industries they want to keep and the industries they deem to be dispensable. The industries they want to keep are protected by subsidies or tariffs or both, while the others are not." Zeus seemed to be finished. After a brief pause, he started again.

"Now let's look at unemployment. The prevailing Theory on unemployment is: 2% or less, is considered to be full employment -- since there is always a portion of the work force which is not employable and is considered to be 'inflationary.' Why? Because there is more money to go around.

"At 6% and more, it signals recession. Why? Because there is less money going around. This is when 'cash is king.'

"However, this applies only to countries with a solid currency. A solid currency implies a solid economy. Right now this includes the Dollar -- including Canada and Australia, Pound, Euro, Swiss Frank and Yen. All other countries, fall into another category, excluding the small oil-rich countries: Kuwait, Qatar, Saudi Arabia and a few others.

"There, an unemployment rate of 10% may be considered normal but inflationary. Therefore, unemployment rates of over 10% are highly inflationary. That is, a 'black hole' exists at about 8% when high unemployment turns from a deflation (recession) to inflation. Traditionally high unemployment, as was about 23% in Germany in 1923, goes hand in hand with high inflation. This is why South America, which is notorious for her high unemployment has high inflation. This is why South America would be a formidable challenge for American ingenuity to rectify. The rewards for Americans and natives alike would not be great--no, they would be stupendous within a few decades...

"Japan and Western Europe have, aside from specific tariffs which protect specific industries, a system of patronage which is the leftover of her recent history -- their feudal systems. In Japan it is the 'Samurai' society and in Western Europe her 'nobility.' Without their blessing, without their patronage doing business is nearly impossible.

"In America this is not so. The Government encourages people to form their own business and be on their way to 'fame and fortune.' That is, entrepreneurs are encouraged, supported and given many incentives, including low interest loans, technical support, tax breaks and much more. Small business is the largest employer in America. Small 'mama-papa' stores, professional groups, consulting, and the service sector employ more people than all the big corporations combined.

"On the whole, America's mode of operation dealing with recession and inflation, while not perfect, is much better and much easier to control. But Americans find it difficult to penetrate both the Japanese and European markets.

"I am here right now to survey this whole situation, because it has great impact on the future..."

"What do you see," I asked.

"I don't prophesise. That's done by mortals. They do that to draw attention to themselves. The patch you see on my eye is from a mild infection. Hera gave me a medication which I applied to the eye. I have changed into this form to be inconspicuous.

"However, in your race we have given you 'free-will.' This way you can make the best choices for yourself. The idea being that eventually you will arrive at the most meaningful environment for yourself. And, while America has many faults, her system has evolved quite nicely I must say..."

"What about the oracles at the various temples, like Delphi..." I started, but Zeus just cut me short.

"These were not prophesies but interpretations of imminent events which were based on the models we used. We never gave only one alternative and we only advised for the near future. Nothing beyond one generation, sometimes even less. The last time I saw Hera we spent a lot of time on her model results. Do you want to hear what they showed? Are you sure you can handle this?" He asked.

"Please tell me!" I exclaimed jubilantly.

"They show a lot of trouble, serious trouble ahead. To begin with there is India pitted against Pakistan over Kashmir. These are some of the two poorest nations on earth with huge populations who have made practically no inroads improving the lot of their people. Pakistan is at the verge of becoming an Islamic republic and India refuses to abolish her caste system. They have nothing to lose in a nuclear shooting war. They are poised to annihilate each other.

"If a shooting war starts, Pakistan will be supported by Bangladesh and Iran. Once Iran joins Pakistan, this could easily turn into a Muslim alliance and a call for Jihad. Then, Afganistan, Indonesia, Malaysia, and the other Muslim states will join on the Pakistani side, including the former Soviet republics in Asia, for they are Muslims. The result can be a nuclear exchange of at least 300 nuclear devices on each side. This alone will cause Nuclear Winter in the Northern Hemisphere. Within a few weeks life will cease to exist, for all practical purposes...

"The emerging power on the Pacific Rim is China. Just recently they acquired Hong Kong which was an economic powerhouse in that region. China is out to annex Taiwan, while North Korea is out to annex South Korea. North Korea is an economically deprived nation, very much like Pakistan. Therefore, they have nothing to lose in a shooting war. Again, a nuclear shooting war could easily result. A nuclear exchange of 200 or so nuclear weapons will decimate that region and create a Nuclear Winter in the Northern Hemisphere.

"This is one reason why Singapore joined the Free Trade Agreement with America, to give it some protection from potential military aggression. I suspect that Australia, New Zealand, Thailand and the Philippines will shortly join the Free Trade Agreement also -- all for the same reason as Singapore. England is no longer a military deterrent in that region -- America is.

"Less than 10 years ago, these alternatives of global disaster were unthinkable. Today they are a reality. Notice that, while Japan is an economic power, she is not a military deterrent to China or North Korea any more. And, while South Korea has a greater GNP than France, she could be overwhelmed. But, this time there would be no winners, only worldwide losers.

"Here are two scenarios by which America could be destroyed without entering a war, without firing a shot but simply because the reaction time to avert these wars is too short. And, as you will see, this is only the tip of the iceberg...

"Let's look at Africa. There, Islam is spreading south from Libya and Sudan across the whole continent. At the same time it is spreading north from Zanzibar, Madagascar, Mozambique to Tanganyika. The battle-scene is now in south-central Africa, from Liberia to the Congo and to Kenya and Somalia. For now, there are no major religious clashes in South Africa. However, that will be the next target. Then, Ghana, Nigeria and Ethiopia will fall.

"Christianity is perceived to be a White-Man's religion in Africa and the White-Man is synonymous with slavery and colonialism. Thus, religion and race are the major factors in that war. Europe and America have withdrawn from Africa. Therefore, it is only a matter of time before the Muslims prevail. Once South Africa is surrounded, she will be sacked.

"Now let's look at Europe....

"For the last 1200 years or so the Pope either called for a Holy war, or sanctioned it. The Pope either directed or orchestrated the religious wars: internal and external Crusades, new conquests in the name of the Church, to the East, to the South, to the North and to the West across the Atlantic Ocean. The Inquisition decimated the population with wanton religious hatred and persecution -- all civilized laws were brushed aside to impose the will of the Church. The Roman Empire was effectively destroyed by the 4th Crusade. The Albi were eliminated. In the New World entire nations were decimated or destroyed. Their civilization was annihilated, their books were burned, they became serfs and slaves. Then came the Counter-Reformation. It ravaged Europe again, for over 30 years. Then came the massacre of the Huguenots. Then Mary Tudor tried to re-install Catholicism in England. I can go on and on. Not one country in Europe was spared this ordeal. The kindest and most gentle religion was perverted by her leaders and was turned into the most vicious and most intolerant faith..."

"But, the current Pope, John-Paul II is a very gentle..." I started, but Zeus did not let me finish. He laced in:

"Pope John-Paul II, is the shield that protects the entire Catholic hierarchy from their complicity in the last holocaust by Hitler. Of course, the new Pope had to be the gentlest, least conspicuous and most persecuted member of their club. The Italian Cardinals did not want to relinquish power, but they had no choice. Each one of them has nasty skeletons in the closet.

"John Paul II, however, was persecuted by the Germans from the time he was Bishop in Poland to the time he was elevated to Cardinal. Then he was persecuted by the Soviets. Therefore, he became the ideal candidate to protect the entire Catholic hierarchy. Here is how it evolved.

"In 1929, Mussolini made a pact with Pope Pius XI, called the Italian Concordat. This endeared Mussolini not only to the Pope but also to the Italian people. The Vatican was created and Mussolini was blessed by the Pope to expand the Italian Empire and haul in the competing Patriarchs. Pope Pius XI supported not only Mussolini but also Hitler. In 1939 he died and Pope Pius XII was elected. He continued to support the policy of the fascists and blessed Hitler's genocide. He supported ethnic cleansing provided that the victims were Orthodox, Jews, Gypsies, heathens and heretics. When Hitler lost the war, the Vatican tried to hush-up her involvement. Pope Pius died in 1958.

"By then the dragnet was on to bring the escaped Nazis to justice. What the Nazi hunters found was that Pope Pius XII was not only collaborating with Mussolini but also with Hitler. This made his Cardinals suspect in their complicity. Pope Pius XII died in 1963 surrounded with much serious evidence against him. Pope John XXIII was elected. He died in 1963 and Pope Paul VI was elected. By 1970, the evidence was irrefutable. It exposed all Popes to be in cahoots with Hitler, starting with Pope Pius XI. In 1978, Pope Paul VI died and Pope John Paul I was elected. He ruled only from August 26 to September 28. Some say he died from embarrassment, for he was a staunch supporter of both Mussolini and Hitler. And, the trial of Eichman in Israel, gave first hand proof of the evidence against them. Therefore, to close this chapter of involvement and complicity a 'pure' Pope had to be found to shield the Cardinals from further embarrassment. That Pope was John Paul II. He rules not because of his ecclesiastical merits but solely to protect the Italian, French and Spanish Cardinals who were deeply and personally involved in Hitler's rampage. But then," Zeus paused briefly, "...they only followed the Vatican's commitment to support the German Concordat.

"Accordingly, Hera's model shows the following scenario in Europe.

"When the Nürnberg trials took place, nobody in the Catholic hierarchy expected to be named as an accomplice to Hitler's genocide. Then, step by step the culprits were exposed.
Europe had to hatch a long term plan to continue the policy of the Vatican. Three things needed to be done.

"First, the criminals at the Nürnberg trial had to be exonerated over a generation or two. This job fell on the International Court of Justice in The Hague. They hatched a plan to convict many war criminals, thereby reducing the culpability of the original lot. The logic was simple: a dozen or two are an abomination, a thousand or more is a statistic. But, most importantly they had to zero in on Americans to give them a taste of their own medicine. Since America is involved in every major conflict or police action, it is only a matter of time before the right victim will be found.

"Second, America's presence brought the Evangelicals and Baptists to Western Europe. On their heels came the Jews. They did good deeds, earned the respect of the population and flaunted many converts. Therefore, starting in the 1960's, both Germany and France brought in Gastarbeiters mostly from the Muslim counties for manual labor. By 1980, this became a flood. The Muslims found a rich and relatively tolerant society which allowed them to flourish. As the Israeli-Palestinian conflict began to escalate many Muslims turned radical.

"Their targets, of course, are the Jews and Jewish Sects--as the Baptists and Evangelicals are labelled in Europe. By 1990, France started passing laws outlawing the existence of all sects, specifically targeting the Baptists and Evangelicals. By 2000, radical Muslims began terrorizing these Jewish sects and the Jews. Now France is forcibly closing the centers of worship of these 'Jewish sects.' Within the next few years the radical Muslims will be unleashed against them. This is expected to create international indignation and then the Muslims can be persecuted in Europe officially. That is, the Muslims will annihilate the Jews and Jewish Sects without much interference from the Governments involved and then, the Muslims will be persecuted for having done the job for the Europeans. Sounds crazy?

"Well, all religious persecutions are crazy. For now, this is the best plan on their drawing board. However, don't be surprised if Europe abandons this plan altogether and starts a new wave of persecutions which will dwarf her prior reign of religious terror.

"According to Hera's model this will depend on: whether or not Israel will survive the present crisis -- in this generation. If Israel does not survive, the next holocaust against the Jews and Jewish Sects will be world-wide and overt. If Israel manages to survive -- with all the Arabs pitted against her -- the next holocaust will be covert and localized to Europe...

"Third, America will be forced out of Europe. This will allow Europe to establish the policies, religious and economic programs in the European Union, to deal with gnostics, heretics, infidels and heathens. This policy will be set directly or indirectly by the Pope. And, once the Pope gets involved in religious matters we all know where that leads, 1200 years of prior history should be abundant evidence.

"Once America leaves Europe, a fierce economic war will start between the European Union and America. Therefore, this is the time to forge the Free Trade Alliance, not when the economic war is in full swing.

"Meanwhile, America must shore up her strength at home. The family must again take center stage. The divorce rate must be reduced, gay marriages should not be allowed, the lawyers must be curtailed in their frivolous suits, the medical profession must be curtailed in their assault on the elderly. There is much to be improved in America, but despite it all, it is still the best and safest place to live in this world..."

"How do we stop this madness of mutual destruction?" I asked.

"You have the tools in place. Create an international court of justice which deals specifically with the clergy. Let that court be composed of three judges from each major religion, excluding the zealots amongst them. This could be done with a permanent panel of humanitarian leaders. Declare universal religious tolerance. Then haul the abusive religious leaders to court. For starters, abolish the titles of Pope and Cardinals, they are the permanent leaders of a huge army which stirs relentless religious wars. Abolish the religious zealots in all other religious including the Jesuits and Dominicans. Banish them to St. Helena or some other deserted island in the middle of nowhere. Let them plot their schemes there. Enforce religious tolerance on a world-wide basis. As soon as you do that, most of the hatred will disappear. From then on, it can be readily monitored and controlled. Only then will you have a semblance of 'peace on earth'...."

"Where would we house this court?" I asked.

"In the Vatican, of course." Zeus replied calmly.

Then, after a brief pause, Zeus continued.

"So far I have given you the most obvious causes of human conflict and a remedy for it. There are still other causes which I have not touched on. These fall into the category of disease and ecology.

"In the area of disease, AIDS is the primary killer of humanity. In Africa it is an epidemic. It has infected over 30% of her population. If unchecked it will devastate the entire continent within the next generation. It has spread to Europe--mostly to Russia -- Asia and America. It is grossly under-reported world-wide. There is no cure for it at this time. And the medication to keep it in check is outrageously expensive. A cure must be found -- and soon. This epidemic alone has the potential to destroy humanity.

"Reckless use of antibiotics has created new strains of old diseases which are immune to your antibiotics. As they emerge, each strain will be more deadly than the one before..."

"How do we control that?" I asked.

"The most effective method is abstinence until marriage. The only sex we ever advocated was sex in marriage. Promiscuity is the cause for most of these diseases..."

"Isn't a successful marriage a rare occurrence these days? Isn't it like buying a cat in a bag. When you open the bag, you may not like the cat?" I asked.

"There is an element of truth in what you say. But for the most part it is because a couple enters marriage without a commitment or purpose on their part. They are totally unprepared for it. Let them take an intensive course for six weeks before they are given permission to marry. Let them formalize their commitment to each other. Education should enlighten them, and if need be, allow a trial marriage of say 2 years or a little more. This would stop the rampant promiscuity.

"Now let me touch on ecology. There are two major problems which will haunt humanity in this 21st century. The 'Green-House Effect' and pollution.

"If the Green-House Effect is not solved, the polar ice caps will melt. The Oceans will rise by about 20 feet. This will inundate humanity in the low-lying areas, destroying about 60% of humanity. The usable land-mass will shrink. The food producing areas will be flooded, which will cause world-wide starvation. To this day this scenario is hushed up and ridiculed. But, within the next few decades it will become reality...

"Pollution is another major problem. While waste is a big issue it is solvable with proper recycling measures. If this is not addressed properly, you will drown in your own sewage. The water supply will be polluted; the beaches made unusable and the marine life will be destroyed. Once you start killing the marine life and flora and fauna, you will kill yourself.

"The nuclear waste, however, is a modern, man-made problem and should be addressed immediately. To begin with, nuclear energy should be banned altogether. It is way too dangerous and for your race has 'everlasting' consequences. Nuclear waste becomes relatively harmless after 1000 years or so. Surely, longer than one human life time.

"Instead you should switch to solar energy. It is abundant, non-depletable, clean and easy to use. Even the most primitive solar panels could reduce your energy needs by as much as 70%. All that is needed is the proper incentives to make them affordable. If that were to be made, solar panels on roofs could provide most of your energy needs 'forever.' Let me moderate this for your race: for a long time. At least two generations or so. The cost must be reduced to the cost of installing a tiled floor, or in your country, to about $4 per spare foot. At that price it will pay for itself within 2 years. Excess energy could be sold. This would make the entire system not only cost effective but also make it a source of revenue or income. Imagine, instead of paying your utility bill each month, you would receive a monthly payment instead. Wouldn't that be a nice change?

"This would eliminate your insatiable need for oil. This would reduce your need for coal -- which in turn would reduce the acid rains. This would reduce the Green-House effect and so on. The advantages are too numerous to mentions..."

"What holds us back?" I asked.

"Your Oil-Lobby, your Coal-Workers-Lobby, your Utilities, your Oil-Barons and so on. They have created a cushy industry for themselves. They don't care that it pollutes, endangers and destroys your environment. All they care about is to make you more dependent on their service. This enslaves you to the job-market to pay their bill. Let's face it: who wants to lose a highly profitable business without a fight?..."

All of a sudden I had the feeling that my visit to the Olympians was over. The scene began fading.

Then I woke up.

Alva Press: The World's Most Notorious Women, 2002.
Andrews, W: The Soviet Union, 1990.
Apocrypha: The Lost Books of the Bible, 1985.
Archimedes: The Sandreckoner, & Measurement of a Circle, 1952.
Aristotle: The Athenian Constitution, 1952.
Augustine, St: On Christian Dogma, & The City of God, 1952.

Bahaly, D.: Outline of Ukrainian Historiography, 1923-5.
Bede, Venerable: Historia Ecclesiastica Gentis Anglorum, 1932.
Bernoulli, D: Hydrodynamica, 1956.
Birmingham, S: Our Crowd, 1967.
Black, E: IBM and The Holocaust, 2001-2003.
Black F & Scholes M: The Pricing of Options and Corporate Liabilities, [U of Chicago & MIT], 1971.
Boyer, C: A History of Mathematics, 1985.
Brinton,C and Christopher,J et al: History of Civilization, 1984.

Carell, P: Unternehmen Barbarossa, 1963.
Cauchy, A: Functions of a Complex Variable, 1985.
Chamberlain, W: Ukraine, A Submerged Nation, 1941.
Chekhov, A: A Dreary Story, & The Duel, 1956.
Chidester, D: Christianity, 1980.
Clark, A: Barbarossa, 1985.
Clausewitz von, K: Vom Kriege, 1985.
Constantine VII: De Administando Imperio, 1969.
Copernicus, N: On the Revolution of the Heavenly Spheres, 1952.
Corvin, O: Illustrierte Weltgeschichte für das Volk, 1880.

Dante, A: The Divine Comedy, 1952.
Darwin, C: The Origin of Species by Means of Natural Selection, 1955
Descartes, R: Method, & Geometry, 1952.
Doroshenko, D: History of the Ukraine, 1940.
Dostoevsky, F: The Gambler, & The Brothers Karamzov, 1966.
Durkheim, E: Division of Labor in a Society, 1966.

Euclid: Elements, 1952. [Aka: Euclidian Geometry.]
Euler, L: Elements of Algebra, 1928.
Eusebius, Bishop: A History of the Church from Christ to Constantine, 1965

Fabozzi, F: The Handbook of Mortgage-Backed Securities, 1985.
Fermi, E: Quantum Mechanics, 1956.
Fermi, M. Atoms in the Family, 1978.
Fleay, F.G: Egyptian Chronicle, 1899.
Fong, G: Bond Portfolio Analysis, 1980.
Fosbach, N: Stock Market Logic, 1992.
Fourier, J: Analytical Theory of Heat, 1952.
Franko, I: Moses, 1955.
Friedman, R: Red Mafiya, 2000.

Galileo, G: Concerning the Two Sciences, 1952.
Gastineau, G: The Options Manual, 1984.
Gibbon, E: The Decline and Fall of the Roman Empire, 1952.
Goethe, W: Faust, 1952.
Gregoras, N: Byzantia Historia, 1988.
Gregory of Tours: The History of the Franks, 1974.
Gurney, G: Kingdoms of Europe, 1990.

Haggard, H: Devils, Drugs and Doctors, 1952
Harvey, J: The Plantagenets, 1971.
Hawking, S: A Brief History of Time, 1988.
Hedwig, W: History of the Goths, 1979.
Herodotus: The Histories, 1952.
Hingley, R: Russia, a Concise History, 1994.
Hitler, A: Mein Kampf, 1966.
Hodgin, T: Theodoric the Great, 1955.
Hohol, N: Vij; Inspector General, & Dead Souls 1962.
Homer: Iliad, & Odyssey, 1952.
Hrushevsky, M: History of Ukraine, 1941.

Ibn Jubair: The Travels of Ibn Jubair, 1952.
Jacobsen, T: The Sumerian King List, 1952.
John Chrysostrom, St.: Ouevres Completes, 1864-7.
Jones G: A History of the Vikings, 1984.
Jordanes: Getica, 1936,
Josephus, F: Jewish Wars, 1960.

Karamazin, N: History of Russia, 1952.
Keegan, J: The First World War, 2001.
Kemeny, J and Snell, J: Finite Markov Chains, 1976.
Kepler, J: The Harmonies of the World, 1952.
Klyuchevsky, V: History of Russia, 1954.
Kobler, F: Juden und Judentum in Deutschen Briefen aus Drei Jahrhunderten, 1935. [Jews and Jewry in German Letters for Three Centuries.]
Kotlyarevsky, I: Aeneid, 1961. [Aka: Travesties of the Aeneid]
Kotlyarevsky, I: Natalka Poltavka & The Moscow Sorcerer, 1932.
Kravitz, D: Who's Who in Greek and Roman Mythology, 1975.
Krusch, B: Fredegarii et Alliorum Chronica, 1888. [Merovingian Chronicle.]

Lancioni, E: The History of the Popes, 1978.
Le Bon, G: The Psychology of a Revolution, 1968.
Leibnitz, G: Calculus of Differentials, 1980.
Lieven, A: Chechnya, 1998.
Life Inc.: Russia, 1981.
Livy, T: History of Rome, 1986.
Lebesgue, H: Functions of a Real Variable, 1980.
Lobachevsky, N: On the Principles of Geometry [the foundation of Non-Euclidian Geometry], 1829.
Lucretius: De Rerum Natura, (60 BC). [First Atomic Model]

Machiavelli, N: The Prince, 1952.
Mango, C: Byzantium, 2002.
Marx, K: Das Kapital, 1966.
Marx, K and Engels, F: Manifesto of the Communist Party, 1952.
Massie R: Nicholas and Alexandra, 1981.
McCombs D and Worth F: World War II, 1983.
Mellenthin, F: Panzer Battles, 1971.
Mendeleyev, D: Principles of Chemistry, 1905.
Michael, the Syrian: Chronicle, 1905-6.
Mierow, C: Gothic History of Jordanes, 1966.
Mommsen, T: Römische Forschungen, 1876.
Moynahan, B: The Faith, A History of Christianity, 2002.
Much, O: The Secret of Atlantis, 1977.
Munch, K: The Code, 1992.

Nahayevsky, I: History of Ukraine, 1966
Nekrasov, N: Who can be Happy in Russia?, 1952.
Neuman von, J and Morgenstern, O: Theory of Games and Economic Behavior, 1947.
Nestor: Chronique dite de Nestor, 1884.
Niehbur, B: Roman History, 1952
Norwich, J: A Short History of Byzantium, 1999.

Oldenburg, Z: Massacre at Montsegur, 1961.
Orchard, A: Norse Myth and Legend, 2002.
Pares, B: A History of Russia, 1962.
Pares, B: Russia, Between Reform and Revolution, 1962.
Pasternak, B: Dr. Zhivago, 1988.
Penrose, A: The Emperor's New Mind, 1990.
Philippatos,G: Financial Management, Theory and Techniques, 1973.
Philip's: Atlas of Word History, 2001.
Philostorgius: Historia Ecclesiae, 1851.
Pipes, R: A Concise History of the Russian Revolution, 1995.
Pirenne, H: Mohammed and Charlemagne, 1957.
Plato: The Republic, 1952.
Platonov, S: Times of Trouble, 1924.
Pliny (the Elder): Natural History & Bella Germaniae, 1970.
Polybius: The Histories, 1972.
Procopius: History of Wars, & Secret History, 1970.
Ptolemy: Almagest, 1952.
Pushkin, A: Gavriliada, 1972. [Travesties of Virgin Mary]
Pushkin, A: The Captain's Daughter, 1972. [His version of the Puhachov rebellion].

Read, A & Fisher D: The Fall of Berlin, 1988.
Reed, J: Ten Days That Shook the World, 1977.
Remarque, E: All Quiet on the Western Front, 1955.
Renouvin, P: War and Aftermath 1914-1919, 1968.
Ridpath, M: Trading Reality, 1988.
Roberts, J: History of the World, 1992.
Roll, R: The Behavior of Interest Rates, 1984.

Salisbury, H: The 900 days, 1970. [Siege of Leningrad]
Schiller, F: Das Lied von der Glocke, 1955.
Setton, K: A History of the Crusades, 1969.
Shaw, K: Royal Babylon, 1999.
Shevchenko, T: Kobzar, 1960. [Minstrels]
Shirer, W: The Rise and Fall of the Third Reich, 1960.
Smith, A: An Inquiry Into the Nature and Causes of the Wealth of Nations, 1952.
Smith, J: Constantine the Great, 1971.
Smith, W & Wace, H: Dictionary of Christian Biography, 1877-87.
Sholokhov, M: And Quiet Flows the Don, 1955. [Aka: Quiet Don.]
Solovyov, S: History of Russia from Ancient Times, 1952.
Solzhenitsyn, A: August 1914, & Archipelago Gulag, 1988.
Solzhenitsyn, A: the Russian Question, 1996.
Sozomen: Ecclesiastic History, 1952.
Spahr, W: Zhukov, 1993.
Spence, L: Egypt, 1996.
Stanley, T: Pythagoras, 1970.
Stark, R: The Rise of Christianity, 1990.
Stearns, P: Word History, 2001.
Strabo: Geographies, 1938.
Sturluson, S: Heimskringla, 1995.
Sykes, P: A History of Persia, 1930.
Sylvester: Slavonic History, 1935.

Tacitus, C: The Annals, & The Histories, 1952.
Theodoret: History of the Church, 1854.
Thomson, E: A History of Attila and the Huns, 1948.
Tolstoy, L: War and Peace, 1952.
Trotzky, L: Geschichte der Russischen Revolution, 1930.
Thomas Aquinas, St: The Summa Theologica, 1952.
Thorp, E: Beat the Dealer, 1966.
Thucydides: The Peloponnesian Wars, 1952.
Time Inc: The Rise of Russia, 1975.

Ukrainian Museum, NY: Treasures of the Trypilian Culture, 1993.

Vasilev, A: Byzance et les Arabs, 1935.
Vernadsky, G: Bohdan, Hetman of the Ukraine, 1941.
Virgil: The Aeneid, 1952.
Voltaire, F: L'Histoire Russe, 1898.
Voltaire, F: Charles XII, 1930.

Wagner, R: The Ring of the Nibelungen, 1995.
Wheler Bush, R: St. Athanasius; His Life and Times, 1888.

Xenophon: Anabasis, 1985. (Aka: Persian Expedition.)
Yahya of Antioch: History, 1952.
Ziegler, P: The Black Death, 1969.
Zonaras, J: Annals, 1868-75.
Zozimus: Historia, 1784.

AAA....: top rating assigned by Moody's rating service.
AA1/AA2/AA3:high grade rating assigned by Moody's rating service.
A1/A2/A3:lowest high grade rating assigned by Moody's rating service.
Aachen.: a German city on the Rhine river, Charlemagne ruled from there. Aka: Emperor City.
Achaean(s): residents of Greece before the Doric invasion.
Adams, John (1797-1801): 2nd President of the USA.
Adams, John Q (1825-1829): 6th President of the USA.
Adenauer, Konrad (1876-1967): Chancellor of West Germany.
Adrianople: a city in the Balkans, part of the Roman Empire.
Aegean.: a civilization, destroyed after the Trojan War.
Aeneas.: legendary Hero of Troy, King of the Dardanians, legendary pre-founder of Rome. His descendants were Romulus and Remus, who were raised by a 'Lupa,' (wolf or loose woman.)
Aetius, (396-454): a Roman general who commanded the Scythians in the battle of Chalons-sur-Marne in 452.
Afrika Corps: a beefed up German division, commanded by General Erwin Rommel in Africa during World War II.
Ahura Mazda: a Persian deity.
Aka....: also known as.
Alans..: a Gothic nation.
Alaric, (370-410): a Gothic King who set out to rescue the Goths in the Roman Empire.
Alberich: mythological ruler of the Dwarfs (Nibelungen).
Albi...: the residents of Languedoc, in Southern France.
Albigense: another name for the Albi.
Alcibiades: a brilliant Athenian military leader who often switched sides between Athens and Sparta in their war for the hegemony of Greece.
Alexander, Nevsky (1220-63): banished Prince of Novhorod when he advocated an alliance with the Tartars. He joined the Tartars in their conquest and was rewarded with a Yarlic (Principality). He chose Volodimir because it included Moscow, which was not a Chartered city. His successors established themselves in Moscow. See Muscovy.
Alexander, the Great (358-323 BC): Macedonian conqueror of the known world.
Alexander I, (1801-1825): Czar of Russia.
Alexander II, (1855-1881): Czar of Russia.
Alexander III,(1881-1894): Czar of Russia.
Algol..: a computer language.
Allemani: a federation of mostly Germanic tribes.
Allthing: a Gothic national assembly.
Alphas.: a base measure in a portfolio.
Amazons: a Gothic-Female warrior nation. Strabo, Cassiodorus and Jordanes claim they were the disgruntled wives of Goth warriors. They formed their own state when their husbands continued to make war and not stay home. Every few years they would get together, during springtime, frolic and exchange children, if any. Boys, after the age of 8 went

back with their father, while girls and younger boys stayed with their mother. Throughout their history, the Amazons were allied with the Goths.

Andrew, St: legend has it that he preached to Ukrainians.

Andrusovo: in the Treaty of Andrusovo in 1667, Muscovy turned over Beralus and the Western part of the Ukraine to Poland for a vague military alliance.

Antioch: a city in Asia Minor.

Antiochus: a general in the army of Alexander the Great, founder of Antioch and ruler of Greece after Alexander's death.

Aphrodite: in Greek (Venus in Roman) mythology, goddess of love.

Apocrypha: writings about Christ or the Christian Church which were rejected by the Church Fathers.

Apollo.: in Greek mythology, the ruler of the sun; hence enlightenment. The keeper of the sun was Helios.

Arcadius, (395-408): Emperor of the Roman Empire.

Archangelsk: a city in Northern Europe, in Russia.

Archimedes, (287-212 BC): mathematician and inventor; developed Integral Calculus,computed the mass of the universe in his 'Sandreckoner,' and much more.

Ares...: in Greek (Mars in Roman) mythology, god of mindless war.

Arial Sharon: current Israeli Prime Minister.

Arian(ism): the Christian teachings of Patriarch Arius.

Aristotle, (384-322 BC): Greek teacher and writer. Teacher to Alexander the Great, created the fundamental knowledge for Western Civilization.

Arius..: first Patriarch of the Christian Church, appointed by the Roman Emperor Constantine.

Armada, Spanish: in May/June (depending on the Calendar) of 1588, 130 Spanish ships sailed for the Low Countries(the Netherlands) to ferry the army under the Duke of Parma to England. (When Elizabeth I was made Queen, England was declared a heretic country by the Pope.) At stake was a bounty set by the Pope of 2 million Ducats in gold for the conquest of England.

In the entire Armada were less than 20-ocean faring ships, while the rest were transport ships from the Mediterranean. While some gunshots were exchanged en route, no ships were lost on either side. When the Armada arrived, the Duke of Parma was not ready. Since the Armada could not wait forever, the fatal decision was made to circumnavigate Scotland for the return journey, as the English blocked the English Channel to the South and a brief skirmish led them to believe that there might be trouble in the Channel. While no ships were lost in the skirmish due to cannon fire, one ship got grounded on a sand bank. As the Armada reached Scotland they got caught in a storm and many of their ships started falling apart. Most wrecks reached Ireland where many Spanish seamen were clubbed to death. Eventually, less than 70 ships of the Spanish Armada made it back to Spain.

Armenia: an independent country in the Caucasus, former Soviet Republic. Armenia converted to Christianity in 301.
Arminius: a Gothic or German chief who defeated two Roman legions in 6 AD.
Artemis: in Greek mythology, goddess of the hunt and legal documents. Diana in Roman.
Arthur, Chester A (1881-1885): 21st President of the USA.
Aryan(s): an Indo-European people who conquered India before the Trojan War. Many historians claim they are Goths, because during a procession Amazons guarded the participants. Since the Amazons were Goths, these conquerors are presumed to be Goths. {Notice, later both Amazons and Goths sided with Troy.}
Askold: a Viking who ruled Kiev with a fellow Viking Dir.
Astrakhan: a city in Russia, on the Northern shore of the Caspian Sea. Formerly a Tartar Khanate.
Athanasius, (293-373): the Bishop of Alexandria who preached against Patriarch Arius. His version of the Christian Faith is called Orthodoxy. It became the dominant Christian Faith with Roman Emperor Valens until Rome broke away in 800 and created her own brand of Christianity: the Roman Faith or Catholicism.
Athene: in Greek mythology, goddess of crafty war, arts and crafts in general. Minerva in Roman.
Atlantic, Battle of the (1939-43): in World War II between the German U-boats and allied navy -- mostly American, to secure the sea-lanes between America and England.
Atlantis: an Island Continent referred to by Plato in his 'Republic.'
Atomic Bomb: initial version developed by Enrico Fermi, as soon as he demonstrated a controlled nuclear reaction in Chicago, December 2, 1944. In Los Alamos, the miniaturization and triggering problems were resolved. Robert Oppenheimer was the administrative leader in Los Alamos. The entire team was dubbed: The Bomb Makers.
Attila, (406-453): warrior chief of the Huns.
Attlee, Clement (1883-1972): leader of the English Labor Party, defeated Churchill in the 1945 elections.
Auger(s): Etruscan priests who interpreted the offerings for the Roman Caesars and Emperors.
Augustine, St., Bishop of Hippo near Carthage (354-430): he started out as a Manichaean Christian and was converted to Orthodoxy by the Bishop of Milan. He set the tone for future Catholic dogma with: 'Confessions,' 'City of God' and 'On Christian Dogma.'
Augustus, Gaius Julius Octavius(63 BC-14 AD):first Roman Emperor.
Ausgleich: a form of geopolitics practiced by Austria. According to Metternich: "Keep all foreigners at maximum discontent, short of insurrection."
Avars..: a Mongol nation.

Azov Sea: a sea off the Black Sea. In antiquity it was called Lake Moesia and the Black Sea was called the Euxine Sea. See Moesia.

BAA1/BAA2/BAA3: the lowest investment grade rating by Moody's.
Babylonian Captivity, 598-538 BC: called a 70 year captivity or exile of the Jews. In that captivity the Old Testament was compiled and written down, during the rule of Persian King Nebuchadnezzar. There was a second Babylonian Captivity when the French Kings installed a Pope in Avignon. It also lasted nearly 70 years, 1309-1377.
Bacchus: in Greek (Dionysus in Roman) mythology, god of re-birth, associated with grapes, wines and spirits.
Badoglio, Pietro (1871-1956) Italian Field Marshal, and first Socialist-Communist leader in 1943, after Mussolini.
Baden..: a province of Germany.
Baku...: a city in the Soviet Union, major oil center.
Balaclava, Battle of (1854): in the Crimea, the basis of Tennyson's poem 'The Charge of the Light Brigade.' (He failed to mention, however, that only the Indian lancers were charging).
Bandera, Stephan (1909-1959): a Ukrainian nationalist leader who fought both the Nazis and Stalin. He was assassinated by Soviet agents in Munich, in 1959.
Barbarians: a word coined by the Greeks to describe non-Greeks. Sometimes referred to uneducated people.
Barbarossa, aka: red beard. See Frederick I, Holy Roman Emperor.
Barollo: a wine from Italy.
Bastogne: a Belgian city. The American forces were encircled by the Germans in the Ardennes offensive, aka: Battle of the Bulge. American general McAuliffe refused to surrender, Montgomery refused to relieve Bastogne thus, general Patton had to cross the Alps and arrived there in the nick of time on Christmas eve 1944.
Battenberg(s): the original name of the English nobility from Germany (Hannover). During world War I, they changed their name to Mountbatten(s).
Batu, (ca 1212-1272), the grandson of Genghis Khan, a contemporary of Kubilai Khan. Batu set out to conquer Europe. The Mongols ruling China were:

Genghis Khan (1162-1227)
Ugudai Khan (1227-1241)
Kubilai Kahn (1259-1294)

Bede, (673-735): the Venerable Bede wrote an account of the invasions by the Angles, Jütes and Sassons (all Goths). The word Sassons is claimed to have been altered to read Saxons in later years. Thus the Anglo-Saxon nation was created.
Belarus: also called Byelorussia. A principality during the Kievan-Rus.

Belgae.: aboriginal people of present day Northern France and Belgium.
Belgorod: a town in the Soviet Union.
Belisarius, (494-565): a brilliant general under Roman Emperor Justinian I.
Bellwether Bond: the longest bond, in terms of time to maturity, of the Government bonds, currently 30 years.
Berezina: a river in Byelorussia.
Berlin.: the capitol of Prussia, now Germany. Founded in the 12th century. In 1709 it had less than 60,000 residents. In 1760 it was raided by Cossacks in the 7 Year War. By 1945 its population swelled to over 4 million. It was captured by Stalin after World War II. Now Germany's capital.
Berlin, Congress of (1878): a conference of Austria, Prussia and England which revoked the mutually agreed Treaty of San Stefano and imposed on the liberated Balkans a treaty of their choice to conform with their mutual geopolitics. See San Stefano.
Bernoulli(s): a family which dominated mathematics for over 200 years in Europe. Jacob Bernoulli called Sir Isaac Newton a plagiarist. Since then their name has been avoided in English prose. Here are some of their members. The ones marked * are universally considered to be the leading mathematicians-physicists of their time:

1623-1708, Nicholas, Sr. moved to Basel.
*1654-1705, Jaques I, advocate of Leibnitz.
1662-1745, Nicholas I, taught at Basel.
*1667-1745, Jean I, advocate of Leibnitz.
*1687-1759, Nicholas II, taught at Padua.
*1695-1729, Nicholas III, taught at St. Petersburg
*1700-1782, Daniel I, taught at St. Petersburg.
*1710-1790, Jean II, taught at Basel.
*1744-1807, Jean III, taught at Berlin.
1751-1834, Daniel II, taught at Basel.
*1759-1789, Jaques II, taught at St. Petersburg.
1782-1863, Christoph, taught at Basel.
1811-1863, Jean Baptiste, taught at Basel.

Bessarabia: a former province of the Ukraine (Moldovia).
Beta(s): the deviation form a linear fit in a portfolio.
Bezier.: a town in Languedoc, sacked by Crusaders in 1209.
Bible..: scriptures of the Old Testament and New Testament.
Bierwag: a modern researcher in financial analysis.
Birger, Jarl (ca.1196-1236): Swedish missionary. Alexander Nevsky, a Prince from Novhorod, slaughtered his delegation at the river Neva and got his name that way. See Alexander Nevsky and Muscovy.
Biron, Ernst J. (1690-1772): advisor and de facto ruler of Russia during the reign of Czarina Anna. Also know as 'Biron the German.' Catherine II restored him to power in Kurland, in 1763. Aka: Biren.

Bismarck, Otto Prince von (1815-98): German statesman.
Black Death: a plague spreading from the Far East, ravaging Europe, notably from 1347 to 1379.
Black Sea: a body of water which connects via two straits to the Mediterranean Sea. A major shipping and trade route in antiquity. The early Greek sagas evolve around the Black Sea. For example: Jason and the Argonauts; which pre-dates the Trojan War.
Black & Scholes: two modern statisticians who developed a fair option price formulation.
Blum...: Lenin's mother's maiden name.
Blücher, Gebhard L (1742-1819): Prussian general.
BNL....: Brookhaven National Laboratory in Upton, NY.
Bock, Fedor von (1880-1945): German Field Marshal, commander of Army Group Center during Hitler's invasion of the Soviet Union.
Bohemia: a Gothic Kingdom in Central Europe. In the 10th century they accepted Christianity from Rome. A leading University of Europe, in Prague, was frequented by the Cossacks from the various Siches.
Bolsheviks: the majority faction led by Lenin in the 1903 Congress of the Russian Social Democratic Party held in Brussels and then in London. In 1917, they took over the Government in Russia, which led to the Revolution, Communism and the rise of Stalin.
Bonaparte: as in Napoleon Bonaparte, see separate entry. Descendants of an Italian family from Corsica, the family dominated Europe during Napoleon's rule:

Joseph (1768-1844) King of Naples, then Spain, then retired in the USA, returned and died in Italy.

Lucien (1775-1840) President of the Council of 500 in France, then King of Holland, retired to Bohemia then to Rome. Louis (1778-1844) son of Lucien, later ruled France as Napoleon III. Jerome (1784-1860) King of Westphalia.

Bordeaux: a city in France and a wine from that region. A Gothic stronghold.
Bordolino: a wine from Italy.
Borgia(s): a ruling family in Italy of Spanish-Habsburg origin. Many Popes came from this family, to begin with:
Rodrigo (1431-1503) as Pope Alexander VI.
Caesare (1476-1507) as Archbishop of Valencia.
Lucretia (1480-1516) was used as a marriage pawn.
Francis (1510-1572) third general of the Order of Jesuits.
Boris..: a martyr in the Ukraine.
Bosnia.: a region in the Balkans, aka: Bosnia-Herzogovina, an autonomous state set up by Austria and administered by Austria after the Congress of Berlin, in 1878. Now policed by the UN.
Bourbon, House of: ruling house of France, related to Capets or the Capetian dynasty (987-1327), followed by the Valois (1328-1589), followed by the Bourbons (1589-1792) until

they were replaced by the French Revolution by Napoleon.
Boyar(s): originally the nobles and warrior Knights in Kievan-Rus. Then the tax-collectors in Muscovy, hence Tartars.
Bradley, Omar N (1893-1981): American general who liberated Paris and let DeGaulle enter first.
Bratislava: the capital of Slovakia. Founded by King Sviatoslav from Kiev in the 10th century.
Brauchitsch, Walter von (1881-1948): German Field Marshal and Supreme Commander of Operation Barbarossa, the invasion of the Soviet Union, replaced by Hitler in December 1941.
Brest-Litovsk: a city in Russia near the German border. In 1918, Trotzky paid off the Germans for funding the Russian Revolution. Kurland, Belarus and the Ukraine were given to the Germans as war reparations.
Brockhaus: a German encyclopedia and dictionary.
Bryansk: a town in the Soviet Union.
Bubus Americanus: an English nickname for Americans.
Buchanan, James (1857-1861): 15th President of the USA.
Buddhism: a religion and philosophy founded by Sidharta Gautama (563-483 BC).
Bukovyna: a Ukrainian province, part of Soviet Union.
Bulgars: a Mongolic people who settled in the Balkans (7th cent.) They accepted Orthodoxy and Slavic customs. [Akin to Hungary, except for the Christian Faith, Orthodox.]
Burgundians: an Asiatic people who settled on the Baltic coast. From there they were displaced to Southern Germany during the Hun invasion. Then they settled in Eastern France after Chalons-sur-Marne in 452.
Busento: a river in Southern Italy.
Bush, George W Jr (2001- present): 43nd President of the USA.
Bush, George W Sr (1989-1993): 41th President of the USA.
Byliny.: a Ukrainian collection of over 10,000 proverbs, sayings and short stories.
Byzantine Empire: a name used by Western historians to downplay the Roman Empire as it continued in Constantinople pitted against the Holy Roman Empire which was started illegally in 800. The focal point, of course, are religious claims. Constantinople was first Arian (313 to 375), then Orthodox (376 to 1453). A schism occurred between the two Christian Churches in 1353, hence religious wars continued to the present.
Byzantium: an ancient city which existed at the time of the Battle of Troy. (In the Iliad, Hecuba, asked one of her sons to take the treasures of Troy to Byzantium). However, in order to conform with the claims of Rome as being the oldest city in Western Civilization, the founding of Byzantium is claimed to be by Byzas of Megara in 657 BC. The Roman Emperor Constantine moved the capitol there in 330 for three reasons.

First, it was more centrally located to run the empire. (Julius Caesar had the same idea and Emperor Diocletian implemented it in 286.)

Second, the Eastern portion of the Roman Empire was rich and productive while the West was not.

Third, with Christianity as a state religion, Rome was burning. Her temples were set to the torch and the heathen priests and priestesses were killed.

Therefore, it was easier to build a new capital, with all the splendor it deserved for the new faith than to rebuild Rome.

C......: a computer language.

Cabotti, Giovanni: in 1497 an Italian captain took a shipload of English colonists to New England, but before he could sail he was renamed George Cabot. Aka: Caboto.

Cadmus.: first Greek King, he came from Egypt or Phoenicia depending on the source.

Caesar, Julius (100-44 BC): Roman general and dictator. Later in the Roman Empire, Caesar was used as a military title, subservient to the title Augustus (Emperor).

Caesarion: the son of Cleopatra and Julius Caesar.

Camillo, Don: a fictitious Catholic priest who is at odds with a communist mayor in a small town in Italy.

Cannae.: a town in Southern Italy. In 216 BC, Hannibal with about 40,000 was encircled by a Roman army of about 70,000. Yet Hannibal not only escaped but defeated the Roman army.

Canute, (994-1035): Gothic King of Denmark and Sweden who also ruled England.

Capet Dynasty: third dynasty of French Kings from Paris, Comte de Paris (940-996) ruled as Hugo Capet. When the French monarchy fell to the revolutionaries, they were guillotined as descendants of Hugo Capet.

Carolingian(s): a dynasty of Frankish Kings who ruled or controlled Gaul from 751 to 987, starting with Carl Martel as Mayordomo and Charlemagne as the first Emperor of the Holy Roman Empire. See Franks.

Carter, James (1977-1981): 39th President of the USA.

Cartier, Jaques (1491-1557): French explorer of Canada.

Cartouche: a dynastic signature or symbol.

Capodistrias Johannes A (1827-1831): secretary of Czar Nicholas I. He became the first modern President of Greece in 1827.

Cassandra: in Greek mythology, Apollo tried to make her his mistress, promising her the gift of prophesy. She accepted his gift of prophesy but refused to become his mistress. Hence, Apollo punished her: nobody would believe her prophecies. When the Trojan war ended, Agamemnon claimed her as his slave.

Cassiodorus Senator: the court historian to Theodoric the Great in Italy. They were Arian Goths and ruled from Ravenna.

Castro, Fidel (1927 --): Cuban revolutionary leader.

Catherine I, (1725-1727): second wife of Peter I, Czarina of Russia.

Catherine II, 'The Great' (1762-96): a German pauper Princes who married Peter III, heir to the Russian throne.When Czarina Elizabeth died in 1761 (under mysterious circumstances), Catherine engineered a coup with her lover Orlov and took over in Russia. Her full name is: Sophia Augusta Frederica of Anhalt-Zerbst. She was history's most successful adventuress to seize power of an empire with a handful of loyal supporters. She imprisoned all legitimate successors or had them killed, like Ivan VI and Tarakanova. Her reign was marred by constant revolts which she suppressed ruthlessly. She enslaved Byelorussia, Poland and the Ukraine and set the pattern for future rulers to do the same.

Cathars: another name for the Albi.

Cauchy, A (1789-1857): French mathematician, formulated Functions of a Complex variable.

Cavour, Camillo B (1810-1861): originally from Savoy, he orchestrated the liberation of and formation of the state of Italy in 1861. (Savoy was later exchanged for Lombardy.)

CBM....: Corporate Bond Model (see RAM.)

CBOE...: Chicago Board Option Exchange.

CDC....: in this context; Control Data Corp.

Celts..: first mentioned in the Battle of Troy, allied with the Trojans. When Troy fell, they migrated to Western Europe. They settled in Switzerland, France, Spain and moved to Ireland.

Cerberus: in Greek mythology, a three headed dog who guards the entrance to the underworld.

Ch == Kh: when the Cyrillic symbol X is translated into the Franco-Germanic it is spelled Ch, in the Anglo-Saxon it is spelled Kh. See KH..

Chaika.: a Viking type boat modified for the use in the Black Sea. It means a swallow, the bird.

Chalons-sur-Marne: in 452 an epic battle took place there. Attila was defeated but not destroyed because Aetius used a ruse to divert the Visigoths.

Charlemagne, (742-814): first Holy Roman Emperor (800) and joint architect of the 'German Concordat' with the first Pope of the Catholic Faith, Leo III. Even though Charlemagne was illiterate, he was an advocate of education and the arts.

Charles V, (1500-58): King of Spain (Charles I) and Emperor of the Holy Roman Empire of Habsburg line, a contemporary of Francis I of France (the architect of the French Concordat), Henry VIII of England and Ivan the Terrible of Muscovy.

Charon.: in Greek mythology, the ferryman who ferried the souls across the river Styx. The river Styx, separated Oblivium on one shore and the Elysian Fields on the other.

Chateau-Neuf du Pape: a French wine.

Chechen: a people, forcibly integrated into the Russian Republic. Their country is called Chechnya.

Cheka..: the secret police founded by Lenin in Russia.

Chekhov, Anton (1860-1904): a Ukrainian writer, dramatist and master of the short story. In order to get published, he wrote much of his work in Russian. But most of it was written in an allegorical style, exposing the Czarist regime. For example: 'The Cherry Orchard,' and much more. Russian censors were not keen enough to relate to his work and much of it passed their scrutiny.

Chernihiv: one of the dynastic cities in the Ukraine. They are: Kiev (ruled by Kings), Lviv (ruled by Kings after 1239), all others were ruled by Princes: Chernihiv, Pereyaslav and Bratislava. The land of the Goths (RUS) was divided into Principalities. In Novhorod ruled the Prince who was the successor to Kiev. The remaining cities had a hierarchy which is lost now. Presumably it was:Kiev, Novhorod, Tver, Minsk, Pskov, Suzdal, Volodimir and so on. Since there were many Princes, most cities did not participate in the rotation of Princes to Kingship. Chernihiv, Pereyaslav, Bratislava and Lviv were some of them.

Chernobyl: a town in the Ukraine, the site of a nuclear meltdown.

Chiang Kai-shek, (1887-1975): a Chinese leader who was evicted from mainland China in 1949 by Mao and settled with his followers in Formosa (Taiwan).

Christianity: the religious followers of Jesus Christ. After the Crucifixion of Jesus his Apostles were hunted by the Romans, especially Peter. Therefore, Peter left James -- the brother of Jesus in charge of the congregation in Jerusalem -- and went into hiding. At least three branches of teaching about Jesus were the result. Those of: James, Peter and Paul who preached to the Gentiles. They were still considered a sect of the Jews.

In Antioch, after the destruction of Jerusalem, the Church Elders met and defined the new religion. The teachings of Paul prevailed. Thus the Old Testament, the Jewish dietary laws and circumcision were brushed aside and replaced with Baptism and the New Testament.

In 313, Roman Emperor Constantine promoted Christianity to a State Religion and issued the Edict of Toleration, creating one Patriarch: Arius and a multitude of Bishops.

In 325, in Nicaea, about 800 Bishops were summoned by Constantine, most of whom were Arian Bishops, to define the essence of Christianity. The result was the 'Creed' which was ratified by all Bishops and endorsed by Constantine. By then there were at least 20 major branches of Christianity. Despite this ratification religious wars among Christians began which continued to the present day.

Chronos: in Greek mythology, the first generation of gods.

Churchill, Sir Winston (1874-1965): British statesman and historian. In 1940, elected Prime Minister of a coalition government in Great Britain, voted out of office in 1945 and into office from 1951 to 1955. Churchill, Roosevelt and Stalin became the 'Big Three' who shaped the world after World War II.

Civil Rights: in America, based on the Bill of Rights. In the Roman Empire the laws governing a Roman Citizen, which were codified by Justinian I. Among the Goths, a three tier system: Royal or Princely court, Veche or Thing and Sbor or Allthing, interpreting the Charter for each Principality. In the Holy Roman Empire, the feudal laws and the religious laws dictated by the Pope, with Church laws having precedence over civil laws. While slavery and serfdom were sanctioned both in the Roman Empire and the Holy Roman Empire, they were not among the Goths. Among the Goths, women had the same rights as men.

Clausewitz, Karl von (1780-1831): author of 'On War,' the 'bible' in Hitler's repertoire and present military.

Cleopatra, (69-30 BC): usually referring to Cleopatra VII, a direct descendant of Ptolemy, one of three major Gothic generals in Alexander's army who became ruler in Egypt after Alexander's death. She had an affair with Julius Caesar and gave him a child: Caesarion. After Julius Caesar was murdered in the Roman Senate, Marc Anthony became governor of the Eastern provinces. Cleopatra had an affair with him and gave him two children. After Octavius defeated Mark Anthony at Actium, she tried to seduce Octavius, but this time her charm failed. She killed herself and Octavius killed her offspring.

Cleveland, Grover (1885-1889): 22nd & 24th President of the USA.

Clinton, William (1993-2001): 42st President of the USA.

Clotho.: in Greek mythology, the goddess who spins the thread of life.

Clovis I (481-511): Merovingian King of the Franks. Clovis was his Latin name. His real name was Cholodoveche or Chlodoveg. (It means: Cholod==Cold, Veche==Assembly.) That is, he was a newly elected King, very likely elected by compromise between the Goths and Franks.

Coalition: an alliance of two or more parties or nations, usually for a specific purpose and limited time frame.

Cobol..: a computer language (Common Business Oriented Language.)

Cold War: a state of diplomatic tension. Primarily used between the USA and USSR from 1946 to 1990.

Collectivization: a program of communal farming, introduced by Stalin.

Colonialism: the dominance and exploitation of other nations or people.

Columbus, Christopher (1446-1501): Genoese explorer in the service of King Ferdinand and Queen Isabella of Spain. He discovered the New World. While Columbus believed he found the Indies, a new era of European colonialism began.

Communism: a theory first advocated by Plato. All property is held in common and all work is done for the common benefit. A major political and economic force in Russia from 1917 to 1992. And just like Plato saw his ideal community collapse, the Russian brand of Communism collapsed also due to economic factors.

Concentration Camps: originally enclosed areas to intern unruly civilians, aliens or undesirables in times of war. In modern times this started in the Boer War (1899-1902) in South Africa with Winston Churchill, and was copied by Hitler (1934-1945), by Stalin and USSR (1924-1990), in Italy (1922-43), Austria (1934-1938), Spain (1938-1946) and others.

Confucius, (551-478 BC): Chinese philosopher.

Conquistadors: a term generally applied to soldiers for profit as to the Spanish soldiers who raided the American Continent in search for gold, mindlessly. In an extended sense, this also applies to: the Internal Crusades in Europe (Albi and others), the Teutonic Knights and the Knights of the Sword who conquered parts of Eastern Europe. They took the land, the property, enslaved the people and imposed their will. The German 'conquistadors' called themselves Junkers.

Conscription: compulsory military service. Peter I, set 40 years as the norm, turning Russia into an armed camp. In addition the peasants paid (60% direct & 20% indirect) taxes.

Constantine, (280-337): Roman Emperor. While he was a sun-worshipper, he never-the-less elevated Christianity to a state religion in his Empire. As Pontifex Maximus, he presided over all Christian councils and his ratification was needed for all decisions. He made Arius, the first Patriarch of the Christian Church. When Constantine was dying, he was baptized by an Arian Bishop.

Constantinople: the new Christian capital Constantine built for the New Christian Roman Empire in 330. The former city of Byzantium was expanded, fortified and the entire Roman nobility and regalia transferred to the new capital. It was taken by Oleh in 911, to get a favorable trade agreement. (His shield still hangs at the main gate.) It was sacked by the Crusaders in 1204 (4th Crusade) and then captured by the Ottoman Turks in 1453. Today it is called Istanbul. The Imperial claims that go with it are guarded by Islam for the benefit of Rome.

Coolige, Calvin (1923-29): 30th President of the USA.

Copernicus, Nicolaus (1473-1543): prominent and revolutionary Polish astronomer.

Coptic Church: the Christian Church in Ethiopia.

Corfu..: an island of Greece, in the Ionian Sea.

Corporates: meaning corporate bonds.

Corsican: from the island of Corsica.

Cos....: a mathematical function called cosine.

Cossacks: a movement which started in the Ukraine in 1444, in response to forceful conversion to Catholicism from Orthodoxy by the Polish Barons in the Ukraine. It advocates the liberty of individuals, called the 'brotherhood of man.' Their leader was called: Hetman. They fought mainly for personal liberties and religious liberties. See Stenka Razin, Puhachov etc. For example: their raiding expeditions into the Ottoman Empire and the Crimea were directed at the major slave markets where they liberated all slaves and Christians. They rose against the Polish Barons, when the Barons demanded forceful conversion to the Catholic Faith in the Ukraine, which was Orthodox. In 1610, they saved Moscow from Tartar rule.

Any freedom minded man was accepted by them as a member. One Hetman was a Karaim Jew, called Karaim. When religious liberty was at stake during the siege of Vienna, in 1683, they rallied with Polish King Sobieski, broke the siege and drove away the Ottoman Turks.

In 1764, the Cossack movement was eliminated by Catherine II in Russia. But, their fame had to be preserved. Therefore, regiments were formed in the regular Russian army which were called Cossacks. These Cossacks have nothing in common with the original movement.

Cray, Seymour (1920-): a contemporary American computer hardware and software architect. For Control data he designed the 6000-series: 6800/6600/6400. Later he designed the Cray Pipe-Line processors.

Cretan.: from the island of Crete.

Crimean War, (1853-56): a war declared by Turkey, Britain, France and Sardinia on Russia.

Croatia: a new country, formerly part of Jugoslavia and before that under Austrian control, hence Catholics. Now a member of the EU.

Croesus, (560-547 BC): last King of Lydia of great wealth.

Cromwell, Oliver (1599-1658): abolished the monarchy in England and granted religious freedom. Later, the Monarchy was restored.

Crusades: traditionally some 10 major Crusades into the Holy Land are counted by Western historians, depending on the author, from the 11th to 15th century -- until the fall of Constantinople in 1453. There were, however, hundreds of Crusades which went unreported because Western history was written mostly by Bishops who protected the Catholic Church by not exposing this practice. To begin with, the 4th Crusade (External) was directed from the beginning to destroy the rival Christian empire: the Roman Empire in Constantinople. The author distinguishes between Internal and External Crusades. External Crusades targeted the infidel, mostly Islam, often in the Holy Land.

There were at least 60 External Crusades. In addition, there were over 200 Internal Crusades. In particular the many Crusades in France, Italy and the East against fellow Christians. The Pope granted special dispensations for the Crusaders: they were absolved of all wrongdoing for the period of the Crusade, their property was placed in safe-keeping with the Roman Church until the safe return of the Crusader, debts were deferred until the Crusader returned and much more. Therefore, it was a win-win arrangement between the Pope and each Crusader. The Crusaders got a license to steal, pillage, rape and plunder while the Pope got to keep the property, free and clear, more often than not -- when the Crusader did not return.

The dispensation was good for 1 year for an External Crusade and 40 days for an Internal Crusade. An internal Crusade was usually preceded and succeeded by the Inquisition to eradicate all remaining vestiges of heresy.

Curzon-Line: the dividing line established by Napoleon between his Empire and Russia, (West and East.)

Cyril & Methodius: two Greek monks who introduced the Cyrillic alphabet to the Goths/Slavs and Bulgars.

Cyrillic: an association of symbols between the Gothic-Runic and the Greek alphabet.

Cz == Ts: Cz is the Anglo-Saxon equivalent and Ts is the Franco-Germanic equivalent to the Gothic z.

Czar == Tsar: a title used by the Gothic Alans. This title was adopted by the rulers of Moscow, starting with Ivan the Terrible for the rulers of Muscovy.

Czarhorod == Tsarhorod: the name used for Constantinople, after it was taken by the Ottoman Turks.

Czechia: when the communist regime collapsed in Czechoslovakia, that country split into Czechia (aka: Czech Republic) and Slovakia. Both countries are members of the EU.

Czechoslovakia: a country established after World War I. It was composed of: Bohemia, Moravia and the former Ukrainian provinces of Slovakia and Ruthenia.

Dacia..: a Roman province on the North bank of the river Danube. Today, roughly the area of Rumania.

Daedalus: in Greek mythology, a gifted architect who built the labyrinth for King Minos of Crete to keep the monster offspring Minotaur (Bull-Man), the result of a liason between his wife and a prime bull. (As punishment to Minos by Zeus for not sacrificing the bull Zeus loaned him to build up his herd for a short time).

Danielo, Romanovich (1214-1264): a Ukrainian King from Galicia. After the Kievan-Rus army was defeated at Kalka in 1238, Danielo was spared. When the Tartars moved back to Sarai, Danielo went to Rome and urged the Pope to launch a Crusade against the Tartars. The Pope agreed, provided Danielo and his subjects convert to the Roman Faith. Danielo agreed and a special Roman Faith was created, called Roman Rite. Danielo and his subjects converted and Danielo was crowned hereditary King of Galicia. But, the Crusade never materialized. (Lviv was made a Catholic Patrirachate, Joseph Slipyj was Patriarch (1892-1984).)

In the 15th century, the Polish Barons descended into the Ukraine. With the Polish Barons came the Jesuit Priests in 1440. They forced the Galicians and the rest of the Ukraine, who were Orthodox to convert to the Catholic Faith. This caused rebellions and the formation of the Danubian Sich in 1444. In this way, two forms of the Catholic Faith are prevalent in Western Ukraine.

Dante Allighieri (1265-1321): Italian poet and statesman from Florence, author of the 'Divine Comedy.'

Danzig == Gdansk: founded by Polish Goths in the 9th century and under Polish rule until 1793. In 1793, it was ceded to Prussia, by force (the three partitions of Poland by: Russia, Austria and Prussia). In 1807 it became a Free City. In 1814, it was returned to Prussia (after Napoleon's defeat in Russia). In 1919, it became a Free City, linked to Poland. In 1939 Hitler demanded its return, and it became his excuse to attack Poland in 1939, which started World War II.

Dardanelles: a narrow strait between the Mediterranean (Aegean Sea) and the Sea of Marmara leading to the Black Sea. Roughly the stretch of land between Troy (in Asia minor) and Gallipoli in the Balkans.

Darius I, (550-485 BC): King of Persia and conqueror. Herodotus described how Darius invaded the Ukraine, was defeated and barely escaped with his life in 'Histories,' in a chapter called: Melpomane.

Darius III, (380-331 BC): King of Persia, at the time of Alexander's conquest. Darius was first defeated at Issus in 333 BC, and then destroyed at Gaugamela in 331 BC.

Darwin, Charles R (1809-82): English naturalist, author of 'The Origin of Species by Means of Natural Selection.'

DAX....: a major index on the Frankfurt exchange in Germany.

Daytona: a town in Florida, USA.

Decembrists: a revolutionary movement in Russia.

Dedekind, Richard (1831-1916): a mathematician, famous for the 'Dedekind Cut.' It proves that there are as many real numbers in the open interval 0 to 1 (0,1) as there are in any other open interval, which led to the notion of cardinality.

DeGaulle, Charles (1890-1970): French general and political leader. He organized the Free French during World War II.

Delhi..: the old capital of India. The new is New Delhi.

Delphi.: a temple dedicated to Apollo and oracle in Greece.

Demeter: in Greek mythology, goddess of the crops, in particular grains, mother of Persephone. Ceres in Roman and French.

Demosthenes, (384-336 BC): Greek orator. He denounced Philip II and Alexander (the Great) of Macedonia. He is said to have lived in a barrel on the beach. When Alexander the Great conquered Greece, he went to see him. They talked and Alexander was impressed with his wisdom and knowledge. Alexander asked him to utter a wish which Alexander was ready to fulfil. Demosthenes replied:'Get out of the sun.'

Denikin, Anton (1872-1947): a general in the Czarist army. He operated in South Russia, mainly in the Ukraine. After he was defeated by the Red Army and pushed to the Black Sea, his troops and their family members were evacuated by English and French forces to (mostly) Jugoslavia. From there, they settled throughout Western Europe.

Denmark: a Nordic country in Europe, now part of the EU. See Waldemar.

Descartes, Rene (1596-1650): French mathematician who broke the grid-lock in Algebra when he introduced zero (0) and zeroes (roots).

Diaspora: dispersion.

Dicke Berta: a super-cannon developed by Austria for the Ottoman Turks, to breach the walls of Constantinople in 1453.

Diderot, Denise (1713-1784): a French writer and collaborator with Voltaire. See Voltaire.

Dido...: legendary Queen of Carthage, lover of Aeneas.

Diem Bien Phu: a town in Vietnam where Colonial France suffered a major defeat by the Vietnamese, formerly French-Indochina.

Dir....: a Viking co-ruler in Kiev. See Askold.

Disraeli, Benjamin (1804-81): British statesman and writer. Prime Minister in 1868 then 1874-80, of Jewish descent, he defined the Arab policy for England.

DIV....: symbol for dividend.

Dnieper: a major river in the Ukraine. Kiev (Kiïv) lies on that river, a major trade route from Novhorod to Kiev to Constantinople, aka: Dnipro.

Dnipro.: see Dnieper.

Doges of Venice: elected heads of the Venetian Republic in Italy. There were 120 Doges from 697 to 1796, when Venice was conquered by Napoleon.

Dollfuss, Englebert (1892-1934): Austrian Chancellor, assassinated by Hitler's agents.

Doomsday Book: survey of England made by William the Conqueror in 1086 mainly for tax purposes.

Donatists: a Christian sect.

Doyle, Sir Arthur Conan (1859-1930): an English mystery writer, created the characters Sherlock Homes, Watson and Moriarity.

Drake, Sir Francis (1543-96): English admiral, opponent to Spanish Armada.

Druzhina: in Ukrainian, a team or a wife.

Duma...:originally in Ukrainian this was the council to the King. When the word was Russified it was replaced with Rada.

Dunkirk == Dunkerque: a French Sea port near Belgium. In 1940, the site of a crushing defeat of the Anglo-French army by Hitler and the heroic rescue effort by England. Over 340,000 soldiers were saved.

DuPont Corp: when Fermi demonstrated the controlled nuclear reaction to the US Government, DuPont Corp. was given

the contract to build the nuclear reactors.
Dwarfs.: human beings of small size.
Dzerzhinsky, Felix (1877-1926): head of the Cheka (KGB) in the Soviet Union under Stalin.

Ebro...: a river in Spain.
Eck, (Johann) Dr. (1486-1543): a learned theologian of the Roman Faith,he challenged Martin Luther to debate his 95 Theses. The debate was held in Ingolstadt. After the debate the German language had a new word: Dreck (or excrement.)
Edict of Milan: in 313, Roman Emperor Constantine made Christianity a valid religion in his empire.
Edison, Thomas A (1847-1931): American inventor. He has over 1000 patents in his name ranging from light bulb, telephone, gramophone and electrical devices for movie cameras.
Effigy.: a portrait, image, burial site or ritual temple.
EFTA...: European Free Trade Association.Consists of the outer 7: Austria, Denmark, Finland, Norway, Portugal, Sweden and Switzerland. This was an alternative to Europa. Now part of EU, except for Switzerland.
Egypt..: an ancient civilization as documented by Manetho,later a Roman province, now an independent Muslim country.
Eichman: one of Hitler's henchmen who escaped to Argentina. He was caught, tried, convicted and hanged in Israel.
Eigenvalue(s): the roots of a system of equations.
Einstein, Albert (1879-1955): mathematician and physicist of German birth and Jewish extraction. He became citizen of the USA in 1940. Major works include:Theory of Relativity, and the formulation how energy is related to mass;E=M*C*C.
Eisenhower, Dwight D (1890-1968): 34th President of the USA. American general, Supreme Allied Commander during World War II in Europe and statesman.
El Alamain: Rommel's Afrika Corps met defeat there in 1942.
Elba...: an island off the Southern coast of France.
Elbe...: a major river which divides Germany. In antiquity, that river divided the Germans and the Goths, except for the Gothic Suevi who had settled along the Rhine river.
Electricity: a form of energy.
Emancipation: the freeing of an oppressed group of people in a society. Examples are: slaves, serfs and women.
Engels, Friedrich (1820-1895): a devout student of Karl Marx.
Empire.: a territory ruled over by an Emperor.
England: technically the southern part of the island of Britain, excluding Wales and Scotland. In the context of this book Great Britain is implied, including Northern Ireland.

Julius Caesar made two expeditions to England but considered the island was not worth conquering. Roman Emperor Claudius (41-54 AD) conquered England. It remained a Roman province until Constantine all but left England in 310 and started his civil war to become Emperor. From then on, England was abandoned by the Roman Empire.

In the 6th century, the Northern Goths moved in, until England was ruled by the Danes. In 1066, the Norman Goths (French Catholics) invaded England and ruled until Henry VIII. With Queen Elizabeth I, England became Protestant and began her development towards an independent nation. The Protestant cause was not settled until Queen Anne died and the Hanoverians took over with George I in 1714, who rule there to the present.

English language: originally a modified Celtic language. When Britain was conquered by the Romans, the official language became Latin. The modifications to the Celtic language became known as Old English. In the 4th century England was abandoned by the Roman Empire and Roman missionaries converted England to the Roman Faith. Again, the official language was Latin and the Old English vernacular was modified. In the 6th century to the 16th century, the British Isles were invaded first by the Angles, Jutes and Sassons (all Goths) and then by the Norman Goths -- with William the conqueror in 1066. The official language remained Latin but the vernacular took on a Norman flavor, a dialect of the French. The Norman line died out with Queen Anne. But when Henry VIII evicted the Roman Church from England and created the Anglican Church, the vernacular underwent major modifications with Queen Elizabeth I who shifted to the Dutch language (this is why Peter I was so impressed with the Dutch language intending to change to Dutch in Russia.)

Enter Shakespeare. Shakespearean English lasted until the Germans took over in 1715, with George I, the Duke and Elector from Hanover. Since that time, English has been gradually drifting towards the German language of Martin Luther and lately towards the language of Goethe, Schiller and Lessing.

Now, with England's entry into the European Union a near certainty (the major banking houses in England and France, the Rothschilds, have already merged),the English language will converge more rapidly towards the German.

Emmanuel III, Victor (1869-1947): King of Italy.

Enron..: a US company which cooked the books (falsified their earnings.)

EPS....: earnings per share.

Erde...: the only known goddess in the German pantheon. In German, earth.

Eris...: in Greek mythology, goddess of feud or discord.

Ermak, Timofeev (1524-1584): a Don Cossack Hetman who conquered the Khanate of Sibir (with the aid of the Ural Sich) and gifted it to Ivan the Terrible, hence Siberia.

Ermanric, (ca 326-376): a Gothic leader who tried to reform the Gothic Empire at the time of the Hun invasion.

Estonia: a country on the South-Eastern Baltic Sea, became a Russian province with Peter I. Became part of Kurland, including Latvia and Lithuania (aka: Livonia). Gained independence after World War I (1919-1939), was allied with Hitler during World War II, was seized by Stalin in 1940, was taken by the Germans 1941-43 and integrated into the Soviet Union in 1945. When the Soviet Union collapsed Estonia again gained her independence. Now part of EU.

Ethiopia: a country in North-East Africa of Christian Faith with her own Patriarch. Their brand of Christianity is called: the Coptic Church.

Etruscans: a nation from Asia Minor who fought in the Trojan War against the Achaeans.After the war they broke up into two groups, one remained while the other migrated into Europe and settled on the Italian peninsula -- from the Alps to the river Tiber. There, they established City-States. Their civilization was highly advanced. They were masters in canal building, city sewers, agriculture, roads and animal husbandry. They maintained a sacred text which was used in the interpretation of sacrifices. They became known as the Roman Augurs. Practically every Roman Emperor and Dictator used such an Augur, including Julius Caesar and so on. Despite it all, they were decimated and absorbed by the Romans.

EU.....: European Union. Is this the 4th Reich?.

Euclid, (ca.350-275 BC): a Greek mathematician, teacher and lecturer in Alexandria, Egypt, (at that time Egypt was the world's cultural center.) He is credited with the 'Euclidian Geometry,' a body of knowledge still taught in our schools just like it was taught in Alexandria by Euclid. The subject was very popular, therefore many complete books have survived, mostly notebooks of his pupils. Today the claim is being made that he was not the author, but rather an editor of existing texts. In any event, his body of knowledge is highly restrictive since it assumes that parallel lines do not intersect. That is, it is valid only in 2 dimensional space.

Lobachevsky showed that a better, spatial Geometry, is more applicable to our earth and for the cosmos. It is 3 dimensional.

Eudoxus: a mathematician from antiquity, he developed the method of exhaustion. Proofs by induction are some of the present uses of his method.

Euler, Leonhard (1707-1783): one of the 3 all-time great mathematicians. The other two being: Archimedes and Daniel Bernoulli.

Euro...: the currency of the European Union.

Europa.: European Common Market (EEC), originally formed by Germany and France which led to the European Union (EU).

Fasolt.: in Gothic mythology, one of the giants who built Walhalla, the abode of the Gothic gods.
Fathers of the Church: in the early centuries, the teachers of the Christian Church, including: James, Peter and Paul. For the most part they preached against heresies and fallacies of the early Church. For example: St. Augustine, Bishop of Hippo, who preached against the Pelagian heresy and so on.
Februs.: in Roman mythology, the god of death. Thantos in Greek.
Federati: in the Roman Empire, the allies who accompanied the Roman legions to battle.
Feldwebel: a military rank in the German army (Sergeant) also in the Russian army, starting with Peter I.
Ferdinand and Isabella, (1452-1516): rulers of Spain.
Fermi, Enrico (1901-1954): an Italian physicist, who received his Nobel Prize in 1939, then made his escape with his family to America. In Chicago (December 2, 1942) he demonstrated a sustained nuclear reaction and developed the Atom Bomb in Los Alamos.
Fibonnaci: a mathematician who developed the series: 1, 1, 2, 3, 5, 8,...etc. (the last two numbers are added to get the next number). This series keeps popping up in nature.
Field-Marshal: a military title above general in Germany and Peter's Russia. The Soviet Union used Marshal. In America, a two star general or higher.
Fillmore, Milard (1850-53): 13th President of the USA.
Florence: the capital of Tuscany, in Italy. Famous for her beauty, art and literature. Florence was controlled by the Medici family. Sister city to Kiev.
Fluxion: a notion of Sir Isaac Newton (for a derivative.) A better and more accepted definition was developed by Leibnitz. He called it a differential and Differential Calculus hinges on Leibnitz's definition.
Fong...: a financial analyst and researcher.
Ford, Gerald (1976-1977): 38th President of the USA.
Ford, Henry (1863-1947): American automobile engineer and manufacturer. He made the Model T (1908) affordable to all Americans, 15 million were sold.
Foreign Legion: founded in 1831, to include foreign nationals in the French army.
Fortuna: in Roman mythology, goddess of luck.
Fortran: a computer language (Formula Translation).
Fouche, Joseph (1759-1820): the chief of secret police for Napoleon (and the monarchy, before and after Napoleon.)
Fractal(s): a notion in mathematics of a minute difference.
Francis I, (1494-1574):King of France, contemporary of Henry VIII of England and his archenemy, the Holy Roman Emperor Charles V. Architect of the French Concordat, in 1515 whereby France paid an annual fee to the Pope in perpetuity and in return the Pope (Leo X) allowed the French King to install the Bishops of his choice, also in

perpetuity. This paved the way for French nationalism. Francis made an alliance with the Ottoman Turks to save France from the Teutonic conquest.

Francis Joseph I, (1830-1916): King of Austria and Emperor of the Holy Roman Empire, a Habsburg. When his nephew, Archduke Franz Ferdinand was assassinated in Sarajevo, Francis led Austria into the attack on Serbia which eventually led to World War I. Today, the Habsburgs are invited observers and advisors to the Council of Europe.

Franklin, Benjamin (1706-1790): American scientist, writer, philosopher and inventor who discovered the nature of electricity.

Franco, Francisco (1892-1975): Spanish general, dictator and leader of the Falangists, the fascist movement in Spain. Franco was allied with Hitler in World War II. Because of the Civil War in Spain (1936-39), only a few divisions were given to Hitler for the invasion of the Soviet Union. After his death the monarchy was restored in Spain. Now part of the EU.

Franco-Prussian War, (1870-71): Bismarck managed to provoke the French into declaring war and Moltke defeated the French armies. Paris fell on January 28, 1871. In the Hall of Mirrors in Versailles, Germany was made an Empire by the victorious Germans by proclamation.

Franko, Ivan (1856-1916): a Ukrainian writer and poet.

Franks.: a coalition of Germanic and Gothic tribes who ruled Gaul. They consisted of the Salian Franks, the Ripurian Franks and Goths. In the end, the Merovingians ruled Gaul for over 300 years.

Frederick I, Barbarossa (1124-90): Holy Roman Emperor, member of the Hohenstaufen family.

Frederick II, The Great (1712-86): King of Prussia, member of the Hohenzollern family.During the 7 Year War against Austria, France and Russia, Prussia was utterly destroyed by the Russians at Kunersdorf and Berlin was raided. But then, the unthinkable happened: his provinces were restored and Prussia was resurrected by Catherine II of Russia in the Treaty of Paris in 1763. When Hitler's war was coming to an end, he hoped for a similar miracle. He could have had his miracle had he unleashed Vlasov and his army in 1942 or as late as 1943. Timing is everything,even in politics.

French Revolution, (1789-99): a series of violent events which overthrew the French monarchy.

Fulton, Mo USA: in 1946 Churchill gave the 'Iron Curtain Speech' there, which led to the Cold War.

G7/G8..: the economic powers: America (USA); France, Germany, Great Britain, Italy, Japan, Switzerland and (Russia).

Galileo, Galilei (1564-1642): Italian astronomer, mathematician and scientist. His main work: 'The Two Sciences.'

Galleon: an early sailing warship of the 14th to 18th centuries.

Gallipoli: a strategic port in the Dardanelles, the location of a disastrous English campaign against the Ottoman Turks led by Winston Churchill during WW I.
Gama, Vasco da (1469-1524): Portuguese explorer of India.
Gandhi, Mahatma (1869-1948): Architect of Indian independence from Great Britain.
Gange, Rolf (860-961): Gothic Viking who settled in France in Normandy, Brittany, Anjou, Aquitaine and Gascony.
Ganymede: in Greek mythology, a servant to Hera.
Garfield, James A (1881-1881): 20th President of the USA.
Garibaldi, Giuseppe (1807-82): Italian leader and patriot. Architect of Risorgimento which led to the consolidation and formation of Italy from 1860 to 1865.
Gastarbeiter: German for, 'guest worker.'
Gaul...: the combined names of the Roman provinces in France. Julius Caesar coined that name from the Gaelic population he encountered there.
Gaulle, Charles De: see DeGaulle.
Gauss, Karl F (1777-1855): German mathematician.
Genghis Khan (1162-1227): Mongol Khan and Emperor of China. His grandson Batu led the Tartar-Mongol invasion into Europe in 1238 with "The Golden Horde."
Genseric, (395-477): Gothic King in North Africa. He sacked Rome in 455. Belisarius defeated the Goths in North Africa in 544 and allowed them to rejoin their kinfolk in Spain.
Geopolitical: using geopolitics.
Geopolitics: a policy practiced by England. Once an enemy was identified, then geography and politics was used to encircle that enemy. That is, the enemy was surrounded and throttled. However, a similar policy was practiced by all royals in Europe -- all Germans. In Austria,it was called Ausgleich; in Germany, Kulturkampf; in Romanov Russia, Russification; in the Soviet Union, stark Tartar terror.
Gepids.: a Gothic nation.
Germanization: the German version of geopolitics. Declare things to be German (by proclamation). Aka: Kulturkampf.
Germany: a modern European country formed in 1871, in Versailles, in the Hall of Mirrors by proclamation.

When Julius Caesar conquered Gaul, he encountered mostly Germanic tribes to the North of Gaul (Dutch, Batavians and Frisians) and across the river Rhine. Eventually Caesar recruited them into his legions. Caesar's famous legion, the 10th, was made up of mostly German legionnaires.

Tacitus, Pliny and Strabo describe the aboriginal German lands as the area between the rivers Rhine and Elbe bound by the North Sea in the North and the Danube river in the South. Only one Gothic nation had settled near the Rhine river: the Suevi. All other Goths were along the East bank of the river Elbe and beyond. During the Hun invasion, the Austrichi (Austrians) and part of the Bayuvari (Bavarians) moved into the Alps, while the Goths, with the Huns at their heels entered Gaul. The German and Gothic tribes from the East bank of the River Rhine and further East became allies of the Huns per force -- these Goths were called the Ostrogoths. After the Hun invasion, the Gothic nations of: Angles, Sassons and Wends were annihilated and Germans began to cross the Elbe river. The coalition of the Franks, eventually gave rise to the Carolingian rulers who were of Germanic origin. Once Charlemagne became Emperor of the Holy Roman Empire and the protector of the Pope (German Concordat) he set up a feudal system starting with the Electors whereby the Germans controlled the election of the Emperor of the Holy Roman Empire (3 Bishops and 4 Dukes). His main cities became: Aachen, Cologne, Mainz, Metz, Trier and Worms. From Germany, he made war on the Avars, who had replaced the Huns in Pannonia. At that time Bohemia and Moravia, both Gothic nations, were allied with Charlemagne and both Gothic nations accepted the Roman Faith. This made them key players and they demanded a voice. Eventually, Bohemia was included as an Elector (Golden Bull). By then, the Germans crossed over the river Elbe, eliminated the remaining Sassons and Wends and created a Mark -- a military zone, called Brandenburg. The Avars were annihilated by the Magyars, at which time Brandenburg began expanding East. Gothic Pomerania was conquered and the Gothic Prussians were annihilated. The Germans used the name Prussia to create a new German state by that name. However, the Polish Goths had converted to the Roman Faith, so they were spared, albeit reluctantly.

During the Crusades, the Teutonic Knights were formed by the Pope, with the mission to conquer the East. They proceeded along the Baltic Sea, bridging the Vistula river and then the Niemen river (Memel in German), conquering parts of Lithuania, Latvia and Estonia which they called Kurland. However, the Lithuanian Grand Duke Vitus defeated them in 1410 and made them sign a treaty whereby the Teutonic Knights were bound by the Vistula river. The Grandmaster of the Teutonic Knights rushed to Rome and the Pope disbanded the Teutonic Knights and chartered a new order called the Knights of the Sword, keeping the same Grandmaster and Knights. This new Crusading order continued beyond the Niemen River until Charles XII of Sweden annihilated that order along the Baltic coast. That is, the Crusades into Eastern Europe lasted for nearly 700 years, from about 1000 to 1708.

In 1701, the King of Prussia (by proclamation) was crowned in Königsberg, East Prussia and Prussia became a dominant power in Europe.

Then, Prussia, Austria and Russia with Catherine II, ganged up on Poland (1772-75) and erased her from the map of Europe -- the 3 partitions of Poland. Later (1804-10), however, Napoleon defeated the Prussians at Jena, occupied Berlin and took a few statues from Berlin to Paris.Prussia became an ally of Napoleon anyway. For that alliance with Napoleon, Prussia received the Dukedom of Hannover from Napoleon (England was at war with Napoleon).

As soon as Napoleon was defeated in Russia in 1812, Prussia joined Russia against Napoleon (1813-15). Therefore, by the end of the Napoleonic wars, Prussia emerged as a near super-power in Europe.

The Franco-Prussian War (1870-71) became her crowning achievement. France was defeated, a German Empire was proclaimed and her statues were taken back to Berlin (winged chariot on the Brandenburg Gate and others). After 1875, Germany, Austria and Great Britain were the dominant powers in Europe.

This changed when Germany began building the Baghdad-Berlin railroad. New alliances were formed in 1901: France, Russia and Japan allied with England. While Germany was allied with: Austria and the Ottoman Empire.

By the end of World War I, the Axis powers of Germany, Austria and the Ottoman Empire were dismembered. From then on, revanche was on their mind (the von Clausewitz motif.) This revanche came with Hitler and World War II. Again, Austria and Germany were destroyed. But, because English geopolitics favors a strong Germany (as a deterrent against Russia), Germany has been rebuilt with American money.

In order to compete among the superpowers, Germany and and France began a trade union (Europa) which made them into a major World Power once 23 European nations joined Europa. Thus, Europa is the Phase I of an all European state. Phase II being a common currency and Phase III a common defense and common foreign policy. Now that the European Union has become a reality, the Franco-German coalition plans to be the next major economic power in the world. The fact that the Rothschild Banks of France and England have merged only proves that England will be part of that triumvirate.

Phase III is the Empire Charlemagne, Napoleon and Hitler were dreaming about. With Phase II nearly completed, we should expect Phase III to start within next decade or so.

Getica.: the definitive history of the Goths, written by Cassiodorus Senator. That version is extinct. Jordanes read that history and wrote a synopsis which is also called: Getica.

Ghea...(aka Gaia): in Greek mythology, the original mother goddess also known as Rhea (Maya in Egypt).

Gneisenau: a German battle cruiser during World War II.

Godunov, Boris (1551-1605): Tartar Czar, ruler of Muscovy.

Goebbels, Joseph P (1897-1945): Nazi propaganda minister.

Göring, Herman W (1893-1946): chief of Hitler's Luftwaffe.
Gogol..: see Hohol...
Goh Chok Tong: current political leader from Singapore.
Gorbachev, Michail (1927-): the leader of the Soviet Union at the time of her collapse.He is a native from the Don area.
Gothland: an island off Sweden in the Baltic Sea. Also called Gotland.
Gotland.: see Gothland.
Goths...: German historians (Mommsen, in particular) and historians serving German rulers (Gibbon) have declared that the Goths are a Germanic people. Furthermore, they have declared that the Goths vanished from the political scene in Europe and the Slavs appeared in the 7th century. However, the historical facts are just not so.

To begin with, the Goths and Slavs merged into one nation in antiquity, prior to the Trojan war. This is recorded in their mythology. They did that by exchanging their King-Judges. They ruled Northern Europe, north of the river Danube and from the river Elbe to the Ural mountains, according to Strabo, Jordanes and other geographers and historians. In population, they were larger than the Roman Empire. Strabo reported that the census by Emperor Augustus, accounted for 5.4 million souls while a similar census made by the Goths produced 5.6 million. By and large, the Goths and the Romans lived peacefully side by side. The Goths emulated the Roman Empire in many ways, except for their form of rulership which was a King-Judge and their concept of personal liberties -- they had no slaves or serfs and women had the same rights as men. Including: education, women could own property and be rulers. Since their land was vast and their population numerous, they organized as Gothic nations.

However, during a national emergency, they had a means of bringing all the Gothic nations together and adopt a common policy. This was called Allthing or Sbor. It was practiced in Russia in the 17th century, when the Tartars in Muscovy were outvoted and Michael Romanov installed as ruler, and in Iceland where the practice continued until the 20th century.

They had a three tier justice system: Royal or Princely court; Thing or Veche -- a court of peers; an Allthing or Sbor -- a national assembly. Their cities were Chartered, guaranteeing certain basic rights for each citizen. Women had the same rights as men.

As soon as the Roman Empire adopted Christianity, the Goths sent a delegation headed by Ulfilas to investigate the new religion adopted by Constantinople. The delegation was treated royally by Emperor Constantine and Patriarch Arius. At that time Arianism was the only legitimate form of Christianity in the Roman Empire.

Ulfilas and his team were impressed with Christianity. They spent the next 10 years in Constantinople. They translated the Bible into Runic (the Gothic language) and returned to their homeland as Christian missionaries -- albeit Arian Christians. (Parts of their translated Bible are still displayed in Uppsala, Sweden.)

However, shortly thereafter the Mongolic Huns invaded Europe. They defeated the Goths and the Goths were on the run, they were in panic. By then, about half of the Goths had converted to Christianity. The converts headed for the Roman Empire. They expected to get sanctuary from their fellow Christians. About 1 million Goths arrived at the Danube in the Balkans in 376 and asked for sanctuary, while another 1.5 million headed for Gaul, crossed the Rhine river in 379 and settled in Gaul between Orleans and Bordeaux.

At that time the Roman Emperor was Valens. But, he had just changed the legal Christian Faith from Arianism to Orthodoxy. The Danubian Goths got sanctuary, but not before they turned over their weapons and gave up their children as hostages in 376. Only then were they ferried across the Danube river. They were promised a rich and fertile province in which they could settle, yet received a portion of Thrace, which was useless for agriculture. Their children were taken away and an attempt was made to convert them to Orthodoxy.When they refused to convert, they were massacred in 377. Eventually, this news reached the Balkan Goths. Unarmed and destitute, they armed themselves the best they could, rebelled against the Romans, and at Adrianople defeated a Roman army and killed Valens in 378. Eventually, they were defeated and their lot became worse than before. They sent messengers to their kinfolk to be rescued.

When word reached the Goths in their homeland, they called for an Allthing in the Trypilian area and elected a new King-Judge to rescue the Balkan Goths, Alaric in 395. Alaric raised an army, crossed the Danube, defeated a few Roman mercenary legions and liberated the Balkan Goths. Then, Alaric proceeded to conquer the rest of the Balkans, which he did. However, he could not take Constantinople. This resulted in a truce. Alaric was promoted to 'Master of the Horse,' a title just below Caesar and Augustus.

Alaric's new title gave him control of all the military supplies in the Roman Empire. He rearmed his Goths as the uneasy truce continued. When he realized there was no future for the Goths in the Balkans, he approached Emperor Arcadius and asked for a Roman province where the Goths could settle peacefully. Arcadius told him, any part of the Western Empire was available to the Goths, including Italy. By then, the Western portion of the Roman Empire had been abandoned anyway and Arcadius promised the Goths safe passage through the Roman Empire. By then, Goths had settled in North Africa, near Carthage, which was a rich and fertile province and Alaric felt his Goths should move there. Alaric assembled the Goths, and his proposal was ratified. They picked up their possessions and moved out of the Balkans.

Arcadius, however, called on his general Stilicho to intercept and to destroy the Goths. As Alaric crossed from the Balkans into Italy, Stilicho attacked him in 403 and nearly defeated the Goths. However, Stilicho was an Alan Goth in the employ of Arcadius. Stilicho and Alaric made a deal. Now, Alaric could continue his trek to Southern Italy. When he came to Rome, Alaric demanded a ransom for the treachery by the Western Emperor Honorius in 408. Honorius paid and had Stilicho executed.Now Alaric allowed his Goths to sack the city in 409, allowing 3 days of rampage. Then, he continued South.

When Alaric arrived in Southern Italy, he died in 410. Alaric was buried in the Busento river and the Goths elected a new leader. He had other ideas. He wanted to link up with the fellow Goths in Gaul (France.) The Goths turned around and trekked North. As they came to Rome, they sacked Rome again. This time, 7 days were allowed to pilfer the city in 411. After that they left Italy and settled in Provence, Languedoc, Gascony and near Bordeaux. Now, practically all of Gaul was inhabited by Goths. Only two enclaves remained which were dominated by other ethnic people. One around Paris, mostly by Gaels and the other in the northern-most part of Gaul, mostly by Germanic people: Batavians, Frisians, Belgae and Walloons.

The Huns settled in Pannonia and from there they raided the Roman Empire; the Balkans, Italy and Gaul. When Attila came to power he decided to conquer the Roman Empire, piece by piece -- Gaul, Italy (Rome) and the Balkans (Constantinople).

In 451 Attila set out to conquer Gaul. He gathered a great army, not only of Huns but also his subjects: Burgundians, Germans and Ostrogoths (heathen Goths). That huge army, said by some historians to number about 1.5 million swarmed into Gaul. All the great cities of Gaul fell one by one until Attila reached Orleans.

By then, the Visigoths (Arian Goths) assembled a great army under Theodoric I, their King-Judge from Bordeaux and met Attila at Chalons-sur-Marne.Theodoric's army consisted of his Arian Goths, Alans and Scythians. The Scythians were brought in by the Roman general Aetius from the Ukraine. That epic battle, saved Western Civilization.

Attila was defeated, however, the victorious Goths did not finish Attila off because Aetius felt that the victorious Goths would be a greater danger to Rome than the defeated Huns. Theodoric was mortally wounded and when he died, Aetius urged his son (Theodoric II) to take the Goths back to Bordeaux to save his succession.

Attila fled to his camp. He was so convinced of an imminent Gothic attack that he burned his armor, shields, saddles and killed his loyal servants and most precious horses. When the Gothic attack did not materialize, Attila broke camp and returned to Pannonia.

The following year Attila raised a new army, invaded Italy and razed the great Northern cities until he came to Rome. There he halted, while Rome was trembling. During that rest period Papa Leo I paid Attila a visit and some sort of truce was reached. Because Attila took his army and returned to Pannonia. There, a young and beautiful Burgundian Princess was waiting for him to be married. They got married and on their wedding night Attila's artery burst and he died in a pool of blood.

Attila had three sons. This presented a unique opportunity to turn the Huns against each other. Legates from Rome and Constantinople were able to turn the three brothers against each another and a battle for succession ensued. In that civil war the Huns nearly eradicated each other. But, when that war was over, the Huns were still a formidable force.

Rome and Constantinople were in a precarious position. While Christianity was a god-send for administrative purposes, it was a disaster in terms of military power. Neither Rome nor Constantinople had an army large enough to take on the remaining Huns.

Julius Caesar had realized that Rome was not ideally suited to administer the empire. When Caesar's affair with Cleopatra reached its height, there was hardly a Roman who did not see the hand-writing on the wall. Caesar had every intention of moving the capital -- probably to Alexandria. Marc Anthony only confirmed that speculation. But, Emperor Augustus dashed these notions and made Rome great again.

However, that seed came to fruition with Emperor Diocletian (284-305), who divided the Roman Empire into two empires and two military zones. Diocletian took the East, because it was rich and gave Maximian, Rome and the West. The two military zones were in Gaul along the Rhine and in the Balkans along the Danube, protecting the border against the Germans and Goths. In the process the titles were changed to reflect the responsibilities. The title Augustus was reserved for the Emperor, while the title Caesar was used for a military dictator in each zone.

However, as soon as Maximian became Emperor (285-305) he abolished that idea. Thus, Rome became once again, the sole capital of the Empire.

When Constantine (310-337) became Emperor (who was a descendent of Diocletian) there was one more compelling reason to change the seat of the Empire: Christianity. Rome was full with heathen temples and once Christianity became the dominant religion, the temples were burning. Therefore, Emperor Constantine picked the best location in the Empire, former Byzantium. He expanded it, built a huge wall, built Churches for the new faith and selected the brand of Christianity he wanted to be practiced in his Empire: Arianism -- while he himself remained a heathen, a sun-worshipper. He was baptized on his death bed and then by an Arian Bishop.

In 330, the new capitol was completed and the patricians of Rome were forced to relocate to Constantinople. During that period all stone construction in the Empire was halted in order to complete Constantinople as soon as possible. (The same tactic was used by Peter I, to build St. Petersburg.)

Once Constantinople was operational, Rome became just another provincial capital. Therefore, starting with Emperor Constantine, the legitimate Roman Empire was in Constantinople. (Later, around 1500, Western historians called it the Byzantine Empire, to give more legitimacy to the Holy Roman Empire.)

The other problem was the military. When Constantine fought for the supremacy in the Roman Empire, 52 Roman legions were strategically positioned in the Empire. With Christianity as the main religion, most of these legions were disbanded. The idea was simple. Since the Emperor designated the Bishops, they owed him direct loyalty. All that was needed was a relatively small militia to guard their city. A Bishop was both a military and religious title. This way, central command was required only in Constantinople and the wars of succession could be eliminated. To a large degree Constantine was right. For example: during Roman rule (27BC to 313) there were 53 Emperors for a period of 340 years. On average, this gave each Emperor 6.4 years to rule. But, the dynastic struggle lasted more than 2 years, which ravaged the Roman Empire. The new Roman Empire from Constantinople, lasted from 330 to 1453 or 1123 years, had 85 Emperors (excluding the six Frankish Emperors after the 4th Crusade), giving every Emperor an average of 13.2 years to rule and an average dynastic struggle of less than 2 months.

However, what was not anticipated was that Christianity itself frowned on military service, encouraged monasticism and advocated to save one's soul rather than one's body. Why? The second coming was around the corner and it was more prudent to save the soul rather than the body. Therefore, by the time we come to Emperor Valens (364-378), which is less than 35 years after Constantine's death, there are no Roman legions left, only a few legions commanded and manned by foreign mercenaries. (Stilicho is a good example.) Therefore, Constantinople had to embark on a new policy of conquest for large military operations. They started hiring entire nations to do battle for them. (A new form of Roman militarism returned with the German Concordat and the Crusades, directed by the Pope.)

Again, the basis of the idea was simple. Recruit the heathens to do battle for you, convert them to the Christian Faith and kill two birds with one stone. The enemy is eliminated and Christianity expands. This became the dominant policy starting with Emperor Arcadius (395-408), with Alaric. That policy backfired, because the Goths were Arian Christians and did not convert to Orthodoxy.

Therefore, when the civil war among the Huns came to an end, the Huns were still too powerful for the Roman Empire to tackle. Thus, under Roman Emperor Leo I (457-74), the Gothic Gepids were hired to annihilate the Huns, which they did. Then the Roman Emperor Zeno (474-491) hired the Ostrogoths, to take up residence in Italy (Italy was pressured by the German Langobards or Lombards). The Ostrogoths moved from the Ukraine into Italy, defeated the Langobards, established Ravenna as their capital and brought peace and prosperity to Italy with their King-Judge and Roman Caesar Theodoric the Great (493-526).

The last payment to the Gepids, however, was not made. Therefore, the Gepids became unruly and started raiding the Roman Empire. Thus, when the Mongolic Avars (ca. 535) appeared on the European horizon, they were hired to eliminate the Gepids. On their way from Asia to Pannonia, they devastated the Ukraine, came to Pannonia and defeated the Gepids. Again, the Roman Empire did not make the last payment to the Avars and the story kept repeating itself. The Avars raided the Roman Empire until another Mongolic nation was found -- the Magyars, who again trekked through the Ukraine, defeated 8 Princes and arrived in Pannonia about 900. There, they eliminated the Avars and settled in Pannonia (Hungary). Again, they were not paid their last installment and they raided the Roman Empire and Gaul. Eventually the Magyars were defeated by Otto I, Emperor of the Holy Roman Empire at Lechfeld in 955. They accepted the Roman Faith and became members of the Holy Roman Empire (eventually under Austrian rule.) Thus, in the end, even that policy worked, but at what price in human life?

Geopolitically, the issue with the Goths, was not settled not by a long shot. To begin with, they were Arian Christians and resisted every attempt of conversion, be it to the Roman Church (which was Orthodox until 800) or the Orthodox Faith.

Therefore, the Roman Empire launched a program of disinformation about the Goths. First, they had to be reduced in size and each group given a new identity. Because, another Alaric type invasion could destroy the Roman Empire. This was initiated with Emperor Justinian I (527-565). Therefore, the Goths beyond the river Danube were called Slavs. The Goths in North Africa, heretics. The Goths in Italy, Ostrogoths and the Goths in Gaul and Spain, Visigoths. And, to make that distinction even more pronounced the Ostrogoths and Visigoths were made a Germanic people, unrelated to any Germanic nation or any German tribe.

By renaming the Goths this way, the umbilical cord was, if not cut, at least severed. Because they had integrated into the Roman society in all respects, except for their faith. They had intermarried and raised their offspring as natives. And, by all accounts they brought peace and prosperity in the areas they ruled: North Africa, Italy, Spain and Gaul.

Nevertheless, Justinian launched his program by eradicating the North African Goths first. Belisarius was sent to Carthage with two legions of mercenaries, and pitting the Christian Donatists against the Arian Christians, Belisarius defeated the Goths but allowed them to rejoin their kinfolk in Spain. Once the Goths were gone, the Donatists were annihilated.

Shortly thereafter, Theodoric the Great died in Italy. Now, Justinian claimed that the contract between Emperor Zeno and Theodoric was only between the two of them and the Ostrogoths had no business being in Italy.

With that he launched his wars against the Ostrogoths. The war lasted from 534 to 565 which devastated Italy but the Goths were evicted and were allowed to join their kinfolk in Gaul. They settled in Provence, Languedoc, Gascony, Aquitaine, Brittany and Normandy. In this war, the Bishop of Rome played a key part. He annulled all marriages between the natives and the Ostrogoths. For that, the Bishop of Rome was elevated to Patriarch by Justinian.

To avoid further religious wars, the Goths in Spain and Gaul began converting to the Roman Faith, in the 7th century. However, while they converted to the Roman Faith, they remained tolerant to other Christian Faiths, gnostic and infidels. (That's why in Gaul, the Merovingians, were called the 'Do-Nothing Kings.')

Again, the policy of the Roman Empire seemed to work, at least partially. However, Islam was on the rise. And when Emperor Heraclites (610-641), tried to convert the

Christian Monophysites in 635, they converted to Islam. Now the richest provinces of the Roman Empire were lost and Constantinople was surrounded by militant Islam.

In 711, Spain was conquered by the Moors. They brought Islam to Spain. The internal religious wars and the lack of a native military nearly ruined both Christian empires. The lack of a native military made both Christian Empires ripe targets for a military takeover. Islam capitalized on this and took over in Asia, Africa and Europe.

To make matters worse, more Goths began descending into both empires. In the West, the Norse or Normans and in the East the Slavs.

The Norse-Goths conquered England in the 7th century. Then the Danes ruled in England and in Scotland until 1066. Then, the Norse-Goths took Paris and in a treaty, gained Normandy and Brittany where they settled. In 1066, the Norman-Goths conquered England and were displaced by the Germans in 1715, when the Hanoverians took over.

Meanwhile, the Norse-Goths pressed further South. By the 9th century they reached Constantinople. Once there, Emperor Basil I (867-886) knew what to do with them. He hired them. They became the Varangian Guard and the new mercenaries in the Roman legions. They dominated the Roman Empire until Constantinople was taken by the Franks in the 4th Crusade in 1204.

For all practical purposes, the 4th Crusade was the end of the Roman Empire. It barely survived until 1453, (all that was left was Constantinople,and it survived because their navy had a 'doomsday weapon' called: the Greek Fire) when it was finally conquered by the Ottoman Turks with the help of the Austrians.

In the 7th century, while Roman Emperor Heraclites was trying to convert the Monophysites, Goths (now called Slavs) began invading the Roman Empire and within a century, the Balkans became know as: Slavland. Croats, Slovenes and Serbs moved in. The Mongolic Bulgars were hired to subdue the Slavs in the Balkans. In the end, the Bulgars accepted the Slavic language, customs and the Orthodox Faith. (A similar case as the Magyars, but in the Balkans).

In the 10th century, the Kievan-Rus-Goths accepted Christianity from Constantinople and for a while a rebirth of Constantinople was in the making. Kiev developed close ties, provided much of the needed military and trade flourished. But, the Tartar invasion, the sack of Kiev in 1240 ended all hopes for the Roman Empire and the Ukraine.

Graf Spee: a German pocket battleship, scuttled in 1939.

Granada: a town in Spain, last Moorish stronghold. Now the site where Muslim Mosques are built.

Grant, Ulysses S (1869-77): 18th President of the USA.

Greece.: now a democracy in South-East Europe. While Greece enjoyed only a short period of liberty in ancient times, about 260 years from 600 to 340 BC, she is still valued highly among Western historians because her ideals became the ideals of Western Civilization -- except for slavery and the degradation of women. By 338 BC the Macedonian Goths under Alexander the Great conquered Greece, by 200 BC the Romans took over and in 1453, after the fall of Constantinople, the Ottoman Turks ruled there.

In 1827, England and Russia liberated Greece from Ottoman rule and Capodistrias, the secretary of Czar Nicholas I became President of Greece. However, this violated the German Concordat and Otto I from Bavaria was installed. A popular revolt in Greece (1967) evicted the German royals and in 1974 a Democracy was installed. Today Greece is part of the EU.

Gregory VII, (1021-85): Pope Hildebrand of Tuscany initiated the struggle called: Investiture.When the Papacy was installed in Rome in 800, Charlemagne became the Emperor and protector of the Papacy according to the German Concordat. As Emperor (Augustus Caesar), he also inherited the title Pontifex Maximus. This title gave Charlemagne the right to install the Bishops throughout the Holy Roman Empire -- which he and his successors did. And, to keep all other ethnic people out of rulership, an electoral college was established which elected the new Emperor of the Holy Roman Empire. These were the Electors. Initially, there were 7 of them. Their title was hereditary.

The title Pontifex Maximus was, however, very valuable, because the office of a Bishop could be sold for a handsome amount of money. By 1075, Gregory VII decided to wrestle that title away from the Emperor and transfer it to the Papacy to invest new Bishops. Thus the struggle ensued and in 1077, Emperor Henry IV had to humble himself before Pope Gregory VII in Canossa in order to remain Emperor. Since then, the Pope invests the Bishops everywhere except in France (French Concordat.) (In 1072, Pope Gregory took the Kievan Kingdom under the protection of St. Peter's Chair.)

Gregory of Tours, St. (539-594): Bishop of Tours and ardent supporter of the Germans in Gaul (France). Author of the 'History of the Franks.'

Guadecanal: an island in the Pacific.

Guadelupe: a town in Mexico. In 1848 a treaty between the USA and Mexico was signed there, where the former Spanish territories (Arizona, California, Nevada and New Mexico) were signed over to the USA.

Guam...: an island in the Pacific.

Guderian, Heinz (1888-1954):Colonel-General of Army Group Center, one of the tank commanders during the invasion of the Soviet Union during World War II.(The other one was Hoth.)

Guelphs and Ghibellines:the struggle over the Investiture created friction among the ruling families in Europe.In Italy they were called the Guelphs and Ghibellines. The Ghibellines were the relations and supporters of the Hohenstaufens who supported the Holy Roman Emperor (Frederick II), while the Guelphs or Wölfs from Bavaria supported the Papacy. This was eventually resolved by passing the baton of the German Concordat to the Habsburgs in Austria.
(Later, in France, the Ghibellines became the Huguenots, while the Guelphs (Guise) the supporters of the French King (Catholics)).
Gulag(s): Stalin's prison colonies in Siberia.
Gustavus I Vasa (1496-1560): King of Sweden. In 1527 he broke with the Catholic Church, becoming Protestant.
Gustavus Adolphus II (1594-1632): King of Sweden. Defender of the Protestants. He died at Lützen, in battle, defending the Protestant cause.
Gutenberg, Johannes (1398-1468): created the movable type in Europe -- the printing press was the result. The first book to be published was the Bible in 1455. Only two complete copies have survived, one of them is in the Library of Congress in the USA.

Habsburg(s), (1276-1918): a German-Austrian line of rulers and protectors of the Pope. After 1425, most Holy Roman Emperors came from that line.Today they are invited observers in the Council of Europe, in an advisory capacity.
Hades..: in Greek mythology, the ruler of the underworld, brother of Zeus. Pluto in Roman.
Hague, The: a town in Southern Holland, the seat of the International Court of Justice (part of UN), where Milosovich is on trial.
Hammurabi, (1792-50 BC): King of Babylon and first recorded lawgiver.
Hannibal, (247-182 BC): Carthaginian general. He invaded Italy 217 BC. He controlled the Italian countryside, and was undefeated for 16 years in Italy. He was recalled to Carthage in 202 BC, when Scipio Africanus Major took the war to Africa. Hannibal was defeated by Scipio Africanus Major at Zama in 202. Hannibal took refuge at the court of Pyrrhus until he was cornered by Roman agents in Magnesia, then he poisoned himself.
Hanoverian(s): a German-Hanoverian line of rulers who have ruled in England since 1715.The Duke of Hannover was an Elector, a title more valuable than King. They are related by marriage to King James I, King of England.
Hansa, (ca. 1350-1530): a commercial naval league initiated by Sweden which later included some German towns -- i.e. Lübeck. Over 80 cities were part of that league,including Novhorod, Danzig, Oslo and London. In the 16th century it

began to decline. By the 17th century, by the end of the 30 Year War, it ceased to be a power.

Harding, Warren G (1921-23): 29th President of the USA.

Harrison, Benjamin (1889-93): 23rd President of the USA.

Harrison, William H (1841): 9th President of the USA.

Hastings, Battle of 1066: Norman victory over the English.

Hayes, Rutherford B (1877-81): 19th President of the USA.

Hedzwiga, (1386-1399): a Polish Princess, who was married off by the Polish Barons to Jagiello in 1386 (although she was already married to Maximilian, the Duke from Austria), to the Grand Duke of Lithuania. She was Catholic, Jagiello a heathen. Consequently, Lithuania converted to Catholicism and Lithuania was Polonized.

Their marriage created the Jagiello Dynasty which ruled Poland and Lithuania until it was partitioned by the three robber Barons: Austria, Prussia and Russia.

Indirectly, however, the Polish Barons were at fault for Poland's subsequent demise. Because, with that marriage the Barons gained special privileges. They were allowed to rule their land as virtual Kings, collecting taxes and keeping their own private army.

By the 16th century, Kingship in Poland was available to anyone (with deep pockets), who kept his own army, did not collect taxes and guaranteed the rights of the Polish Barons. This way, the central power was undermined. (Even Ivan the Terrible had notions of becoming a Polish King, but he was advised against it.) Alternate spellings: Hedwig, Yadwiga or Jadwiga...

Heesh, Heinrich: a German mathematician, a leading researcher in the 'Four Color Problem.'

Heimskringla: a history of the Norman Goths, reconstructed from songs and ballads by Snorri Sturluson in the 13th century in Iceland.

Heisenberg, Werner (1901-1968): leading German physicist. Hitler was counting on his doomsday weapon. He worked on an Atom Bomb, just like Fermi. But, Fermi came in first and thus saved Western Civilization.

Hellenized: a Greek form of geopolitics. For example: Alexander the Great was a Macedonian Goth, yet he is, more often than not, counted as a Greek. This despite the fact that the Greeks in his army were mercenaries. (And, when the Greeks rebelled, he razed Thebes.) When Alexander died, his empire was divided among his Macedonian Gothic generals: Antiochus got Greece; Ptolemy got Egypt and Seleucus got Persia. See Moesia.

Hephaestus: in Greek (Vulcan in Roman) mythology, god of crafts, in particular in gold, bronze and weapons.

Hera...: in Greek mythology, the sister and wife of Zeus, protector of the home and marriage. (The Egyptian custom to preserve divinity was to have brothers and sisters marry one another. Since Greek culture came from Egypt, with Cadmus, that tradition was preserved among the Olympians.) Juno in Roman.

Heraclites, (610-641): Roman Emperor who tried to subdue the Monophysites, a Christian sect. They converted to Islam instead and Constantinople faced a larger foe.

Heresy.: a declared doubt about the faith by an authority.

Hermes.: in Greek mythology, the messenger and herald of Zeus, his father. Mercury in Roman.

Herodotus, (485-425 BC): Greek historian, author of 'Histories.'

Herzl, Theodore (1860-1904): Hungarian Jew, founder of Zionism, author of 'Der Judenstaat' (The Jewish State.)

Hestia.: in Greek mythology, goddess of childbirth. Vestia in Roman. The Vestal Virgins in Rome served in the temples.

Hetman(s): duly elected Cossack leader(s).

Hetmanshina: a period in Ukrainian history, when many Hetmans ruled, most of them by appointment of the Moscow Czar. A Czarist scheme to undermine the power of the original Hetman(s).

Hilbert, David (1862-1943): mathematician and founder of modern system analysis, native of Königsberg.

Hill, Sir Rowland (1795-1879): postal reformer. He invented the postage stamp in 1840.

Hindenburg, Paul von (1847-1934): German general and president of the German Republic. He was forced to include Hitler as Chancellor in his cabinet when Hitler's party boycotted in the Reichstag.

Hinduism: one of the major religions of India dating back to about 1000 BC.

Hipatiev: a Ukrainian scribe (Ipatiev in Russian). He coined the word Ukraine in the 11th century. According to his definition, the Ukraine was the land of the Kievan-Rus which was administered by: Kiev, Chernihiv and Pereyaslav (three major Princely cities.)

Hiroshima: a city in Japan. The first Atom Bomb was dropped there on August 6, 1945.

Hitler, Adolf (1889-1945): President, Chancellor and dictator of Germany from 1934 to 1945, called 'Der Führer.' Author of 'Mein Kampf.'

Hittite(s): an extinct civilization in Asia Minor, claimed to be of Gothic origin, about 2000 to 1200 BC.

Hlib...: a Ukrainian martyr, Gleb in Russian.

Ho Chi Minh, (1890-1969): communist political leader of North Vietnam. He defeated the French at Diem Bien Phu in 1954.

Hohenstaufens(s): a German line of rulers from Würtemberg.

Hohenzollern(s): a German line of rulers from Brandenburg, later Prussia and Europe.

Hohol, Nikolai (1809-52): Ukrainian writer, who ushered in the 'golden age' of 'Russian' literature, Gogol in Russian. He abhorred the Czarist regime, but since the only way to get published in Russia was to write in Russian, he did. However, he wrote most of his novels in Naples, Italy. He also wrote a great deal in Ukrainian. He died in Naples from 'spaghetti el dente.'

Holland: a province of the Netherlands. The Counts of Holland are descendants of Charlemagne. In 1477, Holland became part of the Habsburgs, hence the Habsburg's claims to the German Concordat.

Holy Roman Empire: created by Pope Leo III and Charlemagne in 800 when the German Concordat was ratified. It was dismantled by Napoleon in 1804, when he crowned himself Emperor. Therefore, it lasted 1004 years.

Homer..: Greek poet and historian, lived circa 800 BC. Author of 'Iliad,' 'Odyssey' and 'Menelaos' (which is extinct but referenced.)

Horus..: in the cult of Isis in Egypt, the son of Isis and Osiris. Part of the Egyptian 'trinity.'

Hoover, Herbert C (1929-33): 31th President of the USA.

HPR....: holding period return, a measure of stock fluctuation.

Huguenots: French Protestants. They were massacred on St. Bartolomy's day on August 24, 1572. Continued persecution by Louis XIII and Louis XIV forced many to flee to Holland, England and the rest of non-Catholic Europe.

Hundred Years War, (1337-1453): between England and France over England's claims in France, on account of Richard the Lion-Hearted. When Richard went on a Crusade he left his brother John in charge as regent for his two sons. Word reached John that Richard was killed, so John killed Richard's sons and heirs. For that John was called to court by the Pope. John refused to go and the possessions in France were forfeited. Eventually John went to see the Pope and signed over the possessions in France except for Calais. When John returned to England, the Barons forced him to sign a document called 'The Magna Carta,' which had no validity whatsoever, since the Pope proclaimed that whoever tried to enforce that document would be excommunicated. This led to the 100 Years War, as England tried to reclaim her lost possessions in France. Joan of Arc proved to be the deciding factor in that war. Yet, when she won the war for her King (France), she was allowed to be captured by the Burgundians. She was then handed over to the English, who burned at the stake as a heretic.

Hungary: a land-locked republic in Central Europe. See Magyars. Now part of the EU.

Hus, John == Jan (1369-1415): Bohemian religious reformer, a forerunner to the Protestants. After he was defeated, John was burned at the stake in 1415. Yet his teachings still prevail in the Moravian Church.

Hydrogen Bomb: the next generation of Atomic Bombs, about 1000 times more powerful than the bombs dropped on Hiroshima and Nagasaki. The Patent was filed by John von Neumann, a Hungarian born mathematician. See E. Teller.

Hyksos.: invaders and rulers of Egypt (1785-1570 BC), believed to be Goths, because their main weapon was a double sided axe, a common weapon among the Goths.

Hypnos.: in Greek mythology, god of sleep.

Ignatius Loyola, St (1491-1556): founder of the Jesuit order, by permission of Pope Paul III.

Ihor...: a common name in Ukraine, (Igor in Russia). Also the first legitimate King-Judge ruler in Kiev (914-45), after the rule by the Huns. While Oleh (870-913) ruled only a few years as regent (910-913) for Ihor, Ihor ruled for 31 years (914-945). Ingvar in Norse. Ihor was married to Olha (Olga), a Christian. She was baptized in 954.

Iliad..: Homer's account of the fall of Troy.

Imperialism: rule over alien peoples and / or colonies.

India..: the sub-continent South of the Himalayas, including the states: India, Pakistan, Bangladesh and Nepal.

Indochina: formerly a French colony in South-East Asia including the states of: Vietnam, Laos and Cambodia.

Indonesia: a republic in South-East Asia made up of many islands. The largest are: Java, Sumatra, Celebes, Borneo (part), Bali and others. They were the Spice Islands of the Portuguese, later the Dutch colony Dutch East Indies. Major oil deposits in South-East Asia prompted Japan to turn her attention there during World War II. When Japan withdrew, an Indonesian Republic was proclaimed. In 1949, the Dutch yielded to Indonesian independence.

Indulgences: the prepayment of future sins. A common practice by the Pope to raise money, starting as early as 950. This became the primary cause for Martin Luther to nail his 95 Theses to the door of his church in Wittenberg in 1517, when a Papal legate (Tetzel) started selling indulgences to his congregation and nobody attended Luther's church. This led to the Reformation and then to the Counter-Reformation until nearly half of the humanity in Europe perished in religious wars. It ended (sort of) with the Treaty of Westphalia in 1648 to be continued again and again.

Indus Valley: location of an ancient civilization in India.

Inquisition: a special ecclesiastical court set up to inquire into allegations of heresy. Torquemada (1420-98) was the best known Grand Inquisitor. Two independent accusations were needed to start an inquisition. Once someone was accused, civil laws were brushed aside and the Inquisition proceeded in secret. Torture was an accepted means to extract a confession. Needless to say, most of those accused confessed, in which case the property was turned over to the Church and the accused burned at the stake.

Interdict: a sentence or decree pronounced by the Pope forbidding public worship, sacraments, burial, marriage, baptism and so on. In some cases an entire country was put under an Interdict, such as England during the regency of John, brother of Richard.

Investiture: the struggle between the Pope and the Holy Roman Emperor as to who had the right to invest (install) a Bishop. In the Roman Empire that right went with the title Pontifex Maximus, which belonged to the Emperor (Augustus Caesar). When the German Concordat was ratified in 800, between Charlemagne and the Pope, that title was passed on to Charlemagne, automatically. In the 11th century, this struggle came to a head and Pope Gregory VII won. See Gregory VII.

Irrationals: numbers which defy a rational representation.

Isabella, (1451-1504): Queen of Castile. See Ferdinand and Isabella.

Isis...: principal goddess in a poplar cult in Egypt. The cult of Isis featured a trinity: Isis-Horus-Osiris opposing Seth, the evil one. (Some claim that Bishop Athanasius, used the cult of Isis to interpret Christian Trinity, which resulted in Christian Orthodoxy.)

Islam..: the religion of about 1 billion Muslims who inhabit mostly Asia, Africa and Europe, but is spreading rapidly to the American continent.

Ismail.: son of Abraham, the common link of Islam and Judaism.

Israel, Republic of: a state in South-West Asia, on the Eastern coast of the Mediterranean Sea, founded in 1949.

Istarte == Isthar: a goddess in the Indus Valley, said to pre-date the civilization in Sumer (Mesopotamia). Some equate her to Aphrodite.

Italy..: a republic in South-Western Europe. Various dates are put forward for her modern founding, all with much merit: 1860 (Garibaldi), 1861 (Garibaldi), 1865 (Cavour) and 1870 (Franco-Prussian War).

Ivan...: the name for many strong and absolute rulers of Muscovy.

Ivan I, (1298-1341): Grand Duke of Vladimir (former Volodimir), he moved to Moscow. Aka: Ivan Kalita or Money-Bags (Tartar tax collector).

Ivan III, (1440-1505): Grand Duke of Muscovy, he stopped paying tribute to the Tartars, yet continued collecting taxes for them from the various Yarlics. He married Zoe (Sophia); the niece of the last Roman Emperor (Byzantine Empire); and proclaimed Moscow to be the Third Rome.

Ivan IV, Ivan the Terrible(1530-84): assumed the Alan title Czar; he defeated the Tartar Khanates of Kazan and Astrakhan adding them to Muscovy. Then, Don Cossack Hetman Ermak conquered the Tartar Khanate of Sibir and gifted her to the Czar (this way the bounty on his head was removed and Ermak was allowed to live and explore Siberia). He tried to make Moscow a Patriarchate which led to Rascol, the division of the Orthodox Church. Thereupon, considered making Muscovy Catholic, but backed out at the last moment.

Towards the end of his rule, the Crimean Tartars attacked and sacked Muscovy, taking the entire non-Tartar population prisoners (over 1 million) and drove them like cattle to the slave markets in the Crimea. Ivan tortured and killed his son and heir Alexis, resulting in the 'Times of Trouble,' lasting 29 years, until 1613.

Ivan V, (1682-96): co-ruler with Peter I. Later his descendants ruled Russia: Anna (1730-40) and Ivan VI (1740-41).

Ivan VI, (1740-41): Czar of Russia, when he was 1 year old. Ivan was imprisoned by the Russian gentry in Schlüsselburg, near St. Petersburg and Elizabeth came to power. When Catherine II seized power the Cossacks tried to liberate Ivan VI in 1764, but the guards killed him.

Ja == rR: a runic symbol, looks like as a rotated R in Cyrillic (Russian and Ukrainian).

Jackson, Andrew (1829-37): 7th President of the USA.

Jacobi, Karl G (1804-1851): a mathematician specializing in linear systems.

Jagiello, (1386-1434): Lithuanian Grand Duke who married Princess Hedzwiga from Poland in 1386 and founded the Jagiello Dynasty, aka: Jagiellon. See Hedzwiga.

Jahweh.: the God in the Old Testament.

James, Jessie: an American outlaw -- applied to Stalin in text.

Janisary(ies): fearsome Islamic Jihad fighters.Enslaved Christian children were forcibly converted to Islam. Aka: Janizary.

Japan..: an empire in East Asia. Japan was groomed by England into an industrial power. England saw great similarity between Japan and herself. An island nation, surrounded by powerful continental neighbors. After Japan was defeated in World War II, American money made her strong again.

Je == r3: a runic symbol looks like a rotated 3 in Cyrillic. Tapestry in France, depicting the Unicorn are inscribed with that symbol. Hence, of Gothic origin. (A letter in the Russian and Ukrainian alphabet.)

Jefferson, Thomas (1801-1809): 3rd President of the USA.

Jerusalem: ancient city in the Holy Land, in the Roman province of Palestine.

Jesuits: members of the Society of Jesus, the shock troops of the Catholic Faith, organized by St. Ignatius, styled like an army, headed by a general etc.

Jesus Christ, (6 BC-30 AD): the Jewish religious leader whom Christians worship as the Son of God.

Jews...: residents in the Roman province of Palestine and Judea. After Jerusalem was sacked by Titus in 70 AD, they were forced to leave, causing a diaspora of the Jews. Many settled in Alexandria, Babylon and other major cities of Europe, America, Africa and Asia. In 1949, the State of Israel was created and many Jews have returned to their

ancestral homeland.
Ji == Ï: a runic symbol in Ukrainian (not in Russian).
Joan of Arc, (1412-31): the Maid of Orleans, she drove the English from France and the Dauphin was crowned in Reims, in 1429, as Charles VII. Seen as Saint by her followers and witch by her opponents. The French allowed her to be captured by the Burgundians who handed her over to the English. She was tried as a witch and burned at the stake in Rouen.
Johnson, Andrew (1865-69): 17th President of the USA.
Johnson, Lyndon B (1963-69): 36th President of the USA.
Jordanes, (531-582) a converted Goth (to the Roman Faith) who read the history of Cassiodorus Senator and rewrote it from recall: Getica. Aka: Jordanis.
Josephus, Flavius (12- 81 AD): a Jewish historian and Roman citizen who wrote about the Jewish wars. (Often his section 'Antiquities of the Jews' is omitted.)
Ju ==I-O: a runic symbol looks like an I with an O attached to it. (A letter in the Russian and Ukrainian alphabet.)
Judaism: the religious beliefs and practices of the Jewish people.Christianity and Islam have their roots in Judaism, with Abraham, Ismail and Jesus.
Jütes == Jutes: a former Gothic nation near Denmark.
Judge..: an official, administrator or interpreter of law and justice in a land. Gothic Kings were both Kings and Judges.
Jugoslavia or Yugoslavia: a state formed in the Balkans after World War I and again after World War II. When the Soviet Union disintegrated, Jugoslavia fell apart along religious lines. Catholic: Croatia, Slovenia and Bosnia. Orthodox: Serbia and Macedonia.Bosnia has a large muslim population.
Julian Calendar: the Egyptian calendar adopted by Julius Caesar, replaced by Pope Gregory in the 17th century and adopted at various times in Europe. (That's why historical accounts of the Spanish Armada don't match.)
Justinian I, (483-565): Emperor of the Roman Empire in Constantinople.

Kalka..: a town in the Ukrainian Kuban. In 1238 a Gothic, Kievan-Rus army was defeated there and opened the Tartar conquest for Batu of Europe. Batu was the grandson of Genghis Khan, a contemporary of Kubilai Khan.
Kapital, Das: a book by Karl Marx describing the Communist theory based on economic conditions found in 19th century England. It is also the basis of Socialism, but modified by Emile Durkheim (1858-1917), Max Weber (1864-1920) and Vilfredo Pareto (1848-1923). Durkheim wrote 'The Division of Labor in a Society,' while Weber wrote about the rise of bureaucracy in modern society. This combination became known as: sociological imagination, or Socialism.
Kashmir: a province contested by India and Pakistan.

Katjusha Rocket: little Kathy in Russian, Stalinorgel in German or Stalin's Pipe-Organ.
Kazakhstan: a former Soviet Republic in Siberia (Muslim.)
Kazan..: a town and former Tartar Khanate, east of Moscow, conquered by Ivan the Terrible.
Keelhaul Agreement: an agreement reached in Yalta between Stalin, Roosevelt and Churchill which allowed the Soviets to repatriate all her former citizens throughout the world. The dividing line became 1923. According to Stalin, anyone living in Russia after 1923 was a Soviet Citizen and was subject to repatriation.
Keitel, Wilhelm (1882-1946): German Field Marshal. He was nicknamed 'Lackey,' for his devotion to Hitler.
Keller.: a German tank commander during World War II.
Kennedy, John F (1961-63): 35th President of the USA.
Kepler, Johann (1571-1630): German mathematician and astrologer.
Kerensky, Alexander F (1881-1970): a Russian political leader.
KGB....: Soviet and present day Russia's secret police.
Kh == X: a runic symbol, spelled differently in Europe: Kh in the Anglo-Saxon world; Ch in the Franco-German world; J in the Spanish-Portuguese world. Conversely, people of Slavic extraction in America pronounce TEXAS as TEKHAS.
Khan...: a title (chief or ruler) used by Mongols and Tartars.
Khanate(s): an area ruled by a Khan, a Mongol ruler.
Kharkiv: a town in the Ukraine (Kharkov in Russian). It was founded by the Lithuanians as a fort against the Tartars in the 14th century. When the Polish Barons descended into the Ukraine, they brought Jews with them who were their money-lenders, tax collectors and inn keepers. Hence, Kharkiv had a large Jewish community and the oldest Synagogues. When the Bolsheviks were forced out of Kiev, they moved the capital of Ukraine to Kharkiv (1919-1926).
Khmelnitzky, Bohdan (1648-1657): Cossack Hetman and Ukrainian leader who established an autonomous Ukraine (1648-61). He defeated and evicted the Polish Barons from the Ukraine in 1648. He attempted to form an alliance with various European powers: Muscovy, Sweden and the Ottoman Empire. (His name is 'Boh-dan,' it translates to 'God-given.' Aka Chmelniki in Polish.)
Kholm..: a town in the Soviet Union.
Kiev...: see Kiïv.
Kievan.: based on Kiev.
Kievan-Rus, (550-1240): the (Russian) name given to the reconstructed Gothic empire after the destruction of the Huns. It should really stand for Kievan-Ryc or Kievan-Rik.
Starting with King Volodimir (979-1015), who was crowned by the Roman Emperor Basil II, Volodimir married Basil's sister and became hereditary King ruling from Kiev.
Kiïv...: capital of the Ukraine, the only legitimate Patriarchate in the East (Kiev in Russian) and former seat of her Kings (Riks). Hereditary Kingship was established with Volodimir

(978-1015) by the Roman Emperor Basil II (978-1025). Volodimir married the Emperor's sister Anna and converted the Kievan-Rus to Orthodoxy.
Kirgistan: a former Soviet Republic in Siberia (Muslim.)
Kleist, Paul von (1881-1954): German Field Marshal and tank commander during World War II.
Knut...: a leather whip with spokes.
Knight.: an honorary military rank or superior military service. In Kievan-Rus they were called Boyars. That title, however, degenerated to tax-collectors in Muscovy.
Kolchak, Alexander V (1874-1920): Czarist general from Siberia. He tried to restore Czarism, but was defeated by the Red Army not far from Moscow.
Kondratieff: Russian economist and statistician. He developed the Kondratieff cycle of economic activity based on the American economy.
Konev, Ivan S (1897-1973): Marshal of the Soviet Union.
Koran..: the sacred scripture of Islam.
Korea..: a peninsula in North-East Asia, a Chinese province occupied by Japan during World War II.
Koreas.: North (communist) and South Korea (free). Today, South Korea is the 4th largest producer nation, eclipsing France and Great Britain.
Kotlyarevsky, Ivan (ca.1769-1838): Ukrainian poet and writer. Famous for his Aeneid (a travesty), Natalka Poltavka and Moscow Sorcerer. Native of Poltava.
Kozak(s): an alternate spelling for Cossacks. The word Cossack has been perverted by the Romanovs (and Soviets) establishing regular army regiments that were called Cossacks. They distinguished themselves with their singular brutality on the population. Many modern Ukrainian writers prefer the new spelling to differentiate the original Cossacks and their struggle for a 'Free Brotherhood of Man.' See Cossacks.
Kremlin: the citadel or fortress, in this context, in Moscow.
Krupp, Family: German armaments manufacturer family.
Kuban..: a former Ukrainian land, forcibly annexed by the Soviet Union into the Russian Republic in 1926. South-East of the Azov Sea along the river Kuban.
Kubilai Khan, (1216-94): Mongol Emperor of China.
Kuchma: current leader in Ukraine from the Old Guard (USSR.)
Kukuruznik: a corn advocate in Ukrainian. Khrushchev tried to grow corn in Kazakhstan, became an ecological disaster.
Kulikovo: in 1380, Moscow Prince Dimitry Donskoi defeated the Tartars there, but it was only a temporary victory.
Kulturkampf: Hitler's version of geopolitics (culture-war.)
Kunersdorf: a town in Prussia. During the 7 Year War, Frederick the Great was defeated there by Russians. His cause seemed hopeless. The Cossacks raided Berlin in 1760. But then, Catherine II, stopped the war and restored Frederick in the treaty of Paris in 1763.

Kuril Islands: islands to the North of Japan.

Kurland: an area on the Baltic Sea, includes portions of Estonia, Latvia and Lithuania. Aka: Livonia in Russian.

Kursk..: founded in the 11th century, a Chartered city in the Kievan-Rus, site of the largest land battle of World War II (June-July 1943). After that defeat the Germans were unable to launch another major offensive against the Soviet Union. Aka: Unternehmen Zitadelle in German (Operation Citadel.)

Kutuzov, Michail I (1745-1813: Prince of Smolensk, Russian Field Marshal who defeated Napoleon. (Technically, a Byelorussian. He was Prince of Smolensk.)

Kuzhukh: a heavy fur overcoat.

-(s)laus, (aka: -laus): an ending in the name of Gothic-Slavic Kings-Judges in the tradition of the earlier Goths. Roman inscriptions changed the letter U into a V, hence the ending -(s)laus became -slavs.

Lakewood, NJ: a town in New Jersey USA. In 1947, a Soviet submarine landed off-shore and forcibly repatriated Americans of Ukrainian and Russian descent in accordance with the Keelhaul Agreement of Yalta.

Language traps: practically every language in Europe includes language traps. The idea is simple: certain letters of the alphabet are not used or spelled differently. This way foreigners can be readily identified. Often their origin can be inferred by how they spell certain words. For example: starting with the Greek alphabet, which was derived from the Phoenician, certain symbols had no matching counterpart in the Greek alphabet.

In Rome, including Latin and modern Italian, the letters K and W are not used. And, the letter U was often written as V. This made, reverse translations difficult, if not impossible. In England the F sound was replaced with the PH spelling. To catch the German spellings certain doubling of letters was eliminated. For example:the German word Hannoverian, is spelled Hanoverian in English. In Russia, certain letters of the Ukrainian alphabet were eliminated by Peter I (H, i, ї etc) and the spelling was changed for others. Often, the i in Ukrainian was replaced with o in Russian. In Poland, the letter V is hardly used and replaced with W, and so on.

Many of these language traps were introduced by Leibnitz, mostly in England and Russia. Therefore, certain new words emerged. For example, when the ending -laus was spelled in Roman, it took on the form -lavs, -lav or -slav. Thus the world slav originated. Also, because of the many different spellings in Europe, the Gothic ending -ryc, found many different spellings. In Latin, it became -rix,-ric and -rik in the Anglo-Saxon world.Language traps are very efficient tools to spread disinformation in

Europe, a tactic which has spread to America.

Languedoc: a former country in Southern France, her capital was Toulouse, it was occupied by Cathars. From 1002 until 1271, the Papacy waged a relentless war of genocide against them to annihilate the entire population, ravishing the country-side and annihilating a prosperous community by calling for incessant (Internal) Crusades against them. See Crusades.

Lao-Tse, (604-531 BC): founder of Taoism in China.

Larousse: publisher of French dictionaries and encyclopedias.

LaSalle, (1643-1787): a French explorer who developed the Territory of Louisiana for France in North America. Napoleon sold Louisiana to America to fund his wars in Continental Europe in 1803.

Latinized: adapted or modified for Latin usage. This included name changes; geographical changes and/or religious adaptations or changes, i.e, Hermes became Mercury.

Lay of Ihor: an epic poem about Oleh and Ihor, 11th century.

League of Nations: an international organization created after World War I, the brainchild of American President Woodrow Wilson, to maintain peace.

Lebensraum: German, living-space. The German justification to subjugate her neighbors. Hitler's premise in 'Mein Kampf.'

Lebesgue, Henri L (1875-1941): French mathematician, developed the notions of Real Variables and Countability of sets.

LeBon, Gustave (1841-1931): author of 'The Psychology of a Revolution.'It is a manual on how to make a revolution successful. It became the bible for Lenin.

Lechfeld: a town in Germany, near Ulm, where the Mongol Magyars (Hungarians) were defeated by Otto I the Holy Roman Emperor in 955. They accepted the Roman Faith and ceased to raid the Roman and Holy Roman Empire from then on. The Habsburgs became their own royal rulers when their line died out.

Leeb, Wilhelm von (1876-1956):German Field Marshal during WW II.

Leibnitz, Gottfried W (1646-1716) (aka: Lubeniecz): the last Renaissance-Man, expert in all fields of knowledge. He invented Differential Calculus in mathematics (we use his notion of a differential to this day); he formulated gravity in Physics; established the Hanoverians to the throne in England (his employer); provided Peter I of Russia with the ideas and means to formulate his reforms: Table of Ranks; marriage into the ruling German line; Holy Synod; etc.

Legny..: a town near Waterloo in Belgium. Napoleon had to split his army to deal with the larger Prussian contingent commanded by Blücher as opposed to Wellington. Even though the French gained a victory there, it was not decisive and the Prussians swarmed into Waterloo to defeat Napoleon with Wellington's forces in 1815.

Lend-Lease Bill: US legislation approved by American President F. D. Roosevelt on March 11, 1941 -- to aid England, later the Soviet Union. About 50 billion was spent, none of which was repaid. In today's Dollars, about $650 billion.

Lenin, (1870-1924): Russian revolutionary and founder of the Soviet Republics, his real name: Vladimir Ilyich Ulyanov.

Leningrad: formerly St. Petersburg (aka: Petrograd.)

Lessing, Gottfried E (1729-1781): a German poet and writer. Lessing, Goethe and Schiller are considered to be the architects of the German language, even though Martin Luther had developed the first but small German dictionary to write the Catechism centuries earlier.

Lesya Ukrainka (1871-1916): a Ukrainian poetess and writer, she is very popular in the Ukraine. She defended the underdog. Her 'hero' in the Trojan war was Cassandra. See Cassandra.

Letho..: in Greek mythology, the spinner of life who determines its length.

Levitt, Arthur (ca.1890-1970): an innovative architect and contractor in America. Levitt made housing affordable to all GI's and Americans after Word War II.

Levittown USA: a concept introduced by Arthur Levitt after World War II, creating affordable housing for Americans.

Lincoln, Abraham (1861-65): 16th President of the USA.

Lisbon.: capital of Portugal. Said to be founded by Ulysses while on his Odyssey.

Liter(s): a liquid measure introduced by Napoleon in Continental Europe, roughly a quart.

Lithuania: after the break-up of the Soviet Union, an independent country.

When Batu stopped his conquest of Europe in 1242, and moved his army to Sarai to attend the Mongol conference to elect a new Khan, the Lithuanians swept into Belarus and the Ukraine establishing themselves as protectors, starting with Grand Duke Gedeminas (1316-1341).

In 1386, Grand Duke Jagiello married the Polish Princess Hedzwiga and was elected hereditary King of Poland and Lithuania. The two countries were formally united in 1569. However, Lithuania was Polonized, hence Polish Barons ruled her lands from 1425 on, including Belarus and the Ukraine. With the Polish Barons came Catholic Jesuits who demanded conversion to the Roman Faith (1440). This spawned the Cossack movement in the Ukraine (1444).

Cossack Hetman Khmelnitzky evicted the Polish Barons in 1648 and looked for an alliance with either: Muscovy, Sweden or the Ottoman Turks.

Muscovy replied first and the Orthodox clergy in the Ukraine clamored for an Orthodox alliance. Khmelnitzky yielded and swayed his Cossacks to ratify the alliance with Muscovy (1654). However, when Khmelnitzky died in

1657 and a new Hetman was elected, and his name was sent in for ratification, Czar Alexis replied: "We take no orders from our subjects." Shortly thereafter, Belarus and the Western portion of the Ukraine were given to Poland in the Treaty of Andrusovo in 1667. (Later the other powers responded and intervened in the Ukraine, with devastating consequences to the Ukraine.)

In 1795, during the rule of Catherine II, Poland and Lithuania were partitioned between Russia, Prussia and Austria. This time, Lithuania, Belarus and the Western Ukraine were taken back by Russia.

After World War I, Lithuania gained independence in 1919 but was allied against the Soviet Union with Hitler. In 1939, Stalin annexed Lithuania into the Soviet Union. When the Soviet Union collapsed, Lithuania became an independent country. Lithuania is now part of the EU.

Livy, Titus Livius (59 BC- 17 AD): Roman historian. According to Livy, Rome was founded in 753 BC.

Lobachevsky, Nikolai I (1793-1856): leading Russian mathematician from Kazan. Founder of the non-Euclidian geometry.

Londanabad: a suggested name for London once Islamic militants take over the rule in England.

London.: capital of England and the United Kingdom.

Lothar, (941-986): grandson of Charlemagne, heir to the Central Kingdom of the Holy Roman Empire, aka: Lothair in French.

Louisiana Purchase (1803): America acquired the Territory of Louisiana (828,000 square miles) from Napoleon for 15 million Dollars or about 18 Dollars for each square mile!

Lucasievicz, Ivan == Jan (1878-1956): Ukrainian mathematician from Lviv. He developed a notation, an algorithm, on how to linearize an algebraic expressions, essential for compilers used by computers. It is called:Polish notation.

The reason it is called Polish notation is that, when he taught in Lviv (1929), the Western Ukraine was occupied by Poland (1917-31). Hence he was called Polish.

Ludendorff, Erich (1865-1937): German general during World War I and supporter of Hitler.

Luftwaffe: German, means Air Force.

Lulu(s): original creation of man (aka: Adam.)

Luther, Martin (1483-1546): Augustinian monk and founder of the (Lutheran) Protestant Church in Europe, which led to the Reformation and then to the Counter-Reformation. The religious question was temporarily settled in 1648, in the Treaty of Westphalia. However, the dispute goes on and on in Europe.

Lviv...: Ukrainian provincial capital of Galicia, aka: Lvov (Russian); Lwow (Polish); Lemberg (German). It was founded by Prince Roman of the Kievan-Rus in the 12th century.

After the destruction of Kiev in 1240, King Danielo ruled from there. See Danielo.

Lypkivsky, W (1864-1921): Patrirach of Kiev. In 1921 he was arrested and vanished in Kazakhstan.

-mir or -mer: in Gothic tradition this ending identified a Gothic King-Judge, mainly applied to Slavs.

M1/M2/M3: notions relating to the money supply.

Maastricht: a town in the Netherlands where Western monetary policies were established in the 1990's.

MacArthur, Douglas (1880-1964): American Supreme Commander in the Pacific during World War II and the Korean War.

Machiavelli, Nicolo (1469-1527): Italian patriot (Florentine) and author of 'The Prince,' a blueprint for Italian rebirth, written with Caesare Borgia in mind. It became Stalin's 'bible.'

Macedonia: an area in North-East Greece.

Macedonians: a Gothic nation originating at the Lake of Moesia (Azov Sea). Alexander the Great conquered Greece and then the Persian Empire.

Madison, James (1809-1817): 4th President of the USA.

Magna Carta, (1215): A wish list of the English Barons. While King Richard was away on a Crusade he left his brother John behind as regent (1199-1216) for his two minor sons. Word reached John that Richard had been killed in the Crusade. Thereupon John killed Richard's sons. This led to an inquest by the Pope and John refused to appear. The Pope slapped an interdict on England and threatened to take away the possessions in France (Aquitaine, etc.) John still refused to show up. The Pope threatened to excommunicate John.

Now John appeared at the inquest. There, John signed over Richard's possessions in France, except for Calais, to the French.

While John was away, the English Barons drafted the Magna Carta, and when John returned, forced him to sign it -- which he did. Now John turned to the Pope who declared that: whoever tried to enforce the Magna Carta would be excommunicated, making the Magna Carta null and void. Ultimately this led to the 100 Years War with France. In the 17th century, Queen Elizabeth I, introduced many reforms which resembled the original Magna Carta.

Magna Grecia: Southern Italy from about Naples to Sicily. It was colonized by Greek settlers. During the Second Punic War, Hannibal found support there. When Hannibal was defeated at Zama, Magna Grecia was conquered by Rome. Their principal city was Capua.

Magyars: a Mongolic nation who was bought by Constantinople to annihilate the Avars in Pannonia in the 9th century. They invaded Europe, eliminated the Avars and settled in Pannonia. From there they harassed the Roman and the Holy

Roman Empire, because they were not paid the last installment. In 955, at Lechfeld, near Ulm, they were defeated by Otto I and accepted the Roman Faith from Rome. Their name was changed in the West to Hungary, while they kept their original name.

During Batu's invasion of Europe they were offered twice to become partners in the conquest of Europe. However, they declined both times and were conquered by Batu. Starting with the 14th century, the most Western Yarlics stopped paying tribute to Batu, including Hungary.

During the 15th century, they were conquered by the Ottoman Turks. In the reconquest which followed, they became subjects of the Habsburgs (Austria).

When Napoleon conquered Europe, Hungary clamored for independence and semi-autonomy was established. Hungary got a Diet, but their Monarch remained a Habsburg (aka: Dual Monarchy.) After World War I, Hungary gained independence but became an ally of Hitler. When World War II ended, Stalin had conquered Hungary and it was integrated into the Soviet Union.

When the Soviet Union collapsed, Hungary became independent. In 2003, Hungary was admitted to the EU.

Mainz..: a town in Central Germany, the seat of a Bishop and Elector.

Malo-Yaroslvets: a small fort a few miles South of Moscow. From there Kutuzov harassed Napoleons forces in 1812.

Manichaean(s): a Christian Faith declared heretic by the Orthodox and Roman Church. Aka: Manichaen.

Manstein, Erich von (1887-1973): German Field Marshal in Hitler's army who led Army Group North during Hitler's invasion of the Soviet Union and nearly took Moscow.

Manzzini, Giuseppi (1805-72): Italian patriot, creator of 'Young Italy,' a revolutionary movement to form a united, Italian Republic.

Mao Tse-tung, (1893-1976): Chinese Communist leader and dictator in mainland China. In 1949, Chiang Kai-shek was defeated by Mao and moved to Taiwan.

Marcus, Aurelius (161-180): Roman Emperor.

Marianne: the symbol of French liberty -- a bare breasted woman leading the revolutionaries. During the French Revolution a Parisian prostitute was made 'goddess of reason' in the Notre Dame Cathedral by that name.

Maria Theresa, (1717-80): Empress of Austria.

Marlowe, Christopher (1564-93): English dramatist.

Markov, Andreii A (1856-1922): Russian mathematician-statistician, originator of 'linked chain events.'

Markowitz: modern mathematician and portfolio strategist.

Marshall Plan: a program launched by US Secretary of State, George C. Marshall on June 5, 1947 to rebuild Europe. Stalin refused to participate in this program.

Marx, Karl (1818-83): Created the basis for Communism and Socialism in his book 'Das Kapital,' based on 19th century England.

Maximilian: a common dynastic name of Austrian Habsburg rulers. An important historical reference is to the husband of Princess Hedzwiga of Poland. The Polish Barons had that marriage annulled and married her off to Jagiello the Grand Duke of Lithuania in 1386.

Maximilian I, (1459-1519): Emperor of the Holy Roman Empire, author of the Treaty of Tordesillas where the world was divided for conquest and exploitation between Spain and Portugal with the blessings of the Pope (1494).

Mayordomo: Mayor of the Palace, chief administrator to the ruling King. The Carolingians were Mayordomos to the Merovingian Kings, when they took over the rule.

McCarthy, Joseph (1909-1957): US Senator, headed the Senatorial Committee on Un-American activities from 1947-52.

McKinley, William (1897-1901): 25th President of the USA.

Mecca..: the birthplace of Mohammed, the most sacred city in Islam.

Medici.: a ruling Italian family. Many Popes come from that family. One notorious member of the Medici was Marie. While she was regent for Louis XIII, she orchestrated the massacre of the Huguenots on St. Bartolomy's Day. See Huguenots.

Mein Kampf: Hitler's book of his intentions on Europe and the World.

Menelaos: husband of Helen, hero of the Trojan war and explorer of the Indian Ocean. However, that work of Homer is lost, only references to it exist.

Menshikov: a slave trader and intimate friend of Czar Peter I. He gifted Catherine, his sex slave (and the future Czarina Catherine I) to Peter and many others including Pushkin's grandfather, a black slave from the Sudan. In return Peter I rewarded him with every honor in his empire short of emperor. When Peter I died, Catherine I came to power and Menshikov became the virtual ruler of Russia. He tried to marry off his daughter to Peter II, but Peter died at age 15 before the marriage took place.

Meroveche: founder of the Gothic, Merovingian Dynasty.

Merovingian: a ruling dynasty of the Goths in Gaul. Clovis or Clodio or Chlodwig (428-447), is considered by Western historians to be the founder of that dynasty, starting with Bishop Gregory of Tours (6th century.) But these were all Latin names. His real (original) name was Cholodveche or Chlodvech which was derived from Cholod == Cold, and Veche == Assembly. The subsequent Kings that ruled, from Meroveche (Merovech) (447-458) and until Childeric III (743-751) were all Goths.

To begin with the 'Ch' is not a Germanic letter, it is a distinctly Gothic letter -- it looks like the letter r, rotated or the letter Kh. And, the ending: '-ric,' 'veche' or 'vech' is a Gothic ending. In German dictionaries, there is not a single native word which starts with the letter(s) 'ch'! (Which is a single letter in Gothic.)

The Franks, were not a nation, but a coalition of German and Gothic nations. Therefore, contemporary Bishops like Gregory of Tours, promoted the deeds of the Germans because they were new converts to the Roman Faith, while the Goths were Arian converts and were not trusted.

Finally, the Merovingians were accused of being 'do-nothing' Kings because they were religiously tolerant and did not persecute the Arians, Manichaeans, Gnostics and Jews in the manner the Roman Patriarch wanted them too -- that's why the Albi survived for as long as they did. Therefore, the support of the Roman Bishops shifted to the German Carolingians, who gradually rose to mayordomos with Pepin I (628-39) and took over the rule with Pepin III in 751. Pepin's son was Charlemagne.

Methodius: a missionary who with Cyril spread Orthodoxy among the Bulgars, Southern Slavs in the Balkans and Eastern Slavs in the Ukraine (Kievan-Rus.)

Metternich, Clement (1773-1859): Austrian Minister, Chancellor and architect of Austrian's form of geopolitics, called: Ausgleich (aka: Metternich System). See Ausgleich.

Michael, Fedorowich (1596-1645): Czar of Muscovy, founder of the Romanov dynasty. The Romanovs were of Prussian-Gothic extraction who had distinguished themselves during the rule of Ivan the Terrible. When Ivan the Terrible died, a 'time of troubles' ensued for Ivan had killed his son and heir Alexis. The Tartars seized power with Boris Godunov. The Zaporozhian and Don Cossacks deposed the Tartars and called for a Sbor or Allthing in Moscow. When the great multitude arrived, Michael was elected as the next Czar of Moscow in 1613.

Michael VIII Paleologus (1224-82): Emperor of the (Eastern) Roman Empire and a famous historian. His line is still very active in European politics. After World War I, the French ambassador to Russia was a Paleologue.

Middle Ages: a period of about 1000 years in Western Europe, 5th to 15th century or 476 to 1453, until the fall of Constantinople.

Midway, Battle of: June 4 to 6, 1942. The most decisive battle in the Pacific, where America broke Japan's naval power.

Milan..: main Italian city in the North. It dates back to Roman times. Seat of a Bishop, became a Duchy in 1395; ruled by the Sforza family; attached to the Crown of Spain (1535-1713); attached to Austria (1713-96) and (1815-59). In 1861, Milan became part of Italy.

In 1455, the Duke of Milan sacked Rome. He allowed his soldiers to plunder, pillage and rape Rome for 9 months. (The sack by Alaric in 410 was 3 days, and Genseric's in 455 was 7 days.)

Milosovich, (1990-), former head of state of Yugoslavia, now on trial at The Hague to downplay the German culpability during World War II.

Milton, John (1608-74): English poet and political writer.

Minos..: King of Crete. Upon his death he became keeper of the book of life to judge the souls on Judgement Day, in Greek mythology.

Minsk..: the capital of the Principality of Kievan-Rus called Belarus. Now called Byelorussia.

Mir....: a village assembly in Russia, based on a Veche of olden days in the Ukraine. In 1861, when the slaves and serfs were emancipated the mir helped the dispossessed. Stalin used that notion to create 'communes.'

Moesia.: in antiquity, the area surrounding the Azov Sea and the river Don (Tanais). Colchis was located there. It was also the original homeland of the Macedonian Goths, according to Strabo. However, by the 7th century 'Moesia' was shifted to the Danube river in the Balkans as the homeland of the Goths. This way it became easier to 'Hellenize' the Macedonian Goths.

Mohammed, (570-623): founder and prophet of the Islamic Faith.

Moldovia: a former province of the Ukraine. Aka: Bessarabia or Moldavia. Now a country which applied to the EU.

Molotov, Vyacheslav M (1890-1986):Soviet diplomat during Stalin's era. In 1943, he and von Ribbentrop tried to negotiate a separate peace, before the Battle of Kursk, but nothing came of it. Hitler wanted the occupied lands while Stalin wanted the original Curzon-Line. The Battle of Kursk had to decide the issue. See Kursk.

Mommsen, Theodor (1817-1903): a German historian. His unfounded claim was that the Goths were a Germanic people. This way the newly formed German Empire in 1871, could raid the literature, art and history of the Goths. He created the notion of Völkerwanderung.

Money..: a medium of exchange for goods and services.

Mongolia: formerly, Outer-Mongolia was part of the Soviet Union, while Inner-Mongolia lies between China and the Soviet Union. After the Soviet Union disintegrated, an independent country was formed.

Historically, the cradle of many invading nations from this area. Collectively they are still called Mongols. However, many historians differentiate between the many nations originally from that area: Avars, Bulgars, Burgundians, Huns, Kalmyks, Khazars, Magyars, Pechenegs and so on.

Monophysites: a Christian Faith persecuted by Roman Emperor Heraclites. They converted to Islam instead in 635.

Monroe, James (1817-25): 5th President of the USA.
Monroe Doctrine: a policy established by American President Monroe (1758-1831), which barred the intervention of European powers on the American continent. However, it sanctioned existing European Colonies. Many consider the Falkland War a violation of that policy.
Monte Casino: a monastery in Southern Italy, near Naples. In 1943, the Germans turned it into a Fort, stopping the Allied advance. Indian and Polish units eventually took it, after it was utterly destroyed by air strikes.
Montsegur: the last stronghold of the Cathars (Albi.)
Moors..: a race of dark-skinned people, of Islamic Faith, who conquered Spain in 711, creating much wealth and prosperity. In 1492, their last stronghold in Granada was conquered by Christians. The Moors and Jews were evicted from Spain and Christian Europe. Today, a Mosque is being built in Granada.
Moravia(ns): the Goths who settled along the river Morava in Central Europe (Czechoslovakia) and created a Kingdom.
Morganatic: a marriage between a royal (or noble) and one of much lesser rank. For example: Grace Kelly and Prince Rainier of Monaco. Prince Rainier received a dowry of 2 million Dollars for marrying Grace Kelly.
Moriarity: arch-villain to Sherlock Holmes, created by Sir Arthur Conan Doyle.
Moriscos: Spanish Muslims who converted to the Christian Faith in Spain after Spain was re-conquered. Despite their conversion to Christianity they were evicted from Spain in 1568.
Moscow.: today, the capital of Russia. See Muscovy.
Moscow Parity: a notion started by Ivan III (when he began claiming that Moscow was the 'Third Rome.' Ivan IV, the Terrible, took it one step further. He tried to make Moscow a Patriarchate. But when that failed he made Moscow a Patriarchate anyway, causing the Raskol in the Orthodox Church. Czar Alexis, took it one step further. Alexis demanded that no title outside of Muscovy could exceed the title in Moscow -- past or present. He backed up his edict by a threat that anyone who did, would be tried for treason, which meant death or exile to Siberia, depending on the gravity of the claim. Starting with Czar Alexis I (1645-76), after Khmelnitzky died in 1657, Moscow demanded that all nations under his control were barred from using higher titles than were bestowed by Moscow. The directive was primarily directed at the Ukraine. From then on, the Kievan-Rus Kings were demoted to Princes and the Ukrainian Patriarchs were demoted to Metropolitans. All violators were sent to Siberia. [This became the main theme for all subsequent Czars and Stalin to degrade the Ukraine].

Peter I, created the Holy Synod, decapitating the Orthodox Church altogether. Catherine II and all her successors enforced the edict of Alexis and Peter's subjugation of the Orthodox Church. Therefore, starting with Alexis all Patriarchs of Kiev were called Metropolitans and all Kings of Kiev were called Princes. What is curious, of course, is that there were many Princes but who was their King? Stalin continued with their policy.

Mountbattens: a German family of nobles who moved to England with the Hanoverians in 1715 when George I took over the rule in England. Their original name was Battenberg. During World War I, that (German) name became an embarrassment to them and they changed it to Mountbatten.Queen Elizabeth II is married to a member of that family.

Muja == Mukha: a common Spanish name. When translated into Ukrainian (j=kh) it means, fly, the insect.

Multivariate: involving multiple independent variables.

Munich.: München in German. The capital of Bavaria, now a province of Germany. Base of the Wittelsbachs, from the 13th to 20th century. In 1805, Napoleon made it a Kingdom. In 1919, Bavaria joined the German Empire. On September 29, 1938 in Munich, Czechoslovakia was handed over to Hitler by Chamberlain, to 'buy peace in our time.' One of the key appeasements which led to Word War II.

Municipals: bonds issued by municipalities in America.

Murat, Joachim (1767-1815): Marshal of France in Napoleon's army and King of Naples.

Murmansk: a city on the White Sea, in Russia. Originally, part of Novhorod during the Kievan-Rus.

Muscovy: derived from the name Moscow. The first reference to Moscow occurs in the Kievan-Rus (Gothic) Chronicles in 1147. Two Princes decided to meet at that watering hole. When Prince Alexander Nevsky was banished by the Novhorodians, the residents of Moscow asked him to rule over them, in about 1238. Alexander Nevsky agreed because it was an unchartered community (village) in Kievan-Rus. Alexander Nevsky collaborated with Batu during the Tartar invasion of Kievan-Rus. Batu's conquest of Europe was spoiled by the poisoning of the chief Khan Ugudai by a jealous concubine thousands of miles away and Batu's presence was required at the election of a new Khan. Batu stopped his conquest at Adrianople (Europe had been conquered to about the river Elbe by then.) Next on his agenda was to conquer the Roman Empire. However, he wheeled his army around and moved to the tent city of Sarai, east of Moscow. From there he went to the election. Batu was not elected chief Khan. He returned to Sarai, from where he doled out Yarlics (Principalities) to the highest bidder in taxes. Alexander Nevsky, because of his loyalty to Batu, received first choice in Kievan-Rus.

Alexander chose Volodimir for it included Moscow. Since Volodimir was a Chartered City, his successors moved the seat to Moscow, with Ivan I Kalita (Money-Bags) (1328-41). From there he could rule in an absolute manner unabridged by civilized law. In time, Moscow expanded with the aid of the Tartars and became a Duchy. It was called the Duchy of Muscovy until the reign of Czar Peter I.

Peter changed the name of that Duchy to Rossija. Voltaire wrote the history according to the specifications provided by Czarina Catherine II. Voltaire preferred the French name Russe or Russia, based on Rus. Thus, the natives call their land Rossija to this day (based on the Dutch world Ross or horse), while the rest of the world calls it Russia. Historically, the following names were used for Muscovy or Russia:

1147 to 1238	Kievan-Rus
1238 to 1380	Tartary (until Kulikovo)
1380 to 1725	Duchy of Muscovy (d.Peter I)
1725 to 1797	Rossija
1797 to 1923	Rossija (by natives), Russia or Russe (abroad)
1923 to 1992	Soviet Union
1992 to Present	Rossija (by natives and Russia abroad)

Muslims: followers of Islam.

Mussolini, Benito (1881-1945): Italian Prime Minister and dictator allied with Hitler during World War II. Aka: Il Duce.

Nagasaki: a port city in Japan.The second, and more powerful Atom Bomb was dropped there on August 9, 1945 when Japan refused to surrender during World War II.

Nanking: former capital of China. In 1937, Japan captured it in what is called: the Rape of Nanking. However, Japan refuses to acknowledge to this day that any atrocities took place there.

Nantes, Edict of (1598): an order issued by King Henry IV of France granting religious freedom to the Protestants. However, by 1685, religious persecution in France was rampant and most Protestants left for the Netherlands and England.

Naples.: a city in Southern Italy, formerly in Magna Grecia. It became Roman in 328 BC and Habsburg from 1503 to 1734. Became capital for the Kingdom of Sicily until 1860, when it joined the Italian Republic.

Napoleon I, Bonaparte (1769-1821): Emperor of France (1804-15). Conqueror of Europe, defeated by Kutuzov in his disastrous campaign into Russia in 1812. Once defeated, his alliances crumbled until he and France were destroyed.

Napoleon III, (1808-73): Emperor of France from 1852 to 1870. Bonaparte was his paternal uncle. Defeated in the Franco-

Prussian war, which resulted in the German Empire by declaration, in Versailles, in the Hall of Mirrors.

Napoleonic Wars: the period of 1803 to 1815 in Europe.

Narses, (478-573): a gifted Roman general in the employ of Roman Emperor Justinian I.

Narva..: a Swedish town on the Baltic Sea. (Founded by Kievan-Rus in 1223.) There the 16 year old boy-King from Sweden, Charles XII, with an army of 12,000 routed Czar Peter I, who commanded 80,000.

NASDAQ.: second largest stock exchange in America, trading mostly in emerging issues. Aka: OTC or Over The Counter.

Nassau.: a German Duchy, now part of Germany. The title, Counts of Nassau was created in 1160. Napoleon created the Duchy in 1806. They are related to the House of Orange and Luxembourg, rulers of the Netherlands, and briefly ruled in England: William III (1650-1702).

Nations, Battle of the: (October 13 to 16 in 1813, aka: Battle of Leipzig), the nations facing a defeated Napoleon after his Russian disaster. The nations facing Napoleon were: Russia; Austria, England and Prussia.

NATO...: North Atlantic Treaty Organization, an alliance during the Cold War of Western European nations, led by America against the Soviet Union.

Navarino, Battle of (1827): a decisive naval battle against the Ottoman Turks, which led to the liberation of Greece. A combined fleet under Sir Edward Coddington commanded the English, French and Russians, defeated the combined Egyptian and Turkish fleets.

Nazi...: member of the NSDAP, or Hitler's Nazi party.

Nebuchadnezzar (604-504 BC): King of Persia.

Nelson, Horatio (1758-1805): English admiral who defeated Napoleon's navy at Trafalgar, thereby snatching away the bounty for England's conquest set by the Pope at 2 million Ducats in gold.

Neman..: See Nieman.

NEP....: New Economic Program. A program initiated by Lenin to allow limited capitalism in the Soviet Union to overcome the ravages of the Civil War, while the Civil War was still raging.

Nestor (ca.1020-1080): a Greek monk in the Monastery of the Caves in Kiev. He wrote about the martyrs Boris and Hlib. His account amputated their lineage to the Goths. A form of geopolitics practiced by the Roman Empire.

Netherlands: a Kingdom of Western Europe on the North Sea. Home of the Gaels (Nervii & Belgae) and Germans (Batavians & Frisians). In 851 the Norse with Roruk and Godfrey settled there. In 1795, the Netherlands was overrun by the French, partitioning Belgium and Luxembourg from it. Now all three are part of the EU.

Neva...: a river near Novhorod.After Prince Alexander of Novhorod butchered the Swedish missionaries led by Jarl Birger,

Alexander became know as Alexander Nevsky.

Nevsky, Alexander (1220-1263): Prince of Kievan-Rus, Prince of Novhorod. He was banished when he advocated an alliance with the Tartars. He became ruler in Moscow and ally of Batu (Tartars). When Batu doled out the Principalities, Nevsky received the Principality of his choice:Volodimir, for it included Moscow. His successors moved to Moscow, because Moscow was not a Chartered city and they could rule there absolutely, in Tartar fashion, starting with Ivan I Kalita, or: Money-Bags.

New Deal: a program devised by US President Franklin D Roosevelt to employ (like TVA), relieve (as SSI) and recover (Farm Relief) America from the Great Depression of 1929. It lasted from 1933 to 1939 and included many social reforms such as: Social Security and price guarantees for small farmers. When Hitler came to power, he copied many of the reforms.

Newton, Sir Isaac (1642-1727): English scientist.

Nibelungen Lied: an epic story about Siegfried, the hero in Wagner's Ring (and his son's name.)

Nicaea.: a town in Minor Asia, the site of the first Christian Council of 325. It was presided over by Emperor Constantine, who was a heathen. It defined the nature of Christianity by adopting the Creed. It was attended by about 800 Bishops 600 or so were Arian Bishops.

Nicodemus: a contributor to the teachings of Jesus Christ. But his works are not included in the New Testament. They are, however, included in the 'Apocrypha,' aka: The Lost Books of the Bible.

Nicholas I (1796-1855): Czar of Russia. He came to power in 1825 and promptly created the 3rd Department, a secret police, to terrorize the minorities in Russia: Byelorussians, Jews, Poles and Ukrainians. He initiated the pogroms. His foreign policy led to the Crimean War.

Nicholas II, (1868-1918): Czar of Russia.He came to power in 1894 taking Russia from one political disaster into another: War against Japan (1905); World War I (1914) and so on. In 1917, this led to the Revolution in Russia and a Civil War ensued which lasted about 17 years, most heavily fought in the Ukraine. By 1934, Russia was economically ruined and Stalin firmly in control.

Niebuhr, Barthold G (1776-1831): Danish historian who debunked the histories written by Bishops, Abbots and other historians in the service of Kings and Dukes for the period of about 400 to 1800 in Europe.

Niemen.: a river which divides Russia and Poland. Aka: Nemen in English and Memel in German. Napoleon and Czar Alexander I, reshaped the map of Europe there. The Curzon Line became the dividing line between East and West in 1806.

Nightingale, Florence (1820-1910): reformer of hospital nursing. Under her care the mortality rate in hospitals dropped from 42% to 2%, on average.

Nikkei.: major Japanese exchange in Tokyo.

Nixon, Richard (1969-76): 37th President of the USA.

NKWD...(aka NKVD): the name of the secret police during Stalin's era. While the names change their methods remain the same. The equivalent of today's KBG.

Normandy: province of France, home of the Gothic Normans, albeit converted to the Roman Faith and speaking a French dialect. All the Kings of England, starting with the Danes in the 6th century until Henry VIII were either Normans or related to the Normans.

Norway.: Kingdom in North-West Europe, home of the Gothic Normans and Varangians. They explored Iceland, Greenland and Vineland (America). Member of the EU.

Novhorod: the second most important Chartered city in the Kievan-Rus. The Prince of Novhorod was the heir apparent -- like the Prince of Wales in Great Britain, a custom transferred by the Gothic invaders to England. Novhorod was not conquered by the Tartars because the spring thaw did not allow them to bring in their heavy siege engines there. Novhorod joined the Hansa, a defensive federation of the Northern Goths. Later-on, some German cities were admitted. When the Hansa disintegrated in the 17th century, Novhorod was first conquered by Ivan III from Muscovy. Later-on Novhorod was sacked by Ivan the Terrible followed by a senseless bloodbath (as many as 50,000 were slaughtered). Many were evicted. They formed the Ural Sich. When St.Petersburg was built, the significance as a trading center on the Baltic was eliminated for Novhorod. (Novgorod in Russian.)

Novhorod(ians): the residents of Novhorod.

Numerals: symbols by which numbers are represented. Originally, letters of the alphabet represented numeric values. Rome introduced the first numerals in the West, but they are not workable. In the 15th century 'arabic numerals' were introduced. A mental block in Western Europe was the numeral zero (0) until it was introduced from the Indian-Arabic world and found acceptance in Europe. The Greeks and Romans did not have a numeral for zero, it was considered to be an absurdity to have a representation for 'nothing.' Homer made mockery of it in his Odyssey; Socrates in his dialogues with Plato and so on.

However, as soon as Descartes began investigating the number zero, Western Civilization leapfrogged past all other civilizations, in particular in mathematics and the sciences. This led to the industrial age in Europe and America, and the high-tech age in America.

Nürnberg: a town in Bavaria, Germany. After World War II the Nazi war criminals were tried there.

NSDAP..: the Nazi Party of Hitler's Germany which he controlled.

NYSE...: major stock exchange in America, in New York City.

Obelisk: an Egyptian stone pillar, often used to record the deeds of a Pharaoh. The text was usually signed with the Pharaoh's sign or cartouche.

ober-..: a common German prefix to a title or rank. For example: Ober-Prokuror, etc. Adopted by Peter in Rossija.

Oceledez: literally, a salted herring in Ukrainian. A long mustache or long pony-tail, however, was fashionable among the Cossacks. It was called: Oceledez.

October Revolution: to begin with, there were two of them, both in the month of October by the Old Calendar. Usually, the second October Revolution was observed by the Soviet Union. It occurred on October 24, 1917 (at night) and was observed on November 7th during the Soviet regime.

Oder...: a major river to the East of the Elbe river in present day Germany. When the Holy Roman Empire began expanding to the East with the German Dukes and Knights, the river Oder became the next major target after Charlemagne's death. First, Brandenburg was created, then the 'Teutonic Knights' expanded to the East beyond the river Vistula until they were defeated by the Lithuanian Duke Vitus (aka: Vitovt) in 1410 at Tannenberg. With that defeat, the 'Teutonic Knights' had to sign a peace treaty which limited their expansion to the Vistula river. The Grand-master of the Teutonic Knights rushed to Rome and the Pope disbanded the Teutonic Knights, creating a new order of Knights called the 'Knights of the Sword.' This new order continued their encroachment into the East. Technically, they were not subject of the treaty signed by the Teutonic Knights -- as perceived by the Pope. The area between the Elbe and Oder became new German territory by declaration. The new German masters called themselves Junkers (von).

The Gothic nations: Angles became Mecklenburg; the Sassons became Brandenburg and the Wends became Saxons. On the right bank of the Oder, between the Oder and Vistula river were the Pomeranians, Poland and Prussians. The Pomeranians and Prussians were conquered, exterminated and the Germans took the Prussian name to boot, creating Prussia. Poland was spared only because she was Catholic. From there they expanded into East Prussia and to the Baltic Sea and called that area Kurland, which included most of Estonia, Latvia and Lithuania.During World War II, the Soviets expanded to the river Elbe -- reclaiming their lost territories.

Present day Germany, has a new border in the East, called the Oder-Neisse Line.

Oder-Neisse Line: the current frontier between Germany and Poland. See Oder.

Odyssey: one of the books written by Homer dealing with the exploration of the Atlantic Ocean. When it was Romanized, the action shifted to the Mediterranean Sea.

Oenophiles: wine lovers.

OGPU...: a name given to the Soviet secret police as an extension of the Cheka, founded in 1918 by Lenin.
OK.....: a typically American expression which is used throughout the world today. The opposite of KO in boxing.
Old Guard:originated with the crack troops of Napoleon's Imperial Guard. Today it is used in the extended sense, the staunch supporter of a prior regime. For example: The President of the Ukraine Kuchma is from the Old Guard (Soviet Union).
Oleh, Oleg(in Russian) (870-913): military leader and regent for Ihor (914-945), the rightful King-Judge for Kiev from the Ruryc (Rurik) line of Gothic King-Judges. Oleh restored Kiev's trade privileges with Constantinople by conquering the city. He arrived with his army of about 900 ships and landed just outside the Golden Horn in 911. There, he had the boats outfitted with wheels and they sailed into Constantinople before they had time to close their gate. He did not sack the city, all he wanted was favorable trade privileges -- which he got. His shield is still hanging on Constantinople's gate, now called Istanbul.
Olha, (Olga in Russian) (946-960): Queen of Kievan-Rus, wife of Ihor, regent for Sviatoslav. She was baptized in 954.
Olympia: sanctuary dedicated to Zeus, site of Greek Olympiads.
Olympiad(s): Olympics started by the Greeks in 776 BC. Chronological time was kept this way. For example, Rome was founded in the 3rd year after the 5th Olympiad or 753 BC, (or 23 years after the first Olympiad.)
Olympians: 12 major Greek gods, to coincide with the 12 signs of the Zodiac, who were said to reside on Mount Olympus in Greece. Also, the participants in an Olympiad.
Olympics: started in 776 BC. It was used as a chronoligical time reference for historic events by the Greeks and early Romans. When Rome conquered Greece, the Olympic games were suspended. When Greece was liberated in 1827, the modern games resumed in 1896, in Athens.
OPEC...: Organization of Petroleum Exporting Countries.
Opium War, (1839-42): When a large quantity of Opium was seized and destroyed by the Chinese (which was illegal in China) from English merchants, England initiated a war to sell the Opium to China anyway. Shanghai was shelled, Hong Kong was taken and the Chinese had to pay an indemnity.
Oppenheimer, Robert (1904-67): American physicist and Director of of Los Alamos Laboratory, where Enrico Fermi perfected the Atom Bomb.
Oracle.: a site devoted to a deity, where a priest or priestess interpreted the signs and answered to a posed question. The most famous Oracle in Greece was located in Delphi, it was dedicated to Apollo.
Oran...: a town in North Africa, site of English beachheads in the allied invasion during Word War II. It was defended by the French.
Orel...: a town in the Soviet Union. During World War II, the

town became a strategic objective during the Battle of Kursk in the summer of 1943.

Orleans: a city in France on the Loire river,a Gothic stronghold.

Orlov..: the lover and biological father of some of the children of Catherine II, Czarina of Russia. At the time of his love-affair with Catherine, Orlov was in charge of the Preobrazhensky regiment which protected the Czar. When Czarina Elizabeth died or was killed, Catherine was facing a permanent life in a nunnery. Therefore, Catherine and Orlov engineered a palace coup, imprisoned Catherine's husband Peter III and Orlov killed him. Now Catherine could assume the throne, stop the 7 Year War and resuscitate Prussia and Frederick the Great in Paris, in 1763.

Orthodox: in Greek, right in opinion. In 1054, the Roman Church and Orthodox Church split over the interpretation of the 'i' in the Creed. It became final in 1353. But that, of course, is a pretext. The real reason was power.

Constantinople was on the decline while Rome was rising in power. It is called: the Schism of the Christian Church over an iota. (Aka: the filioque clause).

Osiris.: Egyptian deity in the Isis cult, husband of Isis.

Ostarbeiter: in German, Eastern Workers. About 10 million Slavs were forcibly repatriated by Hitler to Germany.

Ostrogoths: claimed to be the Eastern Goths by may historians. That is, the Goths were divided into the Visigoths (Western) and Ostrogoths (Eastern) Goths arbitrarily. To begin with there were many Gothic nations - see Jordanes. However, solid evidence shows that this division is not correct. The Eastern-most Goths were the Alans, they were defeated first by the Huns. Only after the defeat of the Alans, did the 'other' Goths engage the Huns. But they were also defeated. After that defeat, roughly 2.5 million Goths sought sanctuary in the Roman Empire, about half of the Gothic nation. Eventually, 1 million of them were ferried across the Danube river, while the rest moved on along the Danube river and crossed into Gaul. However, about 2.5 million Goths stayed behind. Why?

There is only one logical explanation: the so called Visigoths were Arian Christians and they had every reason to believe that the Roman Empire would grant them sanctuary, because they had just converted to the Christian Faith, taught them in Constantinople. (Little did they know that the Roman Empire had just switched to a new brand of the Christian Faith: Orthodoxy, under the Roman Emperor Valens. To the Orthodox Christians, the Arian Christians were now heretics and all heretics were actively persecuted by the Roman Emperor Valens.)

However, the Ostogoths were heathens at that time. They had no choice but to stay behind in their homeland. Eventually they converted to the Christian Faith, albeit to the Arian Faith, since the missionaries who stayed behind, were of Arian faith. Therefore, a much better subdivision of the Goths is: The Visigoths were Arian Christians, while the Ostrogoths were heathens. See Goths.

Ostland: German, Eastern land. Without being specific, it meant the Soviet Union.

Ostpolitik: the formal name by which Hitler's policy against the Slavs was known. According to that policy, Slavs had to be enslaved (Untermensch == sub-human) and made to work for the Aryan master race (Herrenrasse == Master Race). This also included the Jews and Gypsies.

Ostracism: in Athens, banishment. Once each year, the Athenian citizens gathered in the market place and wrote a name on a broken piece of pottery. Whoever got the largest number of names was ostracized. The Athenians considered this practice as a safety-valve to banish politically popular individuals to preempt a dictator. Today we mean: a community shunning.

Otto I, (912-73): Emperor of the Holy Roman Empire who defeated the Magyars at Lechfeld in 955. He was married to a distant cousin of the Roman Emperor.

Otto I, (1815-1867): King of Greece from 1832 to 1862, from the House of Wittelsbach (Bavaria).

Ottoman Empire: created by Othman, a devout Muslim, dedicated to Holy War (Jihad) and plunder. They ruled most of the Old World from about 1200 to 1918, to the end of World War I, when the empire was dismembered by England and France.

Ovid, (43 BC - 17 AD): Roman poet.

Pakistan: a Muslim country bordering on India.

Palatine: the Count of Palatine, was elevated to Elector in the Holy Roman Empire in 1369, an extremely important hereditary title, much higher than King or Duke. Main city was Heidelberg.

Palestine: a region in Asia Minor, referred to as the Holy Land.

Panama Canal: a canal consisting of a series of locks, suitable for ocean going vessels, to travel between the Atlantic and Pacific Oceans, built by the USA in 1914. The immediate area surrounding the canal is called: Canal Zone.

Pannonia: a Roman province, roughly present day Hungary.

Papacy, the (800 to present): The name given to the office held by the Pope.

Papal States: parts of Italy ruled by the Pope. (Umbria, Romagna, the Marches, and the Patrimony.) The Papal states became a formidable stumbling block to the formation of an Italian State. Eventually, the Papal States were just taken away from the Pope and an Italian Kingdom was formed under Sicily in 1861. Later, re-alignments occurred in 1865 and Italy was finally fully formed in 1870. Meanwhile, the Pope locked himself up and refused to communicate with his flock. Mussolini, found a solution to this dilemma: the Italian Concordat was made in 1929. The Vatican was created as a state within the state of Italy.This solution was universally accepted in Italy and abroad.This endeared Mussolini to the Pope and the Italian People.

Paris..: the capital of France.

Paristanbul: a potential Islamic name for Paris.

Parma..: a city in Spain, governed by a Duke.

Parteigenosse: fellow party member (in German).

Pascal.: a common computer language, in honor of the French mathematician by the same name.

Pascal, Blaise (1623-62): French mathematician.

Patriarchs: in this context, the duly appointed leaders of the various Christian Churches, established by the Roman Emperors. Since they occurred in a specific sequence, the pecking order is in that sequence.

First and foremost was Constantinople, since it was also the seat of the Roman Empire. Initially, there was only one Patriarch, Arius, he was in Constantinople and he was appointed by the Roman Emperor Constantine.When Athanasius won the dispute against Arius, Emperor Valens created three more Patriarchs: Jerusalem (origin of the Christian Faith); Alexandria (because Bishop Athanasius was from there and his brand of Christianity prevailed) and Antioch (because this is where the Christians had separated themselves from the Jews and established a new religion).

During the reign of Justinian I, Rome's Bishop was elevated to Patriarch, because he supported Justinian I against the Ostrogoths who ruled in Italy at that time.

Emperor Basil II, created a Patriarchate in Kiev, he installed Patriarch Leontiy (991-1004) there, and made Volodimir hereditary King and married off his sister Anna to him.

Later, Armenia was elevated to a Patriarchate because they were the first nation to accept Christianity in 301 and Ethiopia was elevated to a Patriarchate because they sheltered Athanasius during his period of persecution by Emperor Constantine and his son.

In all, there are 8 Patriarchates and 8 Patriarchs. This is still symbolized in the Orthodox Church with the 'eight-ended cross' and 'eight-ended' decorations in their churches -- two overlapping squares.

The role of the Patriarch was to legitimize minor variations in customs for a Christian Church. For example, rather than using Latin or Greek, the local vernacular could be used in Church service; Priests had to be married or be monks; a Bishop could only be installed if his spouse had died (remarriage was frowned upon for priests); a brother of a deceased husband was encouraged to marry the widow (minimizing step-fathers) and so on. However, they also interpreted the Scriptures and their interpretation was final in their Patriarchate. Technically, therefore, Orthodoxy has 8 forms of Christianity.

However, as soon as the Bishop of Rome was elevated to Patriarch, he began claiming supremacy with 'Primus enter Pares.' (First among equals.) When that did not work, he created a second Christian Empire with a proper protector: Charlemagne. Since then, the two main branches of Christianity have been at odds with each other, to this day.

A brief list of Ukrainian Patriarchs is provided here. In all, there were 79 Patriarchs in the Ukraine. Here are the Patriarchs from Kiev who were in charge during the pivotal times in the Ukraine:

Leontiy (991-1004), first official Patriarch sent from Constantinople, during the reign of Volodimir the Great. Twenty one Patriarchs later:

Josyf I (1236-1241), during the sack of Kiev by the Tartars. Twelve Patriarchs later:

Hryhor (1458-72) during the start of the Cossack movement. Eighteen Patriarchs later:

Antoniy (1642-1655), at the time Bohdan Khmelnitzky ratified the Moscow alliance in 1654. Four Patriarchs later:

Yuriy (1708-1714), when Mazepa and Charles XII were defeated at Poltava in 1709. Two Patriarchs later:

Atanasiy (1729-1746), at the time when Elizabeth ruled in Russia. Two Patriarchs later:

Philipp (1762-1778), when Catherine II, destroyed the Zaporozhian Sich and banished all Cossacks. Six Patriarchs later:

Josaphat (1817-1837), when all Patriarchs in Kiev were officially outlawed by Czar Nicholas I.

However, despite the Czarist edicts Patriarchs were elected in Kiev and promptly exiled to Siberia by the Czars. And so, the list is large if all martyrs are to be counted. Of course, the situation during the Soviet regime was not much better. Again, all elected Patriarchs were sent to Siberia. See Lypkiwsky.

With the fall of Constantinople, many of the wars and political aspirations started to evolve around 'whoever controlled the Patriarch,' controlled Orthodoxy, hence Christendom. Therefore, starting with Ivan III, Moscow tried to control the Patriarchs, while Rome tried to eliminate them.

When Ivan III in Muscovy married Zoe, the niece of the Roman Emperor, he started making his claims: Moscow was proclaimed to be the 'Third Rome,' hence Moscow was the protector of Orthodoxy.

Next, Ivan the Terrible wanted Moscow to be elevated to a Patriarchate and the Patriarch of Jerusalem was invited to confirm Patriarch Philip. Instead a break, Raskol, of the Orthodox Church was the result. Philip was not confirmed and the Patriarch of Jerusalem pointed out a few errors in their liturgy. Then, Ivan the Terrible installed

Job as Patriarch in 1589 anyway. Now there were two Patriarchs in the East. One in Kiev, the other in Moscow.

Czar Alexis made Nikon, Patriarch of Moscow in 1653 and outlawed the Patriarch of Kiev. However, despite this, a Patriarch continued in Kiev. When Peter I came to power, the Moscow Patriarch was Adrian. By 1700, the situation of legitimate Patriarchs was as follows:

Constantinople was in the hands of the Ottoman Turks -- as was Antioch, Alexandria and Armenia. The Patriarch of Rome had elevated himself to Pope. This left 3 legitimate and active Patriarchs: Jerusalem, Kiev and Ethiopia.

Mazepa invited the Patriarch of Jerusalem, who confirmed the Patriarch in Kiev and the Patriarchate of Kiev, in effect countermanding the decree of Czar Alexis.Therefore, Peter I decided to eliminate all Russian Patriarchs and create the Holy Synod.

In 1878, Czar Alexander II, liberated the Balkans and Russia occupied Constantinople. As soon as that was done, a Patriarch was elected. But, as soon as England, Prussia and Austria imposed the treaty of Berlin the same year, that Patriarch fled to Greece and from there to Cyprus.

Patrician: a member of the aristocracy or of a privileged class.

Patton, George S. (1885-1945): American general during World War II. Patton broke the German siege of Bastogne during the 'Battle of the Bulge.' Vlasov tried to surrender to Patton, but general Eisenhower would not let Patton accept Vlasov's surrender condemning Vlasov and his officers to death, and his soldiers to a 'Siberian vacation.'

Paulus, Friedrich P. von (1890-1957): German Field Marshal, in charge to take Stalingrad during World War II.

PC.....: personal computer.

Pearl Harbor: a major US naval port in Hawaii. On December 7, 1941, the Japanese launched a sneak attack on that base and did substantial damage. However, the big ships, the flattops were out at sea (Pearl Harbor was too shallow for them.) Therefore, while America took a heavy toll, her power and muscle was preserved. This unprovoked attack led to America's entry into World War II. At Midway, the flattops broke Japan's naval power in June, 1942.

Peleponnesian War, (431-404): the war for the hegemony of Greece between Athens and Sparta. Even though Sparta won, her glory was short lived because, in 371 the Spartan were defeated by the Thebans at Leuctra and at Chaeronea in 338 the Greeks were defeated by Philip II and Alexander, the Macedonian Goths. Then, Alexander the Great conquered Greece and proceeded to conquer the Persian Empire.

Penrose, Archibald: contemporary English mathematician.

Pepone.: a fictitious Italian mayor of a small town, who is in conflict with the local Catholic priest: Don Camillo.

Perestroika: a program to 'retrofit' the Soviet economy by Michail Gorbachev (from the Don area). This and Star Wars, led to the collapse of the Soviet Union.

Pereyaslav: a Princely city in the Ukraine, where Cossack Hetman Khmelnitzky assembled all Cossacks and gave a passionate speech to accept the alliance offered by Muscovy -- mainly because they were Orthodox. With disastrous consequences for the Ukraine in years to come.

Perez..: a Spanish name, translates into pepper in Ukrainian.

Pericles, (495-429 BC): Athenian benevolent tyrant.

Persephone: in Greek mythology, daughter of Demeter, who was abducted and married by Hades.

Persia.: the name for Iran in antiquity.

Persian Wars, (499-449 BC): attempts by the giant Persian Empire to conquer the tiny city-states of Greece. Three major battles shaped the outcome of the war:

1) Marathon in 490, where a Persian fleet -- while attempting to disembark -- were attacked by a handful of Athenians. The Persian losses were staggering, whereas the Athenians suffered only a few casualties. However, that Greek victory did not deter the Persians.
2) Thermopylae in 480, a few Greek defenders held back an army of over 1 million at a mountain pass by that name (according to Greek historians.) But a traitor led the Persians around the pass. All Greeks retreated except the Spartans under their King Leonidas, 300 of them. They perished to a man. Later the Greeks erected a monument there, which reads (roughly translated): 'Wanderer, if you come to Sparta, tell them you saw us lying here as the law commanded it.'

   Meanwhile, the Athenians rushed a messenger to the Delphi oracle to inquire what to do next. The oracle answered: 'Defend yourself behind wooden walls.' To some Athenians this meant to erect a wooden wall around Athens and take up defensive positions there. However, Themistocles argued that the message was clear: the wooden walls were the Greek ships.

   So, he urged all Athenians to man the ships, and most did. Those that stayed behind the wooden walls in Athens were handily overcome by the Persians. What developed was: the isthmus was held by the Spartans and other Greek allies, while the Athenians in their ships guarded the shallow bay and their flank. A sort of stalemate ensued.

   However, Themistocles was anxious for battle, which the Persians refused to give, because their ships were much larger and there was a great number of them. They wanted to engage the Greek fleet in the open sea. So, Themistocles resorted to a ruse (inspired by Athene.) He sent his trusted slave to the Persian King Xerxes with the message: 'Hurry master, finish the Greeks, for they are about to flee.' Xerxes took the bait and ordered his navy to attack the Greeks, while

Xerxes had himself a huge platform built from where he was going to watch his great victory.

As the Persian naval squadrons entered the bay, the Greek ships went right at them. Then, at the last moment before impact, they would swerve and cut the oars of the Persian ships. Once they were without oars, they became easy prey for the Greeks. In this way, the entire Persian fleet was destroyed -- at Salamis. Xerxes was horrified and decided to return home. But, yet another problem arose. In Asia Minor were large Greek settlements and when word reached them of the great victory at Salamis, they revolted against the Persians, cutting off the return road for Xerxes. Now, Xerxes sent a delegation to the Goths, asking to use their country to travel back to Persia. The Goths gave him permission and Xerxes returned to Persia by land via the Ukraine and the Caucasus.

3) Even though Xerxes returned with his entourage he left most of the army behind to destroy the Greeks. Next year the Greeks were ready to take on the Persians at Plataea where they routed them.

In this entire sequence of events Salamis, was the most important battle.In it the Greeks not only destroyed the Persian fleet but they totally demoralized the Persian army, who watched helplessly from the shore as each ship was first crippled and then sacked by the Greeks. The bay ran red with Persian blood, while the Greek losses were relatively insignificant. Thus, from the outset at Plataea, the Greeks, while outnumbered by about 3 to 1, carried the psychological advantage of invincibility into the battle of Plataea and it ended up being nearly a slaughter.

Petain, Henri P (1856-1951): French Marshal and political leader, allied with Hitler (Vichy France).

Peter I, the Great (1672-1725): Czar of Russia from 1696. While Peter is acclaimed as a great reformer and innovator, there is much evidence that this was not so. He killed his son and heir, Alexis, just like Ivan the Terrible did. He ruled without any moral authority. He caused another split in the Orthodox Church. He persecuted the minorities ruthlessly. Usually, the word 'great' is reserved for two occasions: first a great military leader, which Peter was not. (A 16 year old boy-King with an army of 12,000 destroyed Peter's army of 80,000. No military 'great' was ever captured by his enemy, then ransomed by his sex slave and had to give up all his prior conquests -- which Peter had to do in the Prut campaign -- to the Sultan no less.)

Second, the word 'great' is reserved for rulers who accepted Christianity, not fragmented it. Which Peter did when he created the Holy Synod.

Without Leibnitz, there may have been few if any reforms. All Peter was capable of was to terrorize the minorities in Russia -- in particular the Ukraine.

Peter II, (1727-1730): Czar of tender age (12), son of Alexis (son of Peter I by 1st marriage, who was tortured and killed by Peter I.) Thus, Peter II was the grandson of Peter I. Menshikov tried to marry his daughter to him. But Peter II died at age 15.

Peter III, (1762-1762): (technically, he was never made Czar) son of Anna (sister of Elizabeth), grandson of Peter I. Heir to the throne, but his wife Catherine II out-foxed him. He paid for that with his life.

As soon as Elizabeth was buried, Catherine staged a coup with Orlov, her lover and commander of the Preobrazhensky regiment. Peter III was captured, imprisoned and killed by Orlov. However, the 7-Year War turn-around was heaped on Peter III (he was an idiot anyway by all accounts), absolving Catherine II who also restored Biron the German in Kurland in 1763.

Petrarch, Francesco (1304-74): Italian poet.

Pharaoh: an Egyptian title for ruler, in antiquity.

Pharos, The:lighthouse at the entrance to the harbor of Alexandria. One of the 7 wonders of the Old World. The others being: (1) the Pyramids at Giza, (2) the hanging gardens of Babylon, (3) the Colossus of Rhodes, (4) the statue of Zeus at Olympia, (5) statue of Artemis, (6) Mausoleum.

Phidias, (431-417 BC): Greek sculptor.

Philadelphia: the 'city of brotherly love' in Pennsylvania, USA. Founded in 1682 by William Penn, a Quaker.

Philip II, (382-336 BC): Macedonian King,father of Alexander III, the Great.

Philip II, (1527-98): King of Spain and Two Sicilies, married to Queen Mary (Bloody Mary) of England. He launched the Spanish Armada against England when Elizabeth I became Queen of England.

Phoenicians: a seafaring nation and colonists of the Old World. One of their colonies was Carthage.

Picasso, Pablo R (1881-1973): Spanish artist.

Picts..: aborigines of Scotland.

Pierce, Franklin (1853-57): 14th President of the USA.

Pirates: sea robbers.

Pittsburg: a city in Pennsylvania USA,port and industrial center. The 'City of Steel.'

Pius XII, (1876-1958): Pope of Roman extraction, implicated in the Nazi holocaust.

PL1....: a computer language: Programming Language 1.

Plantagenets, House of (1154-1399): rulers of England and portions of France: Normandy, Brittany, Aquitaine and Gascony -- the area occupied by the Norman Goths.

Plato, (427-348 BC): Greek philosopher.

Plebeian: a member of Greek and Roman lower classes.

Pliny, the Elder (23-79 AD): Roman geographer and historian.
Podolia: a Western province of the Ukraine.
Poland.: a Republic in Eastern Europe, between the rivers Oder-Neisse (border of Germany) and Niemen (border of Byelorussia). The Piast Kingdom (850-1370) was under constant German attack, but for the most part Germans were held in check. The Jagiello Dynasty (1386-1550) made Poland a dominant county in Europe. The Polish Barons carved up Poland into large (personal) estates and disintegration followed until it was taken by Austria,Prussia and Russia.

Poland accepted the Roman Faith in 962. The marriage of Polish Princess Hedzwiga and Lithuanian Grand Duke Jagiello created the largest state in Europe (1386), including (roughly) present day Poland, Lithuania, Byelorussia and most of the Ukraine. Disintegration set in when the Ukraine was forced to convert to Catholicism and evicted Poland (1648). But, in the Treaty of Andrusovo (1667), Byelorussia and the Western part of the Ukraine were turned over by Muscovy for a vague military alliance.

Then, Catherine II orchestrated the 3 partitions of Poland, with Austria and Prussia: 1772, 1773 and in 1775 when Poland ceased to exist on the map of Europe.Napoleon, restored a small enclave around Warsaw in 1810 to please his lover Countess Maria Walewska.In 1815,after Napoleon's defeat, that enclave was taken over by Russia. In 1917, Poland was liberated by the Germans and after World War I, the Polish state was created in 1919.

In 1939, Hitler and Stalin partitioned and annexed Poland. In 1945, Stalin integrated Poland into the Soviet Union, as a semi-autonomous Republic. When the Soviet Union fell apart in 1990, an independent Poland was created. In 2003, Poland was accepted into the EU.
Polk, James (1845-1849): 11th President of the USA.
Polo, Marco (1254-1324): Venetian traveller and author.
Polybius, (205-125 BC): Roman historian.
Pomerania: a Gothic nation on the Baltic Sea, next to Poland. It was annihilated by The Teutonic Knights and annexed to German Prussia.
Pompey, (106-48 BC): Roman general and politician.
Pontifex Maximus: a title held by Julius Caesar and every Roman Emperor which made them the head of every religion in the Roman Empire.
Poseidon: in Greek mythology, god of the Oceans and brother of Zeus. Neptune in Roman.
Potemkin, Grigori (1739-1791): Russian Prince and lover of Catherine II.
Potsdam Conference: the third of the 'Big Three' conferences held in Potsdam, an outskirts of Berlin, from July to August 1945. By then, Churchill was not elected and England was represented by Clement Attlee; Roosevelt had died and the

new American President was Harry Truman. Therefore, from the original deal-makers only Stalin was left and he wanted to collect the promises made to him at Yalta and Teheran.

Prague (Praha): the capital of Czechia (Czech Republic.) After World War I, Czechoslovakia was created from the former Bohemia, Moravia and Slovakia. In 1938, Hitler received the Sudetenland as appeasement from England and took over Czechoslovakia, making it a German protectorate called Bohemia and Moravia.

After World War II, Czechoslovakia was restored but integrated by Stalin as a semi-autonomous Republic into the Soviet Union. When the Soviet Union fell apart in 1992, Czechoslovakia broke up into two countries: Czechia and Slovakia. Today, both Czechia and Slovakia have been accepted into the EU.

Preobrazhensky regiment: one of two regiments responsible for the safety of the Czar and/or Czarina. The other was Semeonov.

Primus inter pares: a term used by the Roman Patriarch to claim superiority among the other 7 Patriarchs, defying the pecking order established by the Roman Emperor. It means first among equals.

Procopius, (500-563): Roman historian.

Prokuror: one of many German titles introduced by Peter I.

Proletariat:the lowest class of workers in an industrial society, a concept defined by Karl Marx and applied in the Soviet Union. In Rome, the roughly equivalent term was: Plebeian. The main difference was: Rome provided 'bread and games' for her plebeians, while the Soviet Union provided military propaganda. Therefore, while both systems abused the lower class, in the Roman system the plebeians were taken care off.

Prometheus:in Greek mythology,a Titan who gave fire to humanity. He tricked Zeus and was punished for it. Hephaestus fastened him to a mountain in the Caucasus, while an eagle tore out his liver daily. Hercules freed him from his chains and released him (with the permission of Zeus).

Propaganda: information, often misleading or downright false, to spread in support of a cause or school of thought. There is a saying: figures don't lie, but liars figure.

Protectorate: rule over an area or country which has not been formally annexed. For example: Austria over Bosnia-Herzogovina; Germany over Bohemia and Moravia (former Czechoslovakia).

Protestant: one who protests. Such as the Lutheran Protestants protesting the religious dogmas of Rome.

Protocol: rules of conduct, ceremony or negotiations.

Prussia: originally a Gothic people situated on the Baltic Sea, next to Poland. When the German Knights expanded Eastward from Brandenburg in the 14th century, they conquered and annihilated the Gothic Prussians and took their name for a German state they called: Prussia (1618) and annexed Pomerania (1640) to it.

German Prussia expanded East to the river Niemen (Memel in German). Napoleon defeated Prussia and Prussia became Napoleon's ally. For that Napoleon gave her the lands of the former Duke of Hanover (who ruled as King of England), making Prussia the largest nation in Central Europe. In 1870, Prussia led a coalition of Germans against France and defeated her. In Versailles in 1871, in the Hall of Mirrors, the German Empire was proclaimed.The Netherlands, Belgium, Luxembourg and Austria were invited to join. However, they refused except for the German Kingdoms (formed by Napoleon): Bavaria, Würtemberg and a few Dukes; Baden, Palatine, Mecklenburg, Saxony; and a few Free Cities: Bremen, Bergedorf, Hamburg, Lübeck and Oldenburg -- all led by Prussia. The new state was called: Deutsches Reich (German Empire). Bavaria and Würtemberg formally joined in 1919.

Prut == Pruth: a river in Western Ukraine.

Prut Campaign: in 1710, while Peter I was in hot pursuit of Charles XII and Mazepa, Peter was surrounded and captured by the Ottoman Sultan. Peter was ransomed by his sex-slave Catherine and Peter subsequently ransomed his army with uncut diamonds, but not before Peter I gave up Azov, took his navy out of the Black Sea and so on. When Peter returned to St. Petersburg, he married Catherine, who ruled as Catherine I (1725-1727).

Pskov..: a Chartered city in Kievan-Rus.

Ptolemy I,(ca.340-283 BC):general of Alexander the Great, a Goth. When Alexander died, Ptolemy got Egypt to rule over. His direct descendant was Cleopatra.

Puhachov, Emelyan I (1740-1775): Cossack Hetman from the Don Sich who led a rebellion against Czarina Catherine II and mimicked her court. Pugachov in Russian.

Puj == Pukh: a common Spanish name, translates into: down (as in a pillow, in Ukrainian).

Punic Wars: the wars between Carthage and Rome for the supremacy in the Mediterranean. They are divided into three wars:

1st Punic War (264-241 BC): Carthage was defeated and Rome became the dominant sea power.

2nd Punic War (218-202 BC): after 16 years without a defeat in Italy, Hannibal was recalled in 202 BC to defend Carthage, for Scipio took the war to Africa, near Carthage. At Zama Hannibal was defeated and Rome became the mightiest land power, in 201.

3rd Punic War (149-146 BC): Rome razed Carthage, plowed the land and put salt down on her former site, so that Carthage would never be settled again.

Pushkin, Alexander S. (1799-1837): Russian poet who glorified the Czarist regime.Russians call him a patriot, in the Ukraine he is called a Czar propagandist.

Putch..: German, the takeover of the government.

PYC == RUS: intended to be pronounced as Rik in Old Slavonic, but because many of the monks, clergy and scribes came from Constantinople, where Latin was the official language and Greek the vernacular they used the first Greek letter followed by two Latin letters. Hence they spelled PYC, which was, however, pronounced later as RUS and not RIK. Since the ending ryc, ryk, rik or ric was the standard ending of a Gothic King-Judge, a delegation was sent to the Varangians (Norwegians) to find a suitable King-Judge family to rule over them. The delegation found such a family in Ruryk. Explained in more detail in text.

Pyramid: stone/brick structures in Egypt, Mesopotamia and on the American continent. The Pyramids of Egypt were considered to be one of the Seven Wonders of the Old World. Is there a common link?

Pythagoras, (580-500 BC): Greek mathematician and philosopher from the island of Samos.

Q Ships: Merchant ships used as decoys to attract submarines, in order to destroy them. They were used by Germany, Japan and the USA during World War II.

QUEST..: Quick Unprecedented Equipment Status Test. The first US software patent granted to the author in 1972.

Quick Basic: a common computer language used on PC's.

Quisling, Vidkun (1887-1945): Norwegian collaborator with Hitler. Norwegian legions joined Finland on the assault on Moscow in 1941. And, American Liberty Ships had to run the gauntlet from England to Murmansk to aid the Soviets. After the war Quisling was tried, convicted and shot on October 27, 1945. (Compare this with Petain!)

Quislings: a name used for Nazi collaborators who helped the Nazis in running (or taking over) their country:

- Austria -- Arthur Seyss-Inquart
- Croatia -- Ante Pavelic
- Czechoslovakia -- Konrad Henlein
- Estonia -- Päts and Laidoner
- Finland -- Carl Mannerheim (even though he had a good reason to be on Germany's side. Stalin tried to take over Finland in 1939.)
- France -- Henri Petain (Vichy France)
- Hungary -- Miklas Horty
- Italy -- Benito Mussolini
- Latvia -- Allied with Hitler
- Lithuania -- Allied with Hitler
- Netherlands -- Adrian Mussert
- Norway -- Vidkun Quisling
- Rumania -- Ion Antonescu

Slovakia -- Josef Tiso
Slovenia -- Allied with Hitler
Spain -- Francisco Franco (Felangist)

This leaves: Albania (overrun by Mussolini), Belgium (overrun by Germany), Bosnia (overrun by Austria), Denmark (even though occupied by Germany engaged in active resistance under their King Christian X), England, Greece (overrun by Germany), Ireland, Luxembourg (overrun by Germany), Portugal, Sweden and Switzerland as the only countries in Europe who resisted Hitler actively. Bulgaria was tricked into submission. Serbia was defeated and forced into submission; while, Portugal, Sweden and Switzerland tried to maintain neutrality.

Rada...: a Ukrainian word for council. Originally, the word Duma was used. When it was misused by the Muscovites, the Cossacks used the word Rada instead.

RAM....: Risk Analysis Model.

Ramses II, (1304-1223 BC): Egyptian Pharaoh and conqueror.

Raskol.: the first breakup of the Orthodox Church by Muscovy during the rule of Ivan the Terrible.

Rasputin, Grigori (1871-1916): Russian monk and mystic who gained power during World War I in Czarist Russia. Through him virtually every office in the Czarist Empire was available for sale. For example: The German national Stürmer became Minister of War. The Czarina was attached to him because he could relieve the sufferings of her son, who was a hemophiliac.

Ravenna: city in North-East Italy, capital of the Ostrogoths under Theodoric the Great.

Razin, Stenka (1570-1571): a Don Cossack Hetman who led a popular uprising against Moscow.

Reagan, Ronald (1981-89): 40th President of the USA.

Recursive: (infinitely) repetitive.

Reformation: a period in Europe, 13th to 16th century, when the dogmas of the Roman Church were challenged and various branches of the Christian Faiths emerged: Baptists, Calvinists, Huguenots, Hussians, Lutherans, Protestants, Quakers and so on. This resulted in the Counter-Reformation by the Roman Church which was bloody and prolonged as the Catholics tried to convert the various Protestants by force or to annihilate them, which was extended to include gnostics, heretics, infidels and heathens. Roughly half of the Western European population perished during that time, 16th to 20th century. A temporary halt was reached with the Treaty of Westphalia (1648), after which the 'ruler determined the religion in his realm.' The savior of the Reformation was the Swedish King: Gustavus Adolphus. However, whenever the opportunity presented itself, conversion and reconquest was resumed. In this sense, the Napoleonic Wars, World War I and World War II can be included as part of the Counter-Reformation.

Reichstag: a building complex in Berlin, seat of the German Government. Originally, the name of a German-type parliament which advised the Holy Roman Emperor in Worms.

Reign of Terror: an expression coined for the French Revolution for the period: June 1793 to July 1794 ruled by Robespierre. Stalin's rule made Robespierre look like a schoolboy.

Reims == Rheims: a city in France, the seat of a Bishop. All Kings of France were crowned there, starting with Clovis. During the 100 year war Reims was held by the English and it was Joan of Arc's mission to recapture Reims and crown the French King there, which she did.

Reinhard, von: a German general during World War II.

Renaissance: rebirth. A term used to describe the rebirth of Western Europe to Greek and Roman ideals. Starting with the 4th Crusade (1204) and when Constantinople was captured by the Ottoman Turks (1453), the books of antiquity were sold on the Italian market and the ancient civilizations of Greece and Rome were rediscovered. It started in the 13th century in Italy and spread to the rest of Europe by the 17th century.

Repin, Ilya R (1844-1930): a famous Ukrainian painter from Kharkiv, who is counted as a Russian.

RFP....: request for proposal.

Rhine..: a major river in Germany (mostly), which (roughly) separates Germany and France.

Rhineland: an industrial area in Germany. In the Treaty of Versailles of 1919, it was supposed to remain demilitarized. Hitler flagrantly violated that treaty when he sent his troops into that area.

Rhodes.: a major Greek island, off the coast of Asia Minor. One of the Seven Wonders of the Old World was the statue of Helios in the harbour (aka: Colossus of Rhodes.)

Rhodes, Cecil (1853-1902): British statesman, colonizer of Africa and founder of a program called: Rhodes Scholars, which indoctrinates future, foreign statesmen in British geopolitics.

Rhodesia: now Zimbabwe. A former British colony in Africa, name-sake to Cecil Rhodes.

-ric...: or -rix, or -rik, or -ryc, or -ryk, or -veg or -weg, the ending taken by a Gothic King-Judge to identify the type of law he practiced. The equivalent form by Slavs was -mir or -mer, -polk, -slav or -laus. The variations are mostly due to the different language translations in Europe: Roman (ric), Latin (rix), French (rik), Italian (ric), German (rich), Nordic (ryc or ryk) etc. Phonetically they are all the same.

Rieman, George F. B (1826-1866): German mathematician.

Risorgimento: resurrection in Italian. This became the rallying cry in Italy to form a national state. Used by Garibaldi, Cavour and Manzzini.

ROA....: an acronym for Vlasov's army while in German captivity: Russian Liberation Army. Vlasov claimed he could raise 30 million soldiers to defeat Stalin.

Robespierre, Maximillien (1758-94): French revolutionary and leader in the 'Reign of Terror.'

Rockefeller, John D (1839-1937): American statesman and tycoon. The foundation by the same name, gifted to the UN 6 city blocks in New York City.

Rokossovsky, Konstantine (1896-1968): Soviet General of Polish extraction, during World War II.

Roland.: a Knight in the 'Song of Roland.' In reality, Roland was to bring up the rear guard on purpose. Roland had raided a Basque town when Charlemagne made an expedition into Spain. The Basques wanted satisfaction and demanded Roland.

Roman Catholic Church: in a 'bean counting' sense, the largest of the Christian Churches. In a real sense, probably not much larger than some of the larger 'Christian sects,' as the other denominations are called by the Catholic Church. By last count in 1990, it numbered roughly 750 million faithful. However, most of the faithful are in the strict sense, at best schismatic and often downright heretic. For example, in South America most Catholic members practice 'ancestor worship,' superimposed on the Catholic Faith -- which is technically a heresy. In Europe, many of the Churches and Cathedrals are empty, some have been converted to museums and so on. A more 'realistic' estimate is probably 50 million or so. Of these, the only true Catholics are the residents of the Vatican and their direct liaisons in the various countries, or about 10 thousand.

Roman Empire: technically the period from 27 BC when Augustus (Octavius) was proclaimed Emperor and to the fall of Constantinople in 1453, when Constantine XI died defending the city. Western historians, however, have fragmented the Roman Empire (into the Roman Empire and the Byzantine Empire) in order to accentuate the Holy Roman Empire.

The Roman Empire begins in 27 BC. But, depending on the historian it ends with:

a) Diocletian,who in 293 actually divided the Roman Empire into the Western and Eastern Empire; or
b) Constantine, who in 330 finished building the new capitol and moved all Roman Patricians there; or
c) Theodosius I (379-395) who founded the Theodosian dynasty in Constantinople; or
d) Justinian I (527-65) who compiled the Roman Codex of law; or
e) Phocas (602-610) the last of the Roman Emperors from the Justinian dynasty; or
f) Baldwin (1204-1205), the first of the Franks or Latin Emperors; or

g) Baldwin II (1228-61) the last of the Latin Emperors. The fact is,there is no agreement among Western historians when the Roman Empire ended and when the Byzantine Empire began. That is, no matter where you make the cut, it represents a grave distortion of the Roman Empire, her body of knowledge and her administrative savvy. The very fact that there is no consensus when the Roman Empire ended should be sufficient proof that it ended in 1453.

Once you choose the end of the Roman Empire, you get the beginning of the ever fluid Byzantine Empire. In the opinion of the author, it is just another piece of disinformation to satisfy the Pope and the Holy Roman Empire. But, since the Roman Empire and the Holy Roman Empire are extinct today, it is time to drop this charade.

Now consider this. The Holy Roman Empire was illegal to begin with. It was created as an insider deal between an ambitious Roman Patriarch, who wanted to be supreme ruler of the Christian Church; who elevated a German as his protector, in exchange giving the Germans a monopoly of rule, with the creation of the Electors. The deal was made so that the Goths and all other ethnic groups in Europe would be locked out from any future rule in Europe.

It was not Holy -- even Dante placed many Popes into Hell. It was not Roman -- none of the Holy Roman Emperors ruled from Rome and few spoke Latin. Some even go so far as to say that it was not even an Empire at all, but an Oligarchy of the Gulphs and Ghibellines.

In any event, it is a pity that two Christian Empires were so much influenced by Christian teachings that they killed each other over it, by failing to come up with the same count of how many angels could fit on the tip of a pin.

Romanized: the Roman form of geopolitics. Taking the culture of minorities and changing it to fit the Roman ideal. For example: Etruscan, Greek and Egyptian.

Romanov(s): the ruling house in Muscovy, elected by due process by the Zaporozhian and Don Cossacks during the 'Time of Troubles' after the Tartars took over the rule in Moscow, in the 17th century. The Romanovs were of Prussian-Gothic origin. The Romanov line came to an end with Catherine II in Russia. Succeeding Czars did not have one drop of Romanov blood in them, starting with Catherine II and until Nicholas II.

The rulers of the Gothic-Prussians were related to the Roman Emperor Augustus Caesar, some 30 generations removed.

Rome...: capital of Italy, seat of the Vatican and the old capital of the Roman Empire -- the new capital of the

Roman Empire was Constantinople (330 to 1453). According to Livy, Rome was founded in 753 BC.

Rommel, Erwin (1891-1944): German General,commander of the Afrika Corps. Later Rommel was assigned to fortify the beaches in Normandy. When his complicity to assassinate Hitler was discovered, he was given two choices: 1) kill himself and be buried as a national hero or 2) be tried and executed as a German traitor. Rommel shot himself and got a hero's burial in Ulm.

Roosevelt, Franklin D (1933-1945): 32st President of the USA. He came to power the same year Hitler came to power. But, he was America's driving force to stamp out tyranny in Western Europe, replacing it with compassion and American generosity.

Roosevelt, Theodore (1901-1909): 26th President of the USA.

Roslavl: a town in the Soviet Union.

Ross...: horse in Dutch. See Rossija.

Rossija: name for Russia, chosen by Peter I. It is based on the Dutch word Ross, meaning horse. Hence, Peter I named his realm 'Land of Horses.' Rossija is still used by natives today. The word Russia was coined by Voltaire when he wrote the 'definitive history of Russia' to the specifications provided by Catherine II. Voltaire liked the word Rus or Russe in French.

Rostiv == Rostov (in Russian): a town in the Don area. Rostiv was the gateway to Georgia, Armenia and Baku.

Rothschild(s): a Jewish banking family in Europe. Recently the banking houses in England and France of the Rothschilds merged into one,foreshadowing England's entry into the EU.

Rousseau, Jean-Jaques (1712-78): French writer and philosopher.

Royals.: a term used to describe the ruling families of Europe of royal lineage. All of German lineage: Borgias, Bourbons, Habsburgs, Hanoverians, Hohenstaufens, Hohenzollerns, Luxembourg, Romanovs and Wittelsbachs.

Rozumovsky, Alexey (1645-1661): the husband of Czarina Elizabeth ruler of Russia. He was a descendent of a long line of Zaporozhian Hetmans in the Ukraine. He had, however, no political ambitions whatsoever. All he wanted to do was to sing in the choir, for he had an 'angelic voice.' He had a brother Cyril, see separate entry.

Rozumovsky, Cyril (1650-1764): Cossack Hetman of the Zaporozhian Sich and Field Marshal in the Russian army.

Rumelia: an area carved out from Bulgaria and given to the Ottoman Turks in the Treaty of Berlin in 1878.

Rundstead, Karl G von (1875-1953): German Field Marshal during World War II.

Ruryc..: or Ruric or Rurik, the Royal family of Goths (Vikings or Varangians) who came by invitation to rule Kievan-Rus or the Ostrogoths from Norway.

Russia.: largest country in the world. She consists of seven time zones stretching from Central Europe to the Pacific

Ocean. However, present day Russia consists of many minorities forcibly integrated into the Russian Republic, such as Chechnya and many others. Many of whom are clamoring for their independence, plus areas that were forcibly integrated into the Russian Republic from other nationalities, such as the Don-Kuban area from the Ukraine plus many others. After the disintegration of the Soviet Union, Russian leaders are determined to hold present day Russia together by force. Because, once the Russian Republic begins to disintegrate, she may be reduced to her kernel enclave: Moscow and the most intense areas of Russification such as St. Petersburg.

Russian history begins with Moscow, and the banished Prince from Novhorod: Alexander Nevsky by the Kievan-Rus. Moscow is first mentioned in the Chronicles in 1147 as a meeting place between two Gothic-Rus Princes. Alexander Nevsky became ruler in Moscow after he was banished from Novhorod. At that time Moscow was only a small village. The invasion of the Tartars and Alexander's alliance with them, catapulted Alexander to Grand Prince of Rus, a title bestowed on him by the Tartars, for his faithful service.

When Batu doled out the Principalities, Alexander Nevsky (1252-63) got to choose first. The Yarlic (Principality) of his choice, as chief tax collector for the Tartars, fell on Volodimir (Vladimir in Russian), a Chartered city by the Kievan-Rus which included Moscow.

His descendants moved to Moscow because the Charter in Volodimir greatly restricted their actions. Dimitry (1277-1294, son of Alexander Nevsky), began the transition.

Ivan I or John I Kalita (aka: Money-Bags), grandson of Alexander Nevsky moved to Moscow. From then on they ruled absolutely. The Nevsky line came to an end with Ivan the Terrible in 1584, who killed his son Alexis and heir. This caused a succession crisis and the Tartars took over and ruled in Moscow with Boris Godunov (1606-1610).

The Zaporozhian and Don Cossacks took Moscow and called for a Sbor (an Allthing in the Gothic tradition, a national assembly, in 1610).

At the Sbor, Michael Romanov was elected ruler and became Czar (1613-1645). The last Romanov, Peter I (1682-1725) left no heir, he too tortured and killed his son and heir Alexis, just like Ivan the Terrible did. This made Catherine I (1725-27), Peter's second wife and a Lithuanian by descent, Czarina and ruler of Russia. But, for all practical purposes, Menshikov, her former slave master ruled in Russia. Menshikov tried to marry off his daughter to Peter II (1727-1730, son of Alexis) but failed only because Peter II died at age 15.

Peter I had many offsprings with Catherine I: Anna, Elizabeth (1741-62), Natalia, Peter, Paul and another Peter. However, all males died at an early age.

Next in line were the descendants of Ivan V (or John V) (1682-1696), who was older and co-ruler with Peter I. Thus, Anna (1730-1740, the daughter of Ivan V), became Czarina. But, she was groomed to rule in Kurland and thus had a German upbringing. When she became Czarina, she moved her entire entourage from Kurland to St. Petersburg, including her lover and actual ruler, Biron the German.

When Anna died, Ivan VI (1740-41) or John VI, the great grandson of Ivan V, was next in line. He was a babe of 1, was deposed and imprisoned in Schlüsselberg by the Russian Gentry, now the descendants of Peter I and Catherine I had their turn, starting with Elizabeth (1741-62),her daughter and then Peter III (the son of her sister Anna). Of these rulers, Peter II was a teenager, Anna slow witted and Ivan VI a babe.

Elizabeth (1741-62) succeeded Ivan VI and took care of her sister's son (Anna) Peter III. However, next in line was her daughter Elizabeth (aka: Tarakanova), then Peter III. But, Peter III was an idiot by all accounts. Still, Elizabeth found him a suitable wife, the future Catherine II, a German from an impoverished line of the Hohenstaufen line. In his will, Peter I had requested, by inspiration of Leibnitz, that henceforth all Russian rulers had to be married to the German Hohenstaufen line. This way, Russia would be eventually in a position to take over the rule of the Holy Roman Empire. Elizabeth abolished the death penalty in Russia in 1752. (It was restored by Stalin.)

Peter III, however, had no interest in Catherine whatsoever. He had his own mistresses and his toy soldiers. He bragged openly that when he came to power he would put Catherine into a nunnery for good. All the while, Catherine had one illegitimate child after another. (Peter was impotent and never consummated their marriage.)

Therefore, when Elizabeth was eliminated in 1762, Catherine II (the German) staged a coup with Orlov, and took over the rule in Russia. She secured the loyalty of the Preobrazhensky regiment with her lover Orlov, who was in charge of it. The Semeonov regiment sided with Peter III (1762) and Tarakanova had to flee Russia. Peter III never assumed power, for his first act would have been to put Catherine, his German wife, into a nunnery.

Catherine's son Paul was the product of her German Chamberlain, even though many Russian historian claim he was the son of Saltykov, a Russian Chamberlain or Poniatovsky, a Polish noble and womanizer at Elizabeth's court. Be that as it may, neither Catherine II, nor her son Paul, nor her grandson Alexander I nor any of the succeeding Czars of Russia had a single drop of Romanov's blood in them. They were all Germans (or part Polish), yet they were still called Romanovs. Therefore, the German-Romanov rule came to an end in 1917, with the abdication of Nicholas II.

Mismanagement, despotism and nepotism caused the Revolution in Russia. While Kerensky tried to continue the policy of the Czars the country was bleeding to death. A Civil War ensued in 1917, lasting until 1934. But, from 1923 on, the Soviets were in control, with Lenin and then Stalin. In 1934, the USA recognized the Soviet regime and gave it legitimacy.

World War II, propelled the Soviet Union into a superpower. But again, economic mismanagement, despotism and nepotism brought about her demise in 1990 to 1992. In 1992, the Russian Republic emerged. However, none of her leaders, starting with Lenin were ethnic Russians: Lenin (Tartar-German), Stalin (Georgian), Khrushchev (Ukrainian) and so on until Gorbachev (Don-Ukrainian), Yeltsin (Tartar-Siberian) and Putin (Lithuanian).

Economic depravation and the misuse of her most precious resource, her people,for 75 years of Soviet rule (1917-92) left the country destitute.But, because she still controls a huge arsenal of nuclear weapons, she must be treated with kid gloves. To the EU,Russia represents the centuries long conflict Germany and France were dreaming about with Napoleon and Hitler. Economic necessity may force Russia into the EU. This will be the final disintegration of the Russian Republic. The only way, Russia can preserve her integrity, even if greatly reduced, is by joining the Free Trade Agreement with America.

Russian Census: current, unofficial estimates of Ukrainians living in Russia is roughly 90 million. They are distributed in European Russia, about 70% and in Siberia the remaining 30%. However, the Russian Census does not reflect these figures. The reason is as follows. When it comes to the question of 'original nationality' the following question is asked: "Do you consider yourself to be a Great Rus(sian) or a Little Rus(sian)." Since nobody wants to be counted as a midget, most Ukrainians reply: "Great Rus(sian.)" Accordingly, the census results are highly distorted. [Do you remember the election of Dewey versus Truman in 1948? A last minute telephone census was made to determine who would win the election. The survey found that Dewey was the winner by a wide margin. The problem was, only the affluent had a telephone and when the election results came in,the pollsters were dumfounded that Truman had won. Yet this tactic is still practiced to this day in Russia, because otherwise the majority in Russia would be Ukrainians.]

Russian Parity: see Moscow parity.

Russian Writers: some of the most famous, so called Russian writers were not Russian at all. Of course, this was an essential part of their 'Russification' program. Here is a

list of the top 7 'Russian' writers or poets in chronological order:
(1711-1765), Lomonosov, a Novhorodian from Denisovka, near Archangel.
(1799-1837), Pushkin, the descendant of a Sudanese slave, who's grandfather was a slave at Peter's court. He was emancipated when Peter died and promoted to minor nobility. Needless to say, Alexander Pushkin, his grandson eulogized the Czarist regime and Peter.
(1809-1852), Hohol (Gogol in Russian), a Ukrainian minor noble and landholder.
(1812-1881), Dostoevsky, a Russian, influenced by Hohol, exiled to Siberia, returned in 1859 to Moscow but was ostracized by the regime.
(1814-1841), Lermantov, a Novhorodian from Penza.
(1828-1904), Tolstoy, a Novhorodian from Tula.
(1860-1904), Chekhov, a Ukrainian.

Russian Orthodox Church: in 988, Volodimir the Great, King of the Kievan-Rus, introduced Orthodoxy to his realm. He married Anna, the sister of Roman Emperor Basil II. Kiev was made a Patriarchate and Volodimir was made hereditary King by Roman Emperor Basil II.

When Kiev was utterly destroyed by the Tartars in 1240, the Monastery of the Caves in Kiev, was spared and with it the clergy. However, incessant raids by the Tartars in subsequent years made life miserable, even for the clergy. Meanwhile, Volodimir, a Chartered city of the Kievan-Rus enjoyed relative safety from Tartar raids, her rulers being chief enforcers and tax-collectors of Tartar rule. A few years prior to the Tartar invasion, a great Cathedral was built there, and starting with Alexander Nevsky, the clergy from Kiev was urged to relocate to Volodimir. At first they balked, but during the reign of Andrew III, Patriarch Cyril (1299) moved to Volodimir with some of the clergy. Ivan I Kalita, Money-Bags in Russian, moved to Moscow (1328-40) (because, it was not a Chartered city.)

However, as soon as the Patriarch left Kiev, a new Patriarch was elected by due process in Kiev. Now there were two Patriarchs, one in Kiev, the other in Moscow.

At first, the two Patriarchs did not interfere with one another, as one was in Moscow or Tartary, while the other was in Kiev, which was occupied by the Lithuanians who set themselves up as protectors of the Ukraine. However, because Moscow was not a Patriarchate all subsequent Patriarchs of Moscow were not legitimate.

After the Lithuanian Grand Duke Jagiello (1386) married Hedzwiga, a Polish Princess, the Polish Barons descended into the Ukraine forcing conversions to the Catholic Faith (1440.) This spawned the Cossack movement in the Ukraine: Zaporozhe, Don and on the Danube river in 1444. The

Cossacks became the protectors of the Orthodox Faith with their main mission to liberate all Christians, regardless of their faith in the Ottoman slave markets, primarily in the Crimea but as far away as Constantinople which fell to the Ottoman Turks in 1453, with the help of the Austrians.

In Moscow, Ivan III married the niece of the last Roman Emperor and staked out the claim that Moscow was the 'Third Rome.' Ivan IV, the Terrible, wanted to have Moscow elevated to a Patriarchate with Patriarch Philip, thus legitimizing the Patriarch. He invited the Patriarch of Jerusalem. But, instead of being elevated to a Patriarchate, the Patriarch of Jerusalem pointed out a few errors in the liturgy and the fact that 3 Patriarchs were needed to establish a new Patriarchate. This caused a 'Raskol' or break in the Orthodox Church. (Now it became official that Kiev was the only legitimate Patriarchate.) Ivan refused to make the changes and the Patriarch of Jerusalem left. Ivan was furious and wanted to change to Catholicism. A Papal legate was sent to accommodate him. While Ivan manhandled Patriarch Philip in Moscow, Philip pointed out the folly of Ivan's actions. In the end, Philip exclaimed: "When the Papal legate enters Moscow in one gate, I'll be out the other." Therefore, the Papal legate was denied entry into Moscow and returned to Rome.

After the death of Ivan the Terrible, a succession crisis developed and the Tartar Boris Godunov took over the rule in Moscow. The Zaporozhian and Don Cossacks took Moscow and called for a Sbor, a national assembly (called Allthing by the Goths). At that assembly Michael Romanov was elected Czar and the assembly was dissolved. Czar Michael assumed the rule (1613-1645).

By 1630, the conversion issue to Catholicism came to a head as conversion was intensified which resulted in open rebellion in the Ukraine. The Zaporozhian Cossacks elected Hetman Khmelnitzky (1648) who combined the Cossacks and led a war of liberation against the Polish Barons. He defeated them and evicted them from the Ukraine in 1648, establishing a Ukrainian state.

However, Khmelnitzky also realized that without a powerful ally or protector the Ukraine was exposed to her powerful Catholic neighbors: Poland, Hungary and Austria. Therefore, he sent delegations to: Moscow, Sweden and the Ottoman Empire asking for an alliance.

Moscow replied first and they accepted an autonomous Ukraine with one stipulation: the newly elected Hetman from Zaporozhe (the most powerful Sich), had to submit his name for ratification by the Czar. The Ukrainian clergy and the Patriarch were elated for it signalled to them that the common faith, Orthodoxy, would prevail in all of former Kievan-Rus. They urged Khmelnitzky to ratify the treaty. Khmelnitzky called for a Veche in Pereyaslav for all Cossacks to attend (called Thing in Gothic). There he delivered a passionate speech in favor of the Moscow treaty. The Cossacks accepted, the treaty was ratified (1654) and the Cossacks disbanded. All was fine until Khmelnitzky died and the next Hetman was elected in 1657. When his name was submitted for ratification, Czar Alexis (1645-76) replied: "The Czar does not take orders from his subjects."

Before the Cossacks could rally, Moscow sent army regulars to occupy the Ukraine. They limited the size of each Sich to 8,000 Cossacks and formed new Cossack garrisons in various towns throughout the Ukraine installing their own Hetmans, while the duly elected Hetmans were told to swear loyalty to Moscow. This period is called: 'Hetmanshina' or the rule of Ukraine by a multitude of Hetmans.

At the same time, the legal Patriarch of Kiev was ostracized by Moscow while the Patriarch of Moscow was made supreme. In fact, Alexis appointed a new Patriarch in Moscow called Nikon (1662-1666).

In 1667, in the Treaty of Andrusovo, Czar Alexis gave about half of the Ukraine and Byelorussia to Poland for a vague military alliance. The Polish Barons descended into the Ukraine again, exacting terrible retribution and enforcing conversions. Khmelnitzky's worst fears had come to pass.

This uneasy situation of two Orthodox Faiths, persisted until Peter I. At that time, the Cossack Hetman in Zaporozhe was Mazepa. When Peter I, was defeated by Charles XII at Narva in 1701, Mazepa invited the Patriarch of Jerusalem to Kiev to confirm the Patriarch of Kiev and to confirm the Patriarchate of Kiev -- which he did. Now, the religious Raskol escalated to a higher level.

In 1709, after Charles XII and Mazepa were defeated by Peter I at Poltava, the situation worsened a great deal for the Ukraine. Even though Peter was captured by the Ottoman Turks (in the Prut campaign), Catherine -- his mistress at that time, ransomed Peter with her jewels and Peter ransomed his army with uncut diamonds from the Sultan. But, before Peter was released, he had to sign a treaty with the Sultan, giving up his recent conquests against the Ottomans: the fortress Azov; return the Black Sea to the Ottomans (remove his navy) and not to make war below a specified latitude (which protected the Ukraine). However, Peter was allowed to administer the Ukraine. Peter vented his anger on the Ukraine. The Cossacks and countless Ukrainian farmers were imprisoned and sent to the swamps to build Peter's city: ST. Petersburg. (Modern estimates range from 1.5 million to 3 million). The

Ukraine was nearly depopulated since the survival rate in the swamps was about 3 months.

Peter had to resolve the issue between the two Patriarchs in the East. Leibnitz provided Peter with a solution: Outlaw both of them and create a new form of Orthodoxy controlled by the Czar. Therefore, when the Patriarch Adrian in Moscow died, in 1700, Peter did not replace him. Instead, he created a Holy Synod, a committee of seven: 4 lay and 3 clerics who elected the new leader of the Orthodox Church. But, that leader could not be called Patriarch, only Metropolitan of Moscow.

In the Ukraine, however, a new Patriarch was duly elected but more often than not, he was arrested and sent to Siberia. Yet the practice remained to this day.

These 3 forms of Orthodoxy are still active in Russia, Ukraine and abroad. For example: in America.

Russification: the Russian form of geopolitics. Taking the culture, literature, history, art, music and language of other minorities in Russia and declaring them to be Russian, in this way depriving the minorities of their identity. This was practiced in: Belarus, Lithuania, Poland and Ukraine. Three Russian rulers, Alexis I, Peter I, Catherine II and Stalin nearly succeeded. That's why the minorities in Russia are clamoring for independence.

Russo-Japanese War, of 1904-5: while Russia coasted on her glory after the Napoleonic War the world was changing around her. When the war broke out with Japan, Russia was beaten on land and at sea. At first, the Japanese imposed a harsh treaty which was moderated by England by the Treaty of Portsmouth in 1905. (For all practical purposes, the counterpart of the San Stefano-Berlin treaties of 1878.) However, it exposed Russia's weakness as a modern military power.

Saar...: an area between France and Germany. Germany's coal basin which often changed hands between France and Germany. Today the Saar is part of Germany.

Saga...: an ancient narrative or story. Used primarily for Greek and Gothic stories. For example: in Greece, the story of Jason and the Argonauts; among the Goths, the sagas of the Norsemen (North Men).

Saipan.: a Japanese island fortress during World War II in the Pacific.

St. Helena: a rock-island in the South Atlantic.

Saladin, (1138-1193): Sultan of Egypt and Syria.

Salamis, Battle of (480 BC): stunning naval victory of the Greeks over the Persians. The Greek commander was Themistocles, he was later ostracized in Athens and lived out his life at the Persian court -- among his old enemies.

Salic Law: old Frankish penal code, it excluded women from holding land or ruling a country.

Saltykov: a womanizer at the court of Czarina Elizabeth. Some Western historians claim that, he was the father of Paul (the mother being the future Czarina Catherine II), future Czar of Russia. However, there are others who claim Paul is the product of Catherine and her German Chamberlain. Still others point to the Polish noble Poniatovsky and so on. One thing is certain, however, Paul did not have a drop of Romanov blood in him, because Peter III was impotent and did not father any children even when his malaise was claimed to have been cured. Most Russian historians deny this, even though whenever Catherine had a child, Peter III would exclaim: "Another immaculate conception."

Samarkand: capital of Uzbekistan in the valley of Transoxania. In antiquity, a major trade center and stop on the land route to China.

Samoilovich, I (1672-1687): Hetman of the Zaporozhian Cossacks during the regency of Sophia for Ivan V and Peter I in Russia (1682-96). Samoilovich had been groomed by Muscovy to be a devout supporter of Muscovy with titles,landgrants and money. Sophia wanted to make a name for herself and initiated a war against the Crimean Tartars in 1686. She let Prince Basil Golitsyn lead that campaign. Since the Cossacks were the only experienced Tartar-fighters, Golitsyn commanded the Zaporozhians to join him. Samoilovich requested that the campaign start no later than the spring of 1686, otherwise the grass was too tall and could be readily set on fire. Golitsyn agreed. But, before the Russian army was assembled it was summer. And, when it arrived in Southern Ukraine, it was early fall. This is when the grass is tallest and driest. Therefore, when Golitsyn arrived with his army, Samoilovich urged him to postpone the campaign to the following spring. Golitsyn would not hear of it and called Samoilovich a traitor and coward. With that the campaign was resumed. But, as soon as the combined army reached the Crimea, the Tartars set the steppe on fire and routed the army and the Cossacks. Golitsyn fled to Moscow and accused Samoilovich of treason. Samoilovich and his family were hauled off to Moscow in fetters. There Samoilovich was stripped of all his titles, his land, and he and his family were sent to Siberia. During the reign of Elizabeth his descendants were allowed to return to Russia but were barred from any significant posts. In 1923, when the White army was evacuated to Jugoslavia, his descendants escaped to the West. This case is interesting because Samoilovich is considered to be a traitor in the Ukraine and in Russia. In the Ukraine, for listening to Golitsyn and in Russia for not preventing Golitsyn from making a cardinal blunder.

Samsonov: a Russian General of the 2nd Russian Army who was defeated at Tannenberg by Hindenburg in 1914. Solzhenitsyn claims that the German general was Francois, not Hindenburg, who was on the Western Front at that time.

Samurai: professional soldier in Japan, pre-1860. Modern Japanese economic Barons are often called Samurai as during their attempted takeover of the US economy in the 1980's.

San Stefano: a town in Serbia. After the Russian liberation of the Balkans, the Ottoman Turks were evicted, the new nations were assembled and agreed on mutually acceptable borders in 1878 -- which they ratified.

These borders, however, did not suit the geopolitical ambitions of England, Austria and Prussia. They convened in Berlin, the same year, redrew the borders, brought back the Ottoman Turks and imposed new borders in the Balkans. Ever since then and to this day the Balkans have remained 'the powder-keg of Europe.'

Santayana, George (1863-1952): Spanish-American poet and philosopher. He coined the phrase:"Those who don't know history are doomed to repeat it."

Sarai..: Tartar tent capital of the 'Golden Horde,' due East of Moscow.

Saratoga, Battle of (1777): major victory of Americans over the British during the War of Independence. After the battle, France recognized the 'United States of America.'

Sarajevo: capital of Bosnia-Herzogovina.

Sassons: a Gothic nation on the East bank of the river Elbe.

Savanarola, Girolamo (1452-98): Italian religious reformer in Florence; when defeated, he was burned at the stake.

Savoy..: a former Duchy between Italy and France. At one time Italian, but was traded for Lombardy to France in 1865.

Saxony.: an area in East Germany centering around Leipzig, an area previously occupied by the Gothic Sassons and Wends.

Sbor...: a slavic term for the Gothic term Allthing; a national assembly. Aka: Semskyj Sbor.

Scandinavia: Northern Europe occupied mostly by Goths, starting about 70 BC; consists of Denmark, Iceland, Norway and Sweden, and Finland which is Finno-Ugric.

Scharnhorst: a German battle cruiser, named after a general.

Schiller, Friedrich (1759-1805): a German poet and writer. Part-architect of the German language. His era was called: 'Sturm und Drang.' The others were: Goethe and Lessing.

Schism.: in 1353, the Catholic Church broke away from Orthodoxy permanently.

Schlieffen, Albert (1833-1913): a German military strategist. He developed the plan of how to defeat France in case of a war. His plan called for a strong right flank, 90 divisions or more, to sweep through the Low Countries and capture Paris. During World War I, Prince Rupert of Bavaria, modified the plan. He reduced the right flank to 60 divisions and the German army stalled 30 miles from Paris.

During World War II, Hitler brushed up the Schlieffen plan, made the right flank strong and France was defeated in 35 days.

Schushnigg, Kurt von (1897-1977): Successor to Dollfuss in Austria, Chancellor of Austria. Hitler called him to Berchtesgaden, reamed him out and demanded 'Anschluss'-- the annexation of Austria into Germany, in 1938. With the Anschluss, Germany became know as: Grossdeutches Reich, or the Great German Empire, aka: Third Reich.Then, Schushnigg was arrested and spent the war in Flossburg concentration camp. When Flossburg was liberated by allied forces, he came to America and became a college professor.

Schwaben: in the 19th century the Gothic Suevi were declared to be German. The name Schwaben was given to them. The area around Stuttgart in Germany.

Scipio Africanus Major, (ca.230-160 BC): a Roman general who took Hannibal's war in Italy to Africa. At Zama, near Carthage, Scipio defeated Hannibal, ending the 2nd Punic War in 201.

Scythians: a Gothic people who inhabited the Ukraine.

SEATO..: South-East Asia Treaty Organization. The Pacific version of NATO.

Security Council (UN): as of 1965 consisting of 10 members, 5 permanent: China, France, Russia, Great Britain and USA. And, 5 members elected for a 2 year term. Military intervention requires a unanimous vote.

Sedition: unrest or commotion leading to rebellion.

Seleucus I, (336-323 BC): a Gothic general in the army of Alexander the Great. After Alexander's death he inherited Persia to rule, founder of dynasty.

Seligman(s): a Jewish family of financiers in America.

Senate.: a governing and/or law-making body, originated in the Roman Empire, today in the USA.

Septuagint: in Latin 70 or LXX. Translation of the Old Testament into Greek. The Jewish translation of the Old Testament for the Jews living in Alexandria. By the 2nd century, the Jews in Alexandria could not read Hebrew. A team of 70 bible scholars were hired to translate the Hebrew version into Greek.

Each scholar translated every passage independently. Then, in a general meeting the translations were compared. If they differed by only one 'iota' in any one of the 70 translations, the entire team of 70 was sent back and tried again. Therefore, it is considered to be the only correct translation by many.

Serbia.: a country in the Balkans.

Seth...: in the Egyptian cult of Isis, the evil god.

Settlement, Act of (1701): English law making Hanoverian rule in England a monopoly (everybody else is excluded.) It also excludes foreigners from all offices.

Sevastopol: now a Ukrainian port in the Crimea (formerly Russian until 1954.) In 1954, Khrushchev gifted the Crimea to the

Ukraine. (Stalin had the Tartars forcibly repatriated to Siberia for their collaboration with the Germans in World War II.)

Seven Wonders of the Old World:
1) The Pyramids of Egypt
2) The Hanging Gardens of Babylon
3) The Mausoleum (in Helicarnassus, Asia Minor)
4) The Colossus of Rhodes (Helios)
5) The Temple of Diana (Artemis) at Ephesus
6) The Statue of Zeus at Olympia
7) The Pharos at Alexandria

Seven Year War, (1756-63): Prussia and Great Britain, fought against: Austria, France and (later) Russia. After Russia conquered East Prussia and Pomerania, and defeated Frederick the Great at Kunersdorf, the Cossacks raided Berlin in 1760. Frederick's cause seemed lost. But then, Catherine II seized power, stopped the war, restored Frederick's provinces and orchestrated the Treaty of Paris (1763), which resurrected Frederick and Prussia.
During the final months of World War II, Hitler pinned his hopes on a similar miracle.But, it never materialized.

Shakespeare, William (1564-1616): English poet and dramatist.

Shanghai: China's greatest seaport. When the Chinese refused to trade with the 'Western Devils' (meaning England), and destroyed the opium of the English traders, the city was shelled, Hong Kong was seized and the Opium War ensued.

Sharavari: colorful, baggy pants tucked into boots, worn by the Cossacks and Ukrainian population.

Shaw, George B (1856-1950): Irish critic,playwright and novelist. A sympathizer of Stalin's regime.

Shevchenko, Taras (1814-1861): Ukrainian writer, poet and artist, repeatedly exiled to Siberia for writing in Ukrainian. A national hero in the Ukraine, a great admirer of George Washington and the USA. He would often exclaim "When will the Ukraine have her George Washington!" in his writings.

Shuvalov, A (ca.1712-1799): a liaison man between Catherine II and Voltaire,who provided Voltaire with the data to write a 'definitive history' of Rossija. But Voltaire changed that name to Russe, in French, which became Russia, in Anglo-Saxon but it remained Rossija to this day in Russia.

Siberia: Russian part in Asia.

Sibir..: a Tartar Khanate in Siberia,conquered by the Don Cossack Hetman Ermak and gifted to Ivan the Terrible to lift the bounty on his head (1576).

Sich...: a Cossack fort. In all, there were 4 Siches: Zaporozhe on the lower Dnieper river; Don on the lower Don river; Danubian on the lower Danube river and Ural in the Ural mountains after Novhorod was sacked by Ivan the Terrible.

Sieges.: major modern military sieges include:
1) 1941-44, Leningrad during WW II. It lasted 900 days. Leningrad was not taken by the German, Spanish or

French armies.
2) 1683, Vienna. The siege by the Ottoman Turks was broken by Ukrainian Cossacks and the Polish army under King Sobieski. Yet the Austrians refused to give them hay for their horse, bread and water for the soldiers -- their saviors.
3) 1453, Constantinople. Was taken by the Ottoman Turks with the help of the Austrians. The end of the Roman Empire.

Siegfried: now a German name, derived from the Gothic name Valdemar in Norse or Volodimir in Ukrainian. (Volody == Lead to Victory, Mir == Peace). Hero of the 'Nibelungenlied.' (In German, Sieg == Victory, and Fried[en] == Peace.). That is, an early Gothic name which was Germanized.

Sikorsky, Igor (1889-1972): American-Ukrainian aeronautical engineer, now in America since 1939.

Sisyphus: in Greek mythology a King who cheated Zeus. He was punished to roll a large boulder up a hill and when he was about to reach the top, the boulder would roll down again. Thus, he had to start all over again.

Slavonic History: a history written by the Greek monk Sylvester to permanently alienate the Goths and Slavs.

Slovakia: originally part of the Ukraine. Ukrainian King-Judge Sviatoslav, founded the capital Bratislava.
In the 13th century she became Catholic and was later ruled by the Habsburgs. After World War I, she was integrated into Czechoslovakia. Now a separate nation. Slovakia has applied for entry to the EU.

Slovenia: a nation in the Balkans, of Slavic-Gothic descent who accepted Christianity from Rome. Now member of the EU.

Smith, Adam (1723-1790): Scottish political economist.

Smolensk: a town in Belarus, called Byelorussia today.

Sobieski, aka: John III (1674-1696): Polish King, who, allied with the Ukrainian Cossacks broke the siege of Vienna in 1683. The ungrateful Austrians denied them feed and water after their liberation.

Socrates, (469-399): Athenian philosopher.When he was ostracized, he preferred to take poison (hemlock) and die, rather than live away from Athens.

Solomon, (986-932 BC): King of the Israelites.

Spam...: canned meat.

Speyer.: a town in Germany, site of the first pogrom in Germany during the 1st Crusade.

Stalin, Joseph (1879-1953): Soviet dictator, native of Georgia. His real name was Dzhugashvili. Since he ran a gang of thieves and robbers in Georgia and to avoid the police he changed his name to Stalin, meaning 'man of steel.' He ruled the Soviet Union from 1923 to 1953. After the disintegration of the Soviet Union, he is still revered in his native Georgia for having 'put one over on the Russian

Tartars.'
Stalingrad: formerly called Tsaritsyn, a town on the lower Volga river and the site of the second massive defeat of the German Wehrmacht from August 1942 to February 1943 during World War II.
Stalinorgel: the German name for the Soviet Katjusha rockets (aka: Stalin-Pipe-Organ.)
Stars and Stripes: the national flag of the USA.
Star-spangled Banner, the: national anthem of the USA, adopted in 1931.
Statue of Liberty: a statue in New York harbor, a gift of the French people, symbolizing America's ideals of 'Liberty and Freedom for all Americans.'
Stettin: a German town in East Germany on the Baltic Sea.
Stilicho, Flavius (359-408): an Alan (Goth) general in the service of the Roman Empire (Constantinople, Arcadius.) He nearly defeated Alaric but struck a deal with him when he realized they were fellow Goths. Honorius, the Western Emperor had him executed in 408. This gave Alaric yet another reason to sack Rome.
Stockholm: capital of Sweden.
Strabo, (64 BC-19 AD): Greek geographer and historian.
Strangelove, Dr: a popular movie depicting MAD (Mutual Assured Destruction.)
Stuart, House of: the royal dynasty which ruled in Scotland from 1371 to 1603 and from 1603 to 1688 in Scotland and England combined. Their ancestry goes back to Brittany in France, to the Norman-Goths.
Stürmer, Boris V. (1848-1917): A German national, who bought himself the post of Minister of War of Russia during the reign of Czar Nicholas II, at the height of World War I, using Rasputin's influence.
Sturluson, Snorri (1178-1244): Icelandic poet and historian.
Sturm and Drang: a period in German literature when the writings from other nations was declared German -- mostly from the Gothic. The period spanned by Goethe, Schiller and Lessing -- the founders of the German language in the 19th century. This spawned German nationalism.
Sudan..: a republic in North-East Africa.
Sudetenland: a term used by Hitler to identify an area in Czecho-slovakia which (in Germany's opinion) was oppressed by the Czechs.
Suevi..: a Gothic nation on the East bank of the Rhine river, roughly present day Würtemberg.
Suez Canal: a waterway linking the Mediterranean with the Red Sea, built by the Frenchman de Lesseps starting in 1859. In 1875, the major shares to the Canal were purchased by the British. In 1956, Egypt nationalized the Canal. In 1967, the Canal was put out of action in the war between Egypt and Israel. The Canal was reopened in 1975.
Suleiman I (1494-1566): Ottoman Sultan. He directed his conquests

(Jihad) against Christians conquering Belgrade in 1521; Rhodes 1522; Hungarians at Mohacs in 1526. He was checked near Vienna in 1532.

Sumer..: an ancient civilization in Mesopotamia.

Suvorov, Alexander (1729-1800): Russian Field Marshal (of Ukrainian descent) during the reign of Catherine II. He hunted down Puhachov, put him into a cage and brought him to St. Petersburg as instructed by Catherine II for a show trial. (One of the few generals who never lost a battle.)

Sun Yat Sen, (1866-1825): Republican leader of China.

Sviatoslav, (960-972): Kievan-Rus, King-Judge who ruled from Kiev, founder of Bratislava.

Sweden.: a Kingdom in Scandinavia of Gothic extraction. In 1818, the Bernadotte line from France was invited to rule. Now a member of the EU.

Switzerland: a Republic in Central Europe of Celtic extraction. Switzerland gained independence from Austrian rule in the 16th century. Their country was poor, all they could do was rent out their males as mercenaries during the wars in Europe. Their pay was sent back to the villages they came from. With that money, major industries were bought. Today, Switzerland is a leading financial power in Europe. The Swiss Guard still guards the Pope. They have no intention of joining the EU.

Sylvester, (ca.1060-1120): a Greek monk, Abbot of the Monastery of the Caves in Kiev (Pecherska Lavra). He wrote the 'Slavonic History,' thereby severing the umbilical cord between the Goths and the Kievan-Rus. Aka: Silvester.

T34....: a heavy duty tank, the nemesis to the German tanks in World War II. The T34 was later modified to SU-122 and SU-152. One key difference was the Soviet tanks used diesel fuel, while the Germans used high grade gasoline. Hence, captured Soviet oil depots were of no immediate use for them.

Tacitus, Publius C. (55-118 AD): Roman historian.

Tactics: the art of manoeuvering armed forces.

Tadzhikistan: formerly a Soviet Republic, now an independent, Islamic country.

Taft, William H (1909-1913): 27th President of the USA.

Taylor, Zachary (1849-50): 12th President of the USA.

Thales of Miletus (624-500 BC): considered to be the first philosopher in Western Civilization. He was of Ionian origin (Asia Minor), but is counted among the Greek philosophers.

Taj Mahal: a tomb to the favorite wife of Indian Emperor Shah Jehan, built in 1632-50, in Agra, India.

Talmud.: Jewish religious books, compiled in Babylon, during the Babylonian Captivity.

Tanganyika: an East-African country, now part of Tanzania.

Tannenberg, Battle of: in 1410 according to the German calendar, a Lithuanian Grand Duke (Vitus), defeated the Teutonic Knights there. In 1914, the Germans defeated Samsonov's 2nd Army. Promptly the location was declared to be Tannenberg and the victor von Hindenburg. Solzhenitsyn writes in detail about that defeat in 'August 1914.' His claim is: the German General was Francois of French extraction. The location was hundreds of miles away from Tannenberg. And, Hindenburg? He was on the Western front at that time.

Tarakanova, (ca. 1752-1786): her name was Elizabeth. She was the daughter of Czarina Elizabeth and Alexey Rozumovsky. However, the Russian gentry refused to acknowledge her. Alexey died in 1761 and in 1762 Czarina Elizabeth was eliminated. Catherine II controlled the Preobrazhensky regiment with Orlov, while the Semeonov regiment sided with Peter III. This forced Elizabeth to flee Russia. She found refuge in Ragusa, Sicily. There, she was well received, lived in peace and took the name Tarakanova. When Catherine II ascended the throne, a German adventuress, she eliminated all potential legitimate heirs to the throne, starting with her husband Peter III. Eventually Elizabeth was located and Orlov was sent to bring her back. He took a fleet to Ragusa and demanded her release. Ragusa, however, was not intimidated. Orlov shelled the city. But the citizens of Ragusa refused to give her up. Then, Orlov used a ruse to lure her onto one of his ships. He pretended to be her lover and Tarakanova fell for it. As soon as she was in Orlov's hands, his fleet headed back to Russia. He brought her back to Catherine II who imprisoned her, for about 22 years until Tarakanova died.

Tarawa.: a Japanese island fortress in the Pacific during World War II.

Tartarus: in Greek mythology, a guarded area by Hades, where the evils forces and incorrigible evil souls were kept.

Tartars: a Mongolic nation hired to defeat the Serbs in the Balkans in Europe in the 8th century. However, they took on the Serb customs, language and religion, and settled in present day Bulgaria. In the 13th century a coalition of Mongols called the 'Golden Horde' invaded Europe for conquest. They were led by Batu, grandson of Genghis Khan.

Tartary: when Batu was recalled in 1242 to elect the Chief Mongol Khan, since Ugudai had been poisoned by a jealous concubine, Batu decided not to continue his conquest of Europe when he returned from the election, but to live off the lands he had conquered. That area of his conquest, stretched roughly from the river Elbe to the Ural mountains, and was called Tartary. Gradually, the Westernmost countries stopped paying tribute altogether and a re-conquest began. In the 16th century, his realm covered present day European Russia until Ivan the Terrible conquered the Khanates of Kazan and Astrakhan and the Don

Cossack Hetman Ermak conquered the Khanate of Sibir. In the 18th century, Catherine II conquered the last Tartar Khanate in the Crimea. After World War II, Stalin exiled the Tartars from the Crimea to Siberia permanently, for their collaboration with the Nazis. When Khrushchev came to power, he gifted the Crimea to the Ukraine in 1954.

Teheran: capital of Persia. The first 'Three Power Conference' was held there in 1943 with Roosevelt, Stalin and Churchill in attendance.

Telemachus: son of Ulysses in Homer's Odyssey.

Televangelists: Christian, Evangelical preachers who use TV as their medium for preaching.

Teller, Edward (1908-2003): an American of Hungarian ancestry, inventor of the Hydrogen Bomb, student of Fermi.

Tesla, Nikolai (1856-1943): an American inventor of Serbo-Ukrainian ancestry. Some of his key inventions include: alternating current, generators, FM radio, lasers, plasma physics and much more.

Teutoburger Wald: a forest in Central Germany, along the Rhine river. In 6 AD, the Roman general Varus was destroyed there with 2 Roman legions by Arminius (Latin spelling). The area was the homeland of the Gothic-Suevi at that time.

When Germany became an Empire in 1871 by proclamation, a commission was formed to 'find that place and erect a statue there for a great German victory.' First, the name of Arminius was changed to Herman. Then, the Suevi were declared to be German -- and called Schwaben. The forest was given a name: Teutoburger Wald. Then, a ravine was found which sort of fitted the Roman description of the battle, and a monument was erected there in 1905!

Teutonic: an adjective applied to (mostly North) German people as in 'Teutonic Menace,' by Clemenceau.

Thailand, aka, Siam: a Kingdom in South-East Asia.

Thales of Miletus, (634-546 BC): Greek philosopher. Considered to be the 1st Greek philosopher. (Yet he was an Ionian.)

Thantos: in Greek mythology, the god of death. Februs in Latin.

Themistocles, (525-460 BC):Athenian naval commander who destroyed the Persian fleet at Salamis in 480 BC. Later Themistocles was ostracized and lived out his old age at the court of the Persian Kings -- so much for Athenian Democracy.

Theodoric I, (419-452): King of the Visigoths in Gaul (France). His capital was Bordeaux. He defeated Attila the Hun at Chalons-sur-Marne in 452, near Orleans.

Theodoric II, (452-466): King of the Visigoths in Gaul, son of Theodoric I.

Theodoric, the Great (454-526): King of the Ostrogoths (who came from the Ukraine by the invitation of Roman Emperor Zeno.) He ruled in Italy from Ravenna. He brought peace and prosperity to Italy and protected Italy from the German invaders. However, he was an Arian Christian and when he died, Justinian I wanted the Ostogoths evicted from Italy. Eventually, they were evicted and settled in Provence, Languedoc and Gascony in Gaul (France.)

Theomatics: the encryption in the Bible, in both Testaments.

Thermopylae: a narrow pass to the North of Athens, where a small band of Greek defenders stopped the progress of the mighty Persian army, said to number 1 million by Greek accounts. However, a traitor showed the Persians a narrow pass thereby allowing the Persians to encircle the defenders. All Greeks left, except for the Spartans, who were by law not allowed to retreat. Leonidas, their King and 300 Spartans stayed and were crushed by the Persians. See Salamis.

Third Reich, (1934-45): flaunted by Hitler to last 1000 years if he came to power. In 1938, with the Austrian Anschluss, it became a reality. But it lasted only 11 years. Why 3rd Reich? The first German Reich was formed by Charlemagne (Karl der Grosse in German) and lasted from 800 to 1804, when Napoleon dismantled it. The second German Empire lasted from 1871 to 1919, when it was dismantled by the Versailles treaty, lasting 48 years.

Thirty Years War, (1618-1648): the height of the Counter-Reformation in Europe. It was temporarily settled with the Treaty of Westphalia in 1648. With that treaty, the ruler determined the religion:'cuius regio, eius religio.'

Thomas Aquinas, St. (1225-74): a controversial Dominican monk. He transcribed Aristotle's works, sprinkled it with a few Christian phrases and called it his own: 'Summa Theologica.' His friends call him the 'Angelic Doctor,' his enemies: 'The Dumb Ox from Cologne.'

Thrace.: an area in the Balkans.

Thucydides, (460-400 BC): Greek historian. He died before he could finish the history of the Peleponnesian War, which was completed by Xenophon. The war started in 431 BC and did not end until 404 BC. Thucydides wrote for the period from 431 to about 412. Thucydides was exiled for 20 years from Athens in 412 BC. Xenophon wrote the rest.

Thuringia: now a German province, east of the river Elbe, formerly a Gothic land.

Tiberius, (42 BC - 37 AD): Roman Emperor.

Tilsit.: a town near the river Niemen (Memel in German). There, in 1806, Czar Alexander and Napoleon met on a barge, mid-way in the river, and reshaped the boundaries of Europe. Called Sovietsk during the Soviet regime.

Timbuktu: a town in Mali, Africa.

Timoshenko, Semyon [Simon] (1895-1970): Soviet Marshal during World War II (Ukrainian). He was responsible for the defense of Moscow in 1941.

Timur, (Tamerlane) (1336-1405): a Tartar who conquered Persia.

Tirene.: an example of alternate spelling for a town in Greece:

Tyrine and Tirine. Common spelling errors in the Roman Empire after 600 AD occurred, when Latin was the official language and Greek the common vernacular.

Tyrol..: an area formerly belonging to Austria which was in part given to Italy after World War I. Once it became Italian, Mussolini formed 'Tomb Squads' to erase the German inscriptions and make them Italian.

Tithe..: originally a Jewish custom to pay one tenth of one's income to the temple of Jerusalem.Christianity,especially the Evangelical Christians, ask for the same Church tax.

Tito, Josip Broz (1892-1980): Yugoslav Communist leader of Croat extraction. When he died, Yugoslavia was on the road to disintegration.

Titus, (79-81): Roman Emperor and general. He destroyed Jerusalem in 70 AD. The Jews were dispersed shortly thereafter.

Tokyo..: capital of Japan.

Tordesillas, Treaty of (1494): a town in the Azores. There a treaty between Holy Roman Emperor Maximilian and Pope Alexander VI was made, dividing the New World into 2 hemispheres of conquest and exploitation. The East was awarded to Portugal (they had already found a passage to the Spice Islands) and the West to Spain (with the discovery of Christopher Columbus). But, the way the world was divided, Brazil fell into the Portuguese sphere of colonization. (This treaty was the primary cause for England's Henry VIII breaking with the Pope and establishing the Anglican Church.)

Torquemada, Thomas de (1420-1498): Inquisitor General in Spain, a Dominican. His 'Reign of Terror' became legendary, even among the most devout Catholics.

Toulouse: a town in Southern France. At one time the capital of Languedoc, the home of the Albi and Cathars.

Trade Routes: established routes of trade which created many key cities. For example:

1) Troy, hub of Europe-Asia trade, ca. 1200 BC.
2) Carthage, hub of Phoenician trade ca. 800 BC.
3) Athens-Ukraine, grain trade, ca. 600 BC.
4) Syracuse-Corinth/Africa, grain trade. 600 BC.
5) Alexandria, Persia-India trade ca. 300 BC.
6) Constantinople, Asia-Europe trade ca. 300 AD.
7) Lisbon, hub of spice trade, ca. 1380 AD.
8) Madrid, hub of New World trade, ca 1500 AD.
9) London, hub of wool & slave trade ca.1700 AD.
10) New York City, hub of World Trade,ca.1970 AD.

Trafalgar, Battle of (1805): a decisive naval battle which dashed Napoleon's hope to collect the bounty set on England's conquest of 2 million Ducats in gold by the Pope.

Transcendental numbers: such as π and e, which have no rational representation. That is, they are not the ratio of whole, rational or irrational numbers.

Transcontinental Railway (1869): linked New York City with

San Francisco (3 time zones), about 3600 miles.

Trans-Siberian Railway (1891-1900): linked St. Petersburg with Vladivostok (7 time zones), about 7200 miles.

Tripoli: a town in Libya. In the Versailles Treaty of 1919, Mussolini got Tripoli as a colony.

Trojan War, (ca. 1200 BC): an epic battle between the Achaeans and Trojans lasting 10 years, according to Homer. Troy was finally taken with a ruse: the wooden horse.

It so happens, that about the same time, a massive eruption occurred nearby. The island of Thera exploded in a massive volcanic eruption which inundated the Aegean civilization. For example: the Etruscans had to leave their homeland etc. Let me put forward a new Theory: what if the walls of Troy came tumbling down during that eruption, exposing Troy, which led to her sack? This would have been not nearly as spectacular, in a poetic sense, but much more effective (and realistic.)

Trotzky, Leon D (Bronstein) (1879-1940): Russian Bolshevik leader and organizer. He formed the Red Army; negotiated the term at Brest-Litovsk of the Russian surrender to the Germans (1918), giving away Kurland, Poland, Byelorussia and the Ukraine as reparations to Germany. When Stalin came to power, Trotzky was exiled in 1932. Later, in 1940, Trotzky was killed by Stalin's henchmen in Mexico.

Troubadours: minstrel poets of Provence and Languedoc, starting about the 12-14th century, in an area occupied by the descendants of the Goths: Albi, Cathars and so on. Among the Goths, being a bard was an old tradition. (As it still is in the Ukraine, to the tune of a Bandura.) This is how Snorri Sturluson was able to reconstruct the Gothic-Norse history in the first place. Of course, once the trend started it was Germanized: they were called Minnesingers.

Truman, Harry S (1945-53): 33nd President of the USA.

Trypilian area: an area in the Ukraine, roughly between Kiev and Lviv, where the Goths often held their Allthing (Sbor), a national assembly. For example: Alaric was elevated to King there and took the Goths on a rescue mission into the Roman Empire. Modern excavations have shown that the area had a civilization dating back to 5000 BC.

Tsaritsyn: see Stalingrad.

Tulip Bulb Disaster: in 1637, a shipment of tulip bulbs was lost at sea. When the holders of put options tried to cash in, the put-writers refused to pay or were unable to pay. Since then, that stigma stayed with put/call options.

Turkmenistan: a former Republic of the Soviet Union, now an independent, mostly Islamic country in Asia.

Turkey.: a Republic in Asia Minor and South-Eastern Balkans, guarding the 'sarcophagus of claims' of the Roman Empire (now that the Ottoman Empire has been dismantled.)

Tuscany: an area in Italy. Formerly a City-State, with Florence as her capital.

TVA....: Tennessee Valley Authority.
Tver...: a Principality and Chartered city of the Kievan-Rus which was destroyed and annexed to Muscovy in the 15th century by Ivan III.
Tyler, John (1841-45): 10th President of the USA.
Tyranny: Greek word, meaning absolute rule. Plato claims that tyrants surround themselves with foreign mercenaries to guard them. Who guards the Pope?

Uganda.: an independent country in East Africa, formerly a colony in the British Empire.
Ugudai, (ca.1226-1241): Chief Khan of the Mongols.He was poisoned by a jealous concubine. (A jealous concubine, thousands of miles away, saved Europe from total destruction.) This ended Batu's conquest of Europe. He was recalled for the election of the Chief Khan. Batu took his army to Sarai and went to the election. Batu was not elected, Kubilai Khan was. Batu returned to Sarai, to his Tent-City, East of Moscow and began auctioning off the Yarlics (Principalities) to the highest bidder in tax revenue for the Tartars.
Ukraine: an independent Republic in Eastern Europe, formerly a Republic in the Soviet Union.

The name Ukraine was coined by the scribe Hipatiev (Ipatiev in Russian) during the reign of King Yaroslav the Wise (1019-54) for the royal Principality the Goth-Rus governed from Kiev. It is often called the 'Kievan-Rus.' From about 550 on (after the Huns were defeated first by the Gepids and the Gepids by the Avars, reconstruction of the former Gothic lands began) until 1240 AD, when Kiev was utterly sacked by the Tartars. Since the rulers of Kiev were very prolific, certain Princes did not participate in the 'rotation for Kingship.' They became secondary Princes who ruled permanently from a designated Chartered city. This way the rule of direct claimants to the throne in Kiev (sons of the King) and secondary claimant such as nephews, cousins and so on was equitably distributed among the many Chartered cities. The main Chartered cities in the Ukraine were: Kiev, Chernihiv, Pereyaslav, Lviv, Bratislava plus many more. In addition there were semi-autonomous Principalities, which were governed by Princes, such as: Novhorod, Belarus (now Byelorussia), Tver, Volodimir (Vladimir in Russian) and so on. They also had primary and secondary Chartered cities. The Prince of Novhorod was heir to the Kingship in Kiev.

The Princes who were candidates for succession ruled in the primary cities according to their rank for succession to the Kingship in Kiev. When the King died, every Prince moved up one notch in that hierarchy.The precise hierarchy is lost today. But, roughly speaking it was: Kiev-Novhorod-Tver-Minsk-Volodimir and so on. There were many more cities. All that we know now for sure is, the successor ruled in Novhorod. That is, the precise pecking order is lost today. But these were some of the primary cities. The secondary cities did not participate in the rotation at all. This is referred to in the Chronicles. One time a delegation of city elders came to Kiev and complained to the King: "Is there not another way to establish succession? Because, each time, just as we fatten-up the Prince, he is moved to another city."

Hipatiev, defined the Ukraine as the lands ruled by the Princes of Kiev, Chernihiv and Pereyaslav.

During that reconstruction period there was a dire shortage of Princes and royal families (King-Judges.) They had left during the prior destruction by the Mongols: Huns (4th century); Avars (6th century); Bulgars (7th century) and Magyars (9th century). By the 9th century Christianity was polarized between Rome and Constantinople and many Goths had converted to the Roman Faith, while the Kievan-Rus was still either heathen or of Arian Christian faith. Therefore, a council of sages decided to invite at least one royal family to rule these Principalities.Their choice fell on the Varangians, the remotest region in Europe, in Norway, which still had the 'old time Goths' living there. A delegation was sent there and the entire royal family (still heathen at that time) accepted their offer: Ruryc (862), his family and his 'knights' moved to the Kievan-Rus. At that time many of the cities had been taken over by Vikings. While the Vikings were Goths, they were not Princes but military adventurers. In Kiev, Askold and Dir, took over. In Novhorod, Vadim had set himself up. Ruryc, stayed in Novhorod to 'clean-up' the mess made by the Vikings and sent his chief warrior companion Helgi or Oleh (Oleg in Russian) with Prince Ingvar or Ihor (Igor in Russian) to Kiev. This way the two major Chartered cities could be cleaned up and the rest would be taken care of later. Ruryc (862-879) disposed of Vadim and sent Oleh and Ihor to dispose of Askold and Dir. Ruryc died in 879, therefore Oleh became regent for Ihor (879-913). Oleh ruled until Ihor reached majority and then turned over the rule to Ihor (913-945). Since Oleh was not a trained King-Judge (and neither was Ihor, because of his tender age) they could not append the ending rik or ryc; or slav.

In 911, Oleh reclaimed Kiev's trading privileges. He invaded the Roman Empire, captured Constantinople and got the concessions he wanted. (His shield still hangs on the main gate in Constantinople.)

Ihor was married to Olga, who was a Christian (but we don't know for sure whether she was an Arian Christian.) During her reign the Cyrillic alphabet replaced the runic as the influence of Constantinople began to dominate their trade. This changed their 'identity' from Goths to Slavs, which conformed with the new policy of the Roman Empire. This change seemed not to be important, because in antiquity, the Goths and Slavs had merged into one people. Therefore, the subsequent Kings replaced the Gothic ending of their name with the Slavic endings: -slav, -polk and -mir, depending on which law they practiced -- just like the prior Goths did.

Ihor was killed in an expedition. His wife Olha assumed rule (945-955) and regency for their son Sviatoslav (955-972). His son was Yaropolk (973-980) and his son was Volodimir the Great (980-1015).

Volodimir accepted Christianity from Constantinople (988), and married the sister of Roman Emperor Basil II, Anna (the only marriage in the existence of the Roman Empire whereby an outsider married into the Imperial family of the Roman Empire.) With this marriage Volodimir became hereditary King by the Roman Empire, and Kiev became a Patriarchate, while Princes were installed in all Chartered cities and ruled the Principalities, from Novhorod to Volodimir, a city founded and Chartered by King Volodimir.

During the 4th Crusade (1204), Constantinople was sacked and destroyed by the Crusaders. The trade with Kiev declined, while the Prince of Volodimir began trading with Persia and his Principality became strong. This brought dissention among the two Principalities: Kiev and Volodimir, resulting in many wars for supremacy.

In 1238,the Tartars invaded the Kievan-Rus and destroyed many cities and with it the Kievan-Rus with the help of Alexander Nevsky, a banished Prince from Novhorod.

In 1252, Batu doled out the Principalities (now called Yarlics) of the Kievan-Rus to the highest bidder in taxes. Nevsky got the first pick and he chose Volodimir, which included Moscow, but Moscow was not a Chartered town. Alexander Nevsky set himself up as Chief enforcer and tax collector for the Tartars. In return the Tartars named him 'Grand Prince of Rus.' Eventually, this led to the rise of Moscow and the Duchy of Muscovy. With Tartar muscle and excess monies collected by the Muscovite Princes, Muscovy began a meteoric expansion, which culminated with Ivan the Terrible. When Ivan died (1584), however, the Ruryc line became extinct and Muscovy depopulated of her non-Tartar population (1571) by the Crimean Tartars. Boris Godunov, a Tartar assumed rule in Moscow.

The Cossacks rallied (1610), took Moscow, called for a Sbor (Allthing in Gothic, a national assembly) and Michael Romanov was elected new Czar in 1613.

Meanwhile, in the Western part of the Kievan-Rus, Lithuania under their ruler Gedimin (1316) began to expand south, into Belarus and Ukraine. They were heathens and set themselves up as protectors against the Tartars.

In fact the Lithuanians were welcomed by the population because they protected the Ukrainians from constant Tartar raids. However, in 1386, the Lithuanian Duke Jagiello married the Polish Princess Hedzwiga. By 1440, the Polish Barons moved in and took over the Lithuanian rule in the Ukraine and Belarus. The Polish Barons demanded conversion to the Catholic Faith. By 1444,the Cossack movement began.

In 1648, Cossack Hetman Bohdan (God-given) Khmelnitzky combined the Cossacks from the various Siches, drove out the Polish Barons and formed a Ukrainian state. However, he realized that in order for the Ukraine to survive among her powerful neighbors -- Poland, Muscovy; Sweden; Crimean Tartars, Ottoman Turks and Hungary he needed to form a strong alliance. He sent delegations to Muscovy, Sweden and the Ottoman Turks asking for an alliance.

Moscow replied first in 1654. The alliance with Moscow was ratified by the Cossacks in Pereyaslav and the Cossacks were disbanded. There was one provision in the Moscow treaty: a newly elected Hetman had to be ratified by the Czar, which was presented as a 'rubberstamp' affair. Khmelnitzky died in 1657 and Ivan Vykhovsky (1657-9) became Hetman. When his name was submitted for ratification, Czar Alexis replied: "We don't take orders from our subjects." And, with that Moscow regulars moved into the Ukraine before the Cossacks could rally. In 1659, Hetman Vykhovsky defeated the Russians at Konotop but that victory was short lived, as Russians came in droves. Moscow occupation undermined the Cossacks, the Siches were limited to 8,000 Cossacks, while Moscow installed new Hetmans, loyal to Muscovy throughout the Ukraine in key cities. This time period is called 'Hetmanshina,' when various Hetmans were pitted against one another according to the policy directed by Moscow. The worst was yet to come. In 1667, Moscow made an alliance with Poland, in the Treaty of Andrusovo, giving Poland roughly half of the Ukraine and all of Belarus to Poland for a vague military alliance. Thus, once again, the Polish Barons moved in, exacting horrible retribution and demanding conversion more forcefully than ever to the Catholic Faith. Within 10 years of Khmelnitzky's death the Ukraine was destroyed.

In 1700, a 16 year old boy-King assumed the Throne of Sweden as Charles XII. His contemporaries were Czar Peter I in Moscow and Hetman Ivan Mazepa (1697-1709) of the Zaporozhian Cossacks. Peter I saw an opportunity to expand Moscow's realm to the Baltic Sea. He attacked the Swedish port Narva. But, the city held and asked for help from their King. Charles XII took his light artillery, 12,000 Swedes and sailed for Narva. There he routed Peter's army of 80,000. Then, for the next 8 years he cleaned up the Baltic coast of Polish and Teutonic encroachment. In 1708, he was done and responded to Khmelnitzky's request for an alliance. (At that time, the Ukraine was still seen as the homeland of the Goths. Even Polish King Sobieski, called himself 'the last Goth.') The Swedish army had swelled to 44,000 and Mazepa felt that 40,000 Cossacks would rise, even though all he could promise was 8,000 he was allowed to keep in the Zaporozhe. Charles XII moved his army into the Ukraine, but at Poltava, Charles XII and Mazepa were defeated in 1709 by Peter's forces. Charles and Mazepa fled to the Ottoman Sultan with Peter in hot pursuit. However, Peter and his army were encircled by the Sultan. Peter surrendered and was taken captive. Catherine, Peter's mistress and sex slave, ransomed Peter with the jewels she had with her. Then, Peter ransomed his army with uncut diamonds. But, before Peter was released, Peter had to sign a treaty with the Sultan to give up his recent conquests in the Crimea (Azov); to remove his navy from the Black Sea and the Sultan set a protective screen over the Ukraine,since he had plans to respond to Khmelnitzky's alliance himself. Peter was not allowed to move his troops below a designated parallel into the Ukraine. However, Peter was allowed to administer the Ukraine.

Peter returned to St.Petersburg, married Catherine and continued his wars against Sweden -- to the North. But during his administration of the Ukraine, he imprisoned and exiled the Cossacks and population to a swamp in the north. There Peter was building his capital St.Petersburg. Survival rates in these swamps were about 3 months. The Ukraine was practically depopulated building his city.

When Peter died in 1725, another succession crisis developed. Peter had killed his son and heir, Alexis -- who had a son Peter II (1727-30). But, Peter I left no instructions on his succession. Thus, a committee determined the order of succession. They determined that Catherine I (1725-1727), Peter's second wife, should succeed him.

While Peter I and Catherine had 6 children, 3 girls: Elizabeth (1741-62), Anne and Natalia and 3 boys: Peter, Paul and Peter -- all the boys died in infancy. Peter's (second) wife became Czarina Catherine I. However, she ruled less than 3 years (1725-27). During her rule, her former slave master and lover Menshikov ruled Russia for all practical purposes. Menshikov tried to marry his 15 year old daughter to Peter II (1727-30) then 13, who died before the marriage took place. Within 5 years two generations of rulers were eliminated. Who was next?

To begin with, there were the descendants of Ivan V, the co-ruler of Peter I, Anna (1730-40) and Ivan VI (1740-41). Thus, Anna (from the Ivan V line) became Czarina. She had been groomed for the court in Kurland and assumed rule in

St. Petersburg in 1730. She brought with her, her German entourage from Kurland, in particular Biron the German, her lover. This period of Russian history is called 'Bironshina.' She died in 1740 and Ivan VI (1740-41) became ruler (also from the Ivan V line). He was deposed and imprisoned by the Russian Gentry and Elizabeth became Czarina (1741-61).She abolished the death penalty in 1742.

During the reign of Elizabeth, the Ukraine experienced a reprieve if not a mild rebirth. Elizabeth had married Alexey Rozumovsky, an offspring from a long line of Zaporozhian Hetmans. While Elizabeth heaped every title on him, Alexey refused all of them, all he wanted to do was to sing in the choir, for he had an 'angelic voice.' However, he had a brother, Cyril, who was studying abroad at that time -- which was the Zaporozhian custom. The Zaporozhians waited patiently until he finished and when Cyril returned, he was elected Hetman (1750-1764). When the Zaporozhians presented his name for ratification, Cyril was not only ratified but also made Field Marshal in the Russian army.

Russia entered the 7 Years War in 1756 on the side of Austria and France, because Frederick the Great had insulted Peter I publicly -- who was Elizabeth's father, from his 2nd marriage to Catherine I. With Russia's entry in the 7 Years War, East Prussia, then Pomerania were quickly conquered by the Russians. At Kunersdorf,Frederick the Great suffered a major defeat by the Russians and Cossacks. Berlin was raided by the Cossacks in 1760. All of Prussia was in panic. Frederick's desperation can be seen in his letters to his Queen mother: "All is lost..." he writes.

But then, seemingly out of nowhere, the Russian army withdrew, Frederick's provinces were restored and in the Treaty of Paris (1763), Prussia was resuscitated.

Elizabeth was eliminated December 1761. Catherine II (1762-96) ascended the throne and repaid Frederick's prior small favors -- big time. Of course, it was all blamed on Peter III (1762) who never assumed rule! (Tarakanova [Elizabeth's daughter] was eliminated when the Semeonov regiment sided with Peter III.)

Next in line for succession was Peter III, grandson of Peter and son of Anne (sister to Elizabeth) -- who was a certified idiot and impotent. In Peter's will, inspired by Leibnitz, was a request which stated that henceforth all Russian heirs must be married to Princesses or Princes of Hohenstaufen line -- to the royals of Europe. This way, Peter wanted eventually to 'take over' the Holy Roman Empire by marriage.

Consequently, an impoverished branch of that line was found, and a marriage contract arranged to marry Sophia Augusta Frederica of Anhalt-Zerbst (future Catherine II) to Peter III. When Elizabeth was eliminated, the mad rush to seize power was on. Peter, her husband, had vowed and bragged openly that his first act in power would be to lock up Catherine in a nunnery for good. At that time, Catherine's lover was Orlov, the commander of the Preobrazhensky regiment, one of two regiments guarding the Czars (the other was Semeonov). As soon as Elizabeth was buried, a brief struggle ensued between the two regiments before Peter III had time to react.Peter III was captured, imprisoned and killed by Orlov. Thus, Catherine II became Czarina. From then on Catherine orchestrated the action in Eastern Europe. First, Poland was partitioned between Russia, Prussia and Austria. Second, the Ukraine was enslaved. The Cossacks were outlawed, imprisoned and exiled to Siberia, the Siches were razed (1764). Then, the Crimean Tartars were conquered. Finally, Catherine initiated the wars of conquest against the Ottoman Turks, starting with Bessarabia (Moldovia in Ukrainian), planned campaigns into Persia an so on. Catherine II turned the Ukraine, Belarus and Poland into provinces of Russia. And, so it remained until WW I.

Starting with Catherine II (1762-1796) and until Nicholas II (1894-1917), all rulers of Russia were Germans. None of them had a drop of Romanov blood in them. Catherine's son Paul, was either the product of her German Chamberlain, or her lover Saltykov, or her Polish lover Poniatovsky. While the historians have not yet agreed on Paul's real biological father, they all agree that he had no trace of Romanov blood in him. His sons, and their sons were all married to German Princesses. Hence, Russian rulers were 'pure' Germans.

World War I, exposed the incompetence, nepotism and brutality of the Czarist (German) regime in Russia. While everybody wanted reform, few wanted a Bolshevik revolution. But, Germany funded the revolution with Lenin. Lenin repaid the Germans again -- big time. In the Treaty of Brest-Litovsk (1918), Trotzky gave away: Kurland (Estonia, Latvia, Lithuania), Poland, Belarus and the Ukraine as war reparations -- while the same countries tried to make a separate peace with Germany.

A Civil War ensued with the Red Army pitted against the various White Armies (Czarist sympathizers) and Western intervention by: USA, Great Britain, France, Italy and Greece to keep Russia in the war against Germany. Yet the Red Army prevailed.

In the Treaty of Versailles (1919), many countries gained their independence, while the Civil War was still raging -- mostly in the Ukraine until 1933. Now, armies of the newly formed republics crisscrossed the Ukraine: Czechoslovakia, Poland, Rumania and Hungary, to name only the major belligerent. An independent Ukraine was formed anyway in 1919 and lasted until 1923, when the Bolsheviks gained the upper hand in the Civil war and took over. (The Bolsheviks were forced out of Kiev and established Kharkiv as the new capital of the Ukraine (1919-1926).) Then, the Ukraine was integrated into the Soviet Union. In 1926, the Ukrainian Don and Kuban were forcibly integrated into the Russian Soviet Republic. By 1933, the Civil War was over and America recognized the Soviet Union in 1934.

This prompted Stalin's purges until 1938. Then Stalin's Collectivization decimated the Ukraine again. In one incident alone, Stalin engineered a famine and an estimated 9 million farmers starved to death. In 1939, Stalin and Hitler made the infamous pact, dividing Poland. Then, Stalin grabbed Bessarabia (Moldovia).

In 1941, Hitler invaded the Soviet Union, while Bandera (a Ukrainian national) fought the Germans and then the Soviets until 1953. Again, the Ukraine was depopulated by the Germans, as roughly 10 million Ukrainians were sent to Germany to work as serf-farmers or factory slaves in the German industrial war complex. Many Ukrainians preferred fighting with the Germans against Stalin, however, hoping against hope for the eventual rebirth of the Ukraine.

When the Soviet Union collapsed 1990 to 1992, the Ukraine became again an independent country, but in name only. The Old Guard (Soviet), is still in control in the Ukraine to this day. Soviet rule has left the Ukraine an ecological wasteland (Chernobyl and other nuclear waste and dump sites) and economically ruined. Yet, the Ukraine has applied for EU membership. When the Ukraine is admitted, the dreams of Napoleon and Hitler will be realized without having to fire a single shot.

Ulfilas, (311-383): a Gothic sage who led a delegation of Goths in 330, to Constantinople, to study the new faith which swept the Roman Empire: Christianity.

They got the royal treatment from both Emperor Constantine and Patriarch Arius. They stayed in Constantinople for 10 years. They translated the Bible into Runic (Gothic) and returned as missionaries to the Goths. Portions of their original translation are still displayed at the University of Uppsala in Sweden.

Ulm....: a town in Germany.

Ulyanov: a small town in the Russian Republic, in honor of Lenin.

Ulysses: a Greek hero who fought in the Battle of Troy for 10 years. Then, he was punished by Poseidon (who had built Troy) to navigate the Atlantic Ocean for another 10 years, in Homer's poem 'Odyssey.' When the poem was translated into Latin (and translated back into Greek), the action shifted to the Mediterranean Sea.

In modern times 'Dr. Zhivago' suffered a similar fate. It could not be published in the Soviet Union (it was considered to be derogatory.) It was smuggled into Italy

and translated into Italian.
Italian became the basis from which all subsequent translations were made. When it was translated back into Russian, the Russian community in America considered it downright 'illiterate.'

UNA....: Ukrainian National Army, led by Bandera who fought both Hitler and Stalin; disbanded in 1953. Bandera retired in München, Germany. He was assassinated by Soviet agents in 1959.

Uniate.: a brand of Catholicism, specifically tailored for the Slavs (from the time when Kievan-Prince Danielo converted to Catholicism and was made hereditary King in Galicia, Ukraine, by the Pope.) Aka: Eastern Rite.

United Nations: a world governing body, conceived in the Yalta conference by Roosevelt in 1944, including Churchill and Stalin. Some of her branches are in New York City; the Security Council and the General Assembly. All other branches of the UN are scattered throughout Europe.

United States of America: the only superpower left (aka: USA or America.)

Unter-.: a German prefix, which became part of the Russian language with Leibnitz's Table of Ranks, which Peter I introduced in Russia.

Untermensch: German, sub-human. A term applied by Hitler to all non-Aryans. In particular against: Jews, Gypsies, Poles, Russians and Ukrainians, even though the Goths are the original Aryans.

Uppsala: a University town in Sweden. Portions of the translated Bible by Ulfilas into runic are still displayed there.

Ural(s): a mountain range in present day Russia, which divides the European region from the Asiatic region.

Uzbekistan: a Republic in the Soviet Union, now an independent Republic in Asia, mostly Muslim.

V1/V2..: German rockets that bombarded England during WW II.

Vadim..: a Viking ruler in Novhorod, defeated by Rurik in 862.

Valens, (372-378): Roman Emperor.

Valois.: a Royal House of France, died out in the 16th century, replaced by the Bourbons who are related to the Habsburgs by marriage.

Van Buren, Martin (1837-41): 8th President of the USA.

Vandals: a Gothic people who invaded Gaul in 406. The word vandalism was pinned on them. They were Germanized in the 19th century.

Vatican City: established by Mussolini for the Papacy in 1929 and with it the Italian Concordat.

Varangians: a name used by the Kievan sages to locate Gothic King-Judges to rule in Kievan-Rus. Also, the name of the Imperial guard in the Roman Empire from about 900 to 1204, in Constantinople, which replaced the Praetorian guard.

Varvara: that's how Barbara is pronounced in Cyrillic.

Veche..: an assembly of peers (in Gothic called: Thing). Also, a popular ending used by the Gothic King-Judges, often modified to -veg. Like in Meroveg, the Merovingian rulers in France.

Veii...: an Etruscan city, about 10 miles from Rome, which was utterly destroyed by the Romans. To this day, we don't know her exact location. We only know of the city, because Livy refers to her sack by Rome.

Verdun.: a town in France. Most famous for two events:
First, after the grandsons of Charlemagne dismembered Lothar's 'central empire,' they signed a treaty there in 843, outlining their borders (Charles and Louis).
Second, during Word War I, when Prince Rupert of Bavaria countermanded the Schlieffen plan for the invasion of France and tried to take the fortress head-on. (He took away 30 crucial divisions.) The end result was: the Schlieffen plan failed 30 miles short of Paris and Verdun became a meat-grinder of the German army.

Verman.: Russian lexicographer, linguist and art critic.

Versailles: a French town near Paris,luxurious home of the French Kings and location of a few major events.
In 1871, in the Hall of Mirrors, the German Empire was created by proclamation after France was defeated in the Franco-Prussian War.
In 1919, the site of the Peace Treaty where France and England dismembered Germany, Austria, Russia (their ally) and the Ottoman Empire. In 1940, Hitler imposed a similar humiliating treaty on France.

Vespucci, Amerigo (1454-1512): Italian navigator. A German cartographer called his charted continent: America in 1507, because Vespucci described it in detail and navigated the continent along her coast.

Vesuvian: pertaining to Mt. Vesuvius near Naples in Italy.

Vichy..: a French town in Southern France. The seat of the French Government created by Hitler where Petain ruled as Hitler's ally.

Vienna.: capital of Austria. In 1683, Vienna was besieged by the Ottoman Turks and ready to fall. Polish King Sobieski and the Ukrainian Cossacks liberated Vienna and drove away the Ottoman Turks. The ungrateful Austrians refused to give them any bread, water or hay for their horses.

Vienna Congress of (1814-1815): Czar Alexander I restored the German ruling dynasties there after the defeat of Napoleon and proposed a 'Holy Alliance,' excluding the Pope -- the forerunner to the League of Nations and the UN.

Vikings: a term applied to Norse-Raiders from the 6th to 13th century. Actually, the word is a verb, meaning to go on a raiding expedition. Aka: Norsemen, Normans and Varangians, mostly of Norwegian-Gothic stock.

Vilna..: a town in Belarus.

Virgil, (70-19 BC): Italian poet and author of 'Aeneid.'

Visigoths: according to Western historians, the Western Goths as opposed to the Ostrogoths or Eastern Goths.Technically, however, this is not correct because, some of the Eastern-most Goths are included among the Visigoths. A much better distinction is whether or not they were Christians. At the time of the Hun invasion, the Visigoths were Arian Christians, while the Ostrogoths were heathens. This is why the Visigoths fled to the Roman Empire. What they did not know or did not appreciate the implications of was that the Roman Empire had just adopted a new brand of Christianity which made them heretics. As heretics they exposed themselves to the ruthless persecution of the Church. In time, the Ostrogoths were converted to the Arian faith (Theodoric, who accepted Roman Emperor Zeno's offer to rule in Italy, was an Arian Christian and that's roughly 1 century later) which indicates that the original (Arian) missionaries were still hard at work converting the heathen Goths, well into the 13th century -- Bogomils and so on. The Church officials, however, had to suppress this information because it would advocate the Arian faith. Therefore, the dividing line was not territorial but religious. See Goths.

Vistula: a river in Poland.

Vitebsk: a town in Belarus.

Vladivostok: a Russian port on the Pacific coast founded in 1860.

Vlasov, Andrei A (1895-1945): Soviet general who defeated the Germans at Moscow in 1941 and threw back the entire German front on average, 175 miles.

When the Germans approached Moscow, Stalin told Vlasov to launch a counter-offensive. Vlasov asked Stalin for the release of the political prisoners to which Stalin agreed. Using the political prisoners, women and whoever else Vlasov could round up, he shifted army units along the entire front and launched the counter-offensive in December 1941. Hitler's army nearly collapsed. Hitler took over the personal command to stem the German retreat and collapse. By the spring thaw, the Counter-Offensive petered out and Vlasov took up headquarters at Volkov, about 70 miles from Leningrad. Now Stalin had second thoughts about the political prisoners. Stalin sent in the NKWD (KGB) to cleanse the army. When the NKWD started probing Vlasov, he knew his time was up. He took his staff and surrendered to the Germans. This spawned the Vlasov movement to oust Stalin. Vlasov claimed he could raise 30 million soldiers against Stalin. Hitler did not believe him. And, Hitler did not want any allies to share his glory. So, Hitler imprisoned Vlasov. In 1944, Vlasov's forces were mobilized by Hitler. Vlasov was defeated. He tried to surrender to General Patton, but General Eisenhower would not allow Patton to accept Vlasov's surrender. Instead, Vlasov was turned over to the British, who surrendered him to the Soviets. Vlasov and his adjutant were whisked to Moscow where they were hanged in Red Square. Vlasov's officers were lined up and shot. Vlasov's soldiers went on a Siberian vacation--20 years of hard labor and loss of human rights.

Völkerwanderung: a notion Mommsen developed to throw the migrations by the Huns, Avars, Bulgars, Magyars and Tartars into one kettle, which no doubt included a few German tribes. That kettle was made German by Mommsen. Therefore, when Germany tried to form her identity in 1871. That kettle became a German grab-bag and the Goths were made German by declaration. Hitler took the next logical step and called that struggle: Kulturkampf(Culture war). In reality, the Avars, Bulgars and Magyars were hired to eliminate Goths and each other.

Volkov.: a town, about 70 miles away from Leningrad in the Soviet Union. During Vlasov's counter-offensive during World War II, December 1941 to March 1942, the site of Vlasov's headquarters. When Stalin sent his NKWD (KGB) to investigate Vlasov, he took his staff and surrendered to the Germans. See Vlasov.

Volodimir, The Great (978-1015): Gothic King-Judge of Kievan-Rus; hereditary King by the Roman Empire of Kievan-Rus; married to Anna, the sister of Roman Emperor Basil II; introduced Orthodox Christianity in Kievan-Rus. During his reign, Kiev was made a Patriarchate and Patriarch Leontiy (991-1004) was installed by Roman Emperor Basil II, for the Kievan-Rus. Volodimir founded a Chartered city by his name: Volodimir (Vladimir in Russian). The Gothic equivalent name is Valdemar or Waldemar. Before he ascended the throne in Kiev, he ruled in Novhorod as Prince and spent a few years 'viking' with his Norse buddies and fellow countrymen.

Voltaire, Francoise-Marie (1694-1778): French historian and author. Among his works, he wrote the 'definitive Russian history,' according to the specifications provided to him by Catherine II, which established Russia as a European nation and degraded all minorities, especially the Ukraine. For his work Voltaire was paid a King's ransom. In addition, a library was dedicated to him in St. Petersburg and a statue of him is prominently displayed in the Hermitage. It should be noted that every Russian historian of name has a dedication to Voltaire in his history. (Diderot collected the last installment when he visited Catherine II.)

Voronez: a small, but strategic town in the Soviet Union during World War II. (Small crow in Ukrainian.)

Vugate.: a Latin translation of the Bible, compiled by St.Jerome in the 4th century. In Latin, the norm.

Waldemar or Valdemar: a common name for Danish Kings. There were many instances when Ukrainians were mistaken for Danes.
One case deserves special mention. In 1206, just after Constantinople had been taken by the Franks in the 4th Crusade, a delegation arrived. The Franks had no idea what they wanted and could not understand them at all. They tried various dialects, but that did not work. They found a Bohemian, who declared that they were Danes.
Accordingly, they sent them to Denmark. There, it was determined that they were from Kiev and wanted to serve in the Varangian guard. But, since the Franks had taken over in Constantinople and they did not want that delegation to fight for the Roman Emperor, who was then in Nicaea (Minor Asia), they sent them back home, to Kiev.

Walewska, Maria (1789-1817): Polish Countess, Napoleon's lover who gave him a son whom Napoleon did not acknowledge but whom Napoleon promoted to rank and he served France in the Chamber of Deputies. (His descendants hold now prominent positions in the French government.)
On account of Countess Maria Walewska, Napoleon resuscitated the Polish State in the enclave of Warsaw (1807). (Prior to that Poland had been partitioned by Russia, Austria and Prussia and ceased to exist in Europe.) When Napoleon was defeated in 1815, Russia set up a Governor there and Poland was Russified until the end of World War I.

Walewski, Comte Alexander F (1810-1868): the son of Countess Maria Walewska and Napoleon Bonaparte.

Warsaw: capital of Poland. In 1795, during the Third Partition of Poland, Warsaw was taken by Prussia. In 1807, after defeating Prussia, Napoleon created an independent Grand Duchy of Warsaw, to please his Polish lover Countess Maria Walewska. In 1815, after Napoleon was defeated, Warsaw became Russian. After World War I, Poland was restored and Warsaw once more became her capital.

Warsaw Pact: created in 1955 by USSR, deterrent to NATO.

Washington, George (1789-1797): 1st President of the USA.

Waterloo: a town in Belgium, the site of Napoleon's final defeat.

Webster, Daniel (1782-1852): American statesman.

Webster, Noah (1758-1843): American lexicographer.

Wehrmacht: German, armed forces or army.

Weisswurst: a popular German sausage.

Wellington,Arthur Duke(1769-1852):British soldier and politician.

Westphalia: an area in Germany and a town by the same name. In 1648, the Protestants (mostly Sweden) halted the Counter-Reformation, after about 50% of the population was killed in that war in Central Europe. A treaty was reached whereby the ruler determined the religion (cuius regio, eius religio) in his sphere of rule.

White Army: When Lenin seized power in 1917, Russia still had many armies throughout the empire. Collectively they were called the White Armies, led by generals or admirals. The major ones were led by: Semenov (General), Kolchak (Admiral), Denikin (General, he died in 1919 and his army was taken over by Wrangel), Yudenich (General) and Wrangel (General). Until 1923, each one of the White armies was larger than the Red army led by Trotzky. But, the White armies were uncoordinated, badly led, ill equipped and were defeated by the Red army one by one. They were generally referred to as Whites as opposed to the Reds. The word White became a word of treachery. Therefore, Belarus changed her name to Byelorussia to avoid that stigma.

White House: the official residence of an American president.

Whites.: Czarist sympathizers during the Civil War in Russia, 1917-1933. As opposed to the Reds, the revolutionaries.

Wilhelm I, (1797-1888): King of Prussia.

Wilhelm II, aka: 'Der Kaiser'(1859-1941): Emperor of Germany, 1888 to 1918.

Wilshire: a stock index of 5,000 stocks.

Wilson, Woodrow (1913-1921): 28th President of the USA. Author of the 14 points, which led to Germany's unconditional surrender during World War I.See Versailles.

Witte, Count Sergei Y (1849-1915): Russian statesman.

Wittelsbach: a German ruling family from Bavaria. Bavaria was a series of Dukedoms which Napoleon forged into a Kingdom. In 1919, Bavaria joined the German Empire.

Wittenberg: a town in Saxony (Germany) where Martin Luther had his church.When Papal legates started selling indulgences, Luther posted his 95 Theses, which led to the Reformation, which led to the Counter-Reformation and so on.

Wonsan.: a coastal town in Korea.

Woops..: the name given to the municipal bond issue in the State of Washington which went bankrupt.

Worldcom: a company which defaulted in the crash of 2000.

World War I: the 'Great War' from 1914 to 1918. This war was to end all wars.

World War II: an even greater war, 1939 to 1945.

Wrangel, Peter (1878-1928): Russian (Czarist) general who tried to restore the monarchy in Russia during the revolution. His army was called: White army as opposed to the Red army led by Trotzky. He operated in South Russia, mostly devastating the Ukraine. See Denikin.

Würtemberg: an area in Germany. Originally, the homeland of the Gothic Suevi. Many of the Hohenstaufens come from there. Napoleon promoted it to a Kingdom. In the 19th century, the Suevi were declared to be German, named: Schwaben. In 1919, Würtemberg joined the German Empire.

Wycliff, John (1320-1382): Religious reformer in England.

Xenophon, (430-354 BC); Greek mercenary, commander and author of the Persian expedition, Xenophon called it: Anabasis.

When Alexander the Great read Xenophon's account, he knew he could conquer the Persian Empire.

Xerxes I, (519-469 BC): King of Persia, see Salamis.

Yalta..: a Crimean resort town.

Yalta Conference: February 4 to 11, 1945, held by the Big Three: Roosevelt, Stalin and Churchill.

Yarl(ic/s): the origin of the English word Earl. After Batu had conquered Eastern Europe to the Elbe river, he auctioned each Yarlic (Earldom or Principality) to the highest bidder in taxes. In the Kievan-Rus these were the original Principalities governed from major Chartered cities.

Yaroslav, The Wise (1019-1054): King of the Kievan-Rus who ruled from Kiev. During his rule, European Kings stood in line to marry a Ukrainian Princess. King Henry I of France married his daughter Anna. Their marriage contract, signed by the Dauphin with a huge X and by Anna in clear legible script, is still on display in Kiev's museum. King Harold of Norway, married his daughter Catherine and so on. During his reign Kiev and Florence became sister cities.

Yeltsin, Boris (1931-): Russian political leader from, native of Siberia (Sibir).

Yudenich, N (1848-1919): Czarist general of a White Army, which nearly captured St. Petersburg at the start of the Bolshevik Revolution. He came within a few miles before the Red Army beat him back.

Zaporozhe(ian): a fort (called Sich) the Cossacks built on the lower Dnieper (Dnipro) river. The word means: Za (beyond) porohy (steps or rapids). In 1775, Catherine II razed the fort and had the Cossacks exiled to Siberia. The official end of the Zaporozhian Sich. Since then only army regular units exit who call themselves Cossacks.

Zeno...: a Greek philosopher famous for his paradoxes of motion.

Zeno, (474-491): Roman Emperor. He invited the Ostrogoths to rule in Italy, with Theodoric the Great.

Zeus...: in Greek mythology, ruler of Olympus, the abode of the Olympians. Eventually, all children of Zeus dwelled among the Olympians, albeit some had a minor role, such as: Hercules and others. Jupiter or Jove in Roman.

Zhitomir: a provincial capital in the Western Ukraine.

Zionism: a Jewish political movement to secure a homeland in Palestine. It started in 1897 by Theodore Herzl and the objective was achieved in 1948.

Zoe, aka: Sophia Paleologa: Ivan III, the ruler of Moscow, married Zoe, the niece of the last Roman Emperor. After the marriage Ivan III made the claim that Moscow was the 'Third Rome.'

Zhukov, Grigori K (1896-1974): Marshal of the Soviet Union. He orchestrated the defeat of the Germans at Stalingrad and Kursk during World War II.